797,885 Books
are available to read at

Forgotten Books

www.ForgottenBooks.com

Forgotten Books' App
Available for mobile, tablet & eReader

ISBN 978-1-330-65947-2
PIBN 10088660

This book is a reproduction of an important historical work. Forgotten Books uses state-of-the-art technology to digitally reconstruct the work, preserving the original format whilst repairing imperfections present in the aged copy. In rare cases, an imperfection in the original, such as a blemish or missing page, may be replicated in our edition. We do, however, repair the vast majority of imperfections successfully; any imperfections that remain are intentionally left to preserve the state of such historical works.

Forgotten Books is a registered trademark of FB &c Ltd.
Copyright © 2015 FB &c Ltd.
FB &c Ltd, Dalton House, 60 Windsor Avenue, London, SW19 2RR.
Company number 08720141. Registered in England and Wales.

For support please visit www.forgottenbooks.com

1 MONTH OF FREE READING

at
www.ForgottenBooks.com

By purchasing this book you are eligible for one month membership to ForgottenBooks.com, giving you unlimited access to our entire collection of over 700,000 titles via our web site and mobile apps.

To claim your free month visit: www.forgottenbooks.com/free88660

* Offer is valid for 45 days from date of purchase. Terms and conditions apply.

Similar Books Are Available from
www.forgottenbooks.com

Beautiful Joe
An Autobiography, by Marshall Saunders

Theodore Roosevelt, an Autobiography
by Theodore Roosevelt

Napoleon
A Biographical Study, by Max Lenz

Up from Slavery
An Autobiography, by Booker T. Washington

Gotama Buddha
A Biography, Based on the Canonical Books of the Theravādin, by Kenneth J. Saunders

Plato's Biography of Socrates
by A. E. Taylor

Cicero
A Biography, by Torsten Petersson

Madam Guyon
An Autobiography, by Jeanne Marie Bouvier De La Motte Guyon

The Writings of Thomas Jefferson
by Thomas Jefferson

Thomas Skinner, M.D.
A Biographical Sketch, by John H. Clarke

Saint Thomas Aquinas of the Order of Preachers (1225-1274)
A Biographical Study of the Angelic Doctor, by Placid Conway

Recollections of the Rev. John Johnson and His Home
An Autobiography, by Susannah Johnson

Biographical Sketches in Cornwall, Vol. 1 of 3
by R. Polwhele

Autobiography of John Francis Hylan, Mayor of New York
by John Francis Hylan

The Autobiography of Benjamin Franklin
The Unmutilated and Correct Version, by Benjamin Franklin

James Mill
A Biography, by Alexander Bain

George Washington
An Historical Biography, by Horace E. Scudder

Florence Nightingale
A Biography, by Irene Cooper Willis

Marse Henry
An Autobiography, by Henry Watterson

Autobiography and Poems
by Charlotte E. Linden

JAMES FREEMAN CLARKE

AUTOBIOGRAPHY, DIARY AND CORRESPONDENCE

EDITED BY

EDWARD EVERETT HALE

BOSTON AND NEW YORK
HOUGHTON, MIFFLIN AND COMPANY
The Riverside Press, Cambridge
1891

Copyright, 1891,
By HOUGHTON, MIFFLIN & CO.

All rights reserved.

The Riverside Press, Cambridge, Mass., U. S. A.
Electrotyped and Printed by H. O. Houghton & Co.

CONTENTS.

AUTOBIOGRAPHY.

CHAPTER	PAGE
I. Parentage	1
II. Newton	11
III. The Latin School	26
IV. Cambridge	34
V. Kentucky	50
VI. Life in Kentucky	66

DIARY AND CORRESPONDENCE.

VII. Mr. Clarke's Early Years	81
VIII. Journals and Letters. 1830–1840	94
IX. The Church of the Disciples	135
X. Europe	171
XI. Meadville	186
XII. The Church of the Disciples. 1853	201
XIII. Anti-slavery	213
XIV. The Unitarian Church	251
XV. The War	268
XVI. Education	292
XVII. Work in the Pulpit	308
XVIII. Varied Activities. 1865–1880	323
XIX. Closing Years. 1881–1888	357
XX. The Man	389
XXI. The End	408
Writings of James Freeman Clarke	416
Index	421

AUTOBIOGRAPHY.

CHAPTER I.

PARENTAGE.

MAGNOLIA, MASS., *July* 21, 1883.

It is just fifty years to-day since I preached my first sermon in Bernard Whitman's church in Waltham. I shall keep the anniversary by beginning the sketch of my life, which my friends have thought may be interesting. I have no remarkable events or adventures to record. But I have lived in an important period; have known many eminent men and distinguished women; have seen great changes in social life, in religious opinion, in private morals and public manners. If I can succeed in making a few suggestive pictures, or memory sketches, it may be a gratification to my children and friends, and possibly contribute matter for the future historian of this period.

In looking back to the time, fifty years ago, when I was about to begin my work in life, that which first strikes me is this: I was then twenty-three; and that past twenty-three years seemed to me more eventful and longer than the subsequent fifty appear now. I believe I felt older then than I do now. I seemed to myself to have gone through the round of human experience. I had read and thought, studied and meditated, mingled in society, had friendships with men and women.

What subsequent experiences can compare with those of our first years, when we have just entered the universe, caught our first glimpse of nature, been amazed by the mystery of the human mind, and made acquaintance with poetry, romance, and some of the great classics of ancient and modern times? The boy is full of hope and eager expectation. The curtain is rising on a stage where he looks for a wonderful drama. As Schiller says, "The boy sets sail on the ocean of life with a fleet of a thousand vessels; the old man reaches the shore at last rescued on a single plank."

Wordsworth's "Ode on the Intimations of Immortality" contains a truth which our experience must confirm. The germs of all that we are to be begin to unfold in our childhood. Those shadowy recollections are the master-lights of our after-being. The truths which awake then never perish. The impressions then made on the soul underlie all others, and determine largely our future course.

My father, Samuel Clarke, was an only child. His father, Samuel Clarke, had one sister (Hepzibah Clarke, afterward Mrs. Swan), but no brother. Both were born in Boston. My great-grandfather, Barnabas Clarke, was born in Harwich, on Cape Cod, and was for some years a shipmaster. Afterward he became a merchant in Boston, marrying Hepzibah Barrett in 1748.

Barnabas Clarke was a lineal descendant of Thomas Clarke, who is reported, by what Thacher calls "a well received tradition" in Plymouth, to have been the mate of the Mayflower, and "the first who landed on Clarke's Island" in Plymouth harbor. If so, he returned to England with the vessel, for he came over as a settler in the Anne, in July, 1623. He lived in Plymouth, Harwich, and Boston. He died in Plymouth, aged ninety-eight, in the year 1697, and his grave and gravestone may be seen on the summit of Burying-ground Hill.

My grandfather, Samuel Clarke, born in Boston in 1754, was at the Boston Latin School in 1766. At the age of nineteen he was sailing as master and supercargo of vessels belonging to his father, Barnabas Clarke, and William Dennie. He was a man of ability, energy, and determination.

He married, in 1778, Martha, daughter of Obadiah Curtis. The same year he went as major of one of Governor Hancock's regiments to Rhode Island, acting in coöperation with the troops of La Fayette. The regiment lay under canvas at Newport during the terrible gale of August 12, 1778, long known as the "French Storm." He here contracted disease of the lungs, of which he died in 1780, in his house in School Street.

His widow long preserved his silk sash, helmet, and military regimentals. These I used to see in the garret of the house, where, as a child, I loved to rummage among the high-heeled shoes, and smoke-jacks, and other relics of the past.

THE CURTIS FAMILY.

My father's mother, who, after my grandfather Clarke's death in 1780, married James Freeman in 1788, was the daughter of Obadiah Curtis and Martha Buckminster, of Framingham. Obadiah Curtis was a lineal descendant of William Curtis, who emigrated from Nazing, Essex County, England, in the ship Lyon, which reached Boston, September 16, 1632. His wife was sister of John Eliot, the apostle to the Indians, who also came from Nazing.

The descendants of William Curtis are numerous, and many of them are still living in Boston and Roxbury. .

Obadiah Curtis probably owed his rise in the world to the energy and ability of his wife, who belonged to the somewhat remarkable family of Buckminsters of Framingham.

After their marriage they went to Boston; and, to help her husband, Mrs. Curtis opened a shop for the sale of English goods at what is now the corner of Bromfield Street and Washington Street. Having accumulated a competence Mrs. Curtis and her husband moved to Newton in 1807, bought two or three acres of the estate of my father, who was their grandson, and built a house in which they ended their days. . . .

Obadiah and Martha Curtis had four children, Anna, Martha, Sarah, and Thomas. Anna married the Rev. Jonathan Homer; and it was said of her that if she heard of any family in the parish who needed better food than they could afford to buy, she would send to them the joint from the spit in her own kitchen; and her husband, good man, meditating on Erasmus and Beza, would make his dinner of boiled potatoes, and never miss the meat.

Martha, the second, was my grandmother, a woman of strong will and quick temper, a little inclined to have her own way. But she was affectionate to those she loved, and as generous to the poor as my aunt Homer. Every Sunday she was driven from Newton to Boston, between six and seven miles, in the ancient carriage, that she might attend services at her husband's church, King's Chapel. This was in summer, which Dr. and Mrs. Freeman always passed on the old estate at Newton. During three or four months of winter, they lived in Boston. My great-aunt, Sally Curtis, the third daughter, was of a more poetic nature than the others. In her small collection of books, I recollect Shenstone and other poets, her favorite passages carefully underlined, after the manner of that day. In the garden borders she diligently cultivated flowers which delighted my youthful eyes.

Thomas Curtis was a merchant in Boston, and a ship-owner, doing a large business. He lived on the highest point of Somerset Street, next to the house of his partner, Caleb Loring. He had five sons and three daughters, which made his house a very entertaining place to visit. Every Christmas they had a family festival prolonged till late at night, at which the Lorings, Stevensons, and other relatives, were present, and the conversation was always bright and entertaining.

The eldest son, Charles Pelham Curtis, is well remembered as a distinguished member of the Boston Bar, and very brilliant in conversation.

Another son, Thomas Buckminster, was first an officer in the navy, then master of merchant vessels, and finally merchant and banker.

James Freeman Curtis, the third son, was a handsome and high-spirited youth. He was a midshipman on the Chesapeake, when she was taken by the Shannon, off Boston, but had his revenge by being an officer of the Constitution when she took the Cyane and Levant. Afterward he commanded an expedition against the pirates in the West Indies, and took by assault one of their strongholds. He spent some weeks at our house in Newton, when I was a child, and built for us a small brig and a three-masted man-of-war, about four feet long, which made a splendid appearance riding at anchor on our fish-pond.

Stories of sea-life made a part of the education of Boston boys sixty years ago, even of those who did not go to sea themselves. . . .

My father, Dr. Samuel Clarke, was born in Boston, in 1779, in a house in School Street, which belonged to his father, who died when his son was a year old. My father, like my grandfather Clarke, myself, and my brothers, went to the Boston Latin School. He ought to have gone to college, for he had a taste for study; but his property was in the hands of his guardian, who refused to advance money for his education. He therefore entered the store of Joseph Coolidge, importer of British goods. About 1800, he went into that business with Joseph Coolidge, Jr. In 1804, he obtained possession of his property, and returned to Newton, where he built a house in a beautiful situation.[1] Next year he married Rebecca Parker Hull, daughter of William Hull, a bright young girl, just out of Mrs. Rawson's school. They were well adapted to each other, being counterparts in disposition. The picture of my father by Malbone represents him as a young man of fine features and intelligent face. He was reserved and silent, while my mother was very sociable. Wherever she went she made acquaintances. She could not go a mile or two from home without bringing back a history of curious people she had met, and strange adventures she had encountered. She lived in many places, — in Newton, Mass.; in Boston; in Vermont; in New Hampshire; in Chicago, Illinois; Newport, R. I.; and in Italy. She wrote to me from Rome, "I am a Roman citizen; I know it, for I have just paid my tax-bill." Everywhere she made herself at home, and found friends. Everywhere she took an interest in the unfortunate, and exerted herself energetically in their behalf.

Having one or two old colored people as pensioners she was led to think that there ought to be a home in Boston for old colored women. It was at the beginning of the Civil War, and many of us thought that the attempt to establish such a home would be more successful if postponed. But my mother was no temporizer. She made me bring up the subject at one of the Wednesday evening meetings of the Church of the Disciples; asked Mr. Grimes, the minister of the colored people's church, to be present, and to state the facts within his knowledge to show the need of such an institution; interested Governor Andrew, Dr. and Mrs. Samuel Cabot, and others; and by their help the institution was established, and the old colored women were installed in their comfortable home. My mother

[1] This house was not long after bought by Dr. and Mrs. Freeman, and this was their home as long as they lived.

said to her daughter in her last sickness, "Sarah, I wish carriages to be sent to take the old colored women to my funeral. I think it will be a great entertainment to them. They do not have many amusements."

Two years after their marriage, my father and mother moved to a farm in Maidstone, Vermont, near Canada, situated on an interval of the Connecticut River. My father's object was to raise merino sheep, the wool of which was very valuable. The young couple drove all the way in a sort of buggy wagon, drawn by two horses, harnessed tandem. It is said that their carriage was the first that ever passed through the White Mountain Notch.[1] My mother had with her an infant, only a year old. The house was lonely, two or three miles distant from any other. It was hard to get any domestics. The bears and wolves killed the sheep. The experiment was unsuccessful, and in a year or two my parents returned to Newton. The best thing they brought back from Vermont was a ghost story, which my mother used to tell with much spirit. Their only domestic, a young woman, was taken sick, and died. My father had to go some distance to find a carpenter to make the coffin, and my mother was left alone with her infant. Evening came on, and my father had not returned. All at once an unexpected knock was heard. It was unexpected, for few visitors ever found their way to the house. My mother went to the outer door, but there was no one there, or anywhere in sight. She returned to the sitting-room, and directly the knocking came again, louder than before, and the door into the room where the body of the young woman was lying slowly opened. My mother, thoroughly frightened, seized her child, and ran out of the house, with the wild purpose of going to the nearest neighbor. As she went round the house, she heard the knocking again, close to her. Looking back she saw a large merino ram butting

[1] That is, the first pleasure carriage.

against the house; which, being slightly built, was shaken by the shock.

My father was a man of varied talents. He was able to excel in so many directions that he never could limit himself to one. He was inventor, architect, artist, mechanic, physician, lawyer, chemist, wool-raiser. But no sooner had he succeeded in starting an enterprise than he lost his interest in it, and wished to do something else. His pleasure was in originating and inventing, not in executing. But he had a very practical knowledge in many arts. He understood machinery, and built mills on new plans. He painted portraits in oils, and made effective sketches with the pencil. In Vermont, he presided with dignity as a judge. He was one of the first, if not the first, in this country to whiten wax, to grind drugs by machinery, sublimate calomel, and manufacture lunar caustic, tartaric acid, and other chemicals. As a physician, he anticipated the present belief in the relative uselessness of drugs. He gave very little medicine, and depended in his practice on the influence of proper food, air, exercise, and mental conditions. He brought hope and courage to the sick-room, and his patients were his friends. His temper was singularly placid, and he had the rare gift of perfect equanimity. He was a man of few words, very reserved, and my mother carried on most of the conversation. He was as fond of solitude as she of society. I find in myself both tendencies. I can be very happy alone. When taking a walk, or writing, or studying, I prefer entire solitude. Thus I love to write my sermons before breakfast, in the silence of the early day. This I inherit from my father. But, like my mother, I enjoy society, and love to talk. Dearly as I love nature, humanity has a greater charm for me. Landing once on Tower Stairs in a dense and dirty fog, I found myself filled with a sudden exhilaration. I sought to analyze the feeling. Why should I be so pleased at arriving in

London? There was no one there I wished to see, scarcely any one whom I knew. At last I discovered that my pleasure came because I found myself in the midst of so many human beings. And though there was in London extreme misery, and much of it, yet, of necessity, the joy of life must much predominate.

My father took pleasure in the details of work, invented the machinery for his mills, understood the properties of iron, steel, wood, stone. He had a fine astronomical telescope, through which, when I was a very little boy, he showed me the rings of Saturn. He took an interest in science and its discoveries. Before phosphorus matches came, and while we still depended on flint, steel, and tinder-box, he lighted his candles by a jet of hydrogen thrown on platina sponge. An old man, who had been my father's foreman during many years, said to me, as we stood beside his coffin: "When your father talked with carpenters they thought he must be of their trade. It was the same with blacksmiths, or carriage-makers, or masons. He seemed to know every man's trade as well as the mechanic himself."

But notwithstanding these multifarious gifts and attainments, and though he was a very hard worker all his life, as well as economical in his habits, he never acquired a competence.

In fact, the estate which he inherited from his father was gradually lost by various disasters. Shortly before his death, a fire destroyed the chemical works and mills in which he had invested most of his remaining property. His insurance had just expired, and the loss was total. But his equanimity did not fail him. The fire was in the night, and I did not arrive at the place until everything was burned to the ground. The firemen had gone, and I found my father, alone, gazing at the ruins. When he saw me, he simply said, with a grave smile: "We may call this, I suppose, the abomination of desolation." This was all his comment. When my mother found that the burning of the chemical works had left my father without property, she determined to do something to support the family herself. She hired a house in Ashburton Place, Boston, and took boarders. Her friends assured her that nothing could be made by keeping boarders; but she was hopeful; and though for some time she found it difficult to let her rooms, she finally succeeded. She had among her boarders those who became her warm friends. Among them was Jared Sparks, the historian; Mr. and Mrs. Devens and their children, one of whom is General Devens; the three daughters of Dr. Nathaniel Peabody, Miss Elizabeth P. Peabody, Miss Mary Peabody, afterwards Mrs. Horace Mann, and Miss Sophia Peabody, afterwards Mrs. Nathaniel Hawthorne. Horace Mann was also a boarder, as was Mr. Edward S. Rand.

I do not know that our family were ever happier than in those days. We were all poor, but all who could were doing something to support themselves. My sister gave lessons in drawing. Two of my brothers were doing what they could. My eldest brother Sam was confined to his bed by rheumatism. But though a great sufferer, he was always cheerful, and when we assembled in his room in the evening, he was the most entertaining member of the group.

After my grandfather Freeman's death,[1] my mother gave up her boarding-house, and returned to Newton to take care of my grandmother Freeman in her declining years.

[1] November 14, 1835.

CHAPTER II.

NEWTON.

THE town of Newton,[1] in which I passed the earliest years of my life, and which was my real home until I went to Kentucky in 1833, was a curious and interesting New England community of the post-Revolutionary period. It was thinly settled by farmers, market gardeners, and others, who were neither poor nor rich, but able to support themselves and their families by constant labor. They were industrious, frugal, honest, and conservative in their habits and opinions. Like most of the people in the country towns of Massachusetts, they were Federalists, having a great horror of Jefferson and Madison. They went to church regularly, attending without fail the two services in the parish church. To keep the Puritan Sabbath and go to church twice a day were the sacraments of their religion. Beyond this there was little religious activity of any kind. Revivals were unknown; Sunday-schools had not been invented; Bible societies and missionary societies were in their infancy. The towns were divided into parishes, and each parish had its Congregational church, supported by taxation. The Congregational Church was the established church maintained by law. Every inhabitant of the town, no matter what his faith or his unbelief, was taxed to support the church of his parish. After a while the law was altered so as to allow him "to sign off," that is, to make a formal declaration of his intention to pay his tax to some other

[1] This chapter of the Autobiography was begun July 3, 1884.

society in the town.[1] Ours was the East Parish of Newton, and during all my childhood my great-uncle, Dr. Jonathan Homer, was its sole pastor. The only other religious society in the large region which constituted the parish was a small Baptist church. This was placed by the side of a pond, where the immersions took place. But these were infrequent; the society was not aggressive, and they were looked upon much as we should have regarded a body of Italians or a colony of Portuguese who might have settled among us. Their ways were not our ways, nor their thoughts our thoughts. We little dreamed that the time would come when a "History of Newton" would be written, chiefly occupied with biographies of Baptist preachers and professors, and in which the Baptist Theological School would be described as the most important institution of the town. But in my boyhood this was all in the future. We never thought of going anywhere but to the parish church. There the population assembled every Sunday, except in cases of severe sickness. Dr. Homer mounted the pulpit, and proceeded to carry on the service in a way altogether his own. He was a kind-hearted, good man, and much loved by the people. They sat quietly while he harangued, though they could not possibly have understood much of what he was saying. But that made no difference. Their duty was to go to church, and sit there for an hour or two, and they did it faithfully. It was not their duty to understand what they heard. Dr. Jonathan Homer was one of the most absent-minded of men; more like Dominie Sampson than any one else I have known. If he met you on the road he would begin to say aloud what he was meditating. For example, he might begin, without preface, thus: "Why Beza should have given that rendering of Corinthians I cannot say. Possibly he may have found it in Erasmus, though I have not been able

[1] Or, eventually, to some other society in the State.

to trace it in either of the early editions. Sir Isaac Coffin has promised to send me the first Geneva; but Tyndall would be better." Having made these cursory remarks he would pass on. He was very faithful in pastoral visiting, and if he found any one in sickness or trouble he would forget Beza, and give him some comforting words of the Lord Christ. Of a summer day he might often be seen going on a gentle trot along the road, his gingham dressing-gown floating out behind him like a banner. He would turn into the house of a parishioner, and if he found no one in the sitting-room, would go into the kitchen, all unconscious of any impropriety.

The Congregational ministers in each parish, being supported by taxation of all the property in the parish, were very independent. They could not be displaced except for some serious offense, which was a very rare event. They were all graduates of some college, and learned according to the scholarship of their day. Their practical independence did not produce indolence or indifference to their duty. But it often developed eccentricity. Every clergyman was a sort of king in his parish. If his tendencies were toward self-assertion, he might become arbitrary and domineering; if unchecked by regard for public opinion and fear of ridicule, he might develop certain oddities of speech and behavior. Many of them remained in the same parish for more than half a century, and christened, married, and buried two or three generations. They directed education in the schools, guided the political course of their parishioners in the town meeting, were an authority to be consulted in practical as well as religious and moral questions. They introduced improvements in agriculture and gardening, and communicated to their flocks whatever important discoveries they met with in reading their newspaper, or heard of at the ministers' monthly meeting. They dined one day with the judge or the governor, and the next day with the farmer or mechanic, and thus became a useful medium of communication between different classes of society. They were the natural mediators between rich and educated, and plain people. There were no poor and no ignorant people.

During the summer months we paid and received visits. We drove over in the old family carriage to see Dr. Morse or Dr. Spring in Watertown, Governor Gore and Theodore Lyman in Waltham, Gorham Parsons and Mr. Pomeroy in Brighton, Mrs. Swan in Dorchester, Jonathan Russell and Barney Smith in Milton, Colonel Perkins and the Buckminsters in Brookline. These little trips were very attractive to a child. Our own home, though large and comfortable, had none of the elegance which some of these old mansions displayed. My father's house was also in Newton, not far off, and I was a great deal there. When I was a small child, my parents lived close by, in my aunt Sally Curtis's house; and so I was with my brothers and sister almost as much as if we had been in the same home. My grandmother Freeman was always borrowing the children of her friends. They loved to come to Newton to gather raspberries, blackberries, and cherries, to dig in the garden, fish in the pond, ride the horses with or without a saddle, and wander into the woods when the chestnuts and hickory nuts began to fall. To shoot birds was not allowed on our place. There was no gun about the house; and the squirrels and robins had their way, and did as they liked. We had so many cherry-trees in full bearing every summer that there were enough for the birds and the children too. I never condescended to eat cherries which had been picked; but when I wanted them I climbed to the top of the tree, where they were the ripest and best, and sat eating, with the robins eating around me. And in those days the peach-trees bore as plentifully, and the peaches strewed the ground under our feet. As for the blackberries, there was a great heap of stones in one of the pastures, which had accumulated by being carried there from the cultivated fields, and this stone-heap was overrun with the best blackberry vines. So that we children could say with Marvell, —

> "What wondrous life is this I lead!
> Ripe apples drop about my head;
> The nectarine and curious peach
> Into my hands themselves do reach."

An old-fashioned garden, full of fruit, berries, and nut-trees, teaches children a love for nature. It brings them naturally into confidential relations with the vital forces working up from the soil and down from the sky. Nature, a tender parent, takes the little ones in her arms, as Jesus did, and introduces them into her kingdom of heaven. So a child associates what he hears of God with what he sees of Him in sunshine and cloud, the softly approaching dawn and the gently departing day. One of the hymns which I heard in early childhood had these lines: —

> "Who spread the ocean round
> About the solid land,
> And made the rising ground
> Above the waters stand."

As our residence was so high that we could see the distant line of ocean on one side, and the pale blue horizon of far-off hills on the other, I supposed, in my simplicity, that this circle of blue was the all-surrounding ocean, and that all the solid land was contained in what met my eyes. When quite young, Scott's poem, "The Lady of the Lake," was read aloud in my hearing, and its pictures took possession of my imagination. One day the family coach and driver came to the door to take some of the household to visit their cousins, the Buckminsters of Framingham. I had heard of a lake in Framingham, and asked if the "Lady of the Lake" lived there. Some one laughingly replied, "Certainly! Miss Buckminster is the 'Lady of the Lake'" I therefore expected to see the fair Ellen Douglas in her boat, and when we came to what is now called Cochituate Lake, I looked through the carriage window with eager expectation, sure that the little skiff would appear shooting out from behind a headland. Thus a child enriches his little world by putting into it all he hears or reads, and has these pictures all about him.

Until I was ten years old, I received most of my tuition from my grandfather Freeman.[1] After breakfast each morning, he taught my elder brother and sister and me Latin, Greek, and mathematics. I did not know at the time what a wonderful teacher he was. He anticipated, sixty years ago, the best methods of modern instruction. In the first place he made our studies interesting to us. Next he removed all unnecessary difficulties, and only required us to learn what was essential. The Latin Grammar which we studied was only twenty or thirty pages in length. It was called "Latin Accidence," and contained the Parts of Speech, the Declensions and Conjugations, and a few of the principal rules of Syntax. The larger grammar was not to be committed to memory, but to be used like a dictionary, for consultation. The more important Latin

---

[1] Almost my first recollection as a child is of one who seemed to me then to be old, who was the friend of us all. In the morning he worked in his garden, and we played by his side; in the forenoon, while he read and wrote, we children studied our lessons under his guidance; as the twilight darkened, he gathered us around him to tell during successive evenings the story of Ulysses, of Sir Huon, of Kehama and Thalaba. As we grew older, we learned to understand the quality of his benignity, his generosity, his manly independence, his sagacious wisdom, his purity, humility, and loyalty to all truth and right. Surely those who have come in contact with such an influence may well love to come together, and for an hour communicate to each other what they remember of this remarkable life. — J. F. C. at Centennial of James Freeman.

words we learned by heart from a "Vocabulary," and the more important Greek words from a small book called "Greek Primitives." Thus provided, we immediately began to translate some interesting story in Nepos or Ovid. He kept up our interest by talking to us about it, explaining the difficult passages, and when it was in verse repeating it so as to bring out the rhythm and melody. When we came to a word we did not understand, he would tell us the meaning, but required us to repeat it again and again till he was sure we remembered it. To those who thought that this method made study too easy, and that it did not discipline the mind, he answered, "The study of a foreign language can never be made too easy. There are always difficulties enough in it. But what mental discipline is there in turning over the pages of a dictionary? I tell these children the meaning of the word, just as the dictionary does; but I save them the time lost in the merely manual operation of turning over the leaves. Real discipline comes to the mind when it acts, not languidly, but with its full energy, and it acts with energy only when it is interested in what it does. Therefore, as soon as I am unable to keep up their interest in what they do, I turn their attention to something else, or send them out to play." The excellence of this method may be seen in the fact that before I was ten years old I had read a good deal of Ovid, some odes of Horace, a little of Virgil, the Gospel of Matthew in Greek, and had gone as far as Cubic Equations in algebra. I also had read through the "History of the United States," Hume's "England," Robertson's "Scotland," Ferguson's and Gibbon's "Rome." I can repeat to-day, after sixty years, many passages of Ovid and at least three odes of Horace, which I committed to memory before I was ten. Nor was I aware that I was doing a great deal, for the study was made almost as entertaining as play. Problems in arithmetic and algebra were treated as a kind of game. I once met with the term "trigonometry," and asked my grandfather the meaning of the word. "Trigonometry," said he, "is a wonderful science. It is all about triangles." "What is a triangle?" said I. "I will show you," he replied, and proceeded to draw on a slate a number of triangles, showing me that each had three sides and three angles, and explaining that if we knew three of these (one being a side), we could find the other three. He told me that by that law we could tell the distances of the planets and the moon. Then he took me out upon the lawn and showed me a tall tree, and explained how by trigonometry I could tell the height of the tree. Thereupon I made myself a little quadrant out of a shingle, and proceeded to measure the height of the trees and houses around me. Though the actual results were probably far from accurate, yet by this little experiment I obtained a very clear notion of the great foundation laws of mathematical astronomy. And I learned this in play. Such studies left plenty of time for outdoor exercise. With my brothers and cousins I learned to ride on horseback with and without a saddle, to swim, to skate, to make bows and arrows and slings, and shoot with them, and to practice all the other athletic sports which boys love. We went to find distant ponds and rivers in which to catch perch and pickerel, and we even rediscovered the speckled trout in some brooks whence they had been thought to have disappeared long before. What happy hours we passed roaming through the woods, clambering over ledges of gray rock, or floating in boats on the omnipresent Charles River which nearly encircled Newton! Amid these studies and amusements there was still time enough for reading. First, when young, we had Miss Edgeworth, — her stories not being bound together under the forbidding title of "Parents' Assistant," but in separate tales, each to be read by itself and read again, — "Simple Susan," "The Little Merchants," "Old Poz," "Eton Montem," etc. Then, too, Walter Scott was writing his novels, and whenever a new one appeared, it was brought from Boston, and read aloud in the family circle. I recollect that when "Ivanhoe" came, I eagerly seized it, and became so absorbed in the story of the tournament that I hid under a bed, and refused to hear the call to study till I had seen the Black Knight and Ivanhoe triumphant in the lists of Ashby-de-la-Zouche. I still think that there are no novels like those, — so full of character, adventure, picturesque incident, and with such an atmosphere of sunshine and good health throughout. Under that magic pen history became living, and the past was present. *We* were the crusaders, *we* the outlaws, *we* the hesitating heroes of the Waverley novels, who always seemed in an interesting dilemma, not quite able to decide between the two ways. Each Waverley novel was a new joy. And so Scott's poems were full of delight and cheer. Their lyric flow, their manly tone, their generous sentiment lifted us into a blessed region of ideal beauty. I remember when I was at the Latin School, I spent my half-holiday one Saturday reading "Marmion," for the first time. As the sun was setting I reached the end of the poem, and in the farewell verses read with astonishment these lines: —

> "To thee, dear schoolboy, whom my lay
> Has cheated of thy hour of play,
> Light task and merry holiday!"

and it seemed as if Scott were close beside me, talking to me in person.

There was an old chestnut-tree in the pasture, in which I had arranged a seat, and there I often sat, surrounded by the thick shady branches, and read the most interesting books I could discover in my grandfather's library. As this consisted largely of books of theology, Latin and Greek classics, or learned works in Spanish, Italian, and Portuguese, I found it difficult to suit myself. There was "Rasselas," which pretended to be a story, but was only a long string of moralizing. But among some numbers of "The Monthly Anthology" I found the translation, by Sir William Jones, of the Hindoo play "Sakoontala," and there was an old edition of Shakespeare in a number of duodecimo volumes. The tradition in the family was, that these volumes came ashore when the English man-of-war Somerset was wrecked on Cape Cod. Some of the volumes were missing, but this on the whole was an advantage, for it gave a certain aspect of infinity to the author. For aught I knew there might be a hundred more plays of Shakespeare. And as we think more of the lost books of Tacitus than of those we possess, because the contents of these unread pages fill the imagination with conjectures, so the plays of Shakespeare which I did not have made an ideal penumbra of beauty round those I was reading. There was also a volume of "Elegant Extracts" in verse, by Vicesimus Knox, which contained very good reading. From that volume I learned something of Spenser and Dryden, Swift and Pope. I even found some amusement in "Bailey's English Dictionary," which often gave little historic and biographic anecdotes about the words, expatiating in a delightful way while illustrating their meaning. I learned from it a little of everything, and can still repeat the names and descriptions of the "Ten honorable Ordinaries" in Heraldry as I there learned them for my amusement. It also contained tables for making Latin hexameters by a mechanical process; and other like matters, which are far below the dignity of a modern dictionary.

I confess to a weakness for such old-fashioned textbooks, which condescend a little to the infirmities of beginners. Schoolbooks now are composed by scholars who wish to show off their learning to other scholars, and who scorn what is elementary. A school treatise on algebra is composed as if intended for profound mathematicians. A Latin grammar prepared for boys ten years old goes into the mysteries of philology. A new edition of Virgil shows that the editor has ransacked all the studies on etymology and syntax in order to make a show of recondite learning in his foot-notes. How much better for boys the old Delphin editions of the classics, which, fortunately for me, were still in use in my days! There the words were arranged in the margin in the order of construction, and the foot-notes gave us explanations which made the matter clear. And at the end what a copious index, which gave us words and phrases! Besides this we had other helps, such as the "Gradus ad Parnassum," and for some books an interlined translation. Instead of the modern astronomies which bristle with mathematical formulas, we had "The Young Gentleman's Astronomy," in which the author announces that it is written, "not to advance learning, but to assist learners," and boldly declares his intention to begin at the beginning.

The English classics in Dr. Freeman's library were of the Queen Anne era. Thus I became quite familiar with the "Spectator" and "Guardian," and writers of that period. If we had not many books to read, we possessed some of the best. It did us no harm to read over again and again "Paradise Lost," Pope's "Essay on Man," "The Vicar of Wakefield," "Robinson Crusoe," and "Gulliver's Travels." The poems of Prior, Gay, and Peter Pindar were also in the Freeman library, in old editions. In my good aunt Sally Curtis's rooms I found some of the novels popular in her time: "Cecilia" and "Evelina," by Miss Burney; "The Scottish Chiefs;" "Thaddeus of Warsaw;" with Thomson's "Seasons;" Falconer's "Shipwreck;" and Shenstone's poems.

I am glad that I early came to know and love Pope. I obtained his complete works as a prize when at the Latin School, and in the same way came into possession of Johnson's "Lives of the Poets," and the poems of Scott, Burns, and Cowper. I am indebted to my aunt Swan for one source of pleasure and culture. When I was a child, recovering from a long illness, she brought to the house for my amusement the large engravings from Hogarth, and a folio volume of engravings from the Orleans Gallery.

It is an advantage to a child to grow up among hills, for then Nature makes a perpetual framework around him for his thoughts. The scenery blends with all he does, and its calm beauty gives dignity and serenity to every emotion. The landscape holds him in its arms like a mother, and caresses him with its tender charm at every hour. Our thoughts are at last so associated with hills and the wide horizon that when we go to live on a level plain, or amid the streets of a city, we suffer from nostalgia. We miss the sweeping outlines of nature, the rolling uplands, the deep silent woods, the far resounding sea. Mr. Emerson, in his "Nature," well describes how the orator bred in the fields and among hills draws inspiration long after from the memories of his childhood, and how the sights and sounds of Nature pass into his speech.

My grandfather Freeman's house, where I lived, was on high land, with a horizon line of ocean in the distance to the northeast, and the blue hills of Weston at the northwest. My grandfather Hull's home, a mile or two away, stood above a valley, through which ran a strong cold stream of water, tumbling in a little cascade out of a deep pond. His was a farm containing some three hundred acres, much of it being a wild wood, and a part low meadow land, with stately elm-trees here and there. The house was a sort of Liberty Hall, where people came and went at their will and did as they liked. Both my grandfather and grandmother Hull were in their dispositions largely hospitable, and this habit of hospitality had been increased by their having lived so many years at Detroit, on the frontier, where, as in all new countries, it is the custom to keep an open house and to receive all comers. The poverty and prudence of New England people prevented such a custom from prevailing among them, and my grandfather Hull's house was the only one I remember, as a boy, where the doors seemed always to stand open, literally and figuratively. As my grandfather had lived somewhat abroad, and had been connected with various families through the Union, strangers would often arrive, bringing letters of introduction from remote regions. Among these, I remember foreigners with hard names, Italian and French gentlemen, who would become members of the family for many days or weeks, and then depart, and be heard of no more. Meantime, while these visitors occupied the rooms above, the great kitchen below was commonly full of another class, who made themselves equally at home. A sort of people who would now be called tramps were generally there, ready to eat their dinner, and when night came find some place to sleep in Judge Fuller's old malthouse. Also the Sam Lawsons of the region would often be found sitting in General Hull's kitchen, giving out the village gossip, and relating the news of the neighborhood.

When I read "Oldtown Folks," I was satisfied that *Old* town meant *New* town, and that the scene was laid in Newton, at my grandfather Hull's place. The author, in describing the good grandmother's kitchen, was evidently giving an account of my grandmother Hull's kitchen. I once met Mrs. Stowe at Governor Claflin's, whose residence stands exactly where General Hull's house stood, and I asked her to say frankly if that very spot were not the scene of "Oldtown Folks."

She made no satisfactory reply to this question, and nothing will convince me that some traditions of the old Hull place did not reach her. It is too exact an account to be a mere coincidence.

How all the visitors, retainers, and hangers-on were supported is a question difficult to answer. My grandfather's means were very modest. He had only a small income beside the produce of his farm. But most of what was eaten in parlor and kitchen came from his garden and fields.

My uncle Abraham, General Hull's only son, was killed at the battle of Lundy's Lane, one of the sharpest conflicts of the war of 1812. He was captain in the United States Fourth, a famous regiment, was bayoneted in advance of the line, while leading a charge, and was buried where he fell, as a mark of distinction for his signal gallantry. Years after, in visiting the place, I was shown the spot by an old soldier who had been in the battle, and who spoke warmly of the courage of Captain Hull. I recalled the lines of Bryant, which may have been written on the very spot, beginning, —

> "Once this soft turf, these quiet sands,
> Were trampled by a hurrying crowd,
> And fiery hearts and armëd hands
> Encountered in the battle-cloud."

In my opinion, it is a disadvantage for children to have much money, and also a disadvantage to be without any. The prayer of Agur, "Give me neither poverty nor riches," applies as well to children as to adults. My brothers and I made our own playthings, our bats and balls, our bows and arrows. We had a museum to which drifted the curiosities of the family, — Indian war clubs, moccasins, and finery; the mouths of sharks rimmed with rows of terrific teeth; the rattles of the rattlesnake, the tusks of the rhinoceros, — evidences of the past connection of some of the household with the wilderness, and of others with the sea.

But some things, like sleds and skates, must be bought; and for such purposes we laid away our small incomes. It was one of my grandfather's principles that every person should have some regular allowance, be it ever so little. He believed that a husband should make a regular allowance to his wife, and parents to their children. When I was a very little boy I had three cents a week, then six, then ten, at last twenty-five cents. But I was required to keep an account book, and put down all I received and spent. I even learned to keep my books by double entry, which also was made an entertaining exercise. I cannot but think that this was a very good thing for us. We were taught the value of money, taught to economize it, so as to use it for an extraordinary occasion.

Thus, after hearing a course of chemical lectures, I had my little laboratory. After a lecture on electricity, I set myself to making a machine; for a cylinder I bought a large bottle of smooth white glass; my non-conducting pillars to support it, and to support the conductor, were cologne bottles; the conductor itself I made of a block of wood on which was pasted tinfoil. My Leyden jars I manufactured in the same way, and I could get a very respectable spark from this simple apparatus.

It was the custom on summer afternoons for many of my grandfather Freeman's friends to drive from Boston, to visit him at his country residence. The reception room was a large parlor on the east, from which there was a beautiful view of the valley below, Nonantum [1] on the left, the spire of Brighton church beyond, and farther away, Charlestown, Boston, and the ocean.

[1] Nonantum is the hill where the apostle Eliot first preached to the Indians.

CHAPTER III.

THE LATIN SCHOOL.

THE Boston Latin School was the first and only school I ever attended. All my early teaching, as I have said, I received at home; and when I entered the Latin School, at the age of ten, I had already acquired a considerable amount of knowledge under that genial home instruction. Every difficult step had been made so easy for me that I enjoyed reading the pleasant stories of Ovid, and even the melodies of Horace; and algebra had been a game full of interesting problems, the solution of which gave a thrill of satisfaction. So that I might seem to be thoroughly prepared for the studies of the Latin School. But one thing I had not learned to do. I had not been taught to commit to memory the uninteresting and unintelligible rules, exceptions, notes, and remarks, of which the school grammar was full. It was the Latin School system, in those days, to have the first year wholly occupied in committing to memory the most abstract formulas of Adams' Latin Grammar. There might be a dull kind of discipline in this; but, as I think, an injurious one. It was a discipline of the power of cramming the memory with indigestible facts and sounds. It taught us to make a strenuous effort to accomplish a disagreeable task. But is not life full enough of such tasks? Is there ever a day in which we do not have to do them? Why, then, take the time which might be occupied in learning something interesting and useful, in learning as a mere *tour de force* that which we should never use? It had a benumbing effect on the mind. It stupefied our faculties. It gave a distaste for study. Latin, Greek, and mathematics, taught in this way, inspired only dislike.

What is mental discipline? Every faculty of body and mind is best disciplined by exercise. Now only that which we enjoy doing fully exercises our powers. We do disagreeable tasks by a strenuous effort, feebly; we do agreeable ones without an effort, with energy. What greater exercise than playing chess? This tasks observation, memory, foresight, the power of combining means to an end, patient continued effort. If chess were drudgery, no one could ever do all this. But the pleasure which attends it tides us over all these difficult mental operations.

The joy which children take in play is an ingenious device by which Mother Nature communicates to them the first and most indispensable knowledge. The playroom and playground are her primary school. There, children intent on ball, top, kite, games of tag, puss in the corner, and so on, are really learning how to exercise their limbs, balance their bodies, quicken their perceptive organs, and learn obedience to the immutable laws of the physical world. While playing, they become acquainted with the nature of things, gravitation, motion in direct lines and curves, the laws of elasticity, action and reaction, equilibrium, friction, and the like. They also learn, by playing in company, how to command and obey, to give up their own wishes for the common good, and to unite with others for a common end. From this varied, delightful, and thorough system of education, we take them to a school, and teach them — what? the dull process of committing words to memory! And we think this is education!

Of course I do not mean that children should spend all their time in play, but I mean that we should study the method of nature, and make what we call work as interesting as play. It can be made even more interesting.

It was a well established tradition in our family that the boys should all go to the Boston Latin School. My father went to it. My grandfather Clarke went to it. My grandfather Freeman went to it. And all my brothers, as well as myself, went to it. And no doubt, notwithstanding its grievous defects in methods, it did us all great good to go there.

First, it taught social equality. There is no aristocracy in a public school but the natural leadership of superior ability. The public schools of England have saved the nation from that separation of class from class which has brought revolution to the kingdoms of the Continent. Public schools teach boys the true equality of human beings, not an equality of powers, of function, of position, of possession, but of human and social rights. The young son of an English nobleman finds he must get the son of a farmer to help him in his studies, finds himself surpassed in his classes by the son of a poor widow, finds himself on the playground obeying, as his chief, the bright-eyed, quick-footed plebeian, who is the natural captain of the little regiment. Thus he learns to subordinate position to faculty, outward rank to native power.

In my division in the Latin School there were sons of the wealthiest, and sons of the least wealthy citizens. They studied, recited, played together, and were thus educated to a true democracy. One of these boys, whose father was a man of limited means, became afterward an eminent engineer. Some forty years after we left the Latin School, I happened to meet a relative of his, and asked after my old classmate. "He is chief engineer," she answered, "to the Emperor of Brazil. In his last letter he described a reception he had given at his villa to the Emperor and his court."

On entering the Latin School I was put into a division of ten or twelve boys in the lowest, or fifth class, and began to commit to memory the first pages of the

Latin Grammar. How well I remember the first sentence: "Grammar is the art of speaking and writing correctly." Having thus defined it as an art, the book went on to teach it as though it were a science. Instead of practical rules and examples of correct and incorrect speech, it gave a minute philological analysis of the linguistic forms. How do children learn to speak their own language? By being taught the difference between a noun and pronoun, an adverb and conjunction? By analyzing language into moods and tenses, number and person? Not at all. They learn by imitation and repetition. They learn thus the use of the most essential words and forms, and only come gradually to the less essential. That is, they learn by practice and observation. They first acquire the phrases which are most necessary for common use, and these they retain because they have to use them so often. Their vocabulary extends itself gradually to an outer circle of less used terms; and so, by gradual expansion, they become familiar with all that they need to know.

If grammar is the art of speaking, writing, and reading a language correctly, it should follow this method of nature instead of that of the schools. Fortunately, the superstition of grammar is rapidly disappearing. Another superstition remains, however,—that of the dictionary. Sensible and practical teachers are now generally aware that, in learning a language, all the knowledge of grammar needed at first is that of the declensions and conjugations and a few rules of syntax. Having acquired these, the pupil is to keep his grammar by his side as a book of reference, turning to it when a difficulty appears which he is unable otherwise to remove. He learns his grammar by practical application, and thus will remember it better. But how about the dictionary?

Great objection is made by teachers to the use of translations. But what mental discipline comes from turning over the pages of a dictionary? Does knowledge enter our minds through the ends of our fingers? Does the mere bodily exercise of thumbing the leaves tend to fix the word in the memory? The dictionary tells the boy the meaning of the term. The translation does exactly the same thing, only saving the time lost in searching for it. A tutor, sitting by his side, if wise, would do the same. The point in each case is to have him remember the meaning after he has been told it. That could be accomplished by his going over his exercise repeatedly, until he remembers it without referring to dictionary, translation, or tutor.

When I entered the Latin School I was put into a small class who were set to committing to memory Adams' Latin Grammar. In this exercise I was very imperfect, and I immediately went to the foot of the class, and there remained. For it was the custom, and I think it a very good one, to excite the emulation of the boys by having each boy who made a mistake change places in the seat with any boy who was below him and could correct him. Thus it happened that the position and rank of the pupil might change several times during a single recitation. At the beginning of each recitation the boys occupied the places they held at the close of the previous one. No record was kept of this rank, and no reward or honor was obtained by it. Thus there was no undue stimulus exercised, and yet enough to arouse the ambition of the scholars. The excitement subsided at the end of each recitation.

From this experimental class the pupils were transferred, according to their apparent merits, into different divisions of the fourth and fifth classes. Finally there remained only one boy beside myself who had not been thus transferred. He was John Osborne Sargent, who has since then become a distinguished man. He had been always at the head of the class, and I at the foot. To my intense surprise he and I were both transplanted to a higher position than any of the rest, namely, into the second division of the fourth class. That Sargent should thus be promoted seemed only just; but on what ground was I sent up with him? It seemed like pure favoritism. Or did Mr. Gould have prescience by which to discern the result? For no sooner was I thus promoted, and, instead of committing the grammar to memory, set to translating Cornelius Nepos, than I became one of the best two scholars in the class, my companion Sargent being the other. My previous instruction at home began to tell. It had taught me to use my faculties freely; it caused me to take pleasure in my studies. I took great pleasure in the music of Ovid, which followed Nepos; and when we came to Virgil, the lovely pastoral pictures in the Eclogues had a charm which still remains. The Æneid I never liked so well. It was very easy reading, but seemed less original and more superficial. The "pious Æneas" I thought a cold-blooded humbug, and I think so still. Virgil's heroes seem hardly more than lay figures, or shells of men, with no substantial humanity within. What a poor creature is Æneas compared with the high-spirited, generous Hector! The episode of Æneas and Dido is far inferior to that of Ulysses and Calypso, from which it was copied, and even to the subsequent *replica* of Rinaldo and Armida in Tasso.

There was one book used in the Latin School when I was there in which the true method of instruction was fully realized. This was Warren Colburn's "First Lessons in Arithmetic." It exercised the mind, not the memory; it began with what was easy, and went on to what was difficult; it interested us by perpetual problems, which tasked but did not tax the mind. We had not to commit to memory unintelligible rules, but made rules for ourselves as we went on. We boys never played a game with more pleasure or more excitement than we had in seeing which would be the first to get the answer to a proposed question. But of course this admirable book was soon banished from the schools by the pedants, who thought that whatever was interesting must be bad. It combined the best training with the best instruction, enabling a boy or a girl to solve any mathematical question likely to arise in the business of life. But though it thus fully attained the end of arithmetic, it did not teach the students to call the processes by the old names, and so it was first mutilated, and then very generally discarded.

But I recollect this incident, which illustrates its value. One of the best teachers I ever knew, Francis E. Goddard, of Louisville, Ky., had a little boy committed to his care by his father, Mr. Garnet Duncan, of that city. The boy, who has since become somewhat famous as a politician, was walking with his teacher through the main street of Louisville, when they came to a store, in front of which two or three of the principal merchants of the city were engaged in animated discussion. "Here comes Mr. Goddard," said one of them; "let us ask him. We have a mathematical question which has arisen in the course of our business which we cannot answer." So he stated the difficulty, and asked Mr. Goddard to write down the problem, take it home, and when he had leisure see if he could solve it. Goddard turned to the little boy by his side and said, "Here, ———, do it in your head." And the boy gave the right answer on the spot. He had been thoroughly trained in Colburn's "First Lessons."[1]

One of the most curious literary deceptions occurred when I was at the Latin School. One of my class, whose father was a highly respectable citizen, but not very wealthy, suddenly appeared to have plenty of

---

[1] We leave this incident as recorded by Dr. Clarke because the facts were as stated; but the explanation proves to lie in the exceptional endowment of the boy, who has retained through life the same power of immediate solution of intricate mathematical problems. ED.

money. He would hire horses and take us to drive, and indulge in other expenditures. Years after he gave me the explanation. John Pierpont had just prepared his Reader for schools, called "The American First Class Book." It was published by William B. Fowle, and had a great success. It was far superior in its selections to those of any other reading-book then extant. The author and publisher had found it very profitable. The boy to whom I refer wrote Mr. Fowle, in the character of a retired literary gentleman who did not wish his name to transpire, offering to prepare a companion volume to that of Mr. Pierpont, containing extracts suitable for declamation. Mr. Fowle answered the letter, saying he would like a specimen of the work, sufficiently copious to enable him to judge of its value. Thereupon my young friend associated a companion with himself, and together they wrote out extracts from speeches, plays, and poems, suitable for elocutionary purposes, and sufficient in quantity to make the first quarter of the volume. Mr. Fowle accepted it, and sent his check for, I think, at least a hundred dollars. They prepared and sent another quarter, and received another hundred dollars. By this time they grew a little careless, and the third quarter was so inferior that Mr. Fowle refused to pay for more, and finished the book himself. But the boys received between them two or three hundred dollars; and I presume that Mr. Fowle never knew who were the compilers of the volume.

CHAPTER IV

CAMBRIDGE.

I ENTERED Harvard College in 1825, being fifteen years old, which was the age of the large majority of the class. We graduated in 1829, at the age of nineteen. Instead of the two hundred who now enter, we were only about sixty; but this enabled every one to know all his classmates. The class became a famous one afterward, having produced eminent men in law, science, mercantile pursuits, and literature; but it did not promise much in college. The curious fact was, that few of the class took any genuine interest in the college studies. Benjamin Peirce, who was born with the genius for mathematics which made him afterward so distinguished a mathematician, went far beyond the college course in that direction. Each class had one day a week in which to take books from the college library; and I recollect that Peirce, instead of selecting novels, poetry, history, biography, or travels, as most of us did, brought back under his arm large quarto volumes of pure mathematics. When we came to recite in the Calculus or Conic Sections, it was observed that the tutor never put any question to Peirce, but having set him going, let him talk as long as he chose without interruption. It was shrewdly suspected that this was done from fear lest the respective *rôles* should be reversed, and the examiner might become the examinee. We also could foresee in our forensic discussions the future eminence of Benjamin Robbins Curtis, who afterward became so prominent at the bar and on the bench of the United States Court. His papers, read aloud to the professor of philosophy, were so strictly logical, and such exhaustive discussions, that it seemed impossible to improve on them. His mind worked, even then, with the accuracy of a machine, doing its work perfectly. In after years his intelligence was enlarged by ampler knowledge, was capable of more extensive research and more sustained investigation; but it worked as accurately in those college papers as when it showed its irresistible force in arguments at the bar or opinions from the bench.

It was not till we were well through college that the talent of Oliver Wendell Holmes became known to most of his classmates. I had become aware of it before, for I sometimes visited him at his father's house, where he lived the first two or three years of his college course. Many an evening I passed in his room, playing chess, eating red apples, and enjoying his bright conversation. He said things then as witty as any that have since proceeded from his tongue and pen. One of his impromptus lingers in my memory. We were talking of metaphysics. "I'll tell you, James," said he, "what I think metaphysics is like. It is like a man splitting a log. When it is done, he has two more to split!"

In our last year we had a periodical called "The Collegian;" and some of Holmes's poems were published in it, which have all the flavor and piquancy of his full-grown Muse.

Peirce, Curtis, and Holmes were men of genius, — one mathematical, one logical, and the third poetical. Genius shows itself very early. But most of the class gave little demonstration of what they were to do afterward. One for whom we felt a mysterious admiration was William Henry Channing, the favorite nephew of Dr. W. E. Channing. He was a beautiful boy, with dark hair and shaded eyes, and an expression of serious thought, earnest purpose, and pure aspiration. The child, in him, was father to the man. But he was silent among his companions, lived much alone, was thoughtful rather than studious. The problems of life already had taken possession of his mind; and often, in an evening walk, we would discuss the great questions of destiny and freedom, human progress, and superhuman influences. From the first he was pure in heart, and high-spirited in his temper. He abhorred everything mean, selfish, earthly. James H. Perkins, his cousin, who knew him from a child, once said to me, " William Henry Channing is the *holiest* person I ever knew. God beset him, behind and before, and laid his hand upon him." He was always seeking to get to the very root of every question, but he was obliged, by the structure of his intellect, to look at both sides. This made him often hesitating and unable to decide.

One of my friends, with whom I maintained a near friendship as long as he lived, was George T. Davis. He was the most brilliant of men in conversation, and was so regarded through life by all who knew him. His memory was prodigious, and he quoted in conversation innumerable passages from all authors, — grave or gay, lively or severe, — and he increased the interest of these quotations by his own delight in them.

I have sometimes wondered that our teachers then, and so many teachers since, could never interest young people in study. There is one element in the human soul which is common to all mankind, — *curiosity*. Why was this motive never appealed to? No attempt was made to interest us in our studies. We were expected to wade through Homer as though the Iliad were a bog, and it was our duty to get along at such a rate *per diem*. Nothing was said of the glory and grandeur, the tenderness and charm of this immortal epic. The melody of the hexameters was never suggested to us. Dr. Popkin, our Greek professor, would look over his spectacles at us, and, with pencil in hand, mark our recitation as good or bad, but never a word to help us over a difficulty, or to explain anything obscure, still less to excite our enthusiasm for the greatest poem of antiquity. But this was not peculiar to Dr. Popkin. It was the universal custom, with but one exception.

Professor John Farrar, in his lectures on philosophy, and in his other teaching, excited a living interest in physics, astronomy, mechanics, electricity, and the other sciences. Consequently we really learned in listening to him, and in reciting to him. I can repeat, to-day, many of his explanations and illustrations in these sciences. He was a man instinct with nervous vivacity, and would be carried away by the fervor of his speech and his interest in his theme, till he would quit his desk, walk to and fro about the room, talking and gesticulating, sometimes stooping till his body almost touched the floor, then rising till he stood on the tips of his toes, in the ardor of his discourse. He was a true teacher, but almost the only one in the whole corps of the professors. We went through Conic Sections with a tutor who never suggested to us, from first to last, that these were the curves in which the planets and comets moved, and that by learning their laws we were able to determine, a thousand years beforehand, an eclipse of the sun or an occultation of Jupiter. We supposed they were barren studies with no practical application. Even a little introduction, giving the history of the discovery of these laws, would have interested us. But nothing was said to awaken our curiosity, which I once heard Dr. James Walker say should be the chief motive appealed to by teachers.

But in fact it is a modern discovery, or perhaps a re-discovery, that the duty of a teacher is *to teach*. It was at that time assumed that it was his duty to hear recitations. Of course, if he gave lectures, he was to communicate information, but never in the recitation room. To explain difficulties to the young men before him, to help them along by happy illustration and comment, to untie the knots too hard for their young fingers to loose,— this would have been thought almost improper, and, certainly, it would have caused great surprise if one of the students had said, "I cannot understand this passage in Horace; will you be so kind as to explain it?" But why not, if we were sent to college to learn?

The root of the evil was that the motive relied on by the college system was not *curiosity*, but *emulation*; not the love of knowledge, but the desire for rank. Everything went to rank; recitations, regular attendance at exercises, good behavior in our rooms and elsewhere,— all were counted to the credit of rank in class. But as the majority of the class soon found that they could not attain a high rank, they ceased to try, and contented themselves with reciting well enough and behaving well enough to escape punishment.

The assumption in those days was,— and it still remains too much the general assumption in the corps of teachers in all colleges,— that young men's minds and hearts will not respond to generous motives, that they must be coerced, restrained, punished, and driven, not led by affection, by good-will, by the love of truth, by the desire for knowledge, by the ardor of attainment. But our real study was done from these latter motives. When I recall what my classmates were interested in doing, I find it was not college work, which might have given them rank, but pursuits outside of the curriculum. They did not put their strength into college themes, but into articles for the "Collegian." They did not read Thucydides and Xenophon, but Macaulay and Carlyle. We unearthed old tomes in the college library, and while our English professors were teaching us out of Blair's "Rhetoric," we were forming our taste by making copious extracts from Sir Thomas Browne, or Ben Jonson. Our real professors of rhetoric were Charles Lamb and Coleridge, Walter Scott and Wordsworth. I recall the delight which George Davis and I took in an old copy of Sir Thomas Browne which we stumbled upon in the college library. We had scarcely heard the name; but by a sure instinct we discovered the wit, originality, and sagacity of this old writer. It was about the time of our senior year that Professor Marsh, of Vermont University, was reprinting Coleridge's "Friend," his "Aids to Reflection," and his "Biographia Literaria." These books I read from time to time during several years, and they gave, in a high degree, incitement and nourishment to my intellect. Coleridge the poet I had known and loved. Coleridge the philosopher confirmed my longing for a higher philosophy than that of John Locke and David Hartley, the metaphysicians most in vogue with the earlier Unitarians down to the time of Channing.

The books of Locke, Priestley, Hartley, and Belsham were in my grandfather Freeman's library, and the polemic of Locke against innate ideas was one of my earliest philosophical lessons. But something within me revolted at all such attempts to explain soul out of sense, deducing mind from matter, or tracing the origin of ideas to nerves, vibrations, and vibratiuncles. So I concluded I had no taste for metaphysics and gave it up, until Coleridge showed me from Kant that though knowledge begins *with* experience it does not come *from* experience. Then I discovered that I was born a transcendentalist; and smiled when I afterwards read, in one of Jacobi's works, that he had gone through exactly the same experience. Thus I became a great reader of Coleridge, and was quite ready to accept his distinction between the reason and the understanding judging by sense. This distinction helped me much in my subsequent studies of theology. It enabled me to distinguish between truth as seen by the reason, and its statement as formulated by the understanding. It enabled me to put logic in its proper place, and see that its function was not the discovery of truth, but that of arranging, methodizing, and harmonizing verbal propositions in regard to it. I could see that those who had the same spiritual experience, and who beheld the same truth, might differ in their statements concerning it, and that while truth was unchanging and eternal, theology might alter and improve from age to age.

This distinction, when once clearly seen, puts an end to bigotry, at least to honest and involuntary bigotry. Take, for example, the doctrinal dispute concerning the person of Christ. The Trinitarian says, "He is God." The Unitarian says, "He is not God." Each thinks that if he is right, the other is absolutely wrong, and is denying an essential truth. If the *truth* is coincident with its doctrinal statement, then one or the other is indeed in very grave error. This was the old way of looking at it. But, according to the distinction of Coleridge, the vital truth perceived by the reason is not the same as the doctrinal statement enunciated by the understanding. The reason sees in Christ something divine, finds in him a visible manifestation of the invisible and eternal. In this intellectual vision both the Trinitarian and the Unitarian may be one, though when they come to express it as a doctrine they differ. The essential fact is the vision of truth as beheld by the reason, not its doctrinal form as worked out by the understanding. Thus Coleridge's metaphysical statement has really put an end to much conscientious bigotry in the modern church.

One injurious result of the college method of making emulation rather than curiosity the chief motive for work was that the recitations under this system wasted the time wanted for study. Three hours each day were given in the Freshman and Sophomore years to recitations. If we had been taught anything during these hours, the time would not have been lost. But the teacher was there, not to teach, but to give marks to each student according to the merit of his recitation. Pencil in hand, he listened in silence to the student's translation or solution of a problem, and having affixed the proper number to his name, went on to the next. As only a few of the class recited well enough for us to learn anything from what they said, those hours were not only wasted, but put us into a condition of mental torpor. We had three lessons a day, each of which ought, by right, to have two hours of study given to it in preparation. That would be six hours of study. Add three recitations, and it makes nine hours. Add one for exercise, one and a half for meals, and how much remains for society, amusement, general reading, writing letters, college clubs, etc. ?

Four hours' confinement to real study is quite as much as the average human brain will endure, and few in the class did more than this. For myself, as Greek was to me the most difficult study, I usually gave to it two hours. As I read Latin with a good deal of facility, I often did not look at my Livy or Tacitus before going into recitation. As mathematics was also comparatively easy to me, I gave it about an hour, thus studying only three hours a day. And I think this about as much as ought to be required of a youth of fifteen. If to this had been added three hours of interesting instruction in the recitation room, we should probably have graduated with some fair knowledge of what we had been devoting five years in school and four years in college to learn. In fact, however, in a class of eighty or ninety young men,[1] not more than a dozen

---

[1] Though the college catalogue gives the number who graduated as fifty-nine, there were, at different times during the four years, twenty-one others who were connected for a longer or shorter time with the class, making the whole number who were at some time members of the class, eighty.

were able, when they took their degree, to read a Greek or Latin book, or to solve a problem in the higher mathematics.

Worse than the absence of knowledge was the want of interest left by this system. In the Boston Latin School I had been interested in Ovid and Virgil, in Anacreon and Lucian, in algebra and geometry. But while in college, Homer and Hesiod, Sophocles and Euripides, became distasteful, and I worried through my mathematics simply to avoid bad marks in recitation, each day forgetting what I had learned the day before. There was an immoral influence in a system which produced such habits in well-disposed boys; which taught them to shirk study, to conceal their ignorance, and to make use of means which they knew were forbidden. One of these prohibited methods was the use of translations. But why should not boys use translations in learning their lessons, if they succeed in being able to read them without the translation? A Latin dictionary is only a collection of Latin words translated into English. Why not prohibit the use of a dictionary, and insist on the student finding out by intuition the meaning of the foreign word?

Notwithstanding these drawbacks, our years at Harvard College were by no means wasted. What we did not learn in the regular course of study, we learned outside of it. What we did not acquire from books, we taught each other. Each class was a little world, a microcosm. Here were collected all the chief varieties of human character; here were displayed the human passions, the little vanities, generosities, fine and coarse impulses, noble and mean motives, with which we were to come in contact in the world. College gave us preliminary experience of all this, which was a good preparation for life. It was a world on a small scale, but where the play of character was more apparent, and the motives of action were hardly concealed. In class intercourse were struggles for precedence, underhand and open attempts to carry points, rivalries for popularity. What ardor we put into our small controversies, how we admired and extolled this or that leader, in our little puppet-show world! It was not a bad preparation for life, and I have observed that the chances of success in the world are much in favor of one who has been through college. He gets a certain mental discipline, a power of self-control, a balance of faculty, and an insight into character, which are very helpful. This comes in part from the habit of systematic study; but still more, as I judge, from this boiling cauldron of juvenile struggles, sympathies, antipathies, successes, and disappointments. Thus I think it a good thing to go through college, even though one should accomplish very little in the student's curriculum.

It so chanced that in our Freshman year, Dr. Follen, recently from Germany, was enabled, by some happy influence, to introduce gymnastic exercises into Harvard College. We began with a large room, fitted up with parallel and horizontal bars, ladders, climbing poles, wooden horses, dumb-bells, and the like. Afterward the triangular piece of ground, called the Delta, where Memorial Hall now stands, was fitted up with a more elaborate apparatus. Beside the rest, there was an upright mast, about seventy feet high, stayed by guys, which ran from the top of the mast in opposite directions to the ground, at an angle of about thirty degrees. Halfway up the mast was a platform, from which large beams ran out on either side, at right angles, supported at each end by strong posts. To this platform one could ascend by a ladder, but from the platform to the top he must climb the bare mast, aided only by a knotted rope.

I was always fond of climbing, having a good deal of the balancing organ, which the phrenologists call *weight*. This is a specimen of the defective nomenclature of phrenologists, arising from the fact that they often gave to an organ a name derived from a single function, instead of a name which should express *all* its applications. A more scientific name for the organ in question would be *momentum*. It is the physical faculty in animals and men by which they instinctively measure the amount of pressure, resistance, moving force, required in any muscular act. Being fond of climbing, and feeling safe at any elevation, I took pleasure on the mast, learning to go up the rope to the top, and even to stand upright on the little iron cap at the summit. These open-air exercises were very conducive to health. While at school, I had frequent attacks of fever and pulmonary trouble, but after two or three years of gymnasium exercise I became free from these tendencies, and the foundation was laid for the physical health which has been one of the blessings of my life.

Boating, which now prevails so largely in Harvard, had not then come. But we had baseball and football in their seasons. The college government also paid a fencing-master, M. Vailly, an old soldier in the Napoleonic wars, to give instruction to four monitors in each class; who, in turn, taught the rest. I was fortunately selected or elected to be one of these monitors, and so was taught to fence by this skillful *maître d'armes*. My classmate, Edward D. Sohier, was another monitor, and excelled us all in this, as in most other athletic exercises. He was M. Vailly's best pupil; and when a rival teacher of fencing challenged our master to a trial of skill, Vailly refused, but offered his pupil, Sohier, as a substitute. Great was our excitement on this occasion. The fencing room, in University Hall, was crowded with anxious students, fearful lest our champion should be defeated. But Sohier played a close and cautious game, contenting himself with parrying the lunges of his opponent, till the latter incautiously left a little opening, of which Sohier instantly availed himself and touched the fencing-master on the breast with the button of his foil, which he then threw aside, and, taking off the wire mask from his face, wisely declined any further contention. I have since sometimes wondered whether he had inherited any of this aptitude for arms from the old knights of Vermandois and Sohier, from whom he is descended.[1]

At the beginning of my Sophomore year I met with an adventure which was exceedingly distressing and a great shock. We were to write our first English theme, and Professor Edward Channing gave us for its subject "The Difficulties of Composition." The themes were to be handed in at the end of a fortnight. I sat down immediately and began mine, and wrote a part of it, carelessly leaving the rough draft on my table. When the themes were sent back by the professor, I found that he had written on mine the name of one of my class, whose room was in the same entry, and whom I will call B. D. I went to him, and he showed me his theme, on which the professor had written my name. On looking at it I perceived that the first part was identical with my own. It had been copied almost *verbatim*, though, fortunately for me, not wholly so,

---

[1] I recollect sometimes going with Edward Sohier very early in the cold mornings of November, to shoot ducks on Fresh Pond. I do not think we shot many; but we imagined we were having sport, while we lay hidden in our punt among the reeds, and were half frozen with cold. How large a part of our pleasures are imaginary! The boy thinks he likes smoking a cigar, though it makes him feel very badly; but he perseveres, because he imagines it a manly enjoyment. To impress on boys the difference between true and false manliness would do them a great good. Every Sunday-school teacher who has boys in his class should make this his aim.

After we graduated, I did not meet Edward Sohier during many years. Meantime he had become a leading lawyer at the Suffolk Bar. One day I had occasion to go to his office. On entering, I saw him standing at his desk at a distance, in an inner room. He lifted his head, recognized me, and said, "How are you, Jim?" I replied, "How are you, Ned?" and we were boys again.

for in some places the copyist had not been able to follow my scrawl. In this instance only, during the course of my life, has my bad writing been an advantage to me. I charged B. D. with copying my theme, which he denied doing, and we went together to see the professor. Each having asserted that his composition was his own work, the professor said, "That is simply impossible. Either one of you has copied from the other, or both of you have copied the part which you have in common from a third party. Settle between you which it is, and let me know." I was thunderstruck at thus being exposed to the charge of having stolen my theme. I knew it was false, but how prove it as long as B. D. also denied the charge? Finally we agreed to leave it to a jury of our classmates, each of us to select six. I recollect selecting Benjamin R. Curtis and William Henry Channing among mine, and that when I asked William Channing to be one of my jurors he took my hand, and said, "Yes, James, and I am quite sure that *you* never did so mean a thing." He never knew what a comfort that expression of confidence brought to me in my sore distress. Perhaps it may be thought that as he was to be on the jury he had no right to prejudge the case. He did not prejudge it, nor did he decide that the other party in the transaction had stolen my theme, but he expressed a confidence in my integrity based on his knowledge of my character; and this I think he had a right to do. This principle I afterward expressed in the lines beginning, —

"Judge the people by their actions — 'tis a rule you often get."

When the jury met, and we had made our statements, each of us was asked when he wrote his theme. B. D. incautiously admitted that he had written the whole of his the night before it was handed in. I proved by the testimony of a friend that he had seen on my table and read that part of the composition which was common to both, a week before the time when they were presented to the professor. This settled the question. But there was another point in my favor. I had quoted, from my reading in Vicesimus Knox's "Elegant Extracts," these lines : —

> "Be careful, when invention fails,
> To scratch your head, and bite your nails."

But B. D. had it in his theme, "*pare* your nails." I asked him to tell the jury where the quotation was from, which he was unable to do. I then said that the lines were from Dean Swift, and pointed out the blunder he had committed in copying from my MS. The result was that the jury decided the case in my favor. B. D. did not confess what he had done until many years after. I had no further intercourse with him while we were in college; but thirty or more years after, he came to see me, expressing great sorrow for the action, and till his death manifested for me a warm friendship. I never knew what tempted him to this act, which would necessarily expose him to suspicion. It was not want of ability, for when he came to read aloud a forensic he showed considerable power. Possibly, when he copied the paper on my table, it did not occur to him that it was the beginning of my theme. But if so, why did he not say so? This event was very painful; for though the matter was decided in my favor, I could not be sure that some mist of suspicion might not rest on my character.

During my second year in the Divinity School, Dr. Spürzheim came to Boston, and gave lectures on phrenology, which I attended. I went with a prejudice against the system, supposing it had a tendency toward materialism. I thought that it attempted to deduce mind from body, and to make the organization the source of thought and feeling. But Dr. Spürzheim's first lecture removed this objection. He contended that the brain is the organ of mind only as the eye is the organ of sight. It is not the eye which sees, nor the brain which thinks. The mind sees by means of the eye, and thinks by means of the brain. It has always been suspected that the brain is the organ of thought. The phrenologists go further, and specialize the functions of the different parts of the brain.

The lectures of Dr. Spürzheim were very interesting, combining large generalizations with minute practical details. Many of the points which the old systems of metaphysics had left obscure were made plain at once by this searching analysis. Memory had been treated as a single faculty, reason as another. But Dr. Spürzheim showed by numerous examples that each organ has its own memory. Thus, one who has a large organ of "Language" but a small organ of "Form" remembers names but not faces, and *vice versa*.

A powerful influence was exerted on the minds of young persons by the coming of Dr. Spürzheim. This influence was beneficial in many ways, and that without regard to the truth or error of his system. His observations on human conduct and character were clear and full; he was so overflowing with anecdotes out of his own experience to illustrate his theme, his views were so comprehensive, kindly, tolerant, and sympathetic, that he roused a new interest in mental philosophy and the study of man. Metaphysics, a doubtful, uncertain study heretofore, with small practical results, at once became interesting and adapted for daily use. Phrenology had a marked influence on the methods of education, as was shown by its becoming the chief motor force in the labors of Horace Mann. It left untouched, indeed, the higher problems of philosophy, the nature of the soul, the principle of freedom, the origin of those conceptions which take hold of the Infinite and the Eternal. But in its lower sphere of action it usually was a great benefit to those who became interested in it. It placed our higher speculations on a basis of positive experience.

One of the real benefits of this study was that it inspired courage and hope in those who were depressed by the consciousness of some inability. So much stress had been laid in our schools on verbal memory that it was a blessing to many a child deficient in this power to learn that memory constituted a very insignificant part of the human intelligence. Phrenology also showed us how, as Goethe says, our virtues and vices grow out of the same roots; how every good tendency has its danger, and every dangerous power may be so restrained and guided as to be a source of good. It explained that the organic tendencies in themselves have no moral quality, but become virtues and vices as they are guided or neglected by the higher spiritual powers. These distinctions were of great value and aided us, quite apart from any judgment on the truth or error of the system.

CHAPTER V.

KENTUCKY.

WHEN the last year of my study in the Divinity School at Harvard was approaching its end, I began to think seriously of my future course. I could either remain in New England, and endeavor to be settled as minister of some existing society, or I could go out to the West and try to build up a society there. The last plan commended itself to my mind for various reasons. It was more of a missionary work. It would be harder at first, but would open a wider field of activity and influence as time went on. I was afraid that if I were settled in an old-fashioned Unitarian society I should gradually subside into routine; while in the West there would be no routine, but I should be free to originate such methods as might seem necessary and useful. Then I wished to test my own power and the value of what I had to say. If I preached Unitarian doctrine to a congregation which already believed it, I should not be able to judge of the efficacy of what I said. But if I could make converts in a community where my belief was unpopular, I should be convinced of its adaptation to human needs, and so be able to speak with more strength of conviction. Also, it seemed probable that my powers, whatever they were, would be better developed in an atmosphere where there was more freedom of thought, and where public opinion carried less weight of authority. On inquiry, I found that the church in Louisville, Kentucky, which had been established a year, needed a preacher, Mr. George Chapman being obliged to relinquish that position on account of ill health. Having agreed to go to Louisville and take his place, I set out directly after graduating from the Divinity School. I preached only once before going. This first service was in Bernard Whitman's church, at Waltham, where the congregation consisted chiefly of those who worked in the Waltham factories. My grandmother, hearing where I was to preach, told me I might take for my text the verse in Proverbs, "She seeketh wool and flax, and spinneth diligently with her hands." However, I took for the text of my first sermon, "Whatsoever thy hand findeth to do, do it with thy might;" and the subject was the enforcement of Carlyle's favorite doctrine, "Do the nearest duty." I recollect that after writing this sermon, I felt as if I had said all I knew, and should never be able to preach another; which is, I believe, a not uncommon experience with beginners.

Traveling in 1833 was very different from what it is now. The only railroad on which trains were drawn by locomotives was a short one crossing the State of Delaware. All the rest of the journey between Boston and Kentucky was performed by the old stage-coach or by steamboat. The stage-coach varied in its rate of motion. From two to three miles an hour was the average in the West, and five or six miles where the roads were better. In many parts of the West we traveled on what was called the corduroy road, which consisted of logs laid side by side over swamps; and as some of these logs would rock, break, sink down, or rise up, riding over them was more of an exercise than a pleasure. In other places, where the roads were of clay, they would be so gullied by the rain as hardly to leave room for the four wheels of the stage. Once, going down a hill at midday, on a walk, the stage-coach in which I was riding overturned, because there was no place left on the road where it could stand upright.

At another time, when I was sitting with the driver, going down an exceedingly steep hill near Winchester, in Virginia, the brake, which kept the wheels from turning, became so bent that it would not work; the horses, accustomed to the brake, could not hold back without it; and the stage began to go faster and faster toward a precipice in front, where the road made a sharp turn. The driver said to me, "I am going to overturn the coach, else we shall go over the precipice; be ready to jump off." So he drove into the bank on one side of the road, and overturned the stage as gently as possible. He and I jumped off as it was going over, but the inside passengers were much surprised at this unexpected event, which, however, was the only way of saving their lives. These drivers, all over the West and South, were mostly from New England, and were intelligent, sober, and faithful men. The horses were usually raised in Vermont or New Hampshire; for those in the South were not strong enough or tough enough to do the work.

Once, in Kentucky, when I was arguing in a newspaper on the evils of horse-racing, my opponent defended the system on the ground that it improved the breed of horses; and I replied by showing that the horses raised for racing in Kentucky were too light for harness and could hardly be used except in the saddle, so that the draught-horses were brought from New England. My reply was considered satisfactory.

Inconvenient as it was to be overturned in the day, it was still worse in the night. This happened to me thrice, and each time in Ohio. The first overturn was on the road from Cincinnati to Cleveland. It was raining hard, we were passing through the forest, and the tall trees on either side completely shut out the light, so that it was impossible to see anything. The wheels on one side went into a ditch, and the coach upset where the mud was very deep and very soft.

There was a lady inside, and after the men had crawled out through the door which was uppermost, we lifted the lady out, and placed her on the side of the coach, while the driver went for light and help. Another time we found ourselves utterly lost in the middle of the night in a wood. In the darkness the horses had lost the road and wandered into the forest. The coach stopped, and the driver said, "You had better get out, for I do not know where we are." Some one struck a light, and we found that the horses had carried the coach to the top of a little hill among the trees. It was one of the grand forests, not uncommon in the West, which had not been touched by the axe, where the undergrowth had disappeared, and the great trees stood so far apart that one could drive a carriage between them over the soft turf. There were seldom any fences beside the road in those days; and once, in Kentucky, having occasion to go from one road to another which was half a mile off, I drove my horse and wagon directly through the forest.

Sometimes serious injuries resulted from accidents of Western travel; limbs were broken by the overturning of the stage, and occasionally some person was killed, but commonly the passengers escaped with bruises. Once, in Pennsylvania, we had ridden all day in the coach, and eaten nothing from breakfast-time until nine in the evening. Then we reached Bedford and had a good dinner, and set off again feeling very comfortable. There were nine passengers in the stage, and most of them soon fell asleep. But I was kept awake by the singular movements of the carriage. The horses were evidently running, and occasionally we banged violently against a root or stone. In fact, the driver was intoxicated, and unable to manage the horses, which were running away. As long as the road was smooth and good no accident happened; but, after a while, the horses got out of the road and dragged us across a rocky field, where the stage was violently overturned and very much shattered. We were all bruised, but too closely packed to be seriously hurt. We succeeded in getting out, and found our driver, partly sobered by the accident, preparing to ride back on one of the horses to bring help from Bedford. A new carriage and driver came, but the man who had overturned us went on also to the next change of horses, where he told a pitiful story to the passengers of what his family would suffer if he lost his place, and most of them signed a paper, against my protest, exempting him from blame. Shortly after, I saw in a newspaper that another stage had been overturned in that neighborhood, probably by the same driver, and that one of the passengers had his leg broken.

The national road from Wheeling, Virginia, to Columbus, Ohio, had been built by the United States Government as the beginning of a system of internal improvements. It had been much opposed on this account by the Democratic party, who thought that the national government ought not to take part in such improvements. They did not prevent the road from being built, but they prevented it from being mended. It was a macadamized road, but had been improperly built, so that when I went over it, it was in stony ruts, and the passengers were tossed about in all directions. On one occasion it took four hours for the stage-coach to go twelve miles on this macadamized road.

Yet there was something by no means wholly unpleasant in these long journeys by the stage-coach. In the summer especially, if one rode on the outside with the driver, as was my custom, he was bathed in a constant current of fresh air, was free from dust, and could enjoy the view of the ever-varying scenery. When we reached the top of the Alleghanies, the eye ranged over a vast panorama of forest and meadow, where green patches indicated farms, and through which the blue streams wended their tranquil way. Sometimes we came to a place where a tornado had cut its resistless course through the trees, making a broad pathway where for miles all the timber was leveled. Once, on reaching the summit of a mountain in Virginia not far from the White Sulphur Springs, early in the morning, we saw the mists rolling like a great ocean below, reflecting from their upper surface the rays of the rising sun, which made them white as snow; while here and there the summits of other mountains pierced through this brilliant ocean, appearing like islands of green in the midst of a vast sea. Another day, during the same journey, the stage-coach stopped to allow the passengers to go to the edge of a wonderful precipice, known as Hawk's Nest. From this ledge we looked down more than a thousand feet into the valley of the Kanawha River. The wall of rock was so steep that one might almost drop a stone into the stream.

The foliage of the woods in the Ohio Valley greatly surprised me by its burning richness of color. I had never seen such hues in New England. The enormous trees in these Western forests also seemed to belong to fairyland, and not to reality. The majestic sycamores leaning their vast trunks and massive limbs over the shallow streams which we often forded, the beautiful gum tree carrying up a tower of foliage toward the skies, the enormous tulip trees, and the cottonwood with its leaves always in motion, were unlike anything with which I was familiar. They recalled to my memory engravings which I had seen, when a child, in a volume belonging to my aunt, Mrs. Swan, who had lent it to me for my amusement when I was recovering from an illness. Among these were landcapes by Gaspar Poussin, Claude, and Salvator Rosa, which contained trees so beautiful and majestic that I had supposed them purely ideal creations. But now I saw before me thes every trees, as beautiful as the finest creations of the artists.

In winter a long stage-coach journey was not so pleasant. And yet sometimes there was a charm and excitement even in this. One night, in the middle of December, we crossed the Laurel Mountain in Pennsylvania. It was twelve at night when we reached the summit and began to descend. Fortunately I was on the outside with the driver, else had I lost one of the grandest impressions ever made on my mind. A dark panorama of mountains circled and opened around us, along the edge of whose summits our road wound like a white thread. Beneath us sank a black, fathomless gulf, from which shot up the stems and trunks of gigantic trees, appearing like white spectres as the light from our carriage lamps fell athwart them. As our sure-footed and fleet horses sped along this Simplon route a complex feeling of being on the brink of danger, yet always safe, was merged in a sense of grandeur inspired by the vast, dim amphitheatre around, the mountain tops, the solitude, the loneliness of the hour, and the rapid movement of the horses plunging forward from the darkness behind into the darkness before.

Another night, in mid-winter, we were crossing the mountains, with a long ascent before us, and the horses were slowly dragging a heavy coach up a difficult road. My feet were cold, and I proposed to one of my fellow-travelers to get out and walk. Moving briskly, we soon left the coach behind. After walking nearly an hour, and hearing nothing of the stage, we determined to wait for it to come up. A very rude log cabin was near the road, and we saw the light of a fire within illuminating the window. We quietly opened the door and went in. There was but one room. The bed stood in one corner; the great logs of hickory or sugar-tree were smouldering and blazing up in the big chimney. We sat down to warm ourselves at the fire, and talked with our unseen host, who lay in bed and talked with us, asking the news of his unexpected guests.

I once came from Kentucky to Boston by what is called the Guyandotte route, which crosses the mountains from western Virginia, following up the valley of the Kanawha River, and passing east by the White Sulphur Springs, and so on to Fredericksburg and the Potomac. Some of the taverns where we stopped on this route were old Virginia homes kept by the representatives of decayed families. In such instances the landlord treated his guests very much as if they were friends come to make a visit. He welcomed us at the front door in the most cordial manner, seated us around the old family dinner-table of dark mahogany, on which were spread all the luxuries at his command; and he felt it his duty to entertain us, while we stayed, with such conversation as he thought would interest us. When we departed, he seemed almost ashamed to receive any payment for his civilities. A friend told me that when making a little journey in Tennessee on horseback he took care to avoid the village inns at nightfall, preferring to pass the night on some plantation. In those early days every planter or farmer felt bound to receive travelers, and was usually glad to do so, since this gave him one of his few opportunities of knowing what was passing outside of his own neighborhood. One evening, about sundown, my friend rode up the avenue of a house to the door where the owner was sitting smoking his pipe on the stoop. The traveler, using the customary formula, said: "Can I get to stay here to-night?" The planter, taking his pipe from his mouth, replied, "Young man, when I was of your age, and was traveling, if I came to a house at sunset, and asked if I could get to stay, and the owner said no, I should reply by swearing that I would stay anyhow. So, 'light, young man, 'light" My friend was treated very hospitably; his horse was taken care of, he had a good supper, a good breakfast, and a comfortable bedroom. He was treated so like a friend that, when ready to mount his horse, he was almost afraid to pay for his entertainment, lest he should give offense to his kind host. But wishing to be on the safe side he stammered out the question, "How much am I indebted, sir, for my entertainment?" The planter considered, and answered thus: "Your supper and breakfast cost us nothing, for we added nothing to our usual meal. Your bedroom cost us nothing, for we have servants to take care of the rooms who have not half enough to do. Your horse, however, ate, I suppose, about as much corn as I could sell for a quarter of a dollar. So you may pay me that amount." My friend paid this minimum sum, and rode away, admiring the hospitality of this unlettered planter, which was joined with a courtesy that would not leave his guest under a sense of obligation.

I cannot but believe that this stage-coach traveling gave one a good opportunity of becoming acquainted with human character. We usually see only those associated with us in our own circle of occupation and social intercourse. Thus we take a narrow or one-sided view of mankind. The lawyer sees the quarrelsome side of man; the clergyman the religious side. The physician sees men whose minds are troubled by disease; the man of business encounters them in the sharp conflict of selfish competition. But when we traveled in the stage-coach we met people of every type, quality, training, and occupation. Six or eight persons riding together day after day necessarily became pretty well acquainted with each other. One saw in these long journeys all sorts of characters; people from every State in the Union, and from foreign lands; people of every type of religious belief or unbelief; philanthropists going about doing good, and border ruffians hungry for a quarrel. The result, on the whole, was to give me a favorable impression of human nature. At first, indeed, I was often filled with distaste, not to say disgust. Some seemed coarse and brutal; men using profane language in every sentence, boasting of their quarrels, drinking whiskey. Others were full of conceit, thinking of themselves more highly than they ought to think. Others were garrulous, talking all the time, and saying nothing. Others were morose, stupid, or sullen. Nevertheless, after riding with them for a day or two, some good points would emerge; the stupid fellow would be found to know something of which I was ignorant; the talker would say something worth hearing; the border ruffian, bristling with bowie knives, would turn out to be a good-natured fellow after all. I found that a good deal of this development would depend on the tone taken at first, or on the influence of some one person. Once, when going through the Cattaraugus woods, where the road was mostly deep mire or rough corduroy, and there was every temptation to be cross and uncomfortable, one man so enlivened and entertained our party, was so accommodating and good-natured, that we seemed to be having a pleasant picnic, and the other inmates of the coach took the same tone. I therefore found it best for my own sake, as soon as we took our places in the coach for a long journey, to manifest an interest in my fellow-passengers and their comfort; offering, for example, to change places with them if they preferred my seat to their own, and paying them such little attentions as are always agreeable. It happened almost always that the other passengers would follow this lead, and take pains to be civil and accommodating.

Sometimes, by way of variety, and sometimes from necessity, we traveled in canal-boats. I journeyed thus for a day and night in western New York, on the Tonawanda Canal, with a party from Niagara Falls. The boat was too full for comfort; and when night came, and we had to arrange for sleeping in the little hanging berths on each side of the cabin, there was a good deal of crowding and discomfort. But some Boston young ladies of our party, instead of complaining, made light of the matter, and filled the cabin with their gayety. An old judge from Canandaigua occupied the berth below me, and I heard him saying to himself after he turned in: "How nice and smart those Boston girls are!"

Never shall I forget that first visit to Niagara. I had been in Kentucky a year, and was on my way home for a summer vacation. I stopped at Buffalo on Sunday and preached, and went to the Falls the next morning, to spend a day or two. The large hotels had not then been built; the crowds had not come; one or two moderate-sized taverns accommodated all the visitors. In the tavern where I stayed, I found the Boston party of which I have just spoken. To meet such a party as this, on my first visit to Niagara, enhanced the pleasure of that experience. The majesty of the Falls was not then debased by a miserable environment of curiosity-shops, peddlers, and shouting hackmen. The roar of the cataract and the tumult of the rapids dominated all other sounds. At night, when we walked on Goat Island, by the light of the full moon which shone through the tall treetops, the whole scene was picturesque beyond description. It seemed to make an epoch in one's life. It filled and satisfied the mind, infusing into it the calmness which the mighty Mother Nature sends to her children's hearts at such hours. I was prepared for the sublimity of the scene, but did not anticipate such overpowering beauty. Everything like fear was swallowed up in this luxury of color, form, sound, and movement. The curves and undulations on the face of the great sheets were like exquisite arabesques in a state of continual change. One could sit or lie upon the rocks above the great British Fall and look down without giddiness into the awful tumult below. The water goes over in a solid transparent sheet with a steady, unhastening movement. It meets the clouds of mist rushing upward from the torment below. From the surface of the fall there burst forth rockets where the air, caught and compressed by the descending mass, explodes in white foam. The deep emerald green of the water contrasting with the snowy mists, and the rainbow tints refracted by the sunshine, make a beauty which one lingers over with no wish for any change.

After leaving the canal-boat, and taking my seat in the stage-coach for Rochester and Utica, — for this was long before the days of the New York Central Railroad, — I found a fellow-traveler whose conversation much interested me. He had a great deal to say, for his mind was full and his temper genial. At first, he talked about various eminent persons whom he had known or knew in the United States; and I discovered that he had had personal intercourse with General Jackson, Henry Clay, John C. Calhoun, and other leading Americans. Afterward, he spoke of European events; and it appeared that he had been with the Prussian army which encountered Napoleon at Waterloo, and had been left on the field at Ligny desperately wounded. He was taken to a farmer's house and nursed for weeks, until he became well enough to return home. Meantime his family had heard nothing of him, and supposed him to be dead. He reached home of a summer afternoon, found the front door open, and went in. He heard the voices of his mother and sister, and listened. They were talking sadly of the death of this dear son and brother, who was only fifteen years old. He walked alive into the room where they were, and we can imagine the scene; or if we cannot imagine it we can remember the picture in the illustrations to Schiller's "Song of the Bell," by Moritz Retzsch, depicting in two tableaux the return of the son from his years of travel. His father and mother, in the first picture, are sitting by their table, and for a moment do not recognize the manly stranger who stands before them. But in the next scene they have recognized him. He has thrown down on the floor his cloak and staff and knapsack, and has fallen on his knees by his mother's chair. His head is in her lap, her own head is on his neck and her arm round his shoulder, while the father, from the other side of the table, is leaning forward, reaching out both hands toward the dear son. Somewhat like this must have been the scene in the little house in Germany, when he who was supposed to be dead returned like one risen from the grave. Then this man of many adventures told us how at twenty-one he volunteered in the Greek war of independence, traveling on foot with some of his fellow-students through Switzerland and France to Marseilles. Scarcely landed in Greece, they were arrested by orders from Russia, and sent back under the charge of an officer. Landed on the eastern coast of Italy, they crossed the peninsula, passing at no great distance from Rome. It seemed impossible for them to lose the opportunity of visiting this city of their dreams; but it was useless for them to try to obtain permission from their guard. So they made their escape when he was asleep, and reached Rome without being overtaken. They wisely decided to go immediately to the Prussian Minister, who, fortunately for them, was Baron Niebuhr. They told him what they had done, and asked his permission to remain a few days in Rome, to see its wonders. Niebuhr looked grave, reprimanded them seriously for their violation of discipline, and told them to come back in the evening, and he would let them know the decision he had reached. After they had gone Niebuhr went into the parlor and told his wife of the affair. She said: "Well, Niebuhr, you will let them stay, will you not?" "Of course I shall," said he, "only I thought it necessary to frighten them a little." So when they returned in the evening, very anxious as to the result, he took them at once into his house, and kept them there for some time as members of his family; and of course the love and reverence which my companion expressed for him knew no bounds. Then he told me of his life in Berlin and his admiration for Schleiermacher, of whom I was glad to hear something more, as I had been so much interested in his published writings. He described how the great church in Berlin where Schleiermacher preached was crowded with an audience consisting of every class in society, from high court officers, students, and professors to the humblest day-laborers, — all of them deeply moved by the mingled depth and feeling of his discourse. After a while I learned that my accomplished fellow-traveler was Dr. Francis Lieber. We kept together as far as Trenton Falls; stopping at different places on the way, in each of which he found the objects most deserving of a visit. I took lessons from him in the art of traveling. He showed me that the people who live in a place seldom know in what its real curiosities consist, and that a careful investigation is necessary in order to find them out. Thus in one place we went to see a weigh-lock, where the canal-boats were floated into a gigantic pair of scales, and the water being drawn off the weight of the boat and cargo is ascertained within two or three pounds. In other towns we visited the institutions for which each was most distinguished; seeing in one place a reformatory, and in another flour-mills, and in another building-yards for canal-boats. When we reached Trenton Falls the water in Canada Creek was so high that the usual foot-path by the side of the river was impassable, and nothing remained for us but to clamber along the edge of the rocky precipice as best we could, above the rushing torrent. Dr. Lieber had practiced gymnastics in Germany. I had been taught them by Dr. Follen at Cambridge. So I succeeded in following where he led the way; finding places with difficulty into which we could insert our toes while clinging with the ends of our fingers to the projections of rock above. I did not wish to be outdone; though I confess I was well pleased when he decided that we could go no farther and must return. After we parted I received some letters from this new friend, one of which contained a German poem to Niagara, which, like myself, he had just seen for the first time. In this poem, as I recollect, he expressed the idea that if Dante had seen Niagara he would have found new images there for his "Inferno."

I saw Chicago for the first time in 1840. My brothers, William and Abraham, had already been living there for some years, and they and my mother occupied a house on the south side of the river near the lake. I think it was upon what was called the Reservation, where originally the Government block-house had stood. Some of the early settlers were still living, such as Mr. Kinzie, Mr. Gurdon Hubbard, and Mr. William B. Ogden. One of these gentlemen showed me a sketch of Chicago as it looked when he first saw it. It consisted of two buildings, one on each side of the mouth of the river: the block-house on the south side, and the Indian Agency on the north side. At the time I first saw it, in 1840, it was a town of 7,000 or 8,000 inhabitants; now (1886), less than fifty years after, it has 500,000, and is still growing with rapidity. In 1840 it was a very pleasant place. There was scarcely anything on the north side of the river; but on the south side the houses were pleasantly situated, with open spaces, gardens, and views of the lake. It was a quiet place, with none of the intense activity which now prevails there.

The easiest way of going to Chicago from the East in those days was to traverse the Lakes in the large and well-appointed steamers from Buffalo by Detroit, Lake Huron, and Mackinaw into Lake Michigan. The voyage was charming, for we had beautiful views of the shores, bays, forests, and promontories near which we passed. We sailed into some of the bays, and found the water so transparent that we could see the beautiful agates and carnelians twenty feet below. At Mackinaw were curious cliffs, and we saw Indians in their tents waiting to receive their pensions from the United States.

No Unitarian church edifice then existed in Chicago. I preached one Sunday in a large room, a second in a Universalist church, and in the evening lectured by request of the minister, Mr. Patterson, in the First Presbyterian Church, on "The Evils of Slavery."

CHAPTER VI.

LIFE IN KENTUCKY.

It was early in the morning when the mail-boat reached the expanse of water above Louisville. Here is the only place throughout its whole extent where the navigation of the Ohio River is interrupted by falls, and these falls have built up the city of Louisville. When the boat stopped at the landing I went to a hotel, and after breakfast called at the office of the gentleman with whom I had corresponded. This was Mr. Simeon S. Goodwin, a native of Plymouth, Mass., who had traveled extensively, and had now been living in Louisville many years. He was a Yankee of the Yankees, practical, energetic, persistent, an excellent man of business, but retaining from his New England origin and education a love of knowledge and an interest in all the old New England institutions. He had given much time and labor to establish public schools in the city, and they were in full and successful operation, the teachers being better paid than in New England towns. He was the first to organize an insurance company, of which during many years he had been the actuary or secretary. Although the Kentuckians recognized his usefulness, and could not do without him, he was by no means popular, for he continually let them understand how inferior they were in their ways to the people of New England. He never hesitated to express his opinions in politics or religion; and on these questions, as on others, he was apt to be on the unpopular side. In politics he was an old-fashioned

Federalist, while the people around him were Democratic. When Jefferson died, in 1826, and the people were lamenting his loss as that of the greatest man in the nation, Mr. Goodwin said publicly that "it was a pity he had not died fifty years before." This remark, which seemed to him a truism, nearly caused him to be mobbed. From New England he had also brought his Unitarian belief, and having established public schools, he next proceeded to found a Unitarian church. He had induced several Unitarian ministers of the period to give courses of lectures in Louisville, with the result of bringing together a small company, consisting mostly of New Englanders, but with a sprinkling of Kentuckians and a few others who favored that doctrine. One of the preachers who made a great impression by the clearness and cogency of his arguments, and by his manly independence of character, was Rev. Bernard Whitman, of Waltham, Mass.

Horace Holley, who had gone from the Hollis Street Church, in Boston, to be president of Transylvania University, in Lexington, Ky., had also preached in Louisville, during his occasional visits to that city; and his oratory was well suited to the taste of the people. He was a fluent extempore speaker, with rather a florid rhetoric and an animated delivery, and always made a great impression. Under these influences and by means of Mr. Goodwin's excellent business management, a church building had been erected and fully paid for. There had been one settled minister before I went to the place, Rev. George Chapman; but ill health had compelled him to leave at the end of the first year.

I found Mr. Goodwin in his office, where he received me kindly. He had engaged a room for me in the same boarding-house in which he and his wife were then living. Nothing could be more bare and desolate than this room. It contained, for furniture, a bed, two chairs, a table, and a washstand. The windows looked down upon one of the noisiest streets of the city, whence came to my ears the barking of dogs, the shouts of negroes, and sometimes the voice of an auctioneer selling a horse, which he rode up and down, crying out, " Forty dollars for the horse ! "

Louisville, which has since become one of the most beautiful cities in the country, was in those days one of the ugliest. It consisted of plain brick shops and houses, without any grass plots, and with hardly a tree. The streets were never cleaned, the rain being expected to do the cleansing. Fortunately the limestone rock on which the city stood was absorbent, and everything soon dried up; so that, on the whole, the health of the place was good. Accustomed as I had been to the hills, the green lanes, and the pleasant shade-trees around Boston, I found the flat expanse on which this city stood very tiresome, and the dirt and ugliness hard to be borne. A little piece of the native forest, called Jacob's Woods, had been left untouched by the axe, and to this I often took my morning and evening walk. During a large part of the year the falls of the river were low, and the flat limestone rocks above them were bare, and I took pleasure in frequently visiting these rocks and falls. On the shipping port bottom-lands below the falls, there stood one solitary majestic sycamore, which measured forty-four feet in circumference, four or five feet from the ground. This tree I often made a terminus of my walk before breakfast. The middle of the day, in the summer, was too oppressive and sultry for walking; and, as I did not wish to lose my habit of pedestrian exercise, I usually took my walk before breakfast, to the great surprise of the Kentuckians, who could not understand why any one should walk who was able to ride on horseback, and they sometimes kindly offered me the use of their saddle-horses, thinking that I walked because I did not own a horse.

When any friend from the North visited Louisville,

and called to see me, I usually took him to this great sycamore tree as the chief curiosity of the region. But what was my horror, one day, to find that it had been cut down and was resting its mighty length upon the ground. On inquiry as to the cause of this destruction, I learned that it had been felled by a squatter who lived in a cabin some little distance away, and who seemed to have no reason for cutting it down except the backwoodsman's ingrained hostility to trees. For in the West the period had returned spoken of in the Bible, "when man was accounted great according as he had lifted his axe against the thick trees." But even as it lay on the ground the tree was a wonder. Though it had decayed at the top, and lost its upper branches, it was about ninety feet long, and the diameter of the butt end was fourteen feet.

During what remained of the first week, beside calling on a few of the people and writing letters to my friends, in the hope of getting answers from them, I was trying to prepare for my first Sunday. In regard to this I made two great mistakes. I had heard that the people in the West preferred extempore speaking, and I thought I must preach an extempore sermon. As I had been accustomed to speak often in debate without difficulty, I imagined that I could preach without notes. But I found it was one thing to answer an opponent in debate, and quite another thing to address a congregation. All the thoughts I had arranged in my mind disappeared, and I found that I had nothing to say. So after talking in a very desultory way for fifteen or twenty minutes, I brought my sermon suddenly to an end. I knew I had made an utter failure, and, mortified beyond expression, I left the house without speaking to any one, and went back to my room. No one in the society said anything to me about this failure, nor did I speak to any one about it. Some twenty years after, in Greenfield, Mass., I met a gentleman who told me that he was in the Louisville church when I preached my first sermon. "You heard a pretty poor one," I said "That's so," said he; "about as bad a one as ever I heard." "Do you know what the people said about it?" I asked. He answered, "Yes; after you had gone some of them stopped and talked about it. One man said, 'We had better let him go back at once to Boston, for he will never do anything here.' But another remarked, 'Do not let us be in a hurry, — perhaps he will do better by and by. I noticed that there seemed to be some sense in his prayer.' So they concluded to wait awhile before speaking to you."

After this experience I took care to write my sermons for Sunday morning. In the afternoon, when there were fewer persons present, I spoke from a brief, or a few notes on paper. But my great and unexpected difficulty was in finding something to say. My mind was sufficiently full of thought. I had read a great many books; I had been deeply interested by such writers as Channing, Dewey, Carlyle, Lord Bacon, and the older English writers; and I had read the largest part of the works of Goethe, Schiller, Tieck, Novalis, and other German writers. But nothing of all this seemed the right material for sermons. Few of my congregation were readers, and the books which interested me would not be interesting to them. So I sat by my table half the day, looking at the blank paper, with my mind equally blank. A great weight of responsibility rested on me. I felt as if I ought to say something very important, but it would not come. As Saadi of Shiraz remarks, I was trying to squeeze the juice from a dried-up brain, and to digest the smoke of a profitless lamp. There was an easy way out of the difficulty, if I had only thought of it. I might have made use of the writings of Channing, Ware, James Walker, and other Unitarians, which would have been entirely new to the people, and which contained just the things they wished to hear. I might have reproduced their thoughts in my own words, and given entire satisfaction. But I was possessed with the notion that I ought to give them only my own thoughts. And, alas! those thoughts were very slow in coming. So I was oppressed by a great sense of duty without any ability of fulfilling it. As I sat at the table, trying to write, I saw through the window a man making chairs, and I envied him, because when he had made a chair he knew he had done something, but I, with all my effort, could not do anything. Those were bitter days. I do not see how one could suffer more than I did for the first month or two. There was no one with whom to consult, no one to give me any sympathy. The only peace I had was in my dreams at night. Then the weight of care was removed, and I was again among my old companions and friends. When I awoke in the morning I immediately felt the pressure of the burden coming back upon me. But it never occurred to me to give up or go away. I worked doggedly on, until I began to see my way more clearly. I was very homesick, but I never mentioned it in my letters. I hung around the walls of my chamber all the souvenirs of home and friends I had brought with me, so as to see them when I looked up, and be refreshed. Before I left Boston, Margaret Fuller had given me a blank-book, or album, richly bound and with a Bramah lock. On the first page of this she had written these mottoes: —

"Extraordinary, generous seeking."

"Be revered
In thee the faithful hope that still looks forward,
And keeps the life-spark warm of future action
Beneath the cloak of patient sufferance."

To this book I confided my perplexities and troubles, and I encouraged myself by reading the mottoes.

There was an important question which had to be

settled before I could go much further. I must decide whether it should be my main object, in preaching, to teach and defend Unitarian doctrines as opposed to the Orthodoxy of the place and time, or to aim chiefly to make people feel the power of religion on the daily life. In other words, should I preach Unitarianism as doctrine, or as practical Christianity? Clearly, the first course would be much the easier, and at the same time more popular and apparently successful. It would give me a larger congregation and build up the society. It was what most of the people wished to hear, and this was the only place in which they could hear it. If the Unitarian doctrine was true and important, was it not my duty to devote a large part of my preaching to its promulgation? Why had the people built the church except for this? Here, in the midst of a peculiarly narrow and bigoted Orthodoxy, it seemed as if it were right to lay stress on a liberal and rational form of Christianity. But though these reasons were strong, they did not convince me. I believed that every church should have for its first object the teaching of positive Christianity, bringing comfort to the sorrowful, making God seem near, dwelling on the duties of human life and the blessed help that comes from divine love. Therefore, I made this the main purpose of my preaching, and seldom went out of my way to engage in controversy. I read the religious books of all denominations, especially such writers as Jeremy Taylor, St. Augustine, Luther, Wesley, Robert Hall, Cecil, Scougal, Doddridge, and Jacob Abbott. From the last writer I received much good. I read his books, "The Young Christian," "The Corner Stone," "The Way to do Good," "The Teacher," etc. In these writings I found the best part of Orthodoxy, disengaged from its dogmatism; and I also learned from him a clear, plain style and the help of appropriate illustrations.

During my first year in Kentucky I wrote between

seventy and eighty sermons; but of all these I preached only one or two a second time. The others I dismissed to oblivion. During my second year I wrote only fifty or sixty, but perhaps six or eight of these were worth repeating. I began to find better things to say. In talking with the people I was able to learn what their difficulties were and what they needed to hear; and this gave me a part of my material. Then I learned to look more deeply into myself and my own experience; and I discovered that as people are much alike, the experience of others would vary little from my own, and what did me good would be likely to help them. And, finally, I began to be more and more interested in the Bible, especially the New Testament. I learned how to study it more thoroughly and put to it more searching questions. And with my own increasing interest the interest of my hearers also increased. I adopted the plan of holding evening meetings in the houses of different members of the society, for the free discussion of religious, moral, philosophical, and social questions. These gradually became interesting, and were very well attended, the parlors being often crowded. Although there was not much reading done by the people, they were independent thinkers, and the questions before us were thoroughly discussed from every point of view and by persons of every shade of opinion. I always presided, and learned a great deal about directing such a conversation and keeping it to one point; which knowledge I found of use afterward when holding similar meetings in the Church of the Disciples, in Boston. Of course there were persons who talked too much and took more than their share of the conversation. It sometimes became necessary to see such persons, and ask them to restrain themselves. I never had any difficulty in doing this; nor, I believe, did I ever wound their feelings. One man, a Scotchman, a Mr. D., was particularly fond of giving to us his theory of religion. It was pure Antinomianism. "We are saved," he said, "by faith, and faith means believing that Jesus is the Son of God, and sent by Him; and if we believe this we shall be saved." "Morality," he said, "had nothing to do with it. No matter how bad a man was, if he only believed in Christ he would be saved." None of us agreed with him in this view; but we were willing to hear it expressed now and then. This did not satisfy him; he desired to reproduce it on all occasions, and I found that this interfered with the interest felt in the meetings. I went to see Mr. D., and frankly told him that he took a great deal more than his share of the conversation. He at once agreed to reduce the amount of his communications. "I will tell you," said he, "what I will do. I will not speak at all until you call upon me for my opinion." "Oh, well," I replied, "that will do." The next meeting happened to be a very full one, and Mr. D. sat behind me, where I did not see him till the end of the evening. Looking round accidentally I caught sight of him. Evidently he had been restraining himself by a mighty effort. He was moving uneasily from one side of his chair to the other, with gestures which seemed to indicate that he was, like Elihu, inwardly fermenting and in great danger of explosion. Then I said, "What is your opinion, Mr. D., of this question?" And his opinion came.

I was much interested in a phase of belief which prevailed to some extent among the intelligent Kentuckians. They had been so often told from the pulpit that if they did not believe every word in the Bible they were infidels, that many supposed themselves to be so. Finding, perhaps, something in the Old Testament inconsistent with what seemed to them true and right, they thought it necessary to reject Christianity on this account. I therefore felt it my duty to explain to them and to others that this doctrine of literal, infallible inspiration of the letter had no foundation, and that one could believe in Christ without believing in Jonah or Joshua.

One day a Louisville lady, Mrs. W., asked me to come and see her, and told me she had no faith in Christianity as a Divine revelation, but felt unhappy, and wished to attain this faith if it were possible. Her objections seemed to her so formidable that she thought they could not be answered. Inquiring as to their nature, I found that they all rested on the doctrine of the infallible inspiration of the whole Bible. She supposed that if she doubted or disbelieved any part, even of the Old Testament, she must give up the whole. And as there were many things, especially in the Old Testament, that she was unable to accept as literal verity, she imagined that she must not believe in Jesus Christ. I convinced her that the Old Testament was no essential part of the Christian belief, however full it might be in many places of genuine inspiration; and that even in the New Testament there were many things which it was not necessary either to believe or to disbelieve. I succeeded in making her see that if we believe in Jesus as one who can bring us to God and be our true guide in religion and life, this is enough. If we find that his teaching satisfies the needs of the mind and heart, this is sufficient reason for taking him as our friend and master. When she reached this conclusion she desired to be baptized and to join our church, which was accordingly done. But this was not the end of her experience. Some time after, I was called up in the middle of the night by her husband, who wished me to come immediately and see his wife, who was in great distress. Her child had died, and she was inconsolable. All I could say to her seemed to have no effect upon her mind. But the next day, when I called again, I found her tranquil and submissive. She then said, " I can understand now why my child is taken. When I first sent for you, desiring to become a Christian, I had a secret feeling that it was sinful not to believe, and that I should be punished for my unbelief. And as I could conceive of no more severe punishment than the loss of my child I feared that he might be taken away, but hoped that if I became a Christian God would spare his life. I see now that my motives were wrong, and that instead of accepting the will of God I was trying to make a bargain with Him. But I now believe that I can sincerely accept his will as wiser and better than my own."

Not a great while after this, Mrs. W. was attacked with pulmonary disease, and was advised by her physieian to go to New Orleans. Before going she had a meeting in her room of some of the members of the church, and together we partook of the Lord's Supper. She bade us good-bye with much tenderness, not expecting to see us again. At New Orleans she was visited by her cousin, Rev. John Breckenridge, of the Presbyterian Church, a brother of the great preacher, Robert J. Breckenridge, and himself a minister of ability. When he found that Mrs. W. was a Unitarian he was much shocked, and began to argue with her on the subject. But she replied, "Cousin John, I formed my opinions when I was well and my mind strong. I do not intend to reconsider them now when my mind is weak. If you will try to strengthen my faith I shall be glad to see you; but if you wish to disturb it, I should prefer that you should not come." He then asked her to tell him what she believed, and on hearing it admitted that it was enough. She was surrounded by Presbyterians, but was so serene, and spoke so tranquilly of her approaching death, with entire faith in God and immortality, that it produced a great impression on those who saw her.

One day I noticed in church a gentleman whom I had not seen there before, whose arm hung over the pew-door, holding in his hand a riding-whip. After church I inquired who he was, and learned that he was Judge Speed, a gentleman who had a farm a few miles out of the city. I was informed that people called him an infidel, but that he was universally respected, and was a very good man. Afterward I became very intimate with him and with his family. He was like a father to me, and his house was like my own home. He had a large farm about six miles out of town on the road to Bardstown. One field of this farm contained eighty acres, and hemp was raised in it every year, and grew ten or twelve feet high. Hemp is an exhausting crop, but the field had produced it for a great many years without any fertilizer being used, the land being among the richest in Kentucky. Walking across this field one day, I found a smooth stone about six inches long. It looked like an Indian axe, but I left it where I found it, and when I reached the house spoke about it to Judge Speed. He asked me where I had found it, and on my reply said, "No, that is not an Indian stone; I know the stone you mean." He seemed to be acquainted with every stone in this eighty-acre field.

Judge Speed explained to me why he was called an infidel. He said, "When I was a boy, and went to meeting, the minister took the Bible in his hand, and said, 'Every word within these lids is the word of God, and if you do not believe it, you will be damned as sure as I kill that fly,' slapping his hand on a fly on the Bible. I was an infidel to this kind of religion, and thought it my duty to protest against it. But I have no hostility to the kind of religion which you and many others now preach. I go from one church to another and watch you all, and see that all the churches are making progress."

Several of Judge Speed's children became members of our society, and all of them were like brothers and sisters to me. One of his sons, Joshua, kept a store at one time in Springfield, Illinois, and there became the intimate friend of Abraham Lincoln, — the most intimate friend, in fact, the President ever had. Lincoln visited Farmington, the Speed place, some time after I left Kentucky. Many years later, when I was revisiting Kentucky, I spent a day with Joshua Speed, who told me many interesting and characteristic anecdotes of his friend.

Although Judge Speed had few opportunities for education, and had spent his life in Kentucky as a farmer, up early and late, riding over his plantation, superintending seventy negroes, and educating twelve children, I possess some letters from him which would be creditable to the most finished scholar. His mind was active, vigorous, and free, ever open to new truths. He thought and read with the ardor of a young student, laying aside old opinions, and accepting better ones when he found them. His heart was as fresh as his mind, throbbing tenderly as that of a woman in answer to a kind word. He was a true and faithful friend, a wise and kind father. When he lost his youngest child, his little daughter Anne, he mourned over her as one who had fully sympathized with her young thoughts and desires. He was called "Judge" because he had been appointed associate judge in one of the court districts. The associate judges were men, usually without legal training, who were put by the side of the chief judge in order to temper his decisions with practical common sense.

Judge Speed was a slaveholder. But he did not believe in slavery. He thought it wrong in itself and injurious to the State, and expected, like most intelligent Kentuckians at that time, that Kentucky would before long emancipate its slaves. Meantime he held them as a trust, and did everything he could to make them comfortable. If one of his slaves was discontented and ran away, — which rarely happened, — he did not try to bring him back. A young man from the

North once said to him : " Your slaves seem to be very happy, sir." He replied, "I try to make them comfortable; but I do not think that a slave can be happy. God Almighty never meant a man to be a slave; and you cannot make a slave happy."

After his death, his children, who had been educated to the same views, finding that Kentucky refused to abolish slavery, set free the slaves whom they had inherited, and gave them farms in Indiana.

Judge Speed was a good representative of a certain type of Kentuckians, — strong-minded, independent, energetic men. They were frank and open, very much interested in political questions and public affairs. They did not read much; but they talked with each other a great deal. Every summer there were held throughout the State what were called political barbecues, where leading speakers discussed with each other the public questions of the day. Candidates for Congress or the Legislature defended their public acts and opinions; and the representatives of each of the great parties were heard by the people in turn. The consequence was a much better and broader knowledge of public affairs than is usual in the Northern States, where each man obtains his knowledge of politics from his own party newspaper.

This system also produced excellent speakers. What was called stump-speaking was simply addressing an audience of both parties and of all shades of political opinion, collected in the fields or woods, and spending the larger part of a summer day in listening to such debates. On these occasions it was customary to have for dinner an ox, baked in the following way. A hole was dug in the ground, and a wood fire built in it; when the wood was reduced to coal and ashes, the meat was put in whole, covered up, and left till thoroughly cooked, and then eaten with other provisions, as at a picnic.

Each speaker was obliged, as in a tournament, to maintain his opinions against all comers. This developed quickness of thought and readiness of speech, and made the best extempore speakers in the country. They united with fluency caution and precision, and knew exactly what to say and how to say it, so as to anticipate objections and conciliate opponents. One of the best of these speakers was said to have been the famous Joseph Hamilton Daviess. I have heard old men, who remembered him, rank him above Henry Clay as a stump speaker, though Clay was regarded as a great master in this kind of oratory. One of Clay's feats as a speaker was at the beginning of the war of 1812. He was candidate for Congress, and his district was opposed to the war, having lost many of its best sons in previous struggles with the Indians. Mr. Clay's opponent had made good use of this state of feeling, and had attempted to show that the war was unnecessary and in every way undesirable. When Clay rose to speak, the feeling of opposition to him and his cause was at its height. He did not attempt to oppose it, but fell in with the current, speaking with much feeling of the evils of war, and expressing warm sympathy with those who had lost sons and brothers in Indian campaigns. Having thus obtained full possession of the minds of the people, he said, "But are we not willing to bear all this for the sake of our country?" and appealed so powerfully to their patriotic feelings as to win them over to his own views.

DIARY AND CORRESPONDENCE.

CHAPTER VII.

DR. CLARKE'S EARLY YEARS.

[The Autobiography with which this book opens was begun by Dr. Clarke in the year 1883. It carries the story of his life nearly to the year 1840. He never revised these chapters; and there are some gaps in them which he probably would have filled. It is to assist the reader that we tie together a few other notes of the same time, taken from other sources.]

JAMES FREEMAN CLARKE was born in Hanover, New Hampshire, on the fourth of April, 1810. His father, Samuel Clarke, was living there for a time in order to study medicine under Dr. Nathan Smith, who was connected with Dartmouth College. When James was a few weeks old, Mr. Clarke brought his wife and children to Newton, where he left them with his mother, Mrs. Freeman, while he went back to Hanover to finish his course of study. Before the end of the year he had taken his degree as doctor of medicine, and returned to Massachusetts, where he entered upon the practice of his profession. They lived first in that part of Newton now called Newtonville, with Rev. James Freeman, well known to every one then in Boston, as the minister of King's Chapel.

This chapel, as its name implies, had been founded by and for the crown officers in Boston, at the time when Andros was the royal governor. It continued as the "King's Chapel" till the last royal governor left

Boston, in 1776. The proprietors of the chapel invited James Freeman to be their minister, and settled him in the year 1782 without the help of any bishop, there being, in fact, no bishop who could have helped them. Mr. Freeman and they, alike, understood that he and they were not to be bound by the articles and creeds of the English Church; and thus it happened that the King's Chapel, after the king ceased to reign in America, became the first Unitarian church, known under that name, in America. It seems worth while to say this, in beginning the life of the grandson of James Freeman, as that grandson was to become a preacher and leader widely known in the Unitarian communion of this country.

In 1810, Dr. Freeman lived, for the greater part of the year, in Newton, from which place it was necessary to drive to Boston, six or seven miles away, for the discharge of his duties there. To his house in Newton, Dr. Samuel Clarke, who was the son of Mrs. Freeman by her first marriage, brought his wife and children on their return from Hanover; and there they remained for the rest of that year. Dr. Clarke then removed to another house in the neighborhood. But Dr. Freeman was fond of his godson James, and always wished to have him as an inmate of his own family. So that it was in Dr. Freeman's house and under his immediate care that James Freeman Clarke spent most of his boyhood. "Dr. Freeman was always looked upon by the children of his stepson, Samuel Clarke, in the light of a grandfather, and his affection and kindness were as great as if they were his nearest blood relatives." [1]

The two houses were near each other, so that the children were not much separated by the arrangement which provided for James a home with Dr. Freeman.

Another grandfather and grandmother, General Wil-

[1] From a letter of Samuel C. Clarke, J. F. C.'s older brother.

liam Hull and his wife, lived about a mile and a half from Dr. Freeman. The autobiography gives an interesting account of the boy's relations with them. General Hull is but little remembered now, except in connection with the surrender of Detroit to the English in the year 1812, and the charge of treason on which he was then tried, at the instance of the weak and incompetent administration of this country, which tried to make him its scapegoat. It is only necessary here to say that General Hull did not lose the regard and respect of his neighbors and fellow-citizens.

Mr. Clarke's autobiography dwells so pleasantly on Dr. Freeman's ways of teaching his grandson that there is no need of saying more of them. But there was no subject on which, in after life, Mr. Clarke loved more to talk than the skill with which he had been lured by his grandfather to learn Latin without being aware of it. He is one more instance in that distinguished list of happy children who have been so fortunate as to be well educated before they went to school, or, like Stuart Mill, without going to school at all.

He speaks of the Boston Latin School, in the Autobiography, with the pride and regard with which almost all the graduates look back to it. He was at the school at a distinguished period of its history. After a long decline, greatly regretted by the best citizens, it had been placed under the charge of Benjamin Apthorp Gould, a young man, an elegant classical scholar, and a master of discipline. The attendance at the school, which had been very small, soon became large, and it was without rival in Boston. Scholars were sent to it from a great distance, to be admitted on special terms and as a favor. On a catalogue of the school at that time, which Mr. Clarke kept and prized as having once belonged to Charles Sumner, there are the names of many persons still remembered for public services. Among them are Epes S. Dixwell, George Stillman

Hillard, Robert Charles Winthrop, Charles Sumner, and Wendell Phillips. Ralph Waldo Emerson and William Henry Furness, from the same school, had entered college in 1817. A letter from Mr. Samuel C. Clarke preserves the memory of a contribution which the schoolboys made for Bunker Hill Monument, when the enterprise of building it was begun. It seems that James Freeman Clarke wrote a poem, which was delivered with the boys' offering. It ended with these lines: —

> "We too, though children, our small boon may give,
> We too may bid our fathers' glory live;
> And we the childish toy will throw aside,
> And bring our stone, to swell the column's pride."

During all this period, his life was, of course, mostly spent in Boston. His father and mother had removed to Dr. Freeman's Boston house, in Vine Street. Vine Street, now shut up a good deal by what are called the improvements of modern times, and crowded with such a population as comes in when the separate rooms of houses are let to separate tenants, was then a new street, pretty, airy, and near the water. The pilgrim must not judge of its aspect then by what he sees to-day.

Young Clarke entered Harvard College in 1825, in a class to which Dr. Holmes has given celebrity by the charming poems which he has read at its frequent meetings. Mr. Clarke's own study of his college life in the Autobiography is very interesting and valuable. Of his part in it, more than one of his classmates have given accounts which show how far, in the boy of sixteen and seventeen, the man could be discerned. It is interesting to observe that Mr. Emerson had returned to Cambridge in the same year, and in 1826 was keeping a school in the Hedge house on Winthrop Square. He lived in Divinity Hall at Cambridge until 1829, so that he and Mr. Clarke must have met each other once and again in those days. I think, however, that they did not form a personal acquaintance until 1832. In that year, in a MS. " Journal of the Understanding" is this note: "Thursday, December 5. Patterson carried me to see Mr. Emerson. Had a conversation on Goethe, German Literature, Carlyle, etc."

Mr. Clarke's own account of his college life is so full that I refrain from adding many of the interesting reminiscences which his classmates have given me. It is clear that he was a favorite, — but I should say that they did not anticipate his career as a leader of opinion. His personal courage, his skill as a gymnast, and his friendly good nature, were all noted then, and characterize the anecdotes told of him. More than one classmate still speaks of his terror when he saw Clarke standing on the top of the tall mast, which he describes, upon the Delta. There was an occasion when an effigy which hung from one window of Hollis was on the edge of capture by a " parietal officer," when " James" appeared from the entry of Stoughton Hall, cut down the offending image just in time, and retired to safe seclusion.

Of his literary work he speaks almost contemptuously. A Bowdoin prize dissertation is preserved in the original manuscript. The subject is, " How far political ignorance in the people is to be depended upon for the security of absolute governments in Europe." It will be remembered that these were the palmy days of the Holy Alliance, and that news of Neapolitan and Greek insurrections was in the air. The essay is the essay of a boy; but it is the essay of a boy who had grown up with James Freeman, and had read or heard Dr. Channing. Early in the paper is this passage: —

" The man of information searches not after liberty because he sees the inhabitants of a country robbed of a few pieces of money, or trampled upon by the horses' hoofs of an insolent nobility, or fathers torn from their families to fight a tyrant's battles while their wives and children sit starving at home. These evils will excite a glow of indignation on the cheek of any generous man, but they may be remedied by a kind despot, and the sudden resentment will pass away. It is not individual suffering that causes, in a man of enlarged views, his hatred of tyranny. It is not the dead body of a Lucretia that kindles his patriotism. It is the suffering nature of man, — it is because he sees the being intended by heaven for improvement in mind and far reaches of soul, bound down and prevented from taking its glorious flights, in order that five or six descendants of kings may sit on their thrones, and stupefy their spirits in debauchery, or play with the happiness of beings mostly superior to themselves in all things truly worthy of the nature of men."

The words are the words of a boy, but of a boy who is the father of the man.

His judicial temperament, which we shall have many occasions to observe, which led him always to study both sides of a question with equal candor, was observed even then. A fellow-student, who was among the near friends of his later life, says that when he first knew Clarke he thought him "double-faced," because he noticed only the eagerness with which he examined all parts in a controversy.

Emerson, as has been said, was living in Divinity Hall, and Clarke, before leaving it, had made the friendship, among many others, of F. H. Hedge, H. W. Bellows, and W. G. Eliot. With William Henry Channing he had been intimate from his Latin School days. They sat there side by side.

This will be a proper place to speak of a certain enthusiastic expectation which at that time quickened the lives of all young people in New England who had been trained in the freer schools of religion. The group of leaders who surrounded Dr. Channing had, with him, broken forever from the fetters of Calvinistic theology. These young people were trained to know that human nature is not totally depraved. They were taught that there is nothing of which it is not capable. From Dr. Channing down, every writer and preacher believed in the infinite power of education. In England the popular wave for the diffusion of useful knowledge had set in; and what was called "the March of Intellect" had begun. The great German authors swayed the minds of our young students with all their new power, and with the special seduction which accompanies a discovery, the study of German being wholly new.[1] For students who did not read German, Coleridge was opening up the larger philosophy. The organization of societies for philanthropic purposes was comparatively new. It promised more than it has ever performed, and even sensible people then supposed that when a hundred men gave each a hundredth part of himself to an enterprise, that enterprise had received an alliance stronger than one devoted man could bring alone.

For such reasons, and many more, the young New Englanders of liberal training rushed into life, certain that the next half century was to see a complete moral revolution in the world. There was no "indifferentism" with them. They were not quite sure what they were to do about it, but they knew that something was to be done. And no one rightly writes or reads the life of one of these young men or women, unless he fully appreciates the force of this enthusiastic hope.

[1] Or almost wholly new. Dr. Bentley, of Salem, read the German rationalistic authors, and had a large library of such literature, as early as the beginning of the century. But the remark in the text may still stand. In 1833 it would have been difficult to buy any German book in Boston excepting Goethe and Schiller. As late as 1843 I rummaged the Philadelphia book-stores for German books, supposing that the large German population of Pennsylvania might have led to their importation. I could buy hardly any German books in Boston, and all the Philadelphia shops offered were Goethe, Schiller, the Bible and the Psalm-book.

At the Cambridge Divinity School, it must be confessed, these young enthusiasts were then kept in pretty close harness. But they respected their wardens, as well they might. Professor Andrews Norton conducted the criticism of the New Testament. To a certain degree, he was indifferent to Hebrew and the criticism of the Old Testament. But he gave signal vivacity to the study of the four Gospels, and the men of that time always went back eagerly to describe their surprise when they found they might study the life of Jesus with such realistic criticism as they would have brought to the history of the American Revolution. The senior Henry Ware was thoroughly read in what was then called "divinity." By this was meant, I suppose, the theories which eighteen centuries of scholarly men had wrought out about the nature of God, the nature of man, and the relations between God and man.

These gentlemen made the eager students whom they had in hand study Hebrew and Greek, and read critically every word of both Testaments. They taught them what they believed, that if they could find out from the four Gospels what Jesus Christ wanted done to-day, they had an all-sufficient answer for every question of to-day. They also believed that it was possible to learn just what the Saviour did wish for every contingency of to-day. John Winthrop and John Cotton were not more sure that the details of Mosaic legislation could be applied in New England townships, than were the teachers under whom Clarke studied that there was in the four Gospels the detailed direction for the exchange, the market, and the factory in the year 1830. I mean to say that they cried, "To the Law and the Testimony," quite as earnestly as Winthrop and Cotton did, though the "Law and the Testimony" were to be found chiefly in the four Gospels. If you had asked whether you were not to go to God in personal prayer for a personal answer in to-day's difficulty, they would have said, "Yes." But I think that in the lessons of the class-room, they would have been apt to tell you to study your New Testament carefully, and to seek in the instruction of Jesus Christ the answer to all inquiries.

Of course, however, it was impossible to teach men to rely on their own reason in deciding between two meanings of a Greek word, and not to teach them at the same time that their own reason would tell them what was right and what was wrong. Indeed, the moment these young persons learned from the Saviour that they were themselves sons of God, they took him at his word, and began to go to headquarters for direct instructions. In this habit, they were encouraged by the dominant influence of the younger Henry Ware, one of the most devout of men. In the year 1830, the younger Henry Ware came to the school from the Second Church in Boston, where he had succeeded Ralph Waldo Emerson. He was a man of rare religious genius, passionately interested in what he would have called the "saving of souls," aggressive as any fanatic revivalist in his Christian enthusiasm, and at the same time, by conviction and on the authority of Scripture, an out-and-out Unitarian. He put into the hands of the divinity students the books of the church mystics, and the biographies of Brainerd and other missionaries. While he quickened them in evangelistic zeal, he led them into close personal communion with God, and into a sense of the power of the Spirit. The "immanence of God" has become a theological phrase since that time. It is clear enough, as one reads the biographies, which begin to appear, of the men who were at work in that Cambridge school of criticism, that criticism itself was bringing them all to that personal sense of the Real Presence which has dominated the Unitarian movement of America for the last half century. These young men could not read their Coleridge or their Goethe without emancipating themselves at once from the wooden philosophy of John Locke, over which they had been made to hammer as undergraduates. They left the school pure idealists, sure of the real presence of God, and sure that society was to be made over again within fifty years.

In the year 1831, John Gorham Palfrey, afterward known as the historian of New England, and an aggressive anti-slavery leader, was appointed to the chair of criticism of the Old and New Testaments.[1] He brought to his duty, not only a very accurate knowledge of the subjects especially given to him, but that acute conscience, that interest in history, and that public spirit, which had distinguished him, and which afterward distinguished him, in his work as a citizen. Not long after this time, his father died in Louisiana, leaving a large property, of which a considerable part was in slaves. The other heirs proposed that their Northern brother should take his part in money and leave them the slaves, but he declined. He himself went to Louisiana, brought with him to the North his portion of the slaves, more than forty in number, and settled them in homes, that they might be made free. He thus ranked as a practical abolitionist, long before he connected himself with the movement which bore the name of abolition. In the intimacies of Mr. Palfrey's home, the students of the Divinity School were most cordially welcomed, and to friendships formed there Freeman Clarke owed much in his after life.

Any one who knew Mr. Clarke intimately in after years, and talked with him on theological subjects, knows how accurately and carefully he went into the school-work of which I have attempted thus to give some account. At the same time he was reading, one would say, everything else; but especially was he reading Goethe. And afterward, in referring to those

[1] He was made Doctor of Divinity in 1834.

happy days, he would always speak with enthusiasm of the larger life which opened upon so many of them, under Goethe's lead. In the chapter of Margaret Fuller's biography which he has himself edited, are allusions to this revelation, and to the eager and hopeful studies which he conducted with her.

Dr. Frederick Henry Hedge, the friend of Mr. Clarke's whole life, in speaking of him to me after his death, said, " You do not get a true estimate of Clarke unless you see him as a poet. He approached all subjects from the poetical side. This poetical habit of looking at everything gave him that fairness which you have observed. The rest of us have written as if we were philosophers. Clarke always wrote, no matter on how dull a subject, as a poet writes. And though he has written very few verses, it is because he is a poet that he has done what he has done."

I believe this remark of this careful observer and thinker to be true, and I shall be sorry if the reader of this volume does not think so, before we part.

After Dr. Hedge had said this to me, I found the following passage in Mr. Clarke's journal of October 16, 1832. It is an interesting early suggestion of the mental habits to which Dr. Hedge alluded, fifty-seven years after.

"I have been idle this term, and dissipated in mind. I must shut myself into my room, and make my duties the absorbing occupation of this year. I wish to study the Bible this year thoroughly, and without any commentaries. I wish to write a good deal, to get an individual style, and to read little, and that principally German. I think of studying the early history of our country, and writing a drama, the object of which shall be to do justice to the spirit of those times, by exciting a respect for our ancestors, to cherish the patriotic spirit which is now languishing. I will make the heroes — the Puritans — look forward to our times, and paint their high hopes of what can be done for humanity by a free, religious, enlightened nation. I have always been prevented from expressing myself well in poetry by the obstacle of the rhyme; here I can overcome this. If I write this, I can follow it by a drama relating to the time of the Revolution or just before it, where the feeling will refer backward in reverence, and forward in yet prouder prophecy."

There is no evidence that he ever took any steps forward in fulfilling this dream of a youth of twenty-two, who, with the same ink which records his intention to "read little," proposes to study the early history of the country for his Puritan Drama.

From his journal. "All growing minds may be divided into two classes, the grasshoppers and father-long-legs. The first collect themselves together, and then the whole body goes at once to a definite point, by a spring. The others thrust out a leg, then another, then a third, as far as they will go, and let the body come after as it can. No. 1 are apt to be special pleaders, one-sided arguers, but coherent and comprehensive. No. 2 are fair and candid in debate, caring for truth and not at all for consequences, but very prone to contradict themselves at every other word. I believe that I am a father-long-legs and M. a grasshopper."

Certainly this joking description of himself shows that he had already found out the judicial quality or determination of seeing all sides which distinguished his after life.

At the end of the divinity course, in those days, the young men of the Senior class began to write sermons, and to preach them as they were asked. It is an interesting thing to find that the text of his first sermon was the text of his life: —

"Whatsoever thy hand findeth to do, do it with thy might."

The manuscript, afterward burned at the edges in an

accidental fire, lies before me. It is indorsed, in ink now brown, "Preached, Theological School; first sermon;"— again, "Preached at Mr. Whitman's, July 21, 1833;"— again, "Preached without notes, December 1, 1833."

After the formal introduction to the sermon, he states the text as meaning, "*What lies at hand;* in other words, *Perform thy nearest duty.*" Such was the resolution with which he went forth to battle.

At the end of the sermon is written this prayer: —

"Grant, O Almighty Father, that as our days on earth are multiplied, we may attain to a clearer sense of the value of time, and a more faithful use of passing opportunities. Save us from indolence, from indifference to truth, from the moral death. May the religion of our Master kindle in our hearts the flame of love and piety. Wilt thou answer our prayers with the influence of thy Holy Spirit, so that, partaking more and more of thy divine nature, we may resemble thee more and more in the constancy of our deeds of active charity; and that, when we enter the dark valley of the shadow of death, we may carry the remembrance of a life full of worship and service. Grant, we beseech thee, that all words of truth that we have heard this day may be grafted in our understanding, and bring forth fruits of good living and action, to the honor and praise of thy name, through Jesus Christ our Lord. Amen."

Such was the consecration which the young knight asked for his resolution.

In the public exercises with which the course at the Divinity School closed, his subject was, "Robert Hall." The solidity of the treatment, and the directness of the statement, immediately arrested the attention of the best judges. Dr. James Walker, the Nestor of another generation, when asked his opinion of the graduating class by an enthusiastic admirer of one of them, instantly referred to these merits as they showed themselves in Clarke's paper.

CHAPTER VIII.

JOURNALS AND LETTERS.

1830-1840.

THERE were of course a thousand temptations to a young man equipped as Mr. Clarke was to accept the charge of some vacant parish in New England, and carry on his work among those with whom he sympathized. But that enthusiasm of young New England, to which I have alluded, would not permit him to enter on a career which seemed to offer so little opportunity for missionary work. He preferred to carry such gospel as he had to a region where there were few churches of the denomination to which he belonged. In his Autobiography he has told us of the motives which influenced him in his decision to accept an invitation to preach in Louisville, Kentucky, where some persons, mostly of New England origin, had formed a Unitarian church.[1] This was in 1833. At that time the signs of the coming of the slavery contest were but few. Still every one in New England knew that Kentucky was not New England, and the whole drift of public opinion there was different from that on which Mr. Clarke and his friends had been borne along. It was not many years, for instance, since some gentlemen of Lexington, Kentucky, had invited Horace Holley, the eminent liberal preacher of Boston, to be the president of the University of Transylvania. Dr. Holley had gone there with all the prestige which any man

[1] Dr. Lyman Beecher went with his family to Cincinnati at the same time, and here Mr. Clarke's acquaintance with them began.

could carry from the East to the West; but the Presbyterian ministers of Kentucky, and those of the other Evangelical churches, were quite too strong for any such inroad. Dr. Holley and his friends were given to understand that there was no need for any such men as they were in that region. This was, I think, the only attempt which had been made, before the establishment of the Louisville Unitarian church, toward the transfusion of the New England religious idea into the strictly orthodox flow of the religious life of Kentucky.

The journey to Kentucky, as will be seen by Mr. Clarke's notes and letters, took more time than a journey to Alaska would take to-day, and it was much more difficult. But he was young and strong; he liked adventure; and all through the period of his life in Louisville, which lasted seven years, he was ready, at the shortest call, to undertake even difficult travel in the interest of the cause to which he had devoted his life. He soon found that no clergyman would exchange pulpits with him, excepting Ephraim Peabody, the Unitarian preacher at Cincinnati, and afterward William G. Eliot, who came to St. Louis in 1834. These three young men were thus knit together by a tie of the closest and tenderest character. Mr. Clarke also formed that acquaintance with the family of Mr. Huidekoper, of Meadville, Pennsylvania, which added so much to the happiness of his after-life.

In that after-life he was very fond of referring to the events, not to say the adventures, of his Louisville life, which, to the decorous life of Boston in that time, were nearly as strange as the adventures of John Smith or of Columbus. In selecting from his notes passages which will illustrate the happy years he spent at Louisville, one is only puzzled by having too much material.

The chapter of his Autobiography which is, alas, the last he ever wrote, contains his general review, made fifty years after, of the memories which he had of travel. In other notes it appears that, on the first journey, the route was by stage from Boston to Providence, steamboat to New York, stage and railway to Philadelphia, stage to Baltimore, stage to Wheeling over the mountains, thence by steamboat to Louisville.[1] During his seven years at Louisville he came back to Boston nearly every year for a short visit. In these journeys he took different routes. One was from Cincinnati by stage to Cleveland; thence the steamboat took him to Buffalo, the stage to Albany, and thence he could come through to Boston by stage, or by steamboat to Providence. The railroad lines between Boston and New York were extending all through these seven years.

The Guyandotte route, which is spoken of in the Autobiography, was by boat to the mouth of the Guyandotte, and then over the mountains to Sulphur Springs in Virginia. The Pennsylvania route was over the Alleghanies in Pennsylvania, passing Laurel Hill and Bedford.

He arrived in Louisville, for the first time, August 4, 1833. He found there a small Unitarian society, which had built a neat and well-proportioned church. The society had been organized by a few earnest Unitarians, mostly from New England. Services had been held for several years in different places, generally in the schoolhouse of Mr. Francis E. Goddard, a man of wide attainments and an able teacher. John Pierpont, Bernard Whitman, and Charles Briggs were among the preachers who, in short visits to Louisville, had interested the worshipers. The church had been dedicated on the 27th of May, 1832. On that occasion Dr. Francis Parkman, and James Walker, afterwards president of Harvard College, took part in the services.

Mr. Clarke's immediate predecessor in this church

[1] The railroad from Boston to Providence, and that from Boston to Worcester, were not opened for travel until June, 1835.

was the Rev. George Chapman, who had entered its ministry in 1832. But at the end of a year he was obliged to leave Louisville on account of failing health; and he died of pulmonary disease in 1834. I write these lines with a renewal of that respect and regard which I had, sixty years ago, for one of my first Sunday-school teachers. George Chapman, as a young man, impressed me, a boy of seven, as perfectly in earnest in what he said, and as leading a life wholly consecrated.

The congregation which Mr. Clarke found was not large; but, looking back upon it, we see it was remarkable. It had been gathered, as has been said, by New Englanders; but, beside a constituency of men and women of what may be called the old Unitarian line of New England, it embraced others from England, from Scotland, from Kentucky, Virginia, Maryland, New Jersey, Indiana, and other States of the Union. His autobiography speaks of one and another of these.

Mr. Clarke's connection with the "Western Messenger" maintained and enlarged his acquaintance with the leaders of the liberal religious movement in America. He printed the papers of Channing, of Emerson, of Hedge, and of many of those, less known then, who have since filled important places in literature. Making every year a journey to Boston, he kept his touch with New England, and he knew very well what was the drift, and, indeed, what was the stagnation, of religious thought in New England. For the kingdom of heaven was not coming in quite as fast as the young enthusiasts of 1831 and 1832 had expected. The Unitarian movement was not outgrowing its critical phase, nor emancipating itself from the social conditions of its origin as fast as he and many of his friends could have wished. From time to time, one and another, for various reasons, urged him to come back to Boston. I have not found among his papers any very definite statement by himself as to the reasons which led him to return to the East; but in the letters of 1840 some of them are suggested. He had never been installed as the minister of the Louisville church; he had simply accepted the invitation, renewed every year, to be its minister for one year more; and he now determined not to accept that invitation for the eighth time. This decision having been made, he eventually left Louisville on the 16th day of June, 1840.

In some notes which were used as a brief of a conversational lecture, he says, "Very green and raw when I reached Louisville.

"Nothing to say, that is, that seemed worth saying.

"Knew no one; very lonely; so for three months."

Again, "Kentuckians, Judge Speed, Judge Nicholas, Judge Rowan, George D. Prentice, Tom Marshall, Humphrey Marshall, Judge and Mrs. John J. Marshall, Garnett Duncan, Colonel Woolley, the Popes."

"Slavery, *mild*. People said, 'All wrong, inexcusable; Kentucky will emancipate.' Lectures, debates, newspapers.

"When I came back to Boston, it was harder to speak of slavery than it had been in Kentucky. I learned my anti-slavery there; a great change afterward in public sentiment in Kentucky.

"Dueling. Graves and Cilley, Tom Marshall and John Rowan.[1]

"Character of people: manly, intelligent, generous, fresh; natural refinement."

---

[1] "When I went to Kentucky, dueling was considered entirely proper and necessary. I preached a sermon against it, on the occasion of a very extraordinary duel which had just taken place; and the father of one of the combatants, who had been a United States senator, was in church that day. He said that he could not understand what had got into Mr. Clarke's head to preach against dueling; he might as well preach against courage." — *Anti-Slavery Days*, p. 27.

In another note he speaks of his work in the schools. Elsewhere he speaks of the bloodthirsty people who existed then, as even now, in certain wild sections of the Mississippi Valley.

A list which he made of some of the distinguished Kentuckians whom he then knew recalls many memories of interest in our history : —

"Judge Rowan, eminent lawyer, senator of the United States. Highly courteous gentleman and scholar; had fought at least one duel.

"Joseph Hamilton Daviess; farmer's son; how he studied law. Wonderful speaker. His trip to Washington; his resistance to Burr; his death.

"George D. Prentice; his attacks on Jackson. His wife's party; I refused wine; he asked why."

To his memories of early life, written after half a century had passed, I add a few extracts from his own letters and those of his correspondents, and a very few from his journals.

TO MARGARET FULLER.

OHIO RIVER, *July* 31, 1833.

During the week[1] many things took place to move me. There were a great many "last times" to feel, last things to do, last words to speak. Our exhibition was to me interesting, affecting. I loved my classmates. . . . You can see my part, for it is to be printed in the next "Examiner," by the suggestion of H. Hedge to Mr. Walker. Mr. Greenwood also treated me with great kindness. On Sunday I preached at Waltham, and in the evening was ordained. . . .

My thought after the ordination was, "God forgive me for having called this a mere ceremony." It was much more, — I was deeply moved. . . .

It was bitter to take leave of grandfather; though you may be sure there was no scene; he simply shook my hand in silence

[1] The week before leaving home for Louisville.

I felt very vacant and unindividual till I got upon the Newcastle Railroad, where, by steam, we travel sixteen miles in an hour and ten minutes. Twilight was deepening into darkness, hastened by a thunderstorm, which came up in terrible might from the west, while a full moon floated on the opposite blue sky. We flew through the rain and lightning, four enormous carriages, chained together, and crossed the Chesapeake amid a continuation of the same storm.

TO MARGARET FULLER.

LOUISVILLE, *September* 13, 1833.

I have just been attending the funeral of one of the first settlers, — one General Breckenridge, aged seventy-eight. He came here in 1780, having been in the Revolutionary War. At that time the settlers were few, and these few lived in a fort, for fear of Indians.

. . . I was asked to perform the service, which was in the city; but he was buried on his own place, six miles out of town, and they wished me to go out and make a prayer at the grave. We passed along an avenue winding through the forest for half a mile, until we reached the house, — a one-story building, the sitting-room decorated with a harpsichord and two old-fashioned card-tables. The family burial-place was at a little distance beyond the house. After the service, one of my friends offered me his saddle-horse to return, and I had a beautiful ride through the forest. The forests of Kentucky are said to surpass those of any part of Europe. This was chiefly composed of sycamores of tremendous size, and lofty, tapering beeches with thick clumps at the top. The trunks of the sycamores are often six and eight feet in diameter. The oak is common also. . . .

Louisville is perfectly flat, and there are few pleasant walks, it is so dusty and muddy. There are many customs odd to a Yankee. For example, nothing is more common than for builders of houses to collect their shavings in the middle of the street, and set fire to them. Every evening, in walking about, one sees half a dozen of these fires. There has been a duel in agitation, and an assassination attempted among some fire-eaters here. The progress of the affair was known to the whole city. It was the common talk that Mr. Prentice had offered Mr. Trotter to fight with rifles at forty-five paces, or with pistols at six, or with swords or dirks. And then it was said that Mr. Trotter had demanded, on account of his near-sightedness, to fight with pistols at each other's breast; and then the negotiation broke off. Presently we heard that Mr. Trotter had shot Mr. P. in the back, in the street, etc. They are rather a bloody set of fellows, and they call their cruelty chivalry. The system of slavery colors everything.

TO W. H. CHANNING.

LOUISVILLE, *October* 4, 1833.

When I arrived here I was at first disheartened by the small number who attend the church, and by the feeling, which for a long time [1] I was unable to conquer, that my efforts were wholly ineffectual, and not likely ever to become less so. Yet, even then, I did not think of yielding till a full experiment had been tried. . . . If I have not faith enough in the truths to which I have solemnly devoted myself to persevere through a few difficulties, I will give up my post to some better man.

The number of my hearers has increased a little. I have written a dozen sermons since I have been here; and with this, a weekly lecture, Sunday-school, temperance societies, attending funerals, parish visiting, getting acquainted with the place and people, my mind and time have been pretty well occupied.

---

[1] He had arrived in Louisville early in August. Evidently he measured time by his feelings, and not by the almanac.

I have become better acquainted with St. Paul's character, and admire him more than ever. When I was a child I disliked him, and kept to the Gospels. . . . We admire in the Evangelists the love which has attached itself to great things without knowing they are great; in St. Paul we sympathize with the intellectual perception which enables him rightly to appreciate things high and low, and to understand the spirit and letter of the gospel, — to grasp it in its essentials and in its details. One of these years I intend to write a life of St. Paul.

I wish to hear regularly concerning both your inner and your outward man, and also concerning C. Robbins and our other classmates. Give them my love, and tell them that, notwithstanding the thousand miles between us, they are nearer to me than when we lived under the same roof. May I trust you for an account of their "weaving and working"?

TO W. H. CHANNING.

LEXINGTON, KENTUCKY, *November* 8, 1833.

I have penetrated thus far into the interior, and have had, on the whole, many reasons for being pleased with what I have experienced and observed. In the first place I must thank Heaven for "the freedom of the mind which has been more than wealth to me," which makes it my habit, wherever I go, to look first for the good, and take it in as I best may, instead of shutting up my sense and putting on it the padlock of personal taste and rigid opinion. Is there danger of my being moulded by each new compression of circumstances? There is danger, I grant, of sometimes being drifted from my *opinions;* but the *truths,* which lie five fathom deep in my heart, I hope never to lose.

I have received attention and hospitable welcome from the Episcopalians of this city, Bishop Smith, President Peers, etc. I presented myself among them with openness and frankness, and I have no cause to complain of my reception.

Secondly. I am pleased with the spirit manifested at this education convention, called from all parts of the State for the purpose of petitioning the legislature to act in behalf of popular education. . . . We are going to do something to rouse the people of the State to the business. There is to be a more general convention at Frankfort, and a State education society formed.

Thirdly. The opinions I have everywhere heard expressed on the subject of slavery are encouraging. The general, boldly expressed sentiment is, that slavery is a curse in every point of view to Kentucky, that there is no excuse for its existing a moment in this State. In the stage with me were two Kentuckians. We met four negroes *chained*, preceding a moving family. It was the first time I had seen such a sight. I expressed my disgust. So did these gentlemen, both slaveholders. One said that slave-dealers were held in such abhorrence that by no effort could the power of their wealth ever bring them into respectable society, even after retiring from business.

Fourthly. The prescriptive manners of the clerical body are abolished in the West, and they are influential only in proportion to actual ability. . . . A free conversational elocution, and an easy rhetoric, crowded with figures and illustrations, and avoiding all cant phrases and solemn phraseology, is the characteristic of every popular preacher. And I have listened since I have been out here to such preaching as in every way surpasses Eastern oratory.

Every day I become more interested in the character of this great Western people. Its simplicity charms me, its openness commands my sympathy, its free, unfettered activity calls for my admiration.

TO W. G. ELIOT.

December 4, 1833.

I think your principle of faith is nobly displayed in Fichte, if by faith you understand, as I do, a realizing sense of spiritual things, the sense by which truths are seen as real and substantial *things,* no less real than the material objects around us, yes, more so, because eternal. Faith is, in my opinion, not the belief of propositions or dogmas of any kind, but a sense of truth, which may be stronger or weaker. All faith is essentially faith in God, inasmuch as God is the source of all truths, the centre of the spiritual world.

You ask me about the West, and a suitable preparation for coming to it. Everything which liberalizes your mind, which enables you to despise the form in comparison with the essence, the letter in comparison with the spirit, everything which increases your faith and submission to the will of God, and patient determination to work for his glory, is a preparation for the West. Everything here is free, open, active. To be useful one must lay aside all narrow tastes and exclusive feelings, and from a pure love to humanity plunge into the life around him. With such a spirit as this I think the West a noble field, it is so stirring, so growing. You feel your life, you feel full of energy, your soul grows and expands with every pulse throb. . . . Oh, how I wish you would decide to come out here. You could be ten times as useful, ten times as happy out here. I think the soul grows as fast as the trees do. You must come, however, determined to regard only what is real, not what is apparent, to trace goodness and evil to their roots, and never be repelled by the surface.

FROM HIS JOURNAL.

1834. September. I propose during the present year to collect materials for the following books, and to prepare some of them for the press. The matter is all to be gathered from actual life and experience.

1. Prayers and Helps to Devotion.
2. Aids to Understanding and Applying Scripture.
3. The Clerical Profession at the Present Day, and Religion among the Educated.
4. Poems. Journal. With Illustrations.
5. The Power of Faith, a National and Religious Epic. Pilgrim Fathers.
6. The Power of Conscience: Another.

1834. October 12. Preached in morning on Dueling. Afternoon on Prayer. Lesson to Sunday-school.

November 1. I feel that as I object to the revival method of driving persons into religion, I ought to be always practising the other method of gentle and steady persuasion. May God give me strength so to do that I may not be unfruitful. I think we should be either at work or at prayer all the time.

TO MARGARET FULLER.

October 22, 1834.

I have lately been a good deal interested in the Poles who are journeying to their lands in Illinois. One, in particular, I have become acquainted with; a young man of education and fine feelings; the son of a general officer, who was cruelly treated by the Russians, and sent into Siberia. His name is Casimir Mickiewicz, from Lithuania.

Mickiewicz was in several battles; he plays beautifully on the piano-forte. He had letters to Cincinnati from General La Fayette. He might support himself by teaching music, but prefers to go with his countrymen to their lands.[1]

---

[1] A good many *Poles* came to *Louisville* in 1834, and Mr. Clarke, with others, made zealous efforts to find employment for them This was a difficult task, because most of the *Polish* refugees were from aristocratic families, had learned no trade, and considered most forms of labor beneath them, — they could fight, but they could not work.

I am stuying mineralogy, at present, with Mrs. Windship, who is altogether a superior person. I expect to become a little acquainted with the materials on which I have been moving about all my days without troubling myself before to examine them. I think that mineralogy and geology are in great want of a Cuvier or Goethe to bring them into systematic shape; putting them, I mean, into a system which shall be no arbitrary collocation, but shall contain the law of its organization within itself, so that every part shall cohere and be dependent on every other part, and all make a whole.

After a good deal of effort all were provided for except three; and for these also, after a time, Mr. Clarke succeeded in obtaining employment in a paper factory belonging to a friend of his, — and a lodging was provided for the three Poles in the factory building.

A few days after this arrangement had been made, Mr. Clarke met these gentlemen in the street. He stopped, and inquired how they were getting on.

"Oh, we have left that place!" said they. "We were obliged to leave it. We could not possibly stay there. Mr. —— treated us very badly; he insulted us; it was out of the question to remain any longer."

"Indeed! I have always had a high opinion of Mr. ——. How did he ill-treat you?"

'Oh, he insulted us; he required us to perform menial offices; he expected us to build our own fires."

"Why, I build my own fire every day," said Mr. Clarke. But the wrath of the offended Poles was not to be reasoned away.

"How do you expect to earn your living?" asked Mr. Clarke.

"We intend to give a concert," said they. "Will you take some tickets?"

Of another of the Poles, Mr. Clarke writes in his diary:

"Brosowski, a Pole, came to see me. Speaks Latin, French, Spanish, German, as fast as possible; plays on piano-forte, guitar, etc.; paints and draws, and cannot earn his bread! He says, 'Non habeo laborum, piget mendicare.' I gave him an old coat, which he took with delight, because he would now look like a 'homo doctus." Also a letter and some money, and he went off fully satisfied."

FROM HIS JOURNAL.

1834. November 17. Went about with Pole. Put him at shop of Mr. Smith.

November 18. Searching employment for Poles.

November 19. Went to Tyler's with Poles.

November 24. Went to see Blumenthal about Schiller's letters. Pole at Mr. Smith's a word of advice. Phelps, dying man; prayer and religious conversation. With Mr. Low, to find a guitar for Mickiewicz.

TO MARGARET FULLER.

November, 1834.

My Poles do not behave themselves very well; they trouble me somewhat by their foolish and childish notions, for which I suppose they are not much to blame, but which make them hard to deal with. . . . George Keats is one of the best men in the world. And I have taken a strong liking to the character of his brother John, which has just dawned on me through the medium of his letters and accounts of his personal history. .

I have learned how to tell stories with ease, and to make them intelligible and interesting to children; and, what is not difficult to one in earnest, to extract a moral, or, rather, to convey a moral influence, by any story in the world. My Sunday-school, therefore, is interesting to me.

TO W. H. CHANNING.

January 15, 1835.

I am hopeful, and consider the great beauty of truth till I think it must prevail. I look away from the wickedness, the woeful entanglement, the deep pollution, the great perversions, the gross worldliness of man, and think of his infinite origin, his immortal home, his likeness to God, and the accomplishments of the few noble. Now this is one-sided, I grant you, but real evil makes itself evident all too soon; let us, therefore, put on the whole armor of faith, that we may be able to stand in that evil day. Whether I shall ever do anything great, I know not, but I will do little things from great motives "She hath done what she could" is the highest praise created beings can receive.

TO G. T. D.

February 20, 1835.

I send you the prospectus of a magazine which we are about getting under way, and which we mean to make the leading Western periodical. We intend to combine literature and other matters with religion, and make it generally attractive. . . . We shall try to get the aid of leading and known men through the land. Whoever helps us helps not *us,* but the cause of freedom and truth. *We* gain nothing but an addition to the weight of labor and abuse which is already upon our shoulders. We intend that it shall be *Western* in its character, and as free from merely conventional restrictions in spirit as may be.

TO MARGARET FULLER.

March 16, 1835.

You ask how many hours a day I study? Perhaps three or four. What? I study Greek; I am determined to understand that language passably. I study the Bible; German theology a little; Goethe not at all; St. Paul, much. I study how to talk so as to impress the minds of children and of men. I study Jacob Abbott's books a good deal. . . .

TO MARGARET FULLER.

Sunday, April 12 1835.

To-day I have been preaching two sermons, and have given a Sunday-school lesson. Our school numbers sixty pupils now. To-morrow I have a Bible-class;

Wednesday, a lecture to write and deliver before a phrenological society; Thursday, a lecture in my church at five P. M.; Friday (Good Friday), another at the same hour; Saturday, to write a sermon or two for Easter, and a story for my Sunday-school children. Beside this I must make calls, and go over to Jeffersonville, and perhaps preach Tuesday night. The worst is that all this toil seems to do no good. Maffitt made a hundred converts here two years ago, of whom five only were in the church six months after. However, matters improve decidedly. Five or ten years hence it will be a good place, and then happy will he be who has grown up with it.

TO MARGARET FULLER.

LEXINGTON, KY., *June* 14, 1835.

I have come to this city, first, to see Miss Martineau; second, to get some subscribers to the "Western Messenger;" third, to preach, and to get acquainted with the people here.

I saw Miss Martineau, and had a capital time with her. I talked with her about four hours. Dined with her, with only Mr. and Mrs. Irwin (Clay's daughter and son-in-law) and Miss Jeffrey. She began immediately to talk about Mr. and Mrs. Furness with great enthusiasm. It seems that she was with them while in Philadelphia, and Fanny Kemble came to see them every day. Mr. Furness is a great admirer of Carlyle, and he converted Miss M., and she admires Carlyle just as enthusiastially as he. She says it is a great mistake to suppose her a mere utilitarian; she is preparing the people for Carlyleism, for they must be fed and clothed before they can be spiritualized.

FROM HIS JOURNAL.

1835. December 10. Left Louisville at 5 P. M. for New Orleans [and Mobile]. A sinking of spirit on my departure showed that I was leaning on outward things. But I commended myself to God, knowing my purpose was pure and would be accepted by Him. On His arm I lean wholly, committing myself and my ways to Him, and believing He will direct my path aright, to His glory and to the good of souls.

TO MARGARET FULLER.

STEAMBOAT LEONIDAS, *December* 14, 1835.

I am on my way to Mobile; what to do there God will determine.

We came out of the mouth of the Ohio River at midnight; I rose and went out on the guard, and looked abroad upon the meeting of the waters. We were already on the "Grandfather of all Rivers," as the Persians would call it; and the "Father of Waters," as it is called by the Indians, those "Western Orientalists."

I preached a sermon yesterday, exhorting my fellow-passengers to consider and confess themselves strangers and pilgrims on the earth, as well as on the Mississippi River. That was sound doctrine, but did not quite convince my own mind. When traveling on the river, I am quite willing to put up with bad company and accommodations for a time, but I do not succumb so quietly to a like necessity in that other journey. "It will soon be over" does not strike me as an argument for patience, equally conclusive in the two cases. I remember that I was ever disgusted by that religious view of life which describes it as something very disagreeable, which cannot be enjoyed, but must be just endured for a little. Unkind I hold it to our fellow-pilgrims, to look them in the face with this saintly expression of disgust; ungrateful to God, who has put us into an admirably furnished *school*, to say the least, fitted up with such cabinets, book-shelves, and varied apparatus, that we ought to feel pleasantly about it while we stay. Yea! even disobedient is it, and the part of a wicked and slothful servant, to bury his talent in the earth, because but *one* is given him, and hide his Lord's money. Oh, grumbling religious, or grumbling irreligious, man, grumble no longer, but fight *now* the good fight of faith; lay hold now, with both hands, of eternal life, and in the midst of the Finite discover an Infinite; begin Eternity, while yet shrouded in the mists of Time.

TO H. T. D.
MISSISSIPPI RIVER, BELOW MEMPHIS,
STEAMER LEONIDAS, *December*, 1835.

It was no slight pain to me to hear of the departure of my grandfather. He was the best friend I ever had, or can hope to have. His love for me was wonderful. .

Last night I was much shocked by the cold-blooded and unfeeling way in which a Natchez man described his exploits in flogging negroes. He told, with a truly fiendish glee, how he flogged a man nearly to death a day or two before on suspicion of stealing. But my head is full of stories about hangings and murders.

TO EDITOR OF "WESTERN MESSENGER."
NEW ORLEANS, *December* 22, 1835.

I arrived on Friday, and preached on Sunday to a large audience in Brother Clapp's church. .

I preached Sunday before last on the steamboat to a most attentive audience, composed of the passengers and crew. I had a good deal of religious conversation with the "publicans and sinners," the blasphemers and gamblers, and found them serious and willing to be rebuked. I find a soul of goodness in things evil wherever I go, and my heart leaps with joy at each new discovery of something pure, some love of truth in the roughest shell, the most thorny husk of humanity. Confidence in men unlocks their hearts. Not by looking on them as totally depraved, but by believing there is something good in them, and speaking to them as if you thought so; *this* breaks down their opposition.

FROM HIS JOURNAL.

1836. Mobile. Tell my object in coming. Not to preach to the religious community, or to those under their influence. But a large class not under their influence cannot be reconciled with it, yet want a religion, have none, feel the need of it. These I want to address, take them on their own ground; they are practical deists and atheists, I suppose. I want to make them Christians; not nominal, but real. I hope to do this, because I have different instruments to do it with, and have seen their influence.

I appeal to your understanding. I hope to give you a reason for everything I ask you to do. I shall not dogmatize. I respect the rights of your conscience. I tell you at the outset what I want to do. I wish to produce repentance toward God and faith in our Lord Jesus Christ. If I can induce any one to repent and believe, I have done what I came for. If not, why, it is either my fault, or your fault, or God's time has not come.

TO H. T. D.

"IRISH JEMMY'S BAR,"
12 miles below Rock Cave, Ohio River,
February 10, 1836.

I reckon you never have received a letter from *Irish Jemmy's Bar* before, and I sincerely hope you never will again from any friend in like circumstance with myself. We are frozen up hard and fast, have been lying here and hereabout a week, and cannot say when we shall get away. We cannot get at stages; we cannot hire horses; the roads are in no condition for walking, or, rather, roads there are none. We have no books nor newspapers, and for those who, like myself, neither gamble, drink, chew, nor smoke, there remains but one resource, writing letters.

I write in complete ignorance of everything which

has happened in Yankee-land or Louisville, since January 1, 1836. I had a letter of that date from mother, since when I have heard no word from friendly lip or pen. I have been seeing, feeling, thinking, and acting, however, — most of the first and last. I have seen the Gulf of Mexico, the magnolia tree, the live-oak, General Gaines, and some half-dozen pleasant men and women of New Orleans, a cotton press, portions of Illinois, Missouri, Arkansas, Tennessee, Mississippi, Louisiana, and Alabama, an immense host of blacklegs and rowdies, and the Mississippi River. I have formed a society at Mobile, and have persuaded the members to subscribe a number of thousands of dollars to build a church; have made some good friends and acquaintances, and have induced some of them to think better of Christianity than before. I have also, in leisure moments, written a review of Butler's "Kentucky," one or two sermons, half-a-dozen letters, a hundred lines of verse.

Then, thirdly, for *feeling*. I have felt disgusted and sorrowful at the perpetual stream of cursing and blasphemy which has saluted my ears ever since I have been on the river; have felt a loathing of the cruelties and horrible tyranny of some of the Southern overseers; have grieved at the reckless spirit defying everything we have been taught to love and revere as sacred.

But I have had joyous feelings also. I was touched with the generosity of the Mobile people to myself, and the enthusiasm with which they entered into church matters. There were half-a-dozen men in Mobile who put aside all regard to the plausible and expedient, and asked only what was true and right. One of these was a young man, born in Kentucky. This youth was all fire and enthusiasm about organizing a society, subscribed $500, and when I left told me my coming to Mobile had been the happiest event in his life. Then there was an older man, a Virginian, formerly a mechanic, very intelligent; a man who said not much, but looked immensities, and acted with a steady unflinching energy which carried all before it. Then there was a Boston man, about twenty-five years old, lately married to a Georgian. He was much respected in the place, and devoted himself to the cause with untiring activity. There was another young man, from New York, whose wife and sister had been members of Mr. W. Ware's society. Another, a man overrun with business, told me at first that he could not take much interest in the movement, but put down a subscription of $500, and afterwards came and put down $500 more.

FROM DR. WILLIAM ELLERY CHANNING TO J. F. C.

NEWPORT, R. I., *February* 19, 1836.

MY DEAR SIR, — I received your letter in the beginning of the summer urging me to write for your periodical. . . . Your appreciation was so earnest, and my sympathy with you, and your brethren in the West, so great, that I could not but do something. . . . I often think of the West and its wants. I cannot conceive a nobler field for Christian efforts. My heart is with you in your work, and had I power, I would send you a host of fellow-laborers. It is a bad sign that our body of Christians take no greater interest in spreading truth and righteousness. I live in hope of seeing a new life in our ministers and churches; in hope of partaking more of it myself. With enlightened and fervent ministers, we might cover the country with churches devoted, not to the propagation of a fixed system and of the low Christianity now in fashion, but to moral and religious progress. I look to the young for something better than has been done, and it cheers me to find, in some who are starting, a holy zeal and philanthropy, which cannot be without effect. You and your brethren in the West may act on the young here by heartiness in the cause, your spirit of self-sacrifice, your bolder tone, your firmer faith. What is wanted here is moral confidence in the power of truth and Christianity; thence preaching has a weakness, wants authority and life. May you do better. Your sincere friend,

WILLIAM E. CHANNING.

TO MARGARET FULLER.

LOUISVILLE, *March* 28, 1836.

I have been to Cincinnati to have the "Messenger" removed to Louisville. In a week or so we shall get out a number. I have also written and sent off a long article on "Kentucky History" for the "North American Review."

I sometimes think that could I go to Boston, and preach in some free church, or start a new society, on rather different principles, speaking more to conscience than to intellect, more to intuitive reason than to speculative understanding, making morality and religion one, not two separate matters, I might find a number who would hear me gladly. But better would it be for me to stay here, could I have a few friends who would give me understanding sympathy.

When I was in Mobile, I saw a leathern bag hanging in a certain place, marked thus: "Letter-bag; Ship Sarah sails to-morrow for Liverpool." I went home instantly, and wrote a letter to Thomas Carlyle, returned, and dropped it in the bag, and am now waiting the result. Do you think *Teufelsdröckh* will take any notice of it, or will he mistake me for a gigman?[1]

[1] "But to look across the 'divine salt sea.' A letter reached me some two months ago, from Mobile, Alabama; the writer, a kind friend of mine, signs himself *James Freeman Clarke*. I have mislaid, not lost, his letter, and do not at present know his permanent address, for he seemed to be only on a visit to Mobile; but you, doubtless, do know it. Will you therefore take, or even find, an opportunity to tell this good friend that it is not the wreckage of the *Liverpool* ship he wrote by, nor insensibility on my part, that prevents his hearing direct from me; that I see and love him in this letter, and hope we shall

TO W. H. CHANNING.

CINCINNATI, *January* 21, 1837.

I ought to have written to you long ago, as two months have passed since I reached home. The first month I had everything to do, and no time to write; the last month I have had nothing to do, and less time, if possible, than before. For you know that when we have once strenuously set about doing nothing, we go very thoroughly about it, and will not even pick up a pin, if we can well help it.

I have been in Cincinnati a month, detained from week to week by the ice. I came up to spend a single week, but have not been able to get back. The river has been full of floating ice. One would think this just the time to write letters, sermons, etc.; but no; when once out of the traces of daily duties I felt relieved from all responsibility, and have consequently been gloriously idle for a month back.

Since I returned from the East I have been much impressed with the value of method and importance of system, and have gone seriously to work to reform my bad habits in that regard, and had made some progress before this visit to Cincinnati threw me back again. I had a book-case made by a carpenter, with pigeon-holes in it, and have taken my books, which before lay about the tables, bureau, and mantelpiece, and set them up in a formal manner. I have also caught my letters, which were flying about in the most desultory manner, and filed and labeled them in little packets. I have served in the same way my accounts and bills, and I can now look, with a decent triumph and modest complacency, at my well-ordered household. I feel more like a responsible man than before this arrangement. The books,

meet one day under the sun; shall live under it, at any rate, with many a kind thought towards one another." — T. Carlyle to R. W. Emerson, April 29, 1836.

thus arranged, indicate that their proprietor is, or ought to be, a man of action and influence in society. " Why all this apparatus, unless you do something?" is their tacit exhortation. . . .

I have these two objects when I enter my pulpit. First, if possible, to convey some clear idea and definite instruction to the minds of those who hear. Second, to leave an impression of a religious kind upon their hearts, to arouse awe and reverence, and the sleeping conscience, and the dulled affections, and to create the feeling that we are God's children, though sinners, and though poor and needy, heirs of an everlasting inheritance.

TO W. H. CHANNING.

LOUISVILLE, *March* 29, 1837.

I want to know whether you are going to accept the call which the Cincinnati society, as I understand, have made you? For if not, then I want to know whether you will come here and stay with me a few months at least, and get under way the ministry at large. You will find no one to interfere with you here, and by God's help, it may be done, and well done. I am almost discouraged about it, I have found it so difficult to get any one to undertake it. The people here would support it, I know, if it was once fairly started. There is a fine old man here, who has always passed for an infidel,— though he has more Christianity in him than nine tenths of the so-called professors of Christianity,— who says he will help us heart and hand in this thing. He says it would be something like Jesus Christ's Christianity, and he will go in for that any time.

TO W. H. CHANNING.

LOUISVILLE, *May* 25, 1837.

Only think how much we could do if we were together. My heart burns within me as I ponder it. Under no circumstances would you come out here? Would you come and be the minister to the society, and I be the minister at large? or would you be minister at large here for one year? If so, I would engage to get enough subscribed to support you. To have you here, we living one year together in our own hired house, what an effort would I not make; could anything prevent our succeeding? How we would edit the "Messenger," and how we would preach consolation to the broken-hearted! Oh heavens! shall this not be?

At any rate, pray give me your views on the matter. I have a Sunday-school here of seventy or eighty children, a fine nucleus to begin with, — and some five or six true Christians who would desire no better boon than to help in getting up such a City Mission here.

WILLIAM ELLERY CHANNING TO J. F. C.

BOSTON, *April* 22, 1837.

MY DEAR SIR, — I send you a discourse, or address, which I have lately pronounced on temperance. My object was, not so much to stir up those already interested in the cause, as to interest others by showing its wide bearings and its connection with all efforts for carrying forward the community.

I remember your visit to me with pleasure. Your position seems to me, as I have told you, very important. One of your great aims must be to produce a mutual action of the East and the West. We, here, are to be benefited by acting on the West, as well as the West on us. Our contact with a newer people must wake us up. Every minister who visits you will come back with a fresher spirit, and will spread life around him. The unhappiness is, that all parts of our country are to be planed down to one surface by the infinite, all-pervading intensity of the passion for accumulation. The West will become as mercenary as the East. What a blessing would our present commercial agony be, would it only free us from the accursed thirst for unbounded gain. What is the strength of slavery? The love of money. This makes the free States the upholders of oppression. Must not some tremendous social revolutions give the race a new start? Can we go on further under the present impulses of the social system? My spirit has groaned so much during what has been called our prosperity that I am not as much troubled as most by our present adversity. By all this I mean to utter no despondence. Our present low, selfish, mercenary activity is better than stagnation of mind. Our present stage of society is one which must be passed through. A true civilization lies beyond it. When I began I intended to write but two or three lines, but the West and Society are topics which open the fountain of thought, and it is not easy to stop.

A blessing on your labors. Very sincerely your friend, WILLIAM E. CHANNING.

TO MR. AND MRS. G. T. D.

LOUISVILLE, *July* 20, 1837.

The greatest of all mysteries is the way in which men live in the midst of mysteries; buying, selling, eating, drinking, without having their heads and hearts crushed by the weight of wonders which is on them. To think that we, who have a little while ago begun to live, and in a little while hence are to die, should take it so coolly, and should look on these two marvelous events (of which, to be sure, the first is infinitely the most marvelous) as we look upon waking in the morning, and falling asleep at night! Truly, says Solomon, "God has put the world in men's hearts so that no one finds out the work which he maketh from the beginning until the end." It is this stupidity, kindly sent to us, which keeps us from running mad with the strangeness of our existence. . . . Is it not likely that our change from this life to the next will be equally gradual, and perhaps as unconscious? We shall find ourselves familiar and at home in another state, before we are conscious of having entered it.

TO G. T. D.

NEWTON, *September* 1, 1837.

I arrived here two days since, just in time for Commencement, after a long and tiresome journey by the way of Cincinnati, Columbus, Zanesville, Wheeling, Pittsburgh, Meadville, Erie, Buffalo, Niagara, Rochester, Utica, Albany, New York, and Providence. . . . Yesterday we had a noble discourse by Mr. Emerson on the American Scholar . . . Henry Hedge said they had not had so sweet a song sung to them for many a year. . . . Have you seen Dr. Channing's letter to H. Clay ? I think it capital.

TO G. T. D.

January 24, 1838.

It happened that last night we discussed Burr's character at a conversational club, which we have here. It is a very interesting club, for all opinions are usually represented. We have old Federalists and young Democrats, stanch Puritans and Southern cavaliers, the sons of old England, old Virginia, and old Kentucky, merchants, doctors, lawyers, priests of every church, a sprinkling of literature and of science. On the whole the colonel was severely treated. Some of our number knew him when in the West, and had personal anecdotes to relate about him.

TO R. W. EMERSON.

LOUISVILLE, *April* 30, 1838.

I received your prospectus and letter with much pleasure this morning. I found I could have disposed of more copies of the "French Revolution" than were subscribed for, and therefore will take on my own responsibility twelve copies of the "Miscellaneous Writings." . . .

My chief companion in the study of Carlyle is George Keats, a brother of the poet. . . . He read "Nature" with much pleasure, but told me that the song, "Take, oh take," which you ascribe to Shakspeare, was from "Rollo," by Fletcher   "Sartor" he likes much, and says that often when debating with the other bank-directors about discounting, etc., he is puzzling himself to find out the meaning of what they are all doing by the application of the Sartor philosophy, to tear off the shows of things, and see their essence. But he has quarreled with the "French Revolution" all along for being so Jacobinical; he thinks that the poor aristocrats do not get any of the sympathy which all others receive, and that Carlyle seems even to enjoy their troubles. . . .

We are just on the verge of May. To-morrow all the school-girls choose their May-queens, and I shall go into the woods, and read Wordsworth's "Ode to May." Our forests are full of beauty and perfume and song. You never saw anything like them in New England. But in the pictures of the "Flight into Egypt" you have seen the same vast old trunks, and cheerful vistas, with soft turf and no underbrush. You will find a Gaspar in every piece of Kentucky forest.

TO A. H.

May 19, 1838.

Not feeling well, I have been spending a week five miles from town, with a family who have the true Kentucky character. I think the genuine Kentuckian is the model of what our national character will one day be. He has the enterprise, coolness, sagacity of the North, and the warmth, frankness, and generosity of the South. . . . I am delighted to have such a place to visit whenever I feel tired of town.

July 9, 1838.

We had a beautiful celebration on the Fourth. Fifty little girls in the choir sang anthems and hymns sweetly.

The church was crowded with all sects. A Methodist gentleman spoke to the children at my request. Within two years how much has prejudice been softened here! We have reason to thank God and take courage. There were three hundred children present that day, — one hundred of our own, and two hundred from other schools. They had a collation afterward. I have some of the sweetest children in the world in my society. We walk together in the forests, and have fine times. About eighty-five attend regularly at our Sunday school.

October 13, 1838.

... A sweet little girl, the pet lamb, the nursling of a family of thirteen brothers and sisters, died on Tuesday. A man was sent to town (they live in the country) to ask me to come out before she died. I reached the house half an hour after sunrise, and found her lying in her shroud. She was hardly seven years old, — one of those little angels of purity and loveliness that never do anything wrong. ... I stayed the day with them, and the next day read the funeral service of the Episcopal Church. Her mother is an Episcopalian, but her own minister is away. The child was buried, as is the custom in the country, in an inclosure on the plantation. It has been quite sickly here, though not so terribly so as the Eastern papers say. I am just getting over a relapse into which I fell after getting well from a fever which kept me in my room a fortnight.

NEWTON, *November* 22, 1838.

... Since my arrival I have had very pleasant conversations with Dr. Channing, Mr. Ripley, Mr. Emerson, Mr. Bartol, F. T. Gray, etc. One man whom I wished much to see I happily met last night at Dr. Parkman's, at the Wednesday-night Club, — John Quincy Adams. No marks of age are about him. His voice is firm, clear, and calm, his eye bright, his whole manner quietly self-possessed. I ventured to converse with him about his anti-slavery speeches. He did not avoid the subject, but spoke temperately of the opposition he had encountered, as one who feared neither "the lightning flash nor the all-dreaded thunder-storm" of hostile encounter and party rage. It gratified me much to see him, as I think him the most extraordinary man in our nation just now.

R. W. EMERSON TO J. F. C.

CONCORD, *December* 7, 1838.

MY DEAR SIR, — Here are the verses.[1] They have pleased some of my friends, and so may please some of your readers, — and you asked me in the spring if I had not somewhat to contribute to your journal.

I remember in your letter you mentioned the remark of some friend of yours that the verses, —

"Take, oh take those lips away,"

were not Shakespeare's. I think they are. Beaumont and Fletcher, nor both together, were ever, I think, visited by such a starry gleam as that stanza. I know it is in "Rollo," but it is in "Measure for Measure" also, and I remember noticing that the Malones and Stevenses and critical gentry were about evenly divided, — these for Shakespeare, and those for B. and F. But the internal evidence is all for one, none for the other. If he did not write it, they did not, and we shall have some fourth unknown singer. What care we *who* sung this or that! It is we at last who sing.

TO A. H.

December 29, 1838.

My intercourse with Dr. Channing was delightful. He took a most fatherly interest in me, and I could have laid my whole heart open before him, so

[1] *The Humble-Bee.*

benign and tender was he. And then his conversation revolves so steadily around the axis of mighty truths, and turns always upward, lifting us all along. Hopes and prayers for a better time, anxious inquiries into the spiritual state of all men and all societies, broad and deep surveys of the questions most vital to human interests, — such are the regular themes of his discourse. And ever and anon there comes an unlooked-for playfulness into his manner, which is unspeakably graceful and winning.

As for Mr. Emerson, so great is my respect for the extraordinary dignity and purity of his character, so profound my feeling of the exquisite keenness of his intellect and the antique charm of his imagination, that I cannot bear the criticisms which must needs seem shallow though coming from good and true men. When we are permitted to meet a man whose life is holiness, whose words are gems, whose character is of the purest type of heroism, yet of childlike simplicity, — shall we stop to find fault with the shape of his coat, or the coherence of his opinions, instead of gratefully receiving this Heaven's gift? Truly there are many in these days who entertain angels unawares. I talk of giving up the "Messenger" to W. H. Channing, Edward Cranch, and C. P. Cranch, to be published once more at Cincinnati.

TO R. W. EMERSON.

LOUISVILLE, *January* 1, 1839.

It is said to be the nature of suddenly acquired and unexpected wealth to create a longing for more. The poor victim of prosperity, being suddenly lifted out of all his old habitual ways, cannot form at once new habits and be contented. He wants more yet. Such also I find the case with editors. Had you not given me those two poems,[1] I should probably never have

---
[1] *Each and All* and *The Humble-Bee.*

asked you for anything; but now I wish you to give me two more, namely, "The Rhodora," and the lines beginning, —

"Good-bye, proud world! I'm going home."

I have them in my possession, though not by Margaret's fault; for she gave them to me accidentally among other papers. But, being there, may I print them?

I forgot to ask you, when I was in Boston, about the last two volumes of Carlyle. I hope they will appear before long. I wish to subscribe for twelve copies. I find I can dispose of them with perfect ease. It is too late to patronize Carlyle.

Margaret allowed me to read an address upon Education which you delivered at Providence. I wish that I might have it to publish also.

I wish you more than a happy new year, — an active, progressive year, — a year which shall open to us volumes of thought, worlds of discovery before unimagined. May strength of body and soul be continued to you, patience and pity for short-sighted, clamorous opposers, good counsel and helpfulness for honest seekers and sympathizers.

TO A. H.

January 22, 1839.

William Channing strenuously opposes removing the "Messenger" to Cincinnati. He says that if I am really tired and need relief, they will take it, but if not, I had better continue it. I am undecided. I do not shrink from work. I love it. I need it. The more the better. But I think with you that it would be better, perhaps, to give myself more entirely just now to my church. The work nearest my heart is preaching the gospel, publicly, and from house to house. One of these days I hope to know how. I think I am growing every year nearer to my standard, though it is yet afar off.

TO A. H.

February 3, 1839.

What should you think of the expediency of my leaving Louisville? I have no such serious purpose, but at times I am "exercised in mind" about the propriety of so doing. It often seems to me as if some one else could do more good than I here, and I do more good somewhere else. I am by no means a popular preacher in this place, nor ever shall be. . . . I am extremely anxious in this matter to be guided solely by duty. .

William Channing urged me so strongly to retain the "Western Messenger" that I have agreed to do so till the end of the sixth number, volume vi. Then I hope they will take it to Cincinnati. C. P. Cranch stayed three weeks with me after I reached home, and I grew to love him very much, and he me.

R. W. EMERSON TO J. F. C.

CONCORD, *February 27, 1839.*

I am very sorry to have made you wait so long for an answer to your flattering request for two such little poems. You are quite welcome to the lines to "The Rhodora;" but I think they need the superscription (lines on being asked, "Whence is the Flower?"). Of the other verses I send you a corrected copy, but I wonder so much at your wishing to print them that I think you must read them once again with your critical spectacles, before they go further. They were written sixteen years ago, when I kept school in Boston and lived in a corner of Roxbury called Canterbury. They have a slight misanthropy, — a shade deeper than belongs to me, and, as it seems nowadays I am a philosopher and am grown to have opinions, I think they must have an apologetic date, though I well know that poetry which needs a date is no poetry, and so you will wiselier suppress them. I heartily wish I had any verses which, with a clear mind, I could send you in lieu of these juvenilities. It is strange, seeing the delight we take in verses, that we can so seldom write them, and are not ashamed to lay up old ones, say for sixteen years, instead of improvising them as freely as the wind blows, whenever we and our brothers are attuned to music.

In regard to the Providence discourse, I have no copy of it; but I will get the manuscript if Margaret Fuller has it, and you shall have it, if it can pass muster.

I shall certainly avail myself of the good order you give me for twelve copies of the Carlyle 'Miscellanies' so soon as they appear. He (T. C.) writes in excellent spirits of his American friends and readers.
Your sister Sarah was kind enough to carry me, the other day, to see some pencil sketches done by Stewart Newton. They seemed to me to betray the richest invention; so rich as almost to say, "Why draw any line, since you can draw all? Genius has given you the freedom of the universe; why, then, come within any walls?" And this seems to be the old moral which we draw from our fable, read it how or where we will, that we cannot make one good stroke until we can make every possible stroke; and when we can make one, every one seems superfluous.

I heartily thank you for the good wishes you send me to open the year, and I say them back again to you. Your field is a world, and all men are your spectators, and all men must respect the true and great-hearted service you render. And yet it is not spectator or spectacle that concerns either you or me. The whole world is sick of that very ail, — of being seen and of seemliness. It belongs to the brave now to trust themselves infinitely, and to sit and hearken alone.

I am glad to see William Channing is one of your coadjutors. Mrs. Jameson's new book I should think would bring a caravan of travelers, æsthetic, artistic, and what not, up your mighty streams, or along the

Lakes to Mackinaw. As I read I almost vowed an exploration, but I doubt if I ever get beyond the Hudson.

TO R. W. EMERSON.

LOUISVILLE, *March* 11, 1839.

I received to-day your kind letter, inclosing the lines, "Good-bye, proud world," for which I thank you. . . .

I am passing my days here happily, having enough to do, and being able to do it naturally and without the constraint which custom, opinion and expectation lay upon the preacher in New England. Preaching is to me a delightful office, and especially in this, that I always seem to be beginning to preach. It seems to me often as I leave the church as if neither I nor any one else had preached since the days of the Apostles, and that there is an untrodden domain of power and influence in that department, when we can find the word which will let us into it. There are three modes of influencing men : through books, through public speaking, and by private intercourse. The second has been tame, formal, and dead, and yet, methinks, it might become a weapon of irresistible power. I have dreams and imaginations of what it may one day accomplish, but whether in this generation I cannot tell. I think that oratory will be carried farther in this land than it ever has been before, for he who can persuade and convince multitudes by his speech is the monarch in our country. But I am talking my crude thoughts to one who has considered the whole matter.

TO A. H.

CINCINNATI, OHIO, *March* 18, 1839.

. . . I called on one of the trustees, and stated to him frankly my views and feelings about the expediency of a change in the pastorate of the society, and requested him to call a meeting of the trustees and communicate those views to them, and ask them to tell me with equal openness their own opinion. I represented to him that it was my sincere wish to remain with the society, and that it would cost me a pang to leave them; that I equally believed every one in the society personally attached to myself. But this mutual attachment did not decide the question: Was I doing as much good as might be done by some one else? This last was what I wanted light upon; on the answer to this question I was willing to rest the other: Should I remain or leave them? If I was doing as much good as any one else could do, I was willing to stay; otherwise I felt that I ought to leave them. I was willing to let the personal question: Could I do more good elsewhere? remain a secondary one, and other points also of a like nature. *The good of the society* should decide whether I stayed or left. I then gave my reasons for thinking that some one else might be found better suited than I to advance its interests. These were: 1. The society, though it had certainly increased, and was increasing under my care, yet as certainly increased but slowly. 2. Other men, of a different manner and turn of delivery, who had visited the city, had apparently excited a greater interest, and the nature of the people seemed to require a man of a different manner.

If I leave Louisville I shall wish to go to a free State. Every day I become more of an abolitionist.

TO A. H.

May 15, 1839.

We had a delightful time at Cincinnati. Mr. Farley, W. G. Eliot, and myself were all who were present to conduct the exercises. Mr. Farley preached the sermon, Eliot gave the charge, and I the right hand. It was on Friday night, May 10th. The church was well filled, and they all said it was the most interesting ordination[1] they ever attended. But so they always say.

Mr. Farley arrived from New Orleans on the Sunday

[1] The ordination of William Henry Channing.

previous, landed at Shippingport at half past ten, took a hack, and drove direct to my church. I was in the second prayer. He came up into the pulpit, and preached for me all day.

I was in Cincinnati Wednesday, Thursday, and Friday, and besides talking much with William H. Channing and William G. Eliot, had to prepare my address for Friday night. On Wednesday I called on a sick lady, and at Mr. Vaughan's, where Mr. Farley stayed; at Mrs. Greene's twice; visited a public school and examined it, and made a speech to the children, took tea at Mr. Vaughan's with Farley, Channing, Perkins and wife, William Greene, and Edward Cranch, and then went to a teachers' meeting with them, where we stayed talking till ten P. M., and then went home with W. H. C., to Mrs. Stetson's, where we talked till twelve. Thursday, engaged in talking with Mr. St. John, writing my "Right Hand," and calling at three places to find a friend. Mrs. Stetson had a dinner party of four or five. After dinner, with my friend S. B. Sumner, who went up with me from Louisville, I again attended an examination of the city schools; then four of us drove in Mrs. Stetson's carriage into the beautiful environs of Cincinnati, and made a call; returning, took tea at home with S. B. S. and Perkins; then went to an inquiry or conversation meeting in the vestry of the church. Afterwards to a great wedding at Dr. Drake's, where we saw a buckeye bowl, holding four pails full of lemonade, dipped out with an Alabama gourd, and the bridegroom and bride married under a bower of buckeye.

I have forgotten to mention our going to Mr. Longworth's splendid garden, and seeing his varieties of cactus in the hot-house, as also our examining a fine church. On Friday William Eliot arrived, and in talking and preparing for the night, another dinner party of friends, and more calls, we consumed the day. Saturday morning I returned home.

TO A. H.

LOUISVILLE, *May* 30, 1839.

The city have made me agent of the public schools. The schools have a vacation through August, but till then I should not wish to be away, as I shall have to learn how to do a good many things. They pay me a salary of $400 a year, and my duties are to overlook the concerns of eight schools. I accepted the office with pleasure, as I thought it would give me an opportunity of doing good to the schools, and also be of service to my church by bringing me in contact with many people whom I should not otherwise see. It was a proof of the liberality of the place that my religious opinions were no barrier. I did not know a single member of the city council personally, and yet the vote was ten to three in my favor.

TO A. H.

July 21, 1839.

The examinations of the schools continue till Saturday, the 3d day of August. On Monday the City Council meets to choose teachers. This 4th of August winds up another cycle in my life, and makes a new epoch. Six years ago, on the 4th of August, I landed in Louisville, a stranger all forlorn, to begin my work, and see if I could do anything in the world for its good. These six years have changed me from a sentimental dreamer into a practical man. Sentiment has been quite worked out of me, imagination toned down; I am but a poor, dull, prosaic, commonplace person now. . . . But courage! my powers are better balanced, disciplined, more manageable, if not so exuberant as formerly.

July 25, 1839.

My time is so full that I am running to and fro from morn till dewy eve. My days are "shingled over," as the Kentuckian says, with engagements, each overlapping the other: examining schools; ditto teachers; writing out lists of scholars; visiting sick parishioners; writing sermons; buying medals for children's prizes; putting advertisements in the paper; answering letters of candidates for situations, which main employments are diversified with a sprinkling of various smaller concerns.

August 1, 1839.

We have spent this week in examining the city schools, and to-day we distributed some rewards. The girls were collected in a large room, to the number of two or three hundred, all neatly dressed, with sweet manners and bright good faces. We gave them twenty-five silver medals and some books.

More work remains for me till Saturday night about the schools, and I cannot leave till Monday or Tuesday. I must vote on Monday, like a good citizen, and then I think I shall leave. . .

This week has been so hot, and I have had so much to do, that I am fairly worn out. It has been the hottest weather I have known in Kentucky. The corn is parched in the fields, and man's blood heated into fever in his veins. I shall be glad to escape for some weeks from this burning atmosphere to the cooler latitude of Meadville.

Half of my society have gone to the East.

In August, 1839, Mr. Clarke was married to Anna Huidekoper, of Meadville, Pennsylvania. A few weeks later they went to Louisville, and Mr. Clarke devoted the winter to his church and to the superintendence of the city schools. This last work occupied a good deal of time. During the winter, he finally made up his mind to leave Louisville. He remained, however, until the middle of June. Mrs. Clarke left a little earlier for Meadville.

TO A. H. C.
LOUISVILLE, *May* 29, 1840.

I have made up my mind to one thing conclusively, *i. e.*, not to commit myself hastily to any new situation or work. What I next undertake, I wish to continue at through life. . . . If I know myself I wish to be useful, and whatever I do, I wish preaching always to be my chief work. I love my profession, see my deficiencies, see my capabilities, and expect and intend to improve.

TO A. H. C.
NEWTON, MASS., *September* 25, 1840.

I find social life in a precious state of fermentation. New ideas are flying, high and low. Every man, as Mr. Emerson remarked to me yesterday, carries a revolution in his waistcoat pocket.

The prevailing idea, however, just now seems to be of a community in which all persons are to live after the fashion of the Rapps or Owens. Mr. Ripley appears fermenting and effervescing to a high degree with these new ideas. The remarkable thing is that everybody has a distinct idea, plan, or project, and no two persons can be found to agree in any.

GREENFIELD, *October* 5, 1840.

I saw Mr. Bacon, of Louisville, the other day. Among other things he said this, which may have truth in it: "The society, when you went there, had no religious interest. It was based on a spirit of opposition, — opposition to Orthodoxy. Now it is different. There is religion and a true spirit in it. You think you have done little in seven years. I do not see how you could possibly do more."

There are many large parishes vacant, where I might settle, and it would be pleasant enough to have leisure for study, but I think I could do more good in a city, and am better suited for that life. What I should like best would be a church founded on elective affinities, — not on the purse principle. I mean a society drawn together because they like me and my ideas. To such I could do much good.

CHAPTER IX.

THE CHURCH OF THE DISCIPLES.

[Dr. Clarke's Autobiography, as the reader has seen, breaks off somewhat abruptly. The remaining part of this memoir, therefore, must be necessarily made up from other materials than that which he had himself arranged. We have used his diaries and journals, and some other "table-books;" his printed notes, which often contain biographical allusions; and his correspondence with friends.]

THE brief notes in his diary show that Mr. Clarke left Louisville at the end of his ministry there, on the 16th of June, 1840. Some of the last of these little memoranda show the range of his life, and are curious after fifty years. "Professor Espy called." This is the gentleman who engaged general attention, at that time, by his scientific study of the weather. "Called upon Mr. Espy, and talked with him upon foreknowledge and decrees." "Talked with Espy. Attended Espy's lecture. He looks in the face like Dr. Hedge, and has his logical turn of mind."

"June 1. Interview at the 'Journal' office with Dr. Yandell and Dr. Wilder. Gave article in defense of Dr. Hall to George D. Prentice." This was the Mr. Prentice celebrated in the politics of the day.

For the rest of the year 1840 he had no regular charge in the ministry, and he spent most of that time at Meadville. The diary shows, however, that he preached almost every Sunday. Among other places, he was at Chicago, where he helped to establish the first Unitarian church in that town. The memoranda in the diary are: "Preached in a Chicago hotel parlor." "Preached Sunday, Tuesday, and Friday." On the 22d of August he left Meadville for Boston, and arrived at Newton on the 17th of September, making several stops by the way. He left Boston again for Meadville, October 22d. "Take Shark, the Newfoundland dog."[1] The route is interesting. He went from Boston to New York, by Providence and steamboat on Long Island Sound; from New York to Albany, "on the steamer;" to Buffalo, by rail and stage; "by steamer from Buffalo to Erie, on the 26th," but was driven back by a storm to the Canada shore. Through November and December he was at Meadville, and was occupied, as he had been through the autumn, in the translation of "Theodore." On the 12th of January, 1841, he left Meadville again, and arrived in Boston on the 18th.

With this chapter, therefore, begins the history of nearly fifty years of very active life. That life is singularly varied, seeing that it is the life of a man who was, through the whole of it, the minister of one congregation in one city. I think that those who write the lives of clergymen usually find it hard to interest their readers in the general course of those lives. In truth, they are sure of one element of romance, for there is in them hardly anything which should be called routine. A working minister wakes in the morning with no idea what adventure he is to try before the day is done. To him, of all men, "the unexpected is what happens." But it is as difficult to describe such a life as it is to describe the leaves of a forest. And my experience of the biographies of ministers does not encourage me in any attempt to make real to the reader the course of a week of Freeman Clarke's life, and far less that of a year. Failing this, however, I beg the

---

[1] Shark proved a difficult traveling companion. The passengers naturally objected to his presence inside the stage-coach, and Mr. Clarke was obliged to ride outside, in a bitterly cold snow-storm, to keep the dog company. At Buffalo Shark was put on a vessel for Chicago.

reader to remember that here is a man who had couse-crated himself to do the duty next his hand, who was on the lookout for that duty, and always did it as well as he could, "the moral purpose entirely controlling such mental aptness or physical habits as he could bring to bear." Thus it happens that his life for nearly fifty years touches every important movement of that time. In the hands of a master it might be made the thread of the history of America for half a century. Whatever else may be said of it, it does not lack variety.

This general remark is specially illustrated in such a life as Mr. Clarke led in Boston between the years 1841 and 1849. Whoever deals with the local history of the town in those years has to attempt the description of a certain local ferment, involving eager expectation and a readiness for new things, which certainly does not characterize the Boston of to-day, and did not characterize the Boston of the beginning of the century. The anti-slavery leaders were at their best; they had a mountain to cast into the sea, and they were loyally going about that business, with little but faith to sustain them. Reformers of every school had broken with all the bonds which the church, in various organizations, had contrived for their repression. In speculation, morals, and the philosophy of the intellect, as in the consideration of religion, the word "transcendental" had begun to be heard, and with it came in the suspicion that the higher law, nay, the highest law, might be found available as an everyday direction. Into the midst of the enthusiasms thus aroused came the prophecies of the psychical experimenters of whatever name, — each one generally adopting a new one, — and they brought their fascinating suggestion that, by rightly developing the fit organs of the brain, we might produce, almost to order, poetry better than Dante's or Milton's, and science more accurate than Newton's or La Place's. In a word, prophecy was in order, — not to say in fashion. There was a general sympathy with St. Paul and George Fox and people of that type, who did not travel in the steps of pharisees or of priests. Mr. Brisbane, by an admirably conducted propaganda, was bringing into notice Charles Fourier's plans, and dear Robert Owen,[1] not meaning to be forgotten, came from England with his own. In Boston, by a sort of natural law, the prophets of new beliefs or new suspicions made rendezvous. When, in 1842, the friends of Bronson Alcott thought to give him, and indeed themselves, a little rest, by sending him to Europe on a summer outing, as he landed at Liverpool he met some correspondents, who with him instantly held a convention at a school which had been named Alcott Lodge in his honor. At this convention it was at once voted that the United States of America was the fittest place for the redemption of mankind to begin. And so, before the summer was over, he returned with a certain Mr. Lane and Mr. Wright, with spirits far more excited than his own, to undertake that redemption. They held new conventions, and established the experiment of "Consociation"[2] to "redeem society

---

[1] In 1844 he was stone-deaf. I had the happy good fortune in my young days to have a voice so loud that I could make him hear. In the winter of 1844-45, I sat next him at a boarding-house table in Washington, and used to interpret to him, as I could, the voices of the time. The dear saint was urging Congress to vote five millions for a fair trial of his "Social Unions," and, till Congress adjourned, after the death-struggle of the annexation of Texas, which occupied every thought of every man excepting him, he really supposed that this appropriation could be made, and that, at seventy-eight years of age, he would see his solution of social evil determined on for mankind. — E. E. H.

[2] "*Fruitlands*," as the colony was called, is well described by Miss Alcott. See *Silver Pitchers*, p. 79. It was before the days of kerosene, and, to avoid killing whales for oil, the company dispensed with the use of lamps. You "conversed" in the dark on a winter evening; and when you went to bed, you carried a torch of twisted newspaper. — E. E. H.

from the institution of property" They were quite successful in this effort, so far as the property-holding members of their own number are to be regarded. This "movement" was a little later in time than the associations which had tried other social experiments at Brook Farm, at Hopedale, and at Florence, not to mention places outside of New England.

Meanwhile, the idolatry of the letter of Scripture bore legitimate fruit in the proclamation, by William Miller, that the world would end in the year 1843, on or about the 20th of March. The mathematical instinct of New England especially approved of the additions and subtractions of figures which were found in the books of Daniel and the Revelation, which, beginning with dates in Rollin's History, came out neatly, by the older calendar, at the beginning of 1843. The Latter-Day Saints, generally known as Mormons, also had an establishment in Boston, where the Golden Book was expounded.

In more decorous quarters, the ferment created by the Oxford Movement in England was scarcely less. The most striking tracts and papers in the English controversy were reprinted in America; and, on a smaller scale, the Protestant Episcopal Church here repeated the discussions, and tried the experiments in ritual, which were thrilling the Established Church of England.

There was hardly one of these interests but engaged Mr. Clarke's attention.

A good illustration of what Boston was may be found in the interest taken in Dr. James Walker's lectures on natural theology, the first in a series founded by Mr. John Lowell, Jr. They were scholarly and thorough addresses, such as he might have delivered to an advanced class in a divinity school. They followed the general lines of Benjamin Constant's book on religion, with elaborate studies of the views of different modern philosophers. To hear these lectures, twice a week, two thousand men and women came together, so as to crowd the Odeon, as the building was called which had been the Federal Street Theatre. The adult population of Boston was then about forty thousand people, and the character of the town is shown in the fact that one twentieth part of them went thus to hear this study of the speculations of the modern world on the being of God.

Under an impulse given by Mr. Samuel A. Eliot, who represented Boston in Congress a few years later, Beethoven's symphonies were performed for the first time in Boston in the same hall; a new revelation of the power of music to most of those who were present. And at these concerts also, the hall was filled to its utmost capacity.

It should be remembered that steam or horse railway communication with the suburbs was unknown, so that the audiences were made up almost wholly of the residents of the town.

Mr. Emerson's career as a lecturer was just beginning. It is hard to say that he was at his best at one period of his life more than at another. But it is on record that Mr. Emerson said that "the usual experience is" that a man thinks his best thoughts between thirty and forty. "When the impulse of youth is on the man he sees most clearly." The group of thinking people who made the centre of the Church of the Disciples were just the people who were sure to be present in Mr. Emerson's audiences.

In the same years, or a little later, William Henry Channing spent some months in Boston, and called together a sympathetic religious society. "If he had told us to take any bootblack from the street into our homes, and clothe him in purple and fine linen, we would have done so,"—these are the words of one of his admirers. For the pure and simple gift of eloquence, so far as it consists in seizing the right word at the right instant, and speaking with all the passion of personal conviction, Mr. Channing had no rival among the men around him. Between him and Mr. Clarke there had been the most intimate friendship, since the days when they sat side by side in the Latin School. They were associated afterwards in writing the life of their friend Margaret Fuller. They always called one another " James " and " William."

For Wendell Phillips Mr. Clarke had a high respect. And here may be as fit a place as any to say that, while Mr. Phillips was a raging lion in denouncing iniquity wherever he found it, among his friends and in his family he was the most gentle and affectionate of men.[1] In the nice distinctions of the anti-slavery forces, it happened that he and Mr. Clarke did not live under the same tent. But it would be idle now to attempt to explain the difference between the "old organization" and the "new organization;" between the abolitionist who could vote and the abolitionist who could not vote; between those who could go to a legislature and those who thought the Constitution was a covenant with hell. It is enough to say that in such distinctions Mr. Phillips was of the old line, pure and simple, regarded all political parties with equal scorn, and had, perhaps, no confidence in any public men. Mr. Clarke, on the other hand, was a free lance here as he was everywhere. He was therefore ready and able to give the strong weight of his personal character to the enterprises carried out by such men as Palfrey, Sumner, and Andrew.

The reader has seen from his Autobiography that he had the counsel and sympathy of the great Unitarian

---

[1] Writing of "Wendell," in 1880, Dr. Clarke said: "I told W. Phillips the first time I met him after his tirade that I had heretofore felt a little neglected, as he had attacked nearly every one else; now my mind was relieved."

leader, Dr. William Ellery Channing, in the gathering of the Church of the Disciples. This sympathy showed itself in many forms after the church was established. The Diary shows that Mr. Clarke frequently visited Dr. Channing. Dr. Channing's health at this time was such that he seldom preached. But his counsels were as wise as ever, and his views of the situation of America in matters of politics, and also of what is called religion, were prophetic. Dr. Hedge, who was as intimate with Dr. Channing as Mr. Clarke was, once said to me, of such visits of his younger friends: —

"I often met Clarke at Dr. Channing's house. He would ask us both to dine there, and we would meet at dinner. There was no gossip at Dr. Channing's; the conversation, if you could call it conversation, was always on some high theme. But in truth it was not conversation; it was simply a monologue by Dr. Channing himself. This, or something about it, led you to feel very much dissatisfied with yourself when you came away. He did not pay the slightest attention to anything you said. If you asked a question, he very probably did not answer it; he went on talking on the thing which interested him. So that my presence there with Clarke did not add much to my knowledge of Clarke or my acquaintance with him. But I think Dr. Channing respected him very highly."

Margaret Fuller, whom the reader has seen in Mr. Clarke's notes of his Cambridge life, had begun her series of "Conversations" in Boston. The description given of them in the Life of her by Mr. Clarke, Mr. W. H. Channing, and Mr. Emerson, is from Channing's pen and her own. Her conduct of these classes, as they were called for want of a better name, was "excellent," to take Mr. Emerson's phrase. She sat at one end of the room, and the body of visitors, or "assistants," arranged themselves as they could, so that they might see and hear her. Nine tenths of them were in the mood of people paying homage, which, indeed, she well deserved. But she would not and did not accept it. The skill, the tact, with which she threw back the ball of conversation, so as to start this listener or that, and the success with which she made him speak and say his best, were clear tokens of her real genius, and, more than anything she said herself, showed that she was the mistress of the company and of the occasion.

The meetings of the class at which I saw her most often, and where Mr. Clarke met her also, were in the parlors of Dr. Nathaniel Peabody's house. The reader would not understand all the scenery of the drama which Mr. Clarke's notes describe, unless he knew what this house was. In the determination of young Boston to keep more in the current of the flow of German and French life, Dr. Peabody and his daughter Elizabeth opened what was an immense convenience for these readers. It was a foreign book-store and reading-room. To the working purposes of this institute — for it was such — they gave the front room of the lower story of the house in West Street which was their home. Here the "Dial" was published. Here any one could subscribe a small annual fee, and carry home the last German or French review. "The 'Revue des Deux Mondes' is a liberal education," said one of the bright girls who first saw it there. Here, when one looked in of a morning or afternoon, he met, as the chance might give, Mr. Allston the artist, Mr. Emerson, Mr. Ripley, Mr. Hawthorne, Mr. Hedge, — not then Doctor, — Mr. Clarke, or the three Misses Peabody, — one of whom became Mrs. Mann, and one Mrs. Hawthorne; the other survives, to sympathize still with every philanthropic endeavor, and as sure as she was then that the good time is coming.

To one who remembers how very "English" the training of young Boston had been till now, — fed on

Blackwood, Fraser, and the English quarterlies, — it will be seen that the opening of this modest reading-room for books printed in France and Germany, with a chance to meet those who read them most, was an enlargement of the means of education.

This will be as good a place as any to tell one of Mr. Clarke's common-sense repartees. Some high-flyer of the time was explaining how in churches the Rig-Veda should lie by the Bible, and passages from both should be read aloud. "In what language will you read them?" said Mr. Clarke. "In English, of course." "Then you understand Sanskrit?" Not he, indeed; it was as much as ever that he could write or spell English. And Mr. Clarke had to explain to him, what was at that time true, but what he did not know, that none of the Vedas existed in the English language.

But first, last, and always, in the midst of all such interests, Mr. Clarke was the minister of the Church of the Disciples. On one or two occasions, especially on his seventieth birthday, he reviewed its history; and some extracts from such reviews will make the greater part of this chapter.

The letters which follow these extracts need but little illustration. It is quite enough to say that, to the more staid and decorous circles of the little town which was now to be his home, the sudden arrival and establishment of this wide-awake young townsman, who had really lived on the other side of the Alleghanies, was a marvel hardly to be explained. The older churches of Boston had run on, in a tenor not much broken, for one or two centuries. The population of the place had increased by slow and regular stages since the Revolution, and occasionally a new Congregational church — Liberal or Evangelical, as circumstances might require — had been added to the historical calendar. But now a company of people came together, and a wide-awake young minister led them, who showed in what they did, rather than in what they said, that more might be expected of a church than churches were in the habit of attempting. What was not nnnatural was that young people of spirit, as they heard of the new church, tried the experiment of attending its services. Not unnaturally they joined the society. The new minister, who was anything but a proselyter, was looked upon, therefore, with a certain grotesque jealousy by some of the older professional brethren. "He is nothing but a thief and a robber," was the doleful ejaculation of one of them, half in joke and half in earnest. Mr. Clarke himself never quarreled with anybody, criticised nobody's methods, but was satisfied to organize his church in his own way.

At this time, after half a century, it is hard to believe that any of the novelties then introduced should have challenged much attention, and harder to think that the criticism should ever have been unkind. First, second, and last, the new church stood for religion. It was to be made up of people who wanted more life, and came to God for it. These people united to take a part in worship and in the forms by which worship was conducted. In what was left of the Puritan ritual people hardly did join, except as a Frenchman "assists" at a play. The minister conducted all the service but that of song; a choir conducted this. The congregation stood in prayer, but said nothing, from one end of the service to another.[1] Once more, the people of the new church wanted to know each other, and expected to give and take, to and from each other, the best results of religious experience. Meetings on week-days, less formal than those on Sunday, meetings for conversation and for work in charity, were not to be accidents fastened upon the movement of the

[1] In the theory of Congregationalism, any church member has a right to speak as the service goes on. But in practice this has scarcely been done since the first generation of New England.

church, but an integral part of its life. The business of the church, indeed, was not to be managed, as in the methods which New England had drifted into, by a secular committee of tax-payers. All was to be done by the church itself, which had covenanted together for closer intimacy with God.

After fifty years, all this might now be said of almost any church in New England, of whatever communion. Mr. Clarke and the Church of the Disciples would hardly claim that they brought about the change in church-life which has come in those years. But it was their good fortune to be in the front rank of the pioneers.

To the end of his life, he tried to persuade himself and others that because he was but one of the people who did good work in the Church of the Disciples, he was the least important of its ministers. He would say to you, in perfectly good faith, that if he could not take the Sunday service, Brother Andrew or Brother Winslow could take it, and he tried to believe, as he also wished to have other people believe, that he was less essential to its welfare than, in most churches, a well beloved minister is thought to be. Those who remember him in the Church of the Disciples know just how far this was true, and just how far it was not true. It was true in theory. But in practice these people always wanted to hear him preach, and always knew that they were making a sacrifice to their principles when they assented to the substitution of another in his pulpit. He did succeed to a great extent in breaking up the wretched habit, which had grown up in Boston, of calling a church by the name of its minister. He and his succeeded in making people say "The Church of the Disciples" instead of "Mr. Clarke's church." And although the Unitarians had given names to churches before, I think that the very happy selection of this name had much to do with the frequency with which such names are given now.

The new church began without any choir for singing, and it has never had any. It soon introduced a hymn-book compiled by Mr. Clarke, and a form of liturgic service also prepared by him, both of which are still in use. It will not escape observation, however, that if all the members had really been "ministers" in the same sense, as in theory they were, the preparation of these hand-books would not have been thrown upon the same person who was regularly conducting the Sunday service. But probably this means, what all history seems to have shown, that whether a church can or cannot exist without an overseer, it is much more apt to have an overseer than not; that the better the overseer, the better the church, and that in proportion as the members of the church are willing to work loyally in the Master's service, in that proportion will the overseer work faithfully and well.

I have said above that most of what were considered novelties in 1841 would now be considered matters of course in most of the churches in New England. The most important matter in which the example of the Church of the Disciples has not been followed is the fundamental principle. In that church the management of the whole enterprise is subject to the vote of the majority of the regular worshipers, and is not left, as in most New England congregations, to the vote of the holders of the church property. A New England lawyer would say that its affairs are governed by the "church," and not by the "society." Of course, when it held no property except a Bible and a few hymn-books, and hired a hall for its assemblies, the distinction was wholly unimportant. So soon as the members subscribed money to build for themselves a meeting-house, so soon the question came in again, who was to say how this meeting-house was to be used. In point of fact, however, that question, so difficult to answer in theory, has never made any practical difficulty in the Church of the Disciples. A board of trustees holds the title to the church, and gives the use of it for such purposes as are agreed upon by those who unite in its covenant.

The new church devoted itself, in its very birth, to all such enterprises of public spirit as came within the wide range of the sympathies of its members. The most resolute and loyal of its members regarded the engagement to its Wednesday evening meetings as taking precedence of all others. At these meetings there was familiar talk on every subject of large and vital interest. It might be speculative philosophy; it might be some important turn in the politics of the nation, the state, or the city; it might be some necessary reform in morals; it might be some detail in the plans of the church; it might be some new book of stimulating interest; it might be some sudden exigency requiring prompt, vigorous action. Nothing was out of place, if it were only large, and especially if it involved some duty. From such meetings came the support of the work of John Augustus, the counselor of prisoners. From another set of inquiries came the establishment of the Temporary Home for Children; from another, the Home for Aged Colored Women; from another, the Children's Aid Society. Where a circle of intelligent and ready men and women met with such regularity, it was natural to bring to their meetings any one who had a story of public interest to tell, or a cause to advocate which needed help. A runaway slave, a European exile, the apostle of a new movement, all were welcome to the friendly hospitalities of the Church of the Disciples. It earned for itself the honor, for which every church should strive, of being a church for weekdays, quite as much as it was for Sundays.

It should be observed, however, in all studies of its constitution, that the Church of the Disciples represented to its founder the idea of a " free church," first, last, and always. By this he meant a church in which one person felt just as free to come in and unite in the service as another. He imagined to himself all the people who came into it on Sunday as coming into it as a man goes upon Boston Common, with no thought that one person or another possesses it, this side of the good God. All His children have a right there. In a letter written sixteen years after the church was founded, when some difficulties of administration annoyed the financial committee, Mr. Clarke said to them, "If it should be thought best to dissolve the society, I should still feel that its past existence had not been useless. If the experiment of a free church fails in our hands, it may succeed with others."

With such hopes, which proved to have good foundations, the church was gathered.[1] The congregation soon determined to hire Amory Hall for their regular Sunday service, and the first service there was held on February 28, 1841. This was a convenient and pretty hall which had come into being to meet the demand for lecture halls created by the "lyceum" system. It was up two flights of stairs above the shops on the northern

---

[1] The memoranda in Mr. Clarke's diary for 1841 relating to the church are these: —

January 24. Preached at Waltham.
January 27. Engaged the Swedenborgian church.
January 28. Preached lecture for Gray. [This means the regular "Thursday lecture," in which he took the turn of Rev. Frederick T. Gray.] Anti-slavery meeting.
January 31. [Sunday.] Preached in the Swedenborgian chapel.
February 4. Preached for Waterston. [Rev. R. C. Waterston. This was probably also the "Thursday lecture."]
February 7. Preached in the evening in Swedenborgian chapel. [On this Sunday and the Sunday before he preached in the morning at Waltham.]
Saturday evening, February 13. Preached in Phillips Place Chapel, on "The Church."
February 23. Decided on Amory Hall.
February 28. Preached for the first time in Amory Hall.
March 21. Introduced new order of services.

corner of Washington and West streets. The Church of the Disciples has since occupied larger and more convenient Sunday homes. But there are still living those who look back with peculiar tenderness to Amory Hall, and even to the long staircases, so distinct are their memories of the light and life and cheerfulness of the service which was rendered there.

From the 28th of February, 1841, to the 6th of July, 1849, Mr. Clarke was engaged in the regular duties of the minister of the Church of the Disciples. Not long after the church was established, one of its members, George G. Channing, a brother of Dr. W. E. Channing, formed the idea of publishing a weekly paper which should present the religious views which were the life of the church, and should also keep constantly before the public the need of applying Christianity to the evils of society. In Mr. Clarke's diary for December 5, 1842, he speaks of writing the prospectus for this paper, and while it continued to be published he contributed to almost every number; sometimes having several articles in one number. On the 20th of November, 1847, he assumed full editorial care. It was, however, continued only one year longer, when it was merged in the "Christian Register." The union shows that there was no longer even a nominal difference between the Church of the Disciples and the other churches. When, in 1849, Dr. Bellows established the "Christian Inquirer," in New York, he at once solicited and obtained Mr. Clarke's coöperation in the conduct of that paper. Mr. Clarke admitted, and the supporters of the paper admitted, that there were truths as well as errors in "Orthodoxy." The Church of the Disciples increased in numbers. Its week-day meetings were recognized as having an interest which does not attach to the functional conferences of ecclesiastical bodies. They were recognized among the living social forces of the community. His visiting list of an early part of the year

1843 gives the names of members of one hundred and forty-four different families in the church.

The laws of elective affinities and natural selection did their work in the building up of the church. Other churches in Boston still represented, to a certain extent, localities in the town. Thus the Second and North Churches were largely churches of "North Enders." The South Congregational, Pine Street, and Hollis Street Churches were largely churches of "South Enders," and something of the sort might be said of every church in Boston, if it were of a large communion. But the Church of the Disciples did not represent one street or one ward. It represented persons who had been brought together by the simplicity, the boldness, and the fervor of the religious doctrine proclaimed in that pulpit and embodied in the constitution of the society. Indeed, at one time so many of the more active members of the church drove in from the suburban towns that it was called in joke " The Church of the Carryalls."

Four years after the church was gathered, a few of its most hearty members were greatly distressed by one of Mr. Clarke's determinations, and felt compelled to withdraw from the company of their friends. Theodore Parker, at the ordination of Mr. Shackford, in South Boston, had preached a sermon which might now be called celebrated, if that word could apply to any sermon, on " The Transient and Permanent in Christianity." That sermon, indeed, marks the beginning of his general reputation as preacher and reformer. The conservative Unitarians were distressed to the last degree that an utterance so radical should be heard in one of their pulpits. Fortunately for them, they had, as they have, no machinery of whatever sort by which they could drive Mr. Parker out of their ministry. He was the minister of an independent Congregational church, and as long as that church chose to retain him and he chose to be retained, no power but death could remove him from his charge. But the Unitarian leaders of that day in Boston tried the poor experiment of making him uncomfortable. They could decline to exchange pulpits with him, for instance; they could put him under the same ban, such as it was, that "Orthodoxy" had put them under, for the better part of a generation. Mr. Clarke had no desire to join in any excommunication, and on the 26th day of January, 1845, he exchanged with Mr. Parker.[1] It was on this occasion that, after much sorrowful and friendly discussion, fifteen valued members of the Church of the Disciples withdrew, and with their friends founded another Unitarian church. The transaction attracted attention even outside the little fellowship of the Unitarian churches, and it had its fair share in introducing Mr. Clarke to that wide acquaintance which to the end of his life he enjoyed among the courageous men of all communions.

Many years after, in writing to a friend who had asked him for the history of this event, he says at the close of his letter: "I have given you this account because you asked for it, not because I care to recall these scenes. I am happy to say that those who left our church, and those who remained being equally convinced of the entire conscientiousness of the opposite party, never departed from friendly relations with each other. We remained friends after the separation, as we were before." We would add that these seceders from the Church of the Disciples were so certain of Mr. Clarke's continued interest in their welfare, that some of them came to consult him about the necessary arrangements for their new church.

There was always an effort on the part of Mr. Clarke,

---

[1] The entry in the diary is, "Black Sunday. T. Parker preached morning and evening. I went to West Roxbury to preach." And the next day's entry is, "January 27. Ministers' meeting at Bartol's. Subject, expulsion of Theodore Parker." Of January 30, the memorandum is, "Attended Anti-Texas Convention."

and of the members of the church, to show their readiness to hold fellowship with churches outside the Unitarian body. Rev. Edward N. Kirk, then the most distinguished of the "Orthodox" ministers in Boston, preached in the church, though he would not have received Mr. Clarke into his pulpit. And more than once Mr. Clarke baptized persons by immersion, when their conscientious scruples required such a service.

The members who withdrew from the church did so on the 15th of February, 1845, and it is interesting to observe that at the next annual meeting of the Unitarian Association, Mr. Clarke was chosen one of the directors of that body. The Unitarian Association is the Home and Foreign Missionary Board of the whole Unitarian body. For the Unitarian communion, this choice of Mr. Clarke was most fortunate. By his residence in the West he had become well acquainted with their best missionary ground, and the largeness of his view and the courage of his convictions were such as to lead him always to a vigorous policy. We shall see that at a later time he became the active executive of the Association.

He had been chosen chaplain of the Senate of Massachusetts in 1844. This choice may probably be referred to the recognition, at so early a period, of his advanced anti-slavery views.

Another chapter of this book is devoted to his energetic work in the anti-slavery cause. This was work in which he had the sympathy of the larger part of his church. It seems more convenient to place in that chapter such references as we can make to it. The reader must remember that the great battle had now fairly begun. The annexation of Texas was first hinted at, then timidly suggested, then assumed as the policy of the Democratic party, in the face, all along, of the anti-slavery feelings of the Northern States. It proved impossible to carry a treaty of annexation through the

Senate of the United States; and instead of this, joint resolutions for that purpose were driven through both houses of Congress, the necessary votes for this, at the last struggle, being bought by the persons interested in Texan bonds.[1] This Texan question gave a well-defined issue, which filled a much larger space in the public eye than the question of the emancipation of slaves in the District of Columbia, with which the Abolitionists had been obliged to satisfy themselves before.

Mr. Clarke had learned his anti-slavery lesson at Louisville, as the reader has seen. He intimates that it was easier to take advanced anti-slavery views in Louisville than in the Boston of those days.[2] Boston could say, in a sense in which Louisville could not say it, that slavery was none of her business. In point of fact, the Boston manufacturers who used Southern cotton, and the Boston merchants who directed the coasting trade with the South, did not want to irritate their Southern correspondents. In political combinations, also, the Whig party of that day was still posing as a national party. Its leaders were very eager to keep in alliance the one or two Southern States which still voted with them. Such eagerness gave great coldness to their anti-slavery expressions.

Mr. Clarke, and all the active members of the Church of the Disciples, entered joyfully and fearlessly into the discussion in every arena of the great national question thus involved.

In 1847 he completed what was a labor of love for

[1] The joint resolution for this purpose passed the United States Senate, March 3, 1845.

[2] Mr. Clarke refers the change of opinion in Kentucky to the effect wrought by the growth of cotton. "I was at Henry Clay's home at Ashland about the year 1837. He had been over his estate on horseback, and returned tired, and lay down on the sofa, and talked to me about slavery. He said he had hoped to see the end of it, at least in Kentucky, but cotton had become so profitable that the Southern States would not give it up."

him, the history of his grandfather Hull's connection with the campaign of 1812. Since the publication of that book, it may be safely said that General Hull's character has been wholly redeemed from the infamous charges made upon him by the politicians in the necessities of partisan warfare.

The reader may now turn to a few passages from his letters of these eight years, which will, I think, require no farther illustration.

TO HIS SISTER.

MEADVILLE, *January* 7, 1841.

. I agree with those who think it a good time to form a new congregation in Boston. If a dozen men can be found, to hire a hall for three months, I will give my services for that time without compensation.

My object would be, not to form a congregation of Unitarians, but a church of Christ. The church — church union, church action, church edification — would be the main thing. Churches have usually been built on coincidence of opinion; those who thought alike on doctrinal Christianity have united together. This church should be built on coincidence of practical purpose. Those who intend to do the same things would unite in it. Our desire would be to help each other to deep and distinct convictions of *truth* by preaching, Bible classes, conversational meetings, Sunday-schools, etc.; to warm each other's hearts, and fill them with *love* by social religious meetings, prayer meetings, and the Lord's Supper; and finally, to help one another to habits of active goodness, for which purpose we would agree, as a church, to devote thought, time, and money to the relief of the poor, to doing away with social abuses, to spreading around us the light and joy of religion. We may have committees on temperance, prisons, the poor, the slaves, etc., which from time to time shall report to the whole church. Believing that Jesus intended to found such a church, as this, we take him for our Head; he is our Master, Teacher, and Saviour; our Prophet, Priest, and King. All who join the church express this faith in Jesus. Those who unite with us join with the purpose and pledge of aiding in the work which the church does; and they dedicate themselves, with all the faculties of mind and body, to the service of Jesus Christ. . This is no new idea with me. I have been studying and preparing for it for years, and have full faith that it can be effected.

TO A. H. C.

BOSTON, *January* 27, 1841.

I spend my time mainly in seeing those persons with whom I can talk of the expediency of establishing a new society in Boston. The following persons approve my plan, and say, "Now is the accepted time:" Dr. W. E. Channing, Mr. Bartol, Mr. Samuel Barrett, Mr. S. J. May, Father Taylor, Mr. Briggs, Mr. Waterston, Mr. Sargent, Mr. Ripley, and others among the clergy; among the laity many energetic persons. Father Taylor said now was the time when great good could be done by the right man. He said he wished me to try what I could do, and promised me his hearty aid.

Finally, I have taken the decisive step of hiring the Swedenborgian chapel for Sunday evening next, *myself*, and advertising a meeting then and there. For I find, as Goethe says, that

"After much consultation and longest deliberation,
The final decision at last must still be the work of a moment."

If I waited for others to move I might wait till spring, there are so many secondary considerations to be dealt with. I have decided that, first, a society is needed here on a somewhat different basis from the old ones; second, that no better man is likely to undertake it than I; third, that there is no better time than the present moment. Therefore, trusting in the help of God, I am about to begin. Next Sunday night I shall preach a discourse on the essentials of Christianity, or "What shall I do to be saved?" The second Sunday night I shall preach on "Justification by faith." The third on "The Church, as it was at first, as it ought to be now, as it *can* be now." After this I shall find a place to preach in both morning and night, and shall begin a series of sermons to show what I consider to be important and true in all the usual doctrines of Orthodoxy and Unitarianism. May God make me an instrument of good in this work, for surely much is needed.

Of the first service he writes : —

February 1, 1841.

I found my hall full, though Dr. Channing preached that evening in Warren Street Chapel to an overflowing audience, and Mr. Briggs, of Plymouth, at Waterston's church to a large congregation. Mr. Gannett and Dr. Parkman were present. There was nothing new or striking in what I said, but only the simple and plain truth of the matter as I understood it. . To-day I spent two hours with Dr. Channing, talking about my plan of operations. He is very much interested in it, and made many suggestions of value.

In the same letter he says, "I went at night to a meeting at Judge Rogers' to talk about the project of a new church. A minister present expressed fears lest individuals should be drawn away from the existing churches, and lest the Sunday evening lectures should seem to compete with another series then being delivered. But if I were to be turned aside from my course by such minute considerations as these I should never be able to take a single step. I cannot let the minutiæ of proprieties stop my work, which seems to me a most important one. I never felt so deeply the tremendous nature of what I was undertaking as on Sunday night last."

Of the second discourse, on "Justification by Faith," he says, "The chapel was full, though there were four other Unitarian services the same evening."

February 11, 1841.

I am to preach my third sermon on "The Church," on Saturday night, in the Phillips Chapel. My object is to show that the church is not a place to put pious and holy people into, and keep them safe, but a place to put hungry sinners into, feed them with living bread, and make them pious and good.

February 18, 1841.

I had a meeting last evening to take measures toward the organization of a new society. It had been snowing, and the walking was bad, yet there were forty or fifty persons there, men and women. I stated to them the objects and principles of the church, and ended by making a distinct proposal, namely, that I would preach for several months on two conditions: First. That a hall, with lights, should be provided for me to preach in. Second. That it should be understood at the outset that when a church is established the three following principles shall be embodied in it:

1. The social principle.
2. The voluntary principle.
3. Congregational worship.

By the social principle I mean frequent meetings for conversation, etc. [on religious subjects].

By the voluntary principle I mean no pews sold, rented, or taxed, but worship supported by voluntary subscriptions.

By congregational worship I mean that to some extent the congregation should join in the hymns and prayers. . . .

A committee was chosen at once to provide the hall,

and it was thought that we were beginning under favorable auspices. We shall probably hold the first of our regular services on the Sunday after next.

Monday, February 22, 1841.

. . . I spent a good part of Friday in trying to find a hall for our services. It is difficult to obtain one suitable in every respect. Five or six religious societies occupy the best ones now. . . . I called on Mr. Gannett, and offered to preach for him on Sunday. I thought he needed the help more than any one else, as he is giving a course of Sunday evening lectures. . . . Accordingly I preached for him, both morning and afternoon, and in the evening went to a crowded temperance meeting at Waterston's, where I spoke.

I delivered the Thursday lecture, and gave my discourse on "Justification by Faith."

He preached for the first time in Amory Hall, Sunday, February 28. "In the morning every seat was full, and many were obliged to go away. At night it was nearly full. It seats about 275 persons." He mentions individuals who were present, among others Dr. and Mrs. William Ellery Channing.

April 7, 1841.

On Sunday I preached in our new hall, which is somewhat larger and better than the other, and better ventilated. It was well filled.

On Monday afternoon I met my Bible-class, and had an interesting talk for two hours, in the course of which we ran into metaphysics. There were twenty-five or thirty present. At night I went to a meeting for religions conversation at Mr. George Channing's. .

I came near being knocked down yesterday by a drunken truckman for interfering to protect his horse, which he was beating with a club. I immediately went to the police court for a constable to have him arrested, but could not find the judge. I then met Edward Winslow, who undertook to see the owners of the truck, and have the man properly rebuked.

April 10, 1841.

On Friday afternoon I saw Dr. Channing, and talked with him about the organization of the church. I told him the declaration of faith which I wished was "In Jesus as the Christ, the Son of God." He preferred "In Jesus as the divinely appointed teacher of truth," or something equivalent, because the first was less intelligible. I contended, however, for the other, on the ground that we wished to connect ourselves, not only with one another, but with the whole church of Christ, the only way of doing which was to adopt a universal confession, and the only one which could be universal was that on which Jesus built his church at the first. Dr. Channing was, however, much pleased with our plan of partaking of the communion by ourselves, socially, meeting for this purpose alone. This he thought would make it more real and heart-felt.

April 15, 1841.

On Tuesday evening we had a meeting of our church to discuss its organization. The snow was deep on the sidewalks, and only three or four women and about twenty men came. But it was a delightful meeting, because there was evidently, with great variety and freedom of opinion on each point discussed, but one heart, one mind. I never knew anything like it. There were three points on which we took votes, points concerning which the opinions were quite various, yet each of these votes was unanimous, and all voted. The first question was whether the time had come to begin an organization. Several present were not ready yet to unite themselves, and opposed it; yet at last, after hearing the arguments, were convinced that it would be better for the church to have a nucleus formed, and voted with the rest in the affirmative. The other two points related to the declaration which is to be the groundwork and basis of union. It is this, as we decided by two unanimous votes : —

"We, whose names are subscribed, unite together in the following faith and purpose : —

"Our faith is in Jesus, as the Christ, the Son of God.

"And we do hereby form ourselves into a Church of his Disciples, that we may coöperate together in the study and practice of Christianity"

We determined to have no other organization but this, not to organize at all as a religious society upon the money basis.

April 16, 1841.

Our church was crowded last night. I went up to Dr. Channing's afterward, to bid them good-by. They go to Philadelphia to-morrow, then to Newport. Dr. Channing gave me his parting advice and counsel. He said the danger would be, a tendency to conform to the old, established ways, as the mass exerted a great power of attraction. He said again, emphatically, that we must be more afraid of formality than of eccentricity.

BOSTON, *Friday, April* 30, 1841.

. . . We had a meeting Tuesday night, and organized our church, forty-eight names being subscribed to our declaration.

NEWTON, *May* 11, 1841.

On Sunday the hall was quite full in the morning, and overflowing at night. Ephraim Peabody, Mr. Gannett, Mr. Farley of Providence, Mr. Thompson of Salem, Dr. Parkman, and one or two more ministers were present at the evening service. In the afternoon, Barnard being sick, I conducted services at the Warren

Street Chapel, and preached a short extempore sermon. I carried Conant, the Illinois farmer student, with me, and made him preach a short discourse before mine. He did it very well.[1]

I went to Newton Sunday night after preaching, and came to Boston again Monday afternoon to my Bible-class. There was a storm of rain, but eight or ten were present. We had our social meeting at night at Dr. Osgood's. There were about fifty present, men and women. The subject was "Lay Preaching." The conservative and radical elements came into warm conflict, but the most perfect good feeling reigned. However much we may differ in opinion, we always agree as to what we shall do. We agreed that it would be well not to have any lay preaching on Sundays, except when the regular preacher was unable to attend, and no other minister could be procured.

---

[1] Rev. A. H. Conant is remembered and loved in the Unitarian Church at the West as a saint and an apostle. The story of his introduction to that church is interesting.

Early in life he was a farmer in Illinois. Coming one day to the store of the Clarke Brothers in Chicago to make some purchases, he saw there a copy of the *Western Messenger*, and opening it began to read. Mr. A. F. Clarke, seeing his interest in the magazine, placed a chair for him, and into this Mr. Conant dropped, and went on reading. When he left, Mr. Clarke gave him some numbers of the magazine to take home with him. In reading these he was moved to consecrate his life to the work of the ministry. He studied at the Cambridge Divinity School, under Henry Ware, Jr., and afterwards was settled in Illinois, his influence extending through all the region about him. As a chaplain during the war he was unfailing in his devotion to the soldiers, whether in camp, in hospital, or on the battlefield. At his death a soldier in the ranks wrote: "The brave and noble chaplain, who never turned aside for bullet or shell, but where balls flew thick and fast sought out the wounded and administered to their wants, is dead. Never while I live can I forget him as I saw him on the field, with his red flag suspended on a ramrod, marching fearlessly to the relief of the suffering; appearing to the wounded like a ministering angel. When we said, 'Chaplain, you must rest or you will die,' he always replied, 'I cannot rest, boys, while you suffer; if I die, I will die helping you.'"

And die at his post he did, in February, 1863.

I found Mr. Gannett's card on my table yesterday, so to-day I called to see him. He showed me a letter in the "New York Observer," in which they speak of my church being Orthodox in its character. Meantime, others call us the transcendental church. Mr. Gannett was very cordial, and assured me that the ministers were disposed to sympathize with me.

The journals of these years are filled with the record of thoughts, of studies, of work; of talks with brother ministers on topics relating to the church, with public men about the state of the country, with his own people on questions of faith and practice. There are copious notes of lectures which he heard from Professor Agassiz and others; notes of his reading, of books planned; here and there a short poem, or a translation of one.

He was much interested in the condition of prisoners, and in his journal considers what methods are most likely to influence them for good. Later in life he took an active part in this work.

He was a constant contributor to the "Christian World," one of whose expressed objects was "to awaken an interest in all the great philanthropic enterprises of the day, by giving constant information on all that is doing in the cause of temperance, peace, freedom, Sunday-schools, moral and social reform, and on questions of politics having a moral bearing."

He took an active interest in the Free-Soil movement, and several times spoke at public meetings held by members of the Free-Soil party.

When the Boston Association of Ministers met at his house in 1844, the question he proposed for consideration was, "What should be the specific object of preaching?" he himself taking the ground that, without a definite plan, the preacher would be as one who beats the air. When the same association met at his house in 1847, the subject he proposed was, "The Aim of

Life." He adds in his diary, "The discussion was serious and interesting."

Frequent reference is made in the Autobiography to the "social meetings" of the Church of the Disciples. A list of topics for conversation at these meetings during the winter of 1845–46 is here given: —

1. What is the true Christian doctrine of regeneration?

2. "There is no instinctive, intuitive, or direct knowledge of the truths of religion, either of the being of God or of our own immortality." — *Andrews Norton.*

3. What is the inspiration of the New Testament?

4. Is sin a negative or a positive evil?

5. "Be ye perfect, as your Father in Heaven is perfect." Is this to be understood and obeyed in a literal or a limited sense?

6. What is the New Testament doctrine of the hidden life?

7. Shall we maintain and urge our opinions always, or sometimes concede for the sake of union?

8. Should the good withdraw from an evil community, or separate themselves from an evil man?

9. What is the sphere of woman, and how shall she best be educated to fill it?

10. What is the Christian idea of the future state, and of the spiritual world?

11. What is the doctrine of Scripture with regard to eternal punishment, and what is the Christian view of future retribution?

12. What views do the Scriptures afford us of a spiritual body?

13. What are the principles and ideas peculiar to Protestantism, as distinguished from those peculiar to the Church of Rome?

14. What is needed by Unitarianism, at the present time, to give it greater influence and success?

The programme which has this list of topics adds: —

"The social meetings of the Church of the Disciples are held once a fortnight, on Wednesday evening, at the houses of the brethren. On the alternate Wednesday, there is a prayer-meeting of the church, at Ritchie Hall. Both meetings begin at seven and close at nine o'clock.

"The subjects will be discussed at the social meetings in the order in which they are printed. The church may, however, substitute by its vote any subject not on the above list which it may think it desirable to consider."

TO S. S. C.

December 13, 1846.

Church matters have begun again this winter in a good spirit; our social and prayer meetings have been good, and our church has been well filled on Sunday. There is some talk of building. I hope we may succeed this time.

At home we are all happy and well. Our house is gradually assuming a comfortable, domestic look. The children's portrait (by Cheney) is done, framed, and hanging in the front parlor over the fireplace. Herman and Lilla go to school every day, and are making rapid strides in all the branches of a liberal education. They can repeat the multiplication table as far as $3 \times 7 = 21$. Lilla can spell words of four letters, Herman a little more. He has also begun to draw on the slate, and makes very respectable houses, the walls of which are often not farther out of the perpendicular than those of the tower of Pisa. .

Anna and I have been to some geological lectures, and been much edified in relation to animals of the Palæozoic times. Now we are hearing Agassiz, who lectures on the unity of plan in creation. These lectures are very interesting and curious.

I went to New Bedford last week to lecture on Joan of Arc, — a heroine whom I much approve for her heroic courage, her wonderful faith, and her gentle womanhood. I intend to give a series of biographical discourses in our church in the evening, on Sundays; on which occasions I shall speak of such persons as Joan of Arc, Martin Luther, John Milton, Fox and the Quakers, Wesley and the Methodists, Cardinal Borromeo, Blanco White, etc.

Our Bible-classes have been interesting. At the last two meetings we have spoken of the sin against the Holy Ghost.

This summer, after we came from Meadville, and after I had delivered my poem before the Φ. B. K. Society (which most of the papers said was not *artistic*), we went to the seashore at Beverly and Rockport, and had a very pleasant time. We took long walks in the woods, and sat on the rocks looking at the waves, or spent mornings in bathing among the rocks. All was very beautiful.

TO S. S. C.

October 4, 1847.

... On Saturday Anna and I walked six miles; and a day or two before that we rowed in a boat from Billerica, where we are now staying, to Concord, a distance of ten miles and ten back. It was a lovely day, and the woods on either bank were changing to beautiful tints of yellow and crimson; the air was soft and warm, but elastic and strengthening. The river winds gently among fields and woods; tall elms and maples shade its banks. At Concord we landed at the foot of Mr. Ripley's garden, — the Old Manse, you know, from which Hawthorne gathered his mosses.

Our church building is going up rapidly, and we shall soon be in it. It will be a pretty building, I think, and will suit us very well. We shall have a famous large vestry below, for a Sunday-school and conference room.[1]

[1] This was the *F*reeman *P*lace *C*hapel.

The new chapel, in Freeman Place, was dedicated March 15, 1848. From Mr. Clarke's sermon at the dedication we give a few sentences: —

. . . We united together seven years ago and established this Church of Disciples. We took that name in sincere humility. We wished to be scholars, learners, sitting at the feet of Jesus. We wished to unite together, to coöperate, to help each other onward and upward. Our creed was faith in Christ, and we included in our body many varieties and even extremes of opinion. Your minister was one of yourselves; he assumed no official authority, he wished that all the brethren should occupy the pulpit; he wishes and hopes for it still. A band of brothers and friends, we sought for a deeper religious life, for a larger view of truth, for a better habit of active goodness. . . .

We enter to-day into this new house, which is to be our home. . We wish and intend that these doors shall be always open to welcome the stranger, the feeble, the wretched. We wish and intend that here the rich and the poor may sit together; that the fugitive slave and the penitent prodigal may feel themselves welcome, as they always have been.

After the mention of the dedication in his diary the next entry there is, —

I intend to have a series of lectures on reforms delivered on Sunday evenings, in our church: —
1. Reforms: Their relation to the Church, to the Age; by J. F. Clarke. 2. The Temperance Reform: Its history, idea, present state. What is wanted now. What ought the Church to do? by E. H. Chapin, or John Pierpont. 3. The Peace Movement; by Theodore Parker, or S. J. May. 4. The Anti-Slavery Movement; by Wendell Phillips. 5. Reforms in prisons, poor-

houses, hospitals, insane asylums, etc.; by Dr. S. G. Howe, or J. A. Andrew. 6. Social Reform; by W. H. Channing. 7. Educational Reform; by Horace Mann.

FROM HIS DIARY.

1848. April 12. There are four elements which ought to exist in a church, and which never have existed together in any Christian church since the first century, namely: —

1. A deep spirit of individual, inward religion.
2. An entire intellectual freedom of thought and expression.
3. A union of hands and hearts. Real brotherhood.
4. A practical direction of effort to elevate and purify mankind.

Separately we find these elements often, but we never find them all combined in any association. . . .

Is the difficulty in the existing forms of church organization? In a paid and professional minister?

FROM HIS DIARY.

1848. July. I know nothing which I can do which would be more useful than to write a little book on The Positive Doctrines of Christianity. In this I would attempt to give the positive contents of the gospel as distinguished from speculative and verbal controversies. . . . Some of the chapters would be on: —

1. The Positive Doctrines of Christianity concerning God.
2. The Positive Doctrines of Christianity concerning Man.
3. The Positive Doctrines of Christianity concerning Christ.
4. Concerning Regeneration, or the Christian Change.
5. Concerning the Future Life.

. . . .

Positive doctrines are also practical in the highest sense.

TO H. W. BELLOWS.

BOSTON, *February* 27, 1849.

I have just read your kind and interesting letter of last week. I thank you for your sympathy in our trial. It was very sudden. The little path our boy dug through the snow a fortnight ago has not yet melted away, and he has been lying ten days in his grave. The day after you left Boston I went with Mrs. Clarke to call on Mrs. Bellows (not knowing you were gone), and we saw Herman standing at the head of Walnut Street. He begged to go with us, and went to Mr. Bartol's door, and said he would sit on the step till we came out. That was the last time I walked with him.

Your words show that we have been led along the same path of discipline. . . .

I am extremely interested in your plans concerning the "Inquirer." I see no reason why it should not succeed. The plan of assistant editors is also good, I should say. Dewey, if he will write, is of course a great help. Osgood has indefatigable industry, and also ready talents. There is Henry Hedge, of Bangor, a man whose mind is full of matter and of the best kind, rich in thought and experience. You must consider that men who are to write every week will tire the readers except they have an artistic style and can charm by new forms of expression. But at all events, secure, if you can, James H. Perkins, of Cincinnati, as a contributor and correspondent. He is an admirable writer of short pieces, — full of point, life, wit, beauty, — and his ideas are very pure and noble.

But above all, remember not to forget George F. Simmons, who is a purely religious man, with insight, talent, knowledge, and a generous theology. Then there is my Orthodox brother Lesley, of Milton, a good writer, and liberal as you please.

I should be very glad to write for a paper such as I believe yours will be.

H. W. BELLOWS TO J. F. C.

NEW YORK, *March* 21, 1849.

We mean to issue the first number on the first Saturday in April. . . . Can you suggest a good Scripture motto for the paper? Is it worth while to add any other and more descriptive epithet or clause to the title "The Christian Inquirer"? I hope we are something more than inquirers. . .

I am persuaded that what we want in our paper mainly is a deeper, truer, more practical religious tone, and I hope you will furnish some articles which have expressly for their aim to kindle religious life in individual hearts. . . . It is our showy, noisy, superficial goodness that lets the world stay unconverted.

CHAPTER X.

EUROPE.

AFTER more than eight years of vigorous work Mr. Clarke, by the kind arrangement of members of his society, passed a summer in Europe, sailing from Boston in the "Plymouth Rock," July 6, 1849.

Eleven weeks were spent in Europe, to his great delight, and the account which he printed afterwards shows his activity during these weeks. Like most American optimists of the day, he believed that universal peace was nearer than it has proved,[1] and he had been named, with his own permission, a delegate to the Peace Congress to be held at Paris. I suppose, however, that he was named a delegate because he was going to Europe, not that he went to Europe because he was a delegate. Napoleon III., with grim sarcasm, welcomed the convention, gave it a hall, and appointed sentries to pace in front and keep it from disturbance.

"I had made up my mind," Mr. Clarke says, "that what I wished to see in Europe was, in the first place, the Alps; secondly, fine paintings and picture galleries; and, in the third place, the old cathedrals." And his

---

[1] "We stand on the threshold of a new age, which is preparing to recognize new influences. The ancient divinities of Violence and Wrong are retreating to their kindred darkness. The sun of our moral universe is entering a new ecliptic, no longer deformed by those images of animal rage, Cancer, Taurus, Leo, Sagittarius, but beaming with the mild radiance of those heavenly signs, Faith, Hope, and Charity." — Charles Sumner, in 1846. Mr. Sumner lived to put on his zodiac Preston Brooks and the heroes of the Civil War.

rules for persons like himself, who "have a taste for art, but no pretense to knowledge," are characteristic: "First: Have faith. Believe that what the testimony of mankind through many centuries declares to be great is really great, though you cannot at first discover its grandeur or beauty. Second: Try, not to see many things, but to see a few things well. Third: One gains much insight into the peculiar genius of the great artists by comparing their styles."

But while he says he has no technical knowledge, it is clear, from his quite full criticisms of pictures, that he carried out his third rule steadfastly. He drew well enough to know what bad drawing was, and he was so much in the company of artists that it was impossible for him to look at a picture without thought of the technical principles involved.

His account of the Peace Congress, written, I suppose, as a letter to the Church of the Disciples, is to be remembered as showing how far there was any hope for universal peace, and how practical was his own notion of such an accord of Europe as might, in practice, lead to disarmament. There was a large attendance of delegates, four or five hundred coming from England. The committee of arrangements had provided that Victor Hugo should preside, and had made the Abbé Deguerry, Curé of the Madeleine, and Athanase Coquerel, the head of the French Unitarians, Vice-Presidents. Mr. Cobden spoke, Emile de Girardin, Amasa Walker, Elihu Burritt, and William W. Brown, a refugee slave.

"On the whole," Mr. Clarke says, "the Peace Congress probably did just as much good as any man could reasonably expect. The effect of these meetings is often exaggerated. To bring together those who hold certain opinions, by means of a convention, does not necessarily increase the number holding such views." It is a pity that these last words could not be written in letters of gold in all public halls. "Indeed, if violent, weak, or extreme opinions are expressed, the convention may injure the cause instead of helping it. The members, however, are seldom aware of this; they enjoy each other's sympathy, and mistake the sentiment of the meetings for public opinion."

"The real good done by the Peace Congress was to call men's attention to the subject."

He does not allude, in his book, to the incident of Salisbury spire, of which the narrative, in later life, terrified his friends. The spire of Salisbury Cathedral is a little more than four hundred feet high. With some friends, Mr. Clarke ascended as far as the interior staircase goes, to what is called the weather-door, about thirty feet from the extreme top of the spire. The others were then satisfied with what they had done; but he went out and climbed up the remaining part of the spire, by iron handles fixed in the walls, these having been arranged for the convenience of workmen who have to attend to the vane, and of hardy visitors. When he arrived at the highest of these, he found a bar above him, running round the spire, which he could reach with his hands. By this he lifted himself to the level of the ball, and, as most versions of this anecdote say, stood on top of the ball, with such support as the lightning rod could give him, surveying the scene. He then returned to the supporting rod, and dropped himself, expecting to find the friendly bolt by which he had ascended. But it was not there, and he reflected, too late, that he had not observed on which side of the spire it was. Then and there he had, so to speak, to work around the spire hanging by his hands; and having unfortunately chosen the least favorable direction, he nearly completed its circuit before he found under his foot the bolt which was to be the first step in his retreat.

This story must be compared with the anecdote of his standing on top of the spar erected on the

Delta, to show what a passion he had for these high elevations.[1]

In a letter written while on the voyage he gives a pleasant description of life on board the sailing vessel. After breakfast came a service in the cabin; and then the ministers, of whom there were a number on board, sat round the table writing in their journals.

In the course of the day they had gymnastic exercises on deck, and in these Mr. Clarke was leader. Two hours every evening were devoted to the discussion of questions relating to peace and war.

One of Mr. Clarke's favorite seats in leisure hours during the day was in the mizzen-top. Here he studied his Ollendorff, and here he wrote the lines called " White-capt Waves," in reading which we also seem to see the ocean from the mizzen-top.

> White-capt waves far round the Ocean,
>   Leaping in thanks or leaping in play,
> All your bright faces, in happy commotion,
>   Make glad matins this summer day.
>
> The rosy light through the morning's portals
>   Tinges your crests with an August hue;
> Calling on us, thought-prisoned mortals,
>   Thus to live in the moment too.
>
> For, graceful creatures, you live by dying,
>   Save your life when you fling it away,
> Flow through all forms, all form defying,
>   And in wildest freedom strict rule obey.

[1] I am quite aware that in the detail of this story there may be some error, for I have heard it told in different ways. But the substance of it, I am sure, is true, and I have verified it from the facts as they are recorded, with regard to the arrangements of the top of the spire about that time. When he told it at a meeting of the Class of 1829, more than a generation afterward, old friends of his found they could not sleep that night in their terror for what might have happened.

Show us your art, O genial daughters
Of solemn Ocean, thus to combine
Freedom and force of rolling waters
With sharp observance of law divine.

A few short extracts from letters written home during his European journey will show how fresh and gennine was his enjoyment of the new scenes which met his eye from day to day.

TO A. H. C.

AMBLESIDE, *August* 1, 1849.

I have done much since I arrived on Thursday last at Liverpool. On Friday I went to Chester, and saw the old town and cathedral. Saturday, saw Eaton Hall and park. Sunday, preached in Liverpool three times. Monday, went by steamer to Bangor and Caernarvon, sailing under the Menai Bridge. Tuesday, rode forty miles through the fine scenery of North Wales, and spent two hours in Conway Castle, then back to Liverpool. Wednesday, to the lakes. Friday, Warwick and Kenilworth. I am glad that I am to stay in London a week, for I am tired of running about the kingdom in such a hurry, and I wish to sit still and look at pictures.

LONDON, *August* 10.

. . . Sunday morning I heard Dr. Hutton preach. In the afternoon I went to the service in Westminster Abbey. It is a glorious place. I sat listening to the chants, but looking up along the endless lines of columns and arches, up, up, to the lofty vaults above, and saw the immensity of the structure, and felt that man cannot live by bread alone. The unnecessary amount of space and building makes it seem like the exuberance of nature, who never counts her leaves and flowers.

SALISBURY, *August* 15.

To-day I have been to Stonehenge, riding over Salisbury Plain, a broad, open, rolling piece of country, as much like a Northern Illinois prairie as can be, except that it is poor land and no grouse, all chalk under a thin surface of soil. But Stonehenge was fine. The air blew cool around us as we sat among these old relics of ancient days. They seemed to talk of the twenty centuries which had drifted by; but just then I looked up, and saw a little sparrow chirping on the top of one of the impostal stones, — the gay child of nature, born yesterday, making merry over these solemn ages. . . . Then we saw the wondrous beauty of Salisbury minster. I went to the very top and stood by the vane, four hundred feet above the ground. It is a noble building. We saw it in the soft light of a warm August afternoon, and it will linger in my mind as a vision of pure beauty.

PARIS, *August* 22.

To-day our Peace Congress met. There were about a thousand delegates, of whom six hundred came from England, Scotland, and Ireland. There were, besides, a thousand spectators. Victor Hugo, the poet and novelist, presided, and made a noble speech. Cobden, Coquerel, and others spoke.

August 28.

The French Government has been exceedingly civil to the Congress. It allowed the members to come and go without passports or custom-house examination. The minister of public works ordered that all the public buildings should be shown us on the presentation of our Peace Congress ticket.

At the Palais du Luxembourg I saw the Senate Chamber, where Napoleon's Senators met, and the Chamber of Peers. Round the last were busts of Massena, Augereau, etc. The guide, an officer, said, "See the men against whom you are working." I replied, "Not against the men, but against the system; we admire courage." He said, "Vous aimez le courage, pas le carnage."

ZURICH, *September* 2.

I too am in Switzerland! I have had my first distant view of the high Alps. I am trying hard to realize it all. . . . From Paris we came by rail the first fifty miles, but in our diligence, which was hoisted by a machine on the rail-car, and hoisted off again and replaced on its wheels when we arrived. . . .

At Strasbourg I went to the minster, and mounted to the top of the spire, the highest in Europe, 474 feet. . . . Leaving Strasbourg, we crossed the Rhine and entered Germany. After a lovely ride we reached Freiburg at 9.30 P. M. Lovely in the moonlight rose the Freiburg minster, more fair and graceful, I must needs think, in its proportions than that of Strasbourg. . . .

After crossing the Rhine at Eglisau, we had our first view of the high Alps. To the pleasure and amusement of the driver, we rose to our feet and gave three cheers. There they lay, exquisitely delicate in outline, their snowy summits glittering in the sunset.

These were the eternal Alps, the inaccessible Alps, seventy or eighty miles off. It was the group around the Jungfrau.

September 5.

On Monday afternoon we ascended the Rhigi. We reached the top in time to see the sun set, only it was enveloped in clouds. But we saw the Alps and other high mountain ranges before it grew dark. Then there came on a violent thunderstorm, and we had an opportunity of testing the truth of Byron's description. I went out into the darkness, rain, and wind to get a sight of it, and from the summit saw the forked lightning dart along, apparently on a level with myself, and the two great lakes, Zug and Lucerne, come out like two immense mirrors to reflect the light, and then disappear again in the darkness. The next morning the sun rose clear, and we saw all the immense panorama of mountains, lakes, forests, and cultivated country come into view. The shadow of Rossberg lay purple on the blue water of Zug, and the colossal shadow of Rhigi stretched far away over Lucerne. It is impossible to suggest by any words the unimaginable beauty of this view. . . .

After breakfast we descended by the footpath to Kussnacht, where we took a boat to Lucerne. The sail on the lake was exquisite. I sketched Mount Pilatus, whose craggy tops, bare of all vegetation, pierced the morning sky like sharp spears. . . . We were about an hour in Lucerne. Then at two, on this day of wonders, began our second sail, in the steamer, on this lake, which Sir James Mackintosh pronounces the most beautiful in the world. . . . We sailed round the foot of the Rhigi, touched at the port of Schwytz, saw the bare rocky Mitres, sailed up the extraordinary bay of Uri, where mountains descend on all sides sheer into the water, so that not even a footpath can be formed along the margin of the lake. We landed at Fluellen, drove eleven miles to Amsteg, and after supper walked twelve more to Wesen. This walk was a constant ascent on the St. Gothard road, and between very lofty mountains. We slept in a Swiss tavern, where we woke the people up at eleven

INTERLAKEN, *September 9.*

We have arrived here, having finished our walk round the Jungfrau. In these six days we have walked, by Murray, 130 English miles, by the guides 160. Besides this we have crossed five mountain ridges, amounting in all to about 17,000 feet of ascent and descent.

CHAMOUNIX, *September 13, 1849.*

It is strange how in this heart of Europe I am cut off from all familiar thoughts and things. There seems to be nothing near me but Nature. I am in her element. Of the revolutions going on around me I hear and know nothing. By accident I read in a little Savoy newspaper that Venice has surrendered, that Hungary is conquered.... Neither my own business nor the world's history affects me. In this clear Alpine air the distant mountains seem close at hand, but the nearest social facts seem far away. The atmosphere of the hills is a telescope with which we look at nature through the eyepiece, but at the world through the object glass; one comes much nearer, the other recedes to an illimitable distance. But there is one constant exception to this: those whom I love are nearer to me than ever.

I went into the little Lutheran church in Untersee, and while I sat there the memory of dear Herman came over me so strongly that I thought my heart would break. Those good German Mädchen who sat near me, and noticed my convulsive sobs, must have thought me some great sinner, awakened and convinced by the powerful preaching, — I, meantime, not knowing the meaning of a word the preacher said.

Monday the sun shone bright, and we set off on foot, for the Gemmi Pass.... We walked twenty-four miles to the town of Kandersteg, which lies high beneath the glaciers and snow-covered mountains of the Glarus Alp. Tuesday morning we rose at five, and set off at once to ascend the Gemmi. It took us two hours of constant climbing to reach the top of the first ascent behind Kandersteg. Our party was six: Mr. Cordner of Montreal and I, who carry one knapsack alternately between us; two Mr. Frothinghams of Montreal, who carry their knapsack alternately; a guide for the day, and another who has come with us from Rhigi, and carries our cloaks. After crossing a valley, the type of desolation, surrounded by bare cliffs, glaciers above, and ruins of rocks below, we ascend another ridge of rocks, and pass on and up, round a lake which has no outlet for its freezing waters, and then, climbing a ridge of rocks, the whole chain of Savoy Alps is in view, Monte Rosa, Mont Cervin, and the rest, white with eternal snow. . . .

GENEVA, *Sunday, September 16.*

Friday dawned clear, and from my window, at half past four, I saw the clear outline of the monarch of mountains and his attendant summits. I watched them till they became rosy in the early sunlight. At eight we set out for the Cross of Flégere, a height on the other side of the valley, from which you have a fine view of Mont Blanc and the surrounding peaks.

The view from that summit I trust I shall never forget as long as I live. Sitting on the edge of this steep declivity we looked over the valley, not more than a mile wide, to the accumulation of peaks and mountains of which Mont Blanc is the highest and central elevation. His bare glittering summit receded far up and beyond all the rest, being eight or ten miles away from us, and two thousand feet higher than the gigantic peaks and domes which surround him. A white vapor, like a fleecy cloud, kept rising from his crest; this was the new-fallen snow blown off by the storms which roar forever around him. . . . I sat with all this vast picture of ice, snow, granite peaks, glaciers, and waterfalls before me, — sat for an hour or more, wondering if indeed this was the Mont Blanc of my school-boy studies, of my childhood's dreams. The intense beauty of the scene exceeded all that I ever imagined. These great peaks seemed so close at hand, this vast glacier was spread under my eye like a map. Mont Blanc, indeed, remained like a monarch, inaccessible, remote. We came close to the kings and princes of his court, but the emperor held himself aloof. . . .

COLOGNE, *September* 27.

On Monday we sailed the length of Lake Leman, walked six miles back to Vevay, and drove part way to Swiss Freiburg. We spent some hours of Tuesday in Freiburg, and went on to Berne, which we left next day; passed the Jura through the gap, spent six hours at Basel, went on to Freiburg in Baden, and from there to Heidelberg and Frankfort; sailed down the Rhine to Bingen, from there to Coblenz and Bonn, and thence to Cologne.

These are the statistics, the skeleton of my days. But how shall I give you the color, or even the rude outline of all the grace and beauty I have been seeing and enjoying?

Berne, with its old minster, and lovely walks beneath chestnut and walnut and linden trees, but above all with its snowy Alps in the distance, will deserve a longer paragraph than I have time to give it now. . . . We arrived just before sunset, and saw a rosy collection of clouds, but not the Alps, which were cloud-covered. Next morning I was out before sunrise, and from the high platform behind the minster I saw the white summits of the Alps growing rosy in the early light. After breakfast I went to the minster and ascended to the top, as is my wont, bought some pictures, saw the old clock go through its evolutions, and departed for Basel.

I had determined to pay a visit to Dr. DeWette at Basel, and was much surprised to hear that he had died in June. I did not hear of it because the steamer that brought the news arrived just after I left America, and when I reached Europe it had ceased to be news. . . . Having been thinking of an interview with him it gave me a shock to be told, when I asked the way to his house, "Mais il est mort!"

. . . There is a very old church at Basel, in which the Council was held four hundred years ago at which popes were elected and deposed. The furniture is all as it was, except that the bust of Erasmus stands in the middle of the room. I sat on the old benches, and went back four hundred years, and considered what opinion I should give about the pope when it came to my turn. Then I looked at Erasmus, and said, "What business has that innovator among us?" Afterward we went into the crypt under the minster, and went back four hundred years more, for that was built in the eleventh century. I paced up and down among the shadows, and thought with alarm that in four hundred years a council would be held above to depose a pope. I had got so far back then as to be quite out of sight of Erasmus and the Reformation.

I love the crypts under these old churches. Solid, compact, with nothing of decoration, they seem to belong to the era of primitive religion, the strong faith which dwelt among the roots of things. . . . You can neither preach nor celebrate mass in a crypt, but on its solid columns rests the church in which the pious multitude pray, and the organ sounds the note of praise.

At Heidelberg we had a lovely day. This grand old castle is an immense pile, not ruined by time, as was Kenilworth or Conway, but destroyed by the hand of man, torn in pieces and demolished by the ruthless policy of kings and generals. You feel pity for the old castle, and wish to turn away your eyes, as when a hero is beaten in battle, or the champion of a hundred fights is utterly vanquished.

Sunday evening, September 30, 1849.

The chimes of the Antwerp minster are now playing their accustomed tune before the great bell strikes nine. The moon, nearly full, illuminates the summit of the lofty spire, whose light tracery I see through my window. . . . Alone in Antwerp, I am happy this Sunday evening. Not a soul here knows me, but I have felt the presence and love of God to-night, as I sat in the dimly lighted cathedral, listening to the organ, looking up to the arching roof, or seeing the worshipers come and kneel at the different altars, and go away again. . . .

I have been enjoying Rubens here. His best pictures are filled with life, energy, and the outflow of an exuberant genius. An infinite variety prevails in his works. Every figure has its own character, every head its own expression. Jews, apostles, soldiers, women, children, all are there in their own persons and style of being. The effect of the whole is of a rushing tide of joyful life, like a fine, fresh, clear, airy morning, when every one feels well.

Loftier and purer than Rubens, yet eclipsed by the meteoric splendor of his genius, the paintings of Vandyck elevate one's nature. I cannot but love and reverence Vandyck, so noble, so dignified is his whole method of art. After seeing Rubens' masterpieces here in Antwerp, I retain the opinion I formed in England, that Vandyck is the nobler artist. . . .

•

The last words of "Eleven Weeks in Europe" are characteristic. The steamer arrived at East Boston late at night, and the passengers knew that the ferryboats to the city proper stopped their trips at midnight. They were trying to persuade the admiralty officer to let them cross in the boat which took the mails. "Just then, looking over the side, I saw a skiff glide up to the vessel, and a man climbed aboard. He had come for the English papers for the newspaper offices. As he went back with his bundle into his skiff, I dropped after him, and in five minutes was at the end of Long Wharf." He did not ask himself what a paternal government would have said to such an exceptional landing.

H. W. BELLOWS TO J. F. C.

NEW YORK, *December* 1, 1849.

I welcome you home with all my heart, and wish I could do it with both hands. I have been sick these few weeks past, or I should have written you the moment I heard of your arrival, to say that our hemisphere was glad to recover its equilibrium, and I with it, to see so efficient a co-laborer back.

I write to say that we are entirely depending upon your invaluable coöperation in the "Inquirer." . . . Osgood and I have the whole burden. With you this would be no great affair. Indeed I would sooner risk the paper upon such a tripod — each leg doing its duty — than upon a centipede foundation, where any sense of individual responsibility would be impossible, and every foot might "claw off."

How capital your "House that Jack built"[1] was!

TO H. W. BELLOWS.

BOSTON, *December* 7, 1849.

DEAR BROTHER, — I thank you for your kind welcome home, and your friendly opinions of my usefulness to you.

I am glad to hear you say that my articles are needed in the "Inquirer," and useful when there.

I should be glad to write in the way of systematic treatment of certain subjects of theology and morals, in series of articles; only I fear the dullness of the thing. Tell me how many people complained of the heaviness of the "Inspiration" papers, and whether any number of persons say they have received good from them. My tendency is to look at things all round; to give the astronomical theory of every subject, giving the whole curve of the comet, and not a picturesque description of the phenomenon in its most interesting phases. All this, I own, seems heavy for a paper.

Again, I think we ought to do justice to socialism, —

---

[1] "The House that Jack built" was a short article in the *Christian Inquirer*, suggested by the tendency of the time to write reviews, and reviews of reviews, literature thus seeming in danger of becoming chiefly criticism.

to say a word in favor of protective unions, model lodging-houses, etc.; and to distinguish between destructive and constructive socialism.

TO S. S. C.

December 21, 1849.

I have now been at home nearly two months, and already my European tour seems floating away from me into thin air, as something I have dreamed, and not lived. It is curious how the two ends of your life will draw together and unite, from each side of such an episode.

Such a journey renews one's life. We have much goods laid up for many years, and the soul can take its fill. One can go into the chamber of the memory, and take down a fine picture and examine it anew with great delight.

CHAPTER XI.

MEADVILLE.

To a young American of curiosity and intelligence, the first voyage across the Atlantic and subsequent journeys in Europe are both tonic and stimulant. There is hardly anything to be compared with it in the experiences of other men. A great Englishman lately said, "I should like to be an American, if it were only that it must be such fun to go to Europe." A man readjusts his perspectives, when he looks at himself and his old life across the ocean. He makes real, for all after life, a great many matters of history which have only existed in imagination before. Notre Dame, St. Peter's, and the Alps are different to him, for all time, after he has looked upon them. It infallibly follows that a man of large life and courageous purpose comes back from his first European tour with plans quite new, both in regard to himself and to his work for the world. This happened to Mr. Clarke on his return from his flying European trip of the summer of 1849. That happened also which has happened to so many other men of spirit, that he overestimated the new physical life given by the tonic and the stimulant, and that he could not keep up to the plans which he laid out for himself while under this influence. The little diary is full of short entries which show how eagerly he was at work, till they are broken by this brief memorandum: —

"January 15, 1850. Taken sick with typhoid fever. Confined to my room three months and more."

This imprisonment ends only on the 24th of April, where is the entry, "Go out to drive round the Common." On the 1st of May he went down to breakfast. The 3d of May records, "Working on my solar microscope." The 4th of May the little entry is, "Rainy and cloudy. Reading 'Pendennis.' Solar microscope." And then follows the sad memorandum, "Letter to B. P. Winslow, recommending the plan of selling the church and investing the money." This plan was adopted; and on the 7th of May, at its annual meeting, the Church of the Disciples recommended to its trustees to sell the church in which they had worshiped.

This was the end for the present of the cheerful and large hopes with which all had begun so eagerly nine years before. On the 26th of June is the memorandum, "Suddenly taken sick with lung fever;" and again he seems to have been shut up for some weeks. On the 11th of August comes the entry, "Last service in the Church of the Disciples. Eight children baptized. I made an address. Lord's Supper. Channing; prayer." (Probably his friend W. H. Channing made the prayer.)

At this point his ministerial life in Boston is divided by a gap of more than three years. In such a break-up of hopes and plans I have not found one word of discouragement expressed in any of the diaries or any of the letters. Yet it would be hard to imagine a more severe disappointment than the physician's announcement that he must give up the energetic and enterprising work which engaged him, and rest himself for an indefinite time. He had overcome the difficulties of a beginning, and his work was successful on all sides. Yet it was work which could not be well entrusted to another; and there certainly seemed danger that his favorite plans in establishing the Church of the Disciples might end in no visible results, if he could not himself oversee them. Now that it is all over, it is easy enough for us to see that he filled those years full. In them he laid the foundation for much of the afterwork for which he is now most fondly remembered. And the publications of those years, and their other appeals to the various audiences to which he addressed himself, give no sign of the life of an invalid gaining strength for after-duty.

The pleasant home in Boston was broken up; and in August, 1850, by the route of Bedford Springs and Pittsburgh, the family went to Meadville, Pennsylvania, the residence of Mrs. Clarke's father.

A few memoranda of dates may be convenient.

From the 6th of January, 1851, to the 7th of February, Mr. Clarke was at Washington, D. C.

From the 6th of May to the 16th of June, the time was spent by Mr. and Mrs. Clarke in a visit to Louisville and the Mammoth Cave in Kentucky. In the month of July there was an expedition to Niagara Falls. In September Mr. Clarke visited Boston, and in that month he preached at the Freeman Place Chapel.

With W. H. Channing he spent some days at R. W. Emerson's in Concord, the three friends working together on the Memoir of Margaret Fuller. The entry in his diary, September 5th, is, "At R. W. Emerson's. Spent forenoon in Mr. Alcott's summer-house,[1] reading Margaret Fuller's Italian letters."

After his return from Boston in 1851, he was asked to become for a time the pastor of the church in Meadville. He agreed to do so; and in his diary for September 28, he says: "To-day I begin my work as pastor of this Unitarian society. My duties will be: on Sundays, to conduct public worship and to give lessons in the Sunday-school; on week-days, to visit the parish, hold meetings, Bible-classes, etc. The theological students to be members of my society."

[1] This was a summer-house built for Mr. Emerson by Mr. Alcott and Mr. Thoreau.

In October he went to Detroit to preach the sermon at the installation of Thomas J. Mumford, thence to Chicago and Milwaukee, preaching in both places, and on his way back preaching one Sunday in Cleveland.

It is clear enough that Mr. Clarke enjoyed the regularity of his life and the freedom from the interruptions of a working ministry in a large town. At the beginning of the year he made a plan for the year's work, as he often did when a year began. This time he had little occasion to rebuke himself that he did not hold to his resolutions. He had now the great advantage which results from a regular engagement with a competent amanuensis.

At the end of 1851, in a summary with which he closes the diary, he says : —

1. I have this year taken journeys to Washington ; to Cincinnati, Louisville, and the Mammoth Cave ; to Erie ; to Niagara, Buffalo, and Rochester ; to Niagara again with Anna ; to Boston, New York, Brooklyn ; to Detroit, Chicago, Milwaukee, and Cleveland (seven journeys in all).

2. Publications : —

The Christian Doctrine of Forgiveness of Sin. Boston, 12mo.

Chapter in Life of S. M. Fuller.[1]

Articles in "Christian Inquirer," viz. : Deacon Herbert's Bible-class ; six chapters. Compromises and

---

[1] About this book there is a curious bit of literary history. It was published in the year 1852. Curiosity was greatly excited about it. It was the work of three writers well known among the literary men of New England. It is very interesting in detail, and, as might have been expected, the sale was large and rapid. A second and third edition were hurried through the press, and there seemed every prospect of a wide popularity to the book, when, *presto*, the sale stopped. Nor has it ever been renewed.

The cause was easily found. *Uncle Tom's Cabin* was published. "The retail book market never can take two enthusiasms at one time."

their Consequences. A Trip to Mammoth Cave. Six poems; letters, etc.

3. Studies.

I have read a few books, but as it seems to me very few.

The home to which Mr. Clarke went for recovery of strength was in the town of Meadville, in the northwest section of Pennsylvania. It is a picturesque region, attractive for its walks and drives, and especially for rides on horseback, over the hills.

The house of Mr. Huidekoper, where the family spent the greater part of the next three years, was a rather large, old-fashioned dwelling, with an extensive lawn, containing many stately forest trees. In front of the house was a long piazza, round whose pillars sweet-brier and climbing roses twined themselves, and not far off great beds of damask-roses perfumed the air. In the early morning might be heard the tapping of little hoofs over the piazza, and a couple of young pet deer would signal to the master of the house that they had come for their accustomed piece of bread and the touch of his friendly hand.

Mr. Huidekoper was not only a friend to animals, but a lover of children, and no time spent in giving them pleasure seemed to him wasted. Every year he invited the children of two Sunday-schools to spend the Fourth of July on his grounds, and to bring with them any near relatives. Sometimes as many as two hundred persons came. If mothers brought their infants they found a roomy tent ready to receive them. Games were provided for children of different ages. Dinner and supper were taken under the shade of a wide-spreading maple tree. The children had a long, happy day, and before sunset all were again safe in their own homes.

But one of the pleasantest things to Mr. Clarke's children in the Meadville life was that they had there so much more of their father's society than was possible in Boston. In the morning one of them had an arithmetic lesson with him in his study. Among his valuable qualifications as a teacher was his unlimited patience, and this scholar cannot recall a single impatient word at these lessons. "No wonder your little head is puzzled," he would say; "my big head is puzzled too, sometimes."

For the entertainment of his own children and their cousins he constructed a little puppet-show and enacted plays for them. But most delightful of all were the stories he told them after they were in bed at night, some of these being taken from Scott's novels, or from the shorter stories of German romance.

Mr. Clarke's study was in a wing of the main house, and had one door opening into the parlor and another on the long piazza. It was a quiet place, and had once been the family school-room. While the western window and door looked across an intervale to the hills beyond French Creek, on the other side of the room was a window through which, in the summer, sprays of a climbing rose entered, and opened their blossoms above his writing table. In this pleasant retreat he wrote the books of which he has spoken, and later, "The Christian Doctrine of Prayer,"[1] "Eleven Weeks in Europe," a translation of Hase's "Leben Jesu," beside many articles for the "Christian Examiner," "Christian Inquirer," and other periodicals. His writing, however, was not always done in the time of roses, but often in the season of snowstorms and a low thermometer.

While in Meadville he much enjoyed his intercourse with the theological students. One of these, Rev. C. A. Staples, has kindly furnished us with his recollections of that period.

"I was at Meadville during the years of which you speak, and saw a good deal of Mr. Clarke. He preached

[1] The Essay on Prayer was not finished until early in 1854.

at the church, and occasionally visited the school. Some of the students spent two or three hours a week with him at Mr. Huidekoper's, in gymnastic exercises, reading, and conversation. Sometimes he invited several of us to pass the evening with him, when he would talk about books, pictures, and subjects that were interesting him. I remember that on one occasion he read to us Theodore Parker's sermon on 'Old Age,' which had just been preached.

"Mr. Clarke was deeply interested at that time in the anti-slavery cause, and, before leaving for Europe [in 1852], gave an address upon the subject in the court house, on a week-day evening. I think he did this without any invitation from the people, as a public testimonial of his abhorrence of slavery, and to free his mind and conscience upon the matter. He also gave one or more addresses in the church on Sunday evenings, upon the same subject.

"Teachers' meetings were held by him, in which he gave pleasant talks upon the Epistles of Paul and the Gospels. His preaching at this time was very earnest and interesting, full of apt illustrations, and appealed to the deepest spiritual experiences. It was stimulating to our minds and hearts, and gave great satisfaction to many of the students, with whom he was very popular. He showed a kindly interest in us, and gladly aided us in our studies whenever we sought his assistance. He seemed to live in a world of pleasant memories and high thoughts, and it was an inspiration to all good purposes to meet him. I think his influence upon those young men who were most intimate with him and were especially drawn to him was very marked, and appeared in their aims and their work in after years."

TO MRS. A. F. C.

STEAMER OHIO, BUFFALO, *August* 12, 1851.

A. and I are on our way back to Meadville from Niagara Falls, where we have been passing five and a half days. We were at the Clifton House (Canada side), where we had the falls in our eyes all day long, and in our ears all night. What think you of being serenaded for two and a half hours by Jenny Lind, with Niagara for the undersong? On Sunday evening Miss Lind sang German and Italian hymns from eight and a half till eleven, only ceasing while she played on the piano various pleasant airs. Her room was directly below ours, and we heard every note. I am to preach at Brooklyn, N. Y., the last two Sundays in August. Perhaps I shall go to Boston for a visit.

TO A. H. C.

BOSTON, *September* 7, 1851.

To-day has been quite warm. Before breakfast, I went to Braman's Baths, and swam in the river.

I preached for Robbins morning and evening, our own people being invited freely to attend. After evening service we went into the vestry, and had a communion service for the Church of the Disciples. About sixty were present at it. I shook hands in the course of the day with some hundred persons. . . .

September 15, 1851.

How much I wish that you could have been here yesterday. The Church of the Disciples met in the Washingtonian Hall, Bromfield Street. The hall was filled with our own people; all the most near and dear. It was delightful to see them again. Theodore Parker and many of his people were there, and some six or eight colored people, including Lewis Hayden. (Parker, Hayden, Walcutt, Dr. Bowditch, and Prentiss were called out just after the sermon began, to attend to a slave mother and child just arrived in a vessel from Virginia.) After church some thirty or forty came and spoke to me.

I went to the marble manufacturer, Carey's, on Saturday, and selected a little white cross and marble foot-stone for our darling's resting-place. . . . On the cross piece I had the one word "Herman" engraved, and on the foot-stone, "Dear Boy"

W. H. CHANNING TO J. F. C.

Did I ever tell you that the last time I saw your sweet Herman was as he stood, in the sunshine on the doorstep, holding out to me Plato's "divine dialognes"? It was but a few days before his death. Ever since I seem to see him in an open portal where the glory streams all over him, reaching forth the "Phædo," with a light as of the skies in his mild blue eyes, and his lips half parted.

In May, 1852, Mr. Clarke attended a Unitarian Convention at Cincinnati, and during this journey lectured and preached.

Early in June, with Mrs. Clarke and their eldest daughter, he went to New York and Boston. On the 10th of June, he says in his diary " call with Anna and Lilian at the Irving House, and see Kossuth."

On the 13th of June, he preached in Freeman Place Chapel, Boston. On the 16th the entry is, "See Church of Disciples, and discuss the matter of its renewal." And on the following Sunday he again preached in Freeman Place Chapel.

After his return from Boston in 1852, he resumed his work in connection with the church and the theological school at Meadville, and continued it until October 13th, when, in accordance with the advice of Dr. James Jackson and Dr. Samuel Cabot, of Boston, he and Mrs.

Clarke went to Europe, to spend the winter in the south of Italy.

The three children were left at Meadville, with their grandfather and their kind aunt, Miss Huidekoper, so that it was unnecessary for the travelers to carry with them any anxieties on their account. They sailed from New York on the 20th of October, on the Cunard steamer "Asia."

In Europe their route was through Paris, Nice, and Florence, and from Leghorn, by steamer, to Naples. At Florence, on the 30th of December, the entry is, "Spent two evenings with Mr. and Mrs. Robert Browning."

They spent the month of January in Naples and the neighborhood, and in February went by land to Rome, where they arrived on the 13th. They remained in Rome till the 1st of April, when they went by *voiture* to Florence. On the 15th they left Florence, were nearly a month in the north of Italy, crossed the Alps by the St. Gothard Pass, and on the 13th of May, 1853, were at Lucerne. Thence their route was down the Rhine by slow stages, and they arrived in London on the 1st of June. They sailed for Boston on the 25th of June, and on Sunday, the 10th of July, Mr. Clarke preached in Boston, meeting his friends at the Lord's Supper in the forenoon of that day.

The following lines record the impression made upon him by the Mediterranean shore: —

RIVIERA DI PONENTE.

I.

On this lovely western shore, where no tempests rage and roar,
Over olive-bearing mountains, by the deep and violet sea,
There, through each long happy day, winding slowly on our way,
Travelers from across the ocean, toward Italia journeyed we, —
    Each long day, that, richer, fairer,
    Showed the charming Riviera.

II.

There black war-ships doze at anchor, in the bay of Villafranca;
Eagle-like, gray Esa, clinging to its rocky perch, looks down;
And upon the mountain dim, ruined, shattered, stern and grim,
Turbia sees us through the ages, with its austere Roman frown, —
  While we climb, where cooler, rarer
  Breezes sweep the Riviera.

III.

Down the hillside steep and stony, through the old streets of Mentone,
Quiet, half-forgotten city of a drowsy prince and time,
Through the mild Italian midnight, rolls upon the wave the moonlight,
Murmuring in our dreams the cadence of a strange Ligurian rhyme, —
  Rhyme in which each heart is sharer,
  Journeying on the Riviera.

IV.

When the morning air comes purer, creeping up in our vettura,
Eastward gleams a rosy tumult with the rising of the day;
Toward the north, with gradual changes, steal along the mountain ranges
Tender tints of warmer feeling, kissing all their peaks of gray;
  And far south the waters wear a
  Smile along the Riviera.

V.

Helmed with snow, the Alpine giants at invaders look defiance,
Gazing over nearer summits, with a fixed, mysterious stare,
Down along the shaded ocean, on whose edge in tremulous motion
Floats an island, half-transparent, woven out of sea and air; —
  For such visions, shaped of air, are
  Frequent on our Riviera.

VI.

He whose mighty earthquake-tread all Europa shook with dread,
Chief whose infancy was cradled in that old Tyrrhenic isle,
Joins the shades of trampling legions, bringing from remotest regions
Gallic fire and Roman valor, Cimbric daring, Moorish guile,
  Guests from every age to share a
  Portion of this Riviera.

VII.

Here the Afric brain, whose story fills the centuries with its glory,
Moulding Gaul and Carthaginian into one all-conquering band,
With his tuskëd monsters grumbling, 'mid the alien snow-drifts stumbling,
Comes an avalanche of ruin, thundering from that frozen land
        Into vales their sons declare are
        Sunny as our Riviera.

VIII.

Tired of these, the mighty mother sought among her types another
Stamp of blended saint and hero, only seen on earth before
In the luminous aureole shining from a maiden's soul
Through four hundred sluggish years; till again on Nizza's shore
        Comes the hero of Caprera
        Born upon our Riviera.

IX.

Thus forever in our musing comes man's spirit, interfusing
Thought of poet and of hero with the landscape and the sky;
And this shore, no longer lonely, lives the life of romance only; —
Gauls and Moors and northern Sea-kings, all are gliding ghost-like by:
        So with Nature man is sharer
        Even on the Riviera.

On the 28th of July Mr. Clarke was again in Meadville, where he resumed his former duties in connection with the church, preaching regularly until after the first Sunday in October, when he left for Boston.

The tie which bound him and the Church of the Disciples together had not been broken by his absence. During the years of separation he received letters from his church friends, and he wrote letters to them, to be read at their communion services. Through all discouragements, both the people and their pastor had held fast to the hope that in time they might again unite and revive the work which had been so suddenly interrupted.

NICE, PIEDMONT, *December* 4, 1852.

To the Members of the Church of the Disciples, assembled together January 2, 1853.

My dear Friends, Brethren and Sisters, — I write this letter amid green leaves and flowers, roses in full bloom, orange and lemon trees covered with fruit, olive trees with silver leaves like willows in June. You will receive it amid frosts and ice, outward Nature rigid with the stern aspect of a New England winter. But it is the state of the heart which makes summer or winter, and I hope it will be all summer in your hearts.

The orange trees which are growing round us here in all the gardens remind me of what George Herbert says, wishing that he could be like the orange tree, "that busy plant," and never want fruit for his Master. For the orange bears fruit, it is said, all the year, and has on it at the same time blossoms, green fruit and ripe. Happy the man who, with perpetual summer in his heart, can be always bearing fruit and always covered with blossoms; whose life is always in its spring, its summer, and its autumn; who can keep his youthful feelings with his manly strength of action and his mature wisdom. For him alone can the orange tree be the suitable symbol.

But it is the beautiful thing in Christian experience that the highest attainments of saints are felt and understood by the humblest and lowliest Christian as realities, though as realities in their germ; and so, if George Herbert, or Madam Guyon, or St. Theresa, or Dr. Channing utter the noblest aspirations of their souls, the chord of Christian experience vibrates in harmony therewith in every Christian soul. Thus we can all feel that it is no imagination, but something very possible for every one of us to have a perpetual summer in our hearts, and to bear fruit without ceasing for our Master. For this, in fact, God destined us when he called us to be Christians.

But how shall we attain this? The answer I read to-day in the Epistle of Paul to the Romans. The gospel is God's power unto salvation upon all who believe, beginning and ending with faith. We are justified, redeemed, and saved by faith. . . . When Paul wrote, he wrote to Gentile and to Jew. We are Gentiles and Jews still, needing to take to ourselves the same instruction, and to translate into the language of our own day the same warnings and promises. . We too need a power of God unto salvation, a perpetual sweetness in the heart, that we may bear fruit every day to God and to Christ.

It is by faith that this must come. The Christian life is a life of faith throughout, in its origin, progress, and termination; in its root, branch, flower, and fruit. Faith is the open eye with which we see God. . .
It is faith in a Divine goodness, in an infinite fatherly tenderness, in a blessed fullness of salvation, which softens the hard, and melts the frozen, heart. We love God when we see his loveliness; we love Christ when we trust to him as a Saviour; we love man when we have faith in man's capacity for excellence. We can only love ourselves in a true way when we can believe in the destiny God has offered us, and feel the work which he has done in our hearts.

This, my friends, is the best message I can send you from this distant land; I have found nothing better, nothing deeper, than this truth, which grows clearer to me every day and year. Among friends, amid the joys and affections of home, it makes them more rich and dear; away from home, on the other side of the world, it surrounds the soul with a heavenly home. In hours of trial and bereavement, trust in a Divine Providence is our only support, as many of you well know. Looking forward to progress in knowledge, to growth of character, to a fuller activity, what can support hope, so often baffled, but faith? And at the table of the

Master, in our consciousness of unworthiness, it is faith in his love which enables us to draw near and sit at his feet, and feel ourselves his friends.

In thinking of you thus met together at the beginning of a new year, I cannot but ask myself whether I shall be permitted before its end to unite with you again. Shall we be together, as in times past, learners in the school of Jesus? I look forward to it now with more hope than hitherto. Yet this and all other personal interests I desire to leave to that Providence who has wisely directed my way thus far, and only pray that no willfulness of choice on my part may lead me to resist his leading hand.

I am here apart from all communion of worship, but I feel myself more than ever at home in the great universal church of the Lord Jesus. In that church is one Lord, one faith, one baptism. Heresies and schisms are unknown in it. Its creed is a trust in God the Father, and love to man the brother. Its worship is obedience and benevolence, doing good and growing good. From this church no one can excommunicate or exclude us except ourselves.

May God bless and keep you forever. Your brother,   JAMES FREEMAN CLARKE.

CHAPTER XII.

THE CHURCH OF THE DISCIPLES.

ON Mr. Clarke's return to Boston he preached several times in the Young Men's Hall, on Bedford Street, and afterwards in Williams Hall; and after earnest conferences in regard to the renewal of regular church services and activities, it was decided that the Church of the Disciples should be reëstablished on the same basis as at the beginning.

On the 1st of January, 1854, Mr. Clarke began anew the pastorate which ended only with his life.

For most of the thirty-five years of this renewed church activity, Mr. Clarke conducted the religious services on Sunday morning; sometimes also giving Sunday evening courses of lectures. He generally had a large class under his personal guidance in his afternoon Sunday-school. This school collected three or four hundred children, many of them of foreign nationalities, from all parts of Boston. To give to these children a happy Sunday afternoon, that, if they gained no other good, they might at least learn the lesson of love, — this was one of his central hopes for this school. And it was not disappointed.

Some months after his death, a man whom I scarcely knew approached me in a street car, and asked me eagerly if it were true that Dr. Clarke was dead. When I told him it was, he expressed the most serious grief: "If only I could have seen him once again!" But it proved that he had not seen him for twenty years, —

not since he was in the Sunday-school of the Church of the Disciples. I tried to draw from him the secret of his sorrow for this death, and to find what was the central lesson which he had gained from Mr. Clarke. "Oh, if you knew, sir, how good he was to us boys! We had such a good time there! How I wish you could have heard him tell us stories at Christmas! Did you ever hear him tell a story?" There was no memory of any scientific theology. But it was clear that, for that boy at least, Mr. Clarke had wrought the miracle which he once proposed as an aim for one of his teachers: "If your scholars have learned the lesson of love, — why, that is the great lesson of life."

Every Wednesday, again, the church met in its regular social meeting. In the theory of the church, I think he attached even more importance to this meeting than to those of Sunday. That is, he would have said that in our social order the Sunday meetings would take care of themselves, but that this Wednesday meeting was distinctive, and belonged to the very life of the Church of the Disciples. The professional reader may wonder how the interest of such a meeting was preserved. The answer is that it was virtually a club, containing in its membership a large number of sensible and public-spirited men and women, who took in hand here every matter which the life of Boston at the time suggested. If an "outside barbarian" from England or France arrived in Boston, coming to study prisons, or botany, or pauperism, or education, he would be very apt to turn up at the Wednesday evening meeting. If there were a fire at Portland or in St. John, and money or clothing were needed, the matter would be practically discussed in the Wednesday meeting. If Mr. Polk, or Mr. Pierce, or Mr. Buchanan had committed the nation to some new imbecility or infamy, the Wednesday meeting took cognizance of it, in discussion or perhaps in action. The Wednesday evening meeting was not so transcendental but that it could send rifles to Kansas;[1] it was not so practical but that it could discuss free-will and foreknowledge.

In his own description of these meetings, written after they had continued for many years, Mr. Clarke says: —

"All is informal conversation; we have no speech-making, we sit in a circle, and no one rises to speak. The meetings have educated the church to thought and its expression. We do not hear at them any religious commonplaces, but each man or woman says something to the point."

This is perhaps an overstatement, but it shows how good a listener he was. He never heard any commonplaces, because in his cordial sympathy he often made more of what was said to him than another hearer would have done.

The determination to "do something about it," which, from the nature of the case, is inherent in all Unitarian consultations, showed itself of necessity in these meetings. It would be hard to say how many enterprises of public spirit received direct material aid from them.

As to the cordial social life which grew up in the church, the account given by Dr. Holmes, in "The Professor at the Breakfast-Table," may well be copied.

"The Church of the Galileans," as he calls it, "is open to all comers. The stranger who approaches it looks down a quiet street, and sees the plainest of chapels,[2] — a kind of wooden tent, that owes whatever grace it has to its pointed windows and the high sharp roof, traces, both, of that upward movement of ecclesiastical architecture which soared aloft in cathedral-spires, shooting into the sky as the spike of a flowering aloe

---

[1] Mr. Clarke writes to a friend, December 3, 1856: "We collected in our small society, last Sunday, the sum of $606 for a Thanksgiving present to Kansas. Last January we sent $535." No doubt these contributions were for food and clothing.

[2] The society then worshiped in Indiana Place Chapel.

from the cluster of broad, sharp-wedged leaves below. This suggestion of mediæval symbolism, aided by a minute turret in which a hand-bell might have hung and found just room enough to turn over, was all of outward show the small edifice could boast. Within there was very little that pretended to be attractive. A small organ at one side, and a plain pulpit, showed that the building was a church, but it was a church reduced to its simplest expression.

"Here, too, Iris found an atmosphere of peace and love. The same gentle, thoughtful faces, the same cheerful, reverent spirit, the same quiet, the same life of active benevolence. But in all else how different from the Church of Saint Polycarp! No clerical costume, no ceremonial forms, no carefully trained choir! A liturgy they have, to be sure, which does not scruple to borrow from the time-honored manuals of devotion, but also does not hesitate to change its expressions to its own liking.

"Perhaps the good people seem a little easy with each other; — they are apt to nod familiarly, and have even been known to whisper before the minister came in. But it is a relief to get rid of that old Sunday — no — *Sabbath* face, which suggests that the first day of the week is commemorative of some most mournful event. The truth is, these brethren and sisters meet very much as a family does for its devotions, not putting off their humanity in the least, considering it, on the whole, quite a delightful matter to come together for prayer and song and good counsel from kind and wise lips. And if they are freer in their demeanor than some very precise congregations, they have not the air of a worldly set of people. Clearly, they have *not* come to advertise their tailors and milliners, nor for the sake of exchanging criticisms on the literary character of the sermon they may hear. There is no restlessness and no restraint among these quiet, cheerful worshipers."

Mr. Clarke and his society did not regard "membership of the church" and "partaking of the elements in the communion service" as interchangeable terms. His own language is, " Our church is not a body of 'professors,' but of students. We do not unite together as communicants to partake of the Lord's Supper, for we see no natural connection between the two acts. We keep them distinct. We should no more say, 'Members of churches in regular standing are invited to partake of the Lord's Supper,' than we should say, 'Members of churches in regular standing are invited to sing the forty-fourth hymn.'"

The evident danger of such parish life as has been described, if your man has anything small about him, is that he will become the flesh-and-blood idol of a little coterie calling itself a church. There is danger that this "church," instead of worshiping God, will fall back on the worship of itself and its minister. I do not know whether Mr. Clarke ever considered this danger, but it is clear enough that he was armed against it. He insisted first, as indeed the Unitarian principle requires, that his church should not occupy itself so much with the salvation of its own members as with the salvation of the world. He was quite as much a missionary in Boston as he had been at Louisville, and his church was a missionary church from the beginning. It sent its own protest to Congress against the Mexican War. It published its own tracts against the annexation of Texas. When John Brown was arrested at Harper's Ferry, John Albion Andrew, afterwards "War Governor" of Massachusetts, came to a church meeting, and proposed a contribution to pay the expenses of his defense. And accordingly several hundred dollars were collected at once in that church, and used for this purpose.

Mr. Clarke himself had an eye upon every interest, and could not be shut up in the details of parochial life.

His sermons and all he printed gained a constantly widening circle of readers, and his correspondence with people who owed to him their emancipation from the chains of dogmatic or of sacramental religion soon made large demands upon his already fully occupied time. From the period of his settlement in Boston, the old personal letters, covering long folio pages of paper, and written to his early friends, grew shorter and shorter, while in their place he was writing instruction, encouragement, or words of inspiration to people whom he had never seen. In another chapter we will try to show how close was his connection with the anti-slavery movement, of which he afterward wrote the narrative for the "Memorial History of Boston." He had no scruple about connecting anti-slavery with politics, and worked in every capacity with the men whose views eventually took form in the action of the Free-Soil party.

But it was with his pen, and as an editor, that he touched the world at the greatest number of points. From the year 1842 he had been a frequent contributor to the "Christian Examiner," and there is hardly a volume without an article by him from that time until it was absorbed in "Old and New," to which journal also he contributed regularly.

Not long after his return to Boston the question of a permanent home had to be considered. "I must be on my anchorage before I can work to advantage," he said. He had a dream, common to many others of a like social temperament, that by combining with a group of friends who should live near each other in the country, each family having a home of its own, but with rooms in common for conversation, music, lectures, library, etc., the advantages of city and country life might be obtained. It happened that in the spring of 1855 Brook Farm was offered for sale. This place, nine miles from Boston, had become somewhat celebrated as the spot where, from 1841 to 1847, a company of intelligent, educated men and women, with George Ripley as leader, had endeavored to carry on a community on socialistic principles. Financially the plan was unsuccessful, and in 1847 the organization was disbanded.

This was the place which Mr. Clarke bought, thinking it adapted to his plan of a neighborhood. But it was too far from the station on the railroad, and too distant from the city, to suit the business friends who formed part of the group with whom he had hoped to be associated. Indeed, it may as well be admitted here that his marked characteristic of hopefulness was rather apt to prevent him from foreseeing difficulties in regard to the business details of life. He held the property, however, for a number of years.

The plan of living on Brook Farm having been abandoned, early in September, 1855, he bought a lot on Woodside Avenue, Jamaica Plain, belonging to his friend and parishioner, George Wm. Bond, whose own home was only two or three minutes distant. A house was in process of building on the place, and this was so far completed that Mr. Clarke moved into it before the end of November. In this home he passed the remainder of this life.

In the spring of 1856, he busied himself in planting trees, making flower-beds, and setting out the smaller fruits. In 1857, he writes that his soulange magnolia is in blossom, and that his dielytra has a hundred flowers on it. The number of trees he contrived to put into a house-lot of one and a half acres was surprising, and soon the place became like a young forest. The nest of the oriole swung from the branch of a large elm, the scarlet tanager flitted in and out of the white pine, the robins built on the pillars of the southern piazza, and the squirrels in their frolics easily leaped from tree to tree all over the place. As the trees grew, the flowers and fruits requiring sunshine gradually disappeared. In the course of time it became necessary to sacrifice a number of the trees for the good of the rest and for the welfare of the house. It was long before Mr. Clarke could accept this measure, but finally he gave his consent, and went away for a few days that he might not hear the woodman's axe striking at the lives which he had fostered with so much pleasure. As the years went on, the sacrifice had to be repeated, and though Mr. Clarke's consent came late and reluctantly, he was always magnanimous enough to say afterwards that what had been done was an improvement. In the autumn of 1887, a number of large trees were taken down. Repeatedly during that winter he spoke with pleasure of the larger extent of sky which had been revealed, and of the better opportunity to see the beauty of the sunsets. The last time he walked across his room he lay for an hour in a reclining chair, looking out on the trees which he had seen grow up, and which he had loved so well.

After the reëstablishment of the Church of the Disciples there was no farther break or pause in its life. Remembering the amount of work which Mr. Clarke put into the years that followed, and the youthfulness which he kept to the last, it is amusing to hear him, at the age of forty-nine, asking whether it were his duty to feel old.

TO T. W. HIGGINSON.

JAMAICA PLAIN, *April* 4, 1859.

Believe me, it was no feeling of coolness which was expressed in my last note, but merely haste. I wrote a hurried line, merely to learn if the other letter had been received.

I believe there is one good thing in my disposition, or in my character, which is that I do not judge people by their actions; but, as I once said in some lines, I "judge actions by their people." I am never in a hurry to impute any fault to people whom I have known. I may not understand their conduct, but I assume that there is something which, if I knew it, would make me understand it in accordance with what I know of them.

This is my birthday, and I am forty-nine. Is it a duty to feel old when one is forty-nine? I value age, for it brings with it many good things; but I cannot feel old. How young are Thought, Devotion, Love! I am as full of hope as I was thirty years ago, when I graduated at Cambridge, looking forward to life expectant, full of plans still. I am always expecting to preach better, always hoping to write some book, or to learn some new subject out and out.

Age brings us many good things, — among the rest, troops of friends. A person ought to make four or five new friendships every year, become acquainted with ten or twenty good new people, and so by the time one is fifty he can hardly help having a multitude about him whom he likes. He has also seen the world moving on; he has seen some who were wild becoming tame, — some crabbed, sour fruit mellowing and sweetening.

However, I did not sit down to write you a treatise "De Senectute," but to acknowledge the receipt of your note, and to say that to-day, of all days in the year, I did not like to be thought "cool" by a friend.

The next year brought his fiftieth birthday, and his parishioners held a reception in the vestry of the Indiana Place Chapel, to which were invited not only past and present members of the church, but also others who had shown an interest in its life. Among the records of this occasion is an address by John A. Andrew, who had become a member of the church a few months after its organization. From this address we take a few sentences: —

"I have been asked to attempt the expression of that

which is, in truth, inexpressible, — the affectionate respect of this congregation of Disciples of Christianity towards him who, as our pastor and as the guest of this festivity, is the central figure of our group. . . . I confess, for myself, that I do not know how I could overestimate the influence of this Home of the Soul on the happiness and welfare of my life. Amid all distractions, and griefs, and bewilderments, I have seen the vision of this temple, and heard its calm voice and hopeful wisdom, encouraging, winning, teaching, and strengthening the love of the best goodness and the highest truth. . . .

"Twenty years of earnest, active, most devoted, and various labor here, as a preacher, pastor, writer, and citizen, have identified James Freeman Clarke not only with this single organization, but also with the ideas, progress, history, and character of liberal Christianity; and when I heard him, just now, regret the past, passing severe judgment upon himself, as if he "had not attained," underestimating what is a part of history, — in view of the loftiness of his ideal, — I wished that I could but make him feel how priceless is the good my own heart confesses that it owes to him, and how many there are who would join with me in the confession. Indeed, this human life is all too short to allow the indulgence of vain regrets. .

"Nor would I forget the ample satisfactions which accompany the mind, as it travels over the broader field, cultivated by one of a catholic spirit and no pent-up sympathies. We all know how closely allied in labor, as in spirit, our pastor has been with the grand movements which have signalized the history of the last quarter of a century. How thankful it makes the heart to find its human lot cast in such an age, such an age of freedom of thought and action, such an age of hopefulness. I will not stay to lament over its follies, its failures, or its reverses. I see in them all only the limitations of *men;* while through them all I also see 'the steady gain of *man.*'

"I desire to render due thanks and due honor to him who has guided and helped our thought and our activity, that, in all the vicissitudes of twenty years, against all temptations, and under all allurements of temporizing policy, he has kept this pulpit free, this church free, its creed as comprehensive as the formulary of the first Apostles, its spirit of brotherhood as expansive as the charity of the Christian faith. Nor had this been possible, save to a man who saw too wide a field, too great a harvest, a world too broad, and a humanity too precious, either for delays, for jealousies, or for strifes; too much to be done, too many ways for doing good, too little difference in the values of methods, to permit the waste of strength and time in questioning the diversity of the manifestation of the same spirit."

The Church of the Disciples outgrew the Indiana Place Chapel, and early in 1868 they took measures to provide themselves with a building better adapted to their needs. Land was bought on Brookline Street, corner of Warren Avenue, and the corner-stone of a new edifice was laid on the 8th of July in the same year. The building, being simple in design, was soon completed, and it was dedicated, February 28, 1869, on the twenty-eighth anniversary of the first religious meeting held after the formation of the church.

TO HIS SISTER.

JAMAICA PLAIN, *March* 14, 1869.

. Yes, we are in our new church. It is all we want. The auditorium is large, cheerful, perfectly easy to speak in, a pleasant room to look at. The rooms below are large, comfortable, convenient, and ample for all our uses. We have had no quarrels, we have no debt, we have all the seats free, every one is pleased and happy. . . . It seems miraculous to us; I cannot quite understand it. I never did so much work in the same time. But I am doing too much, and I shall have to resign my professorship at Harvard, I think, as well as my place on the Massachusetts Board of Education.

CHAPTER XIII.

ANTI-SLAVERY.

At our earnest request, Dr. Clarke's classmate and friend, Rev. Samuel May, of Leicester, has prepared this valuable narrative of his work in the anti-slavery movement, which culminated in the emancipation of the slaves of America. From the nature of the case, Mr. May has been compelled to condense severely the material in hand; for there was no work of Mr. Clarke's life in which he was more interested than this. E. E. H.

It was to a slaveholding State that James Freeman Clarke's steps were directed, when, his term of study at the Cambridge Divinity School being closed, he sought a field of work, with a high purpose of self-consecration. The Unitarian church at Louisville needed a minister, called him, and he went there early in August, 1833. He was earnest to make no delay in preaching the higher form and better views of Christianity which he had learned from his spiritual father, Dr. James Freeman; and to which, by the guiding of Dr. Channing, the Wares, and other witnesses to the truth, and by his own maturer studies, he had come to devote himself with all the strength of a nature as deep and brave as it was calm and self-possessed. Probably the matter of slavery had nothing to do with his decision to go to Kentucky; and it is not likely that he had given much attention to it until he went there. During the whole time of his study at the Cambridge Divinity School, a society of the students had existed for the purpose of considering questions of practical benevolent action. The prisons and jails were thus considered; the temperance cause; the cause of seamen; peace and war, and so forth. In this way there came in review before the students all the various topics and movements which were then engaging the attention of philanthropists and the churches. These the students discussed in the presence and with the aid of the professors, or listened to invited speakers who, from official position or special study, could best present them. But it is not remembered that the subject of slavery in the United States came before this "Philanthropic Society" in any way whatever, as a wrong to be righted, as a sin to be repented of and put away, or as a great national peril, and therefore a subject for a Christian minister's study and action. Perhaps no greater proof of the deadness of the public conscience concerning slavery could be adduced than this, that in the theological school of the freest and most advanced denomination in New England, where thoughtful and humane men like the Wares, Follen, and Palfrey had office and influence, men who subsequently, in different degrees and ways, became strong and outspoken opponents of slavery, three years of study and preparation for active ministerial duty could be passed, from 1830 to 1833, with no special recognition of that great wrong.

Mr. Clarke himself says, "I was a citizen of the State of Kentucky from 1833 to 1840. Slavery existed there, it is true, in a comparatively mild form. But its evils were such that I learned to look on it with unmixed aversion. I learned my anti-slavery lessons from slavery itself, and from the slaveholders around me."[1]

And what was American slavery? may be asked by readers who have come upon the stage since slavery ceased to exist. The answer must be sought elsewhere; and there can be no difficulty in finding it. Mr. Clarke himself has named a book to which he was indebted for full and particular knowledge of the practical character

[1] *Anti-Slavery Days*, by James Freeman Clarke, p. 22. New York, 1884.

and working of slavery in the United States. It was entitled "American Slavery as it is; Testimony of a Thousand Witnesses," a compilation made by Theodore D. Weld, and issued by the American Anti-Slavery Society. Similar in character to it, but of twenty years later date, is the "Key to 'Uncle Tom's Cabin,'" compiled by Mrs. Harriet Beecher Stowe, the author of that well-known book.

From the earliest introduction of kidnapped Africans to America, where they were sold as slaves to the highest bidder, condemnation of their enslavement, protest against it, and prophecy of evil consequences from it, had not been wanting. John Wesley, founder of the Methodist Church, — who had been in Georgia in early life, and who had kept up his knowledge of affairs in America, — just before his death, in 1791, besought Mr. Wilberforce to persevere in his labors for the abolition of the slave-trade, "till even American slavery, the vilest that ever saw the sun, shall vanish away." Thomas Jefferson, slaveholder as he was, declared slavery to be full of evil and peril to the country. "I tremble for my country," he said, "when I reflect that God is just, and that his justice cannot sleep forever." And he said that, in a contest between the enslaved and their oppressors, not improbable, in his judgment, "the Almighty has no attribute which can take side with us in such a contest."[1] A confession of judgment perhaps unparalleled, and sufficiently decisive of his belief that slavery was evil, evil only, and that continually.

Nevertheless, heedless of the example of Washington, who had given freedom to his slaves by will, heedless of the warnings of Jefferson and of others whom they professed to honor, the Southern States chose slavery, and sought to make it perpetual. What if it defied God and debased man, trampled on the Declaration of Independence, and made their country a by-word and

[1] *Notes on the State of Virginia*, 8th edition, 1801, p. 240.

reproach? It was gainful, and that answered every objection. So they demanded what Daniel Webster afterwards called "solemn guarantees" for slavery in the new constitution of the republic, and obtained them; demanded and obtained that the African slave trade should go on unmolested for twenty years. The evil spirit encroached more as it gained more. It found that it could silence Northern men by threats to dissolve the Union; that it could even command their service, through fear of losing profitable trade. It was as early as 1835 that Governor McDuffie, of South Carolina, declared that "domestic slavery, instead of being a political evil, was the corner-stone of our republican edifice." The sentiment, in a thousand forms, was echoed from all the Southern States, and more than a generation passed before the dull North understood its meaning. "It is all a hallucination," said a leading journal of Virginia, "to suppose we are ever going to get rid of African slavery, or that it will ever be desirable to do so. . . . The negro is here, and here forever, is our property forever, is never to be emancipated, is to be kept hard at work and in rigid subjection all his days."[1] We recall these passages now, that present readers may see with what perverted ideas and seared consciences the anti-slavery men of Mr. Clarke's day, in every part of the country, had to contend.

What must have been the effect upon the generation coming upon the stage when such ideas prevailed, and when the acceptance of them in American thought and life was a part of education; when opposition to slavery, especially in the laws, was denounced as unpatriotic and treasonable, and made a crime subjecting the offender to a felon's penalties? What, we ask, would be the moral standard of the young when required by law and custom to bring their natural conceptions of right and justice to the level of positive inhumanity?

[1] *Richmond Examiner*, October, 1854.

Not long after Mr. Clarke arrived at Louisville he saw one Sunday, in church, a rather striking-looking man, listening attentively, and holding in his hand, which hung over the pew, a riding-whip. This was Judge Speed, whose farm was several miles from the city, and who had ridden to church on horseback. Mr. Clarke soon formed the acquaintance of Mr. and Mrs. Speed and of their sons and daughters; and when he visited them he found a circle intelligent and refined and of the greatest hospitality. Judge Speed held slaves. On one occasion Mr. Clarke took a young friend from Boston to call upon some of his friends near Louisville. The first visit was to the plantation of the Marshall family, holding slaves. Mrs. Marshall was a sister of James G. Birney, afterwards well known as the candidate of the political anti-slavery party for President. "My Boston friend," says Mr. Clarke, "believed that abolition was fanaticism; and he said to Mrs. Marshall that he thought the Northern people who attacked slavery were very much mistaken. Mrs. Marshall replied, 'It will not do, sir, to defend slavery in this family. The Marshalls and the Birneys have always been abolitionists.' The Boston gentleman was greatly surprised to hear such an avowal. We next drove to the house of my dear old friend, Judge Speed, who took us about his plantation, and showed us the negro cabins, having in them various comforts and ornaments. My companion said, 'Judge, I do not see but the slaves are as happy as our laboring classes at the North.' 'Well,' answered the Judge, 'I do the best I can to make my slaves comfortable, but I tell you, sir, you cannot make a slave *happy*, do what you will. God Almighty never made a man to be a slave, and he cannot be happy while he is a slave.' 'But,' continued the Boston visitor, 'what can be done about it, sir? They could not take care of themselves, if set free.' 'I think I could show you three men on my plantation,' replied Judge Speed, 'who might go to the Kentucky legislature. I am inclined to believe they would be as good legislators as the average men there now.'"[1] It is evident that Mr. Clarke's first acquaintance with slaveholders was an exceptionally favorable one.

In the volume of Mr. Clarke's, entitled "Anti-Slavery Days," from which the above passages are taken, the open manner in which slavery was at that date discussed in Kentucky, in public as well as in private, is quite fully described, and instances of such discussions are given. In them Mr. Clarke was not silent. He took part in a public debate in Louisville, lasting three nights, which ended with a majority against slavery. And in the Louisville "Journal," then edited by George D. Prentice, he wrote in opposition to slavery. But his chief field and opportunity for making his sentiments known, not in Louisville only, but throughout an extensive Western region, were furnished by his editorial connection with the "Western Messenger," of which we must now give a somewhat particular account.

In April, 1836, Mr. Clarke assumed the editorship of the "Western Messenger," a monthly magazine, of which eight numbers had already been published in Cincinnati. In the first number published in Louisville, he printed copious extracts from Dr. W. E. Channing's work entitled "Slavery," which had just appeared in Boston. These extracts occupied about twelve pages of the "Messenger," and gave Mr. Clarke the opportunity to manifest the attitude which, as an editor of a Christian journal, he felt it his duty to take on the subject

---

[1] At a later day, two sons of Judge Speed carried out the lessons of their home in a way to make them effective in the country's history. Joshua Speed was the intimate friend of Abraham Lincoln, and in daily intercourse with him, for five years of their early life in Springfield, Illinois James Speed, another son, was called by Mr. Lincoln into his Cabinet, in 1864, as Attorney General of the United States, — a man of the highest personal character and of eminent legal ability.

of slavery. Mr. Clarke says, "We heard of this book from all quarters before we saw it; and that an edition of three thousand copies had been sold immediately." He speaks of various criticisms for and against the work, and says, "Now, having read it we pronounce it, in our judgment, the best production of its author. In thought, unanswerable; in expression, clear, concise, and strong; in spirit, not merely religious, but Christian. Springing from the deepest fountain of duty, it flows out in the purest current of love. How many there may be in Massachusetts that would object to such a publication we know not; but this we know, that in Kentucky their number is very small. The people of Kentucky have never been afraid of discussing this subject, or of having it discussed before them. We have heard lectures, we have participated in debates, in which everything was said that could have been spoken in a free State."

After occupying twelve pages with extracts from Dr. Channing, Mr. Clarke adds, "The substance of the book seems to be, Slavery is a wrong and evil; but it does not follow that immediate emancipation is right, or that the slaveholder is a sinner. No good man should sleep over this subject; he should think and pray upon it. But it rests with the slaveholding States, and no others, to point out the time and way in which slavery is to cease. The people of the North have a right to form and express opinions on this subject; but they must do it so as not to endanger the peace and tranquillity of the South, and must never address the slave, but only his master. To all which we say, Amen." In May, Mr. Clarke, in a brief notice, commends the Colonization Society; and in the August number, in answer to a communication, he says, "I consider the system of slavery a monstrous evil, moral, economical, and physical, to remove which from a single State I would willingly devote my life; but the principles of Abolitionists I consider false, and the consequences of their efforts evil to the master and the slave. The false position which all Abolitionists take is this, that if a system or institution is wrong, all who support it are committing sin. . Though the system of slavery is a wrong one, I deny that to hold slaves is always to commit sin. The *system* must be judged by its consequences, the man by his *motives*. If his motive in holding the slave is to perpetuate the system for his own selfish ends, though he sees its general evils, then his act is a sinful act. If his motive is to preserve the peace of the community and the welfare of the slave till the time comes when emancipation is safe and wise, then it is not a sinful act." Then follow arguments against the advisability of immediate emancipation. In closing the article, Mr. Clarke protests that he is not to be suspected of having acquired a love of slavery by residence in a slave State. He says, " Acquaintance with slavery has only increased my disgust and horror at the misery flowing from it."

In proof that liberty of speech prevailed in Kentucky Mr. Clarke cites the case of Mr. Birney, who had preached and lectured all through the State against slavery, showing it to be politically bad, economically injurious, morally wrong, and socially dangerous. But when Mr. Birney proposed to set up an Abolition paper in the town of Danville, the opposition was so strong that he left Kentucky, to publish his paper in Cincinnati. Mr. Clarke thinks it was a mistake in him to throw away the vantage ground which he possessed as a native Kentuckian, and to go elsewhere "to write and print an Abolition newspaper. He descended [in so doing] to a level which any Garrison could occupy as well as he." But freedom of thought and speech was necessary to Mr. Birney, and we cannot call that free speech, in this case, which did not include the right to print and publish his thoughts. Mr. Birney was under the necessity of establishing himself elsewhere in order to discharge his conscience in the matter of slavery; and so his course was not to be considered a descent, but the reverse, as it proved his high purpose, while it showed that in some parts of Kentucky, at least, a free press was impossible.

In after years Mr. Clarke learned to think otherwise of Mr. Garrison, and to coöperate with him to a considerable extent; and, when slavery fell, to join by word and deed in the public recognition of those great services of Mr. Garrison's life which made the nation forever his debtor. In "Anti-Slavery Days" (p. 22), Mr. Clarke says, speaking of those early years in Kentucky, "At that time I knew nothing of Mr. Garrison or his movement, and supposed, as others did, that he was merely a violent fanatic. After I returned to Boston in 1841, I had the advantage of knowing him and his fellow-laborers, and seeing something of their grand and noble work."

In the "Messenger" of December, 1836, Mr. Clarke printed in full the stirring lines of Whittier, on the passage of Pinckney's "Resolutions" and of Calhoun's "Bill of Abominations," beginning

> "Now by our fathers' ashes! — where 's the spirit
> Of the true-hearted and the unshackled gone?
> Sons of old freemen, do we but inherit
> Their *names* alone!"[1]

In the "Messenger" of February, 1837, Mr. Clarke says, "We have have read Dr. Channing's letter to Mr. Birney with great pleasure. It is a noble vindication of the outraged rights of free discussion." He again has a friendly word for the Colonization Society, but is "not surprised that the negroes are so suspicious of this society as to believe that those who embark for Liberia are never carried there, but are sold as slaves. The African has received too much wrong from the white

[1] In the later editions of Mr. Whittier's poems, these lines begin thus: "Men of the Northland," etc.

man to make us wonder at such suspicions." In the December issue, Mr. Clarke reviews a book called "The Bible against Slavery," in which he takes occasion to speak of "Abolitionists of the ultra sort, whose object is not to convince, but to bear down by a storm of popular feeling." Perhaps, as an individual judgment, this is as harsh as any of those by Abolitionists which Mr. Clarke censures. Abolitionists in those days were the victims of such storms, as witness Mr. Clarke's repeated rebukes of mob violence, and they had little power, even had they the disposition, to excite such storms against others. In a later number Mr. Clarke quotes approvingly Dr. Channing's words: "No communities can withstand just, enlightened, earnest opinion; and this power must be brought to bear on slavery more zealously than ever."

The destruction by a mob of the printing press of Rev. Elijah P. Lovejoy, of Alton, Ill., and the death of Mr. Lovejoy at the hands of the mob, brought from Mr. Clarke the following outburst: "We must add our voice to the sound of rebuke which has been uttered by the press almost unanimously from North and South, from East and West. One or two persons have attempted to divert the public attention from this terrible outrage to the imprudence of Mr. Lovejoy. . . . A man whose mind at such a time can dwell for a moment on Lovejoy's imprudence or mistakes, on the folly of Abolitionism, or the mischief which Abolitionists are doing, shows either that he has a very imperfect idea of the transaction, or a very imperfect notion of right and wrong. Abolitionism is not now the question. The question is of American freedom, of liberty of thought and speech, of the freedom of the press, of which Hume's famous maxim declares that 'the liberty of the people must stand or fall with it.'"

In the "Messenger" for February, 1838, Mr. Clarke re-affirms his belief that immediate emancipation would be wrong; that some kind of education and preparation should precede emancipation.

Some of his Alton subscribers had withdrawn their subscriptions, and the editor thus addresses them: "Are you wise in discontinuing on account of our notice of Mr. Lovejoy's murder? We think not. What you ought to pray for just now is, that every editor, far and wide, shall speak out his abhorrence of this deed in tones which shall rebuke the spirit of mob-ism in your borders. You have silenced your own press, and you are actually under the rule of a mob. Opinion governs everything, and the opinion of your city is in favor of mob law. . . . We know that you have good men and true amongst you, but be assured it is a mistaken patriotism which would now refuse to listen to tones of rebuke."

The "Messenger" for May, 1839, contains extracts from the letter of Dr. Channing to Jonathan Phillips, of which the chief topic was a recent speech of Mr. Clay, of Kentucky. Mr. Clarke says: "We do our readers the best service in our power by presenting them with these extracts. Many of our Southern and Western friends may have no other opportunity of becoming acquainted with the views of one who speaks upon the great subject of interest before the American people with equal sympathy and candor. May the day soon come for that frank and friendly interchange of thought which all, as Christians and brethren, must desire."

After October, 1839, the "Messenger" was edited by Rev. William H. Channing; but in the August number of 1840, Mr. Clarke writes of the case of Rev. George F. Simmons, compelled to leave Mobile on account of his sermons against slavery. He states the facts, which are honorable to Mr. Simmons, but gives reasons "which induce us to believe that a Christian minister, in a slaveholding State, ought not, under present circumstances, to preach on the subject of slaveholding." He says the "subject of slavery cannot be handled in any way in the South without producing instant and violent excitement;" for "the public mind is in a diseased and irritable condition."

This abstract of the "Western Messenger's" course in regard to slavery, during the three and a half years of Mr. Clarke's editorship, is given because its evidence, we think, is conclusive of Mr. Clarke's early principle against slavery, his sincere and strong desire that it should cease, and his determination to speak his thought about it carefully, yet plainly. He was in a community where prominent men and families, some of them his personal friends, held and openly expressed anti-slavery sentiments, and in a State extensively believed to be ripe for emancipation, which belief he shared. There was ground for hope of it when men like James G. Birney, Cassius M. Clay, and Robert J. Breckenridge, besides such as have been already named, representing the best intelligence and character of the State, could publicly advocate and practice emancipation, as then and later they did. That this belief was an error in time appeared, as Mr. Clarke sorrowfully acknowledged. "In those days every Kentuckian said that Kentucky would be the first State to emancipate. Alas! it was one of the very last." [1]

Here, as he leaves Kentucky, we may record his own judgment of slavery, which, though expressed at a later day, was evidently the firm conviction of his mind after his seven years' residence in a slave State. "Abolitionists have stated the evils of slavery very strongly, but they never have been overstated. It was a condition of perpetual warfare. Not only were untold cruelties inflicted on the slaves almost as a matter of necessity; but among the whites deeds of violence, duels, street-shootings, death by lynch-law, mob violence in all its forms were common. The young men grew up in the midst of license and self-indulgence of all kinds." He

[1] *Anti-Slavery Days*, p. 26.

testifies to exceptions in the persons of upright, honorable, pure men and women, who felt responsibility for the proper care and comfort of their slaves. "But the system itself," he adds, "was so evil that it made their best efforts almost useless." [1]

It was a noteworthy fact of his life in Louisville that he openly attacked the custom of dueling, then almost unquestioned, and that he preached against it; even men of note and character deeming him singularly warped or blinded in doing so. A friend of his, a judge, said, "He might just as well preach against courage."

Leaving Louisville in June, 1840, he came in the same year to Boston, and gave himself to his long-cherished purpose of forming a Christian society in accordance with his ideas of equal discipleship and co-operation. The hold which the question of slavery had upon him soon appears. In the mass of his manuscripts in these early years are sermons upon such themes as "the national sin of slaveholding;" "the sin of holding in bondage three millions of our brethren;" "slavery in the United States," and that all have a duty to do for its abolition, against Texan annexation, against the Mexican war, and so forth. In a sermon in 1847, when his topic was, "Slavery must be destroyed or it will destroy us," he said: "If I were in the Senate of the United States, I would end every speech as Cato ended his speeches in the Roman Senate; whatever his subject, he always ended by saying, 'And besides, Senators, it is my opinion that Carthage should be destroyed.' So, whether I spoke of tariff or of banks, of manufactures or of commerce, of relations with France or with China, I should think it logical to add, 'And besides, Senators, it is my opinion that slavery should be destroyed.' For what sort of prosperity can we hope to have in any direction, while this deadly foe is attacking our heart and life?"

[1] *Anti-Slavery Days*, p. 21.

In 1844, a letter had been received from British Unitarian ministers, addressed to their American brethren, on the subject of slavery, and a brief reply in acknowledgment had been made. Such had been the growth of anti-slavery opinion that it was widely felt among the Unitarian ministers that they should take some united action on the subject; and at a public meeting, held at the Bulfinch Street vestry in Boston, May 29, 1845, it was resolved to issue a protest against slavery as unchristian and inhuman; that all the ministers should have opportunity to sign it, and that it should then be published and distributed. A committee of eleven ministers — of which Mr. Clarke was one, Rev. Caleb Stetson, of Medford, being the chairman — was chosen to draw up this protest, and Mr. Clarke was requested by the committee to write it. This he did with care, and at some length. It was accepted essentially as it came from his hands. "All who have seen it," said the chairman, "are exceedingly well pleased with it."

The protest bore its "solemn testimony" against slavery, because "We owe it to three millions of slaves, our fellow-men and brethren, to do what we can to undo their burdens by calm and earnest appeals to the reason and consciences of the slaveholders," and because "We owe it to the slaveholders, our fellow-men and brethren, to speak a word of warning concerning the moral evil and inhumanity" of slavery. The fact that the gospel of Christ cannot be fully preached at the South; the fact of Northern complicity in upholding slavery; and the fact that all the principles upon which the Unitarian faith is based are violated by slavery, are especially given as reasons for the protest.

"And we do hereby pledge ourselves," it is said in conclusion, "before God and our brethren, never to be weary of laboring in the cause of human rights and freedom, till slavery be abolished and every slave made free." The protest was signed by one hundred and seventy-three Unitarian ministers.

Soon after coming to Boston he became a frequent writer for "The Christian World," established and edited by Mr. George G. Channing. At a later period, 1847-48, he was himself its editor. From an imperfect file before us it appears that slavery, and subjects connected with it, were frequent topics with him; as also with another correspondent, John A. Andrew, afterwards known as the "great War Governor" of Massachusetts, but at that time a young lawyer in Boston, a personal friend and parishioner of Mr. Clarke. The duty of every Northern man to give his influence for the termination of slavery is set forth in letters, in leading articles, and in sermons. The especial duty of Unitarians to make application of their distinguishing principles to this subject is urged. The paper had much influence in bringing the Unitarian ministers to unite in the protest against slavery already spoken of. Mr. Clarke and Mr. Andrew also wrote often in its columns against the war with Mexico, so obviously a slaveholders' war. A protest against that war went to Congress from the Church of the Disciples, in Boston, of which Mr. Clarke was the minister. It was signed by one hundred and thirty members of that church.

For several years, subsequently, he was the Boston correspondent ("Shawmut") of the New York "Christian Inquirer," edited at different times by Rev. Samuel Osgood and Rev. Henry W. Bellows. We find him writing therein on the Fugitive Slave Law, and the consternation it caused among both escaped slaves and free colored people in the Northern States. He describes one such exodus, of which he was himself a witness, of colored residents of the State of Pennsylvania. Meetings and lectures against that law are reported by him. The indictment of Rev. Theodore Parker for words spoken in Faneuil Hall hostile to that law; the duty of taking one's religious principles into the political contest against slavery; the New England Emigrant Aid

Society's work in saving Kansas from slavery; the Dred Scott case, with the humiliating decision of the United States Supreme Court, and the dissent of Judges McLean and Curtis therefrom, — these, and whatever other phase of the great question might present itself, were treated plainly and fearlessly. In the protracted effort to remove Judge Edward G. Loring from the office of Judge of Probate for Suffolk County in Massachusetts, because of his act, as a United States Commissioner, in giving up Anthony Burns to slavery, — an effort delayed by Governor Gardner's refusal to comply with the request of the Legislature, but afterwards carried into execution by Governor Banks, — Mr. Clarke was greatly interested, contributing to its success by his articles in the "Inquirer."

In October, 1856, he addressed a public letter to his fellow-townsman, J. Thomas Stevenson, reviewing the political course of Daniel Webster as a senator of Massachusetts, and as a member of President Fillmore's Cabinet. Mr. Stevenson was a personal and political friend of Mr. Webster; and it was generally understood that Mr. Webster's support of the Fugitive Slave Law was a thorough surprise and grief to him. The letter appeared in a New York paper, signed "A Citizen of Massachusetts;" but its authorship was not a secret. Mr. Clarke points out, with faithful plainness, the causes of Mr. Webster's change and fall. "We all know," he said, "that he had a majestic intellect and a large soul; but we know equally well that the one was not infallible, nor the other immaculate." Step by step Mr. Webster had subdued the tone of his early condemnation of human slavery, and of whatever and whoever supported it, till at length he is found consenting to, and voting for, that slaveholders' extreme measure, the Fugitive Slave Law; a measure which proved a fatal one to him and all its authors, a load too grievous for the long-divided and dishonored North to endure.

Mr. Clarke was a contributor to the "Christian Examiner" for many years. We can only refer here to the chief instances in which he wrote therein of slavery. There was published in Boston in 1854, "A South Side View of Slavery; or, Three Months at the South in 1854. By Nehemiah Adams, D. D." Dr. Adams was pastor of a Boston church. His motive in visiting the South, and in publishing the book, must be sought in the book itself. It may be referred to, now, as evidence of the kind of work which an educated New England minister of that day was willing to do. Mr. Clarke examines this book ("Christian Examiner," January, 1855) in a very thorough manner. No abstract of his review, within any brief compass, could do it justice. For keen analysis, sound criticism, effective and witty reply, it is a good model. "We have spoken strongly," he says in conclusion, "in censure of this remarkable production, but no more strongly than the case demands. . . . When a Northerner enjoying the blessings of freedom, when a minister of the gospel which was sent to break every yoke and to let the oppressed go free, goes South to find excuses for slavery, and comes home in order to publish them, we think the case demands plain speaking, — that there are no words too strong to use for its condemnation."

In like manner, in the pages of the "Examiner," he reviews two other books, of similar purport; one by Rev. Nathan Lord, D. D., president of Dartmouth College, the other by John H. Hopkins, D. D., bishop of the Episcopal Church in Vermont. Dr. Lord issued, in fact, two pamphlets; the first, anonymously, as a "Northern Presbyter." The American Presbyterian Church, of which he was a member, had taken a decided stand against slavery in 1794; and, in 1818, had declared it to be the duty of Christians to obtain the complete abolition of slavery throughout Christendom, and, if possible, throughout the world. Dr. Lord, however, in 1854, overrides this position of his church, — a position, indeed, which that church itself had long before abandoned.[1] He maintains that slavery is an institution of God, according to natural religion, and that it is a positive institution of revealed religion, an institution which may profitably be extended, and that Christians, instead of opposing slavery, ought to oppose the men who seek to abolish it. He admits abuses, and condemns them; but claims that they are not inherent in it. Mr. Clarke states Dr. Lord's position as not only excusing slavery, but defending, and justifying, and admiring it. "He declares he would own slaves, if necessity or convenience should require it." This position so greatly "out-Heroded Herod," even at a time when the anti-slavery movement had but little countenance, that it unquestionably shocked the general sense of the community. It afforded Mr. Clarke an excellent opportunity for his critical powers, his fund of information, and his clear, controlling sense of justice, in all which qualities he compares most favorably with his Presbyterian opponent. Mr. Clarke says, "In an age of light, Dr. Lord has chosen darkness." "His writings will not strengthen slavery; but they will promote infidelity. When Dr. Lord argues that slavery is a 'positive institution of revealed religion,' no man will believe any more in slavery; but many will disbelieve in revelation. . . We wish no harm to Dartmouth College, but rather good, in desiring that it may be speedily relieved from the injury of having at its head a man of such extreme and bitter fanaticism."[2]

Of Bishop Hopkins's book, which was entitled "The American Citizen," six chapters of which are given to the citizen's duties in connection with slavery, Mr. Clarke treats in the "Examiner" of September, 1857.

[1] *The American Churches the Bulwarks of American Slavery*, by James G. Birney.
[2] *Christian Examiner*, November, 1856.

It was a book of contradictions, representing slavery as a part of the divine plan, sanctioned by the church; and yet something to be got rid of; and this to be effected by sending the slaves to Africa. It was difficult to deal patiently with such a book, but the weary work was done. "We are ready," Mr. Clarke concludes, "for any other bishop, pious South Side traveler, metaphysical president, or other dignitary, who may next enter the lists in defense of our national sin, or raise a cry of exultation over our national shame. We are sorry to read such books, but not sorry to criticise them."

He made the condition of the colored people a special study. His note-books abound in memoranda concerning them, especially such as had ever been slaves. Long lists of names are given, showing occupation, standing and reputation, ownership of property, habits as to temperance, church attendance, number of children in schools. In 1850, a serious illness had obliged Mr. Clarke to give up, for a time, his connection with his church in Boston; and, in the autumn, he went to Meadville, Pennsylvania, for rest and recovery. When partially restored, he became minister of the Meadville society, continuing about two years. During this period he visited Cleveland and Cincinnati, and made an extended inquiry into the character and circumstances of the colored people, recording the facts obtained at much length. He consults at Cincinnati the city records of taxable property; finds that two hundred colored citizens pay taxes on real estate; that one of them has a property of $26,000; another, of $15,000; another, of $10,000; three others have $4,000 each, and so on; that they have six churches ("W. says that all the colored people attend church"); that they have four schools, with four hundred and fifty children in them; that fifty of their older children are sent to advanced schools and colleges, at Oberlin and elsewhere; that they labor under many difficulties in getting employment, even when having unquestioned qualifications; that, in spite of these, they maintain a respectable position and repute. A well-conducted hotel was kept by one; and one, with larger property than those before named, has "the best retail grocery in the city." He gives a list of thirty-six different trades or pursuits in which they are engaged. He made like inquiries concerning the colored people of St. Louis, Baltimore, and Philadelphia; and during all the time of his residence in Boston, and especially after returning there in 1853, he kept himself informed of the resident colored people, and personally acquainted with many of them. In an article in the "Christian Examiner" of September, 1857, he says that he had "taken some pains to examine into the condition of the free negroes in Boston, Philadelphia, Cleveland, Cincinnati, and other places," and gives the results.[1]

When in Washington, in the winter of 1851, Mr. Clarke sought the society of members of Congress and others, prominent as opponents of slavery and of its rule in national affairs. The house of Mr. Gamaliel Bailey, editor of the "National Era," was the usual place of their gathering. "I met there," he says, "Seward, Giddings, Chase, Hale, Julian, Slade, Horace Mann," and others. "These men were unpopular in Congress; were in a small minority; their influence was supposed to amount to little."[2] To these meetings also came "other gentlemen of their way of thinking from different parts of the country." It is not difficult to imagine the interest or the importance of these meetings, their cheering influence on those attending them, and their salutary bearing on the public counsels. "As the wheel of time revolved, these men came to the summit," he says. Even then the questions of the settlement of Kansas and Nebraska were looming up in

[1] See, also, *Anti-Slavery Days*, p. 96.
[2] *Anti-Slavery Days*, p. 62.

the horizon; questions which, of immediate importance in themselves, were destined to have a far more extended effect as touchstones of men and parties; questions in which Mr. Clarke himself was preparing to take a deep interest and active part.

On Whitsunday, June 4, 1854, he preached an emphatic discourse on the rendition of Anthony Burns to slavery, a deed then just done in Boston with the co-operation of the civil and military powers of the city and State. Its publication was called for, and an edition of two thousand copies was printed, followed speedily by two thousand more. In it he said, "I blame to-day the churches and clergy of Boston; for if they had been faithful to their Master, this thing could not have happened. And especially I blame the Unitarian churches, for they have had the especial and rare fortune of having their greatest and best teacher on the side of justice and humanity, and they have fallen away from his teaching and his example. Dr. Channing's writings read to-day as history, not prophecy. He announced beforehand, in his clear mind, all that has since come upon us. And yet out of the Unitarian churches of Boston have come those who have done the most in this community to lower its moral sense on this subject. The man who voted for the [Fugitive Slave] law at Washington, and many of those who defended and have enforced it at home, were members of our Unitarian churches." "True," he said, "we have also been represented at Washington by a John Quincy Adams, a John G. Palfrey, a Horace Mann, and a Charles Sumner." He remembers that it is Whitsunday. "Last Friday, Christ was crucified again in the form of the poor negro slave. This morning I feel in my heart that he has arisen from the grave, and that his spirit is poured out on many a mind and heart," for the servants of Christ, he said, will everywhere be "speaking with new tongues, as the spirit gives them utterance."

He attended on the 1st of August, 1857, at Abington, Mass., the celebration of the anniversary of emancipation in the British West Indies, and "addressed the meeting," said the "National Anti-Slavery Standard," "in a speech characterized by ability of reasoning and happy illustration, which we give nearly in full." Only a few extracts can be given here. After alluding to the scarcity of holidays in this country, he proceeded: "But the people of New England have found another holiday; and they have found it on this day, on which we meet to celebrate — what? To celebrate what never happened in the world before the 1st of August, 1834, namely, the acknowledgment of the fact, by a nation, that it was bound by the great laws of right and wrong just as much as individuals are bound by them. That is what we celebrate to-day, and that is worth celebrating. . . . We can learn from that act this: that it is a safe thing to emancipate the slaves of the United States. You know that the constant outcry has been that those who wish to have the slaves emancipated are wishing to have the throats cut of the masters, their wives, and their children; and you know, too, that when these 800,000 West India slaves became free men there was not a single throat cut, nor the least act of violence committed, throughout the whole of the British possessions. You know this very well, because we have read, over and over again, descriptions of the beautiful solemnity of the peaceful and happy thanksgivings with which these slaves, turned into freemen, welcomed the great boon of liberty." He spoke of the plain practical lessons which that grand act of emancipation had for the United States, and said, "I make two parties in this country, and only two. I do not call them slaveholders and non-slaveholders, because I know that among the slaveholders are some of the most generous and noble souls in the world. I have lived among them; I have known them; I know there were men among

them, — and I suppose there are still, — who, while technically and nominally slaveholders, were yet, in the whole influence of heart and life, anything but slaveholders. . The two parties which I should make are, those who are *doing something* against slavery, and those who are *not doing anything* against slavery. . . . I believe the great influence that is to overthrow slavery is Christ and his church. I believe that Christ is present where any two or three meet together to do any act of righteousness, any act of generosity, any act of humanity. I find my church, whether it is called a church or not, wherever I find men with whom I can work in the cause of God on earth, which is the cause of man. That is my church as long as I live.
There Christ dwells, my master, my friend, the friend of humanity and of human rights. I believe he is here. . . . So, friends, I say go forward! If you think the dissolution of the Union is the thing to strive for, strive for that. If you think that in any other way you can best labor for the cause of the slave, I will not hinder you, I will help you as well as I can, and, by the blessing of God, the day will certainly come when we ourselves, or our children, or our children's children, shall meet in this beautiful grove, hearing the sweet song of these pines over our heads, to celebrate the day, not of West India emancipation, but of the emancipation of the slaves in the United States of America."

The "Boston Courier," no longer edited by the Hon. Joseph T. Buckingham, censured Mr. Clarke for attending this meeting of the Massachusetts Anti-Slavery Society, and giving countenance to the disunion Abolitionists. He sent a letter to that paper stating, as he had done at the meeting itself, the points in which he differed from the Anti-Slavery Society; and also the points, which he deemed of far more practical importance, of essential agreement; and showing the real danger to be in the policy of concession to the demands of the slave power.

Besides sermons in 1855, urging the present need of anti-slavery work; and, in 1856, on "Clerical Defenses of Slavery" by "prophets who prophesy falsely;" on "The Demoralization of the North by Slavery;" and on the duty of anti-slavery voting, we note a published sermon of November 6, 1859, on the "Causes and Consequences of the Affair at Harper's Ferry," in which he said: "You may call John Brown's act madness, but it is the madness of Curtius leaping into the gulf which yawned in the Forum; the madness of Arnold of Winkelried gathering into his bosom the deadly sheaf of spears; the madness of the Three Hundred who went to die at Thermopylæ. It is a kind of insanity of which a few specimens are scattered along the course of the human race, and wherever they are found they make the glory of human nature, and give us more faith in God and man."

Mr. Clarke had formed a high estimate of the integrity, sincerity, and moral heroism of John Brown, a feeling which he kept to the end of his life; while he could not fully approve his violent or warlike acts. His position can be fully apprehended only by reading the whole of this masterly discourse. Had such been the tone of the American pulpit generally, during the long agitation of the question of slavery, the nation would have been saved from many a harm, and very probably from the war itself. A brief abstract of the sermon is all that is here possible. His text was, "Herod feared John, knowing that he was a just man." He says that John Brown's "whole course has been so convincingly conscientious, manly, truthful, and heroic, that his enemies have been compelled to honor him   North and South seem united in one opinion and one sentiment" about him, namely, that "his attempt was unwise and unwarranted;" that "the man himself" was to be regarded "a hero."[1]

---

[1] Governor Andrew had publicly said, "Men may say what they please of John Brown's methods. — *John Brown himself was right.*"

"An attempt has been made," he said, "to ascribe this event to the teaching of the Anti-Slavery party in this country. Well, they are the cause of it, in one sense, just as Samuel Adams and Josiah Quincy, James Otis and Patrick Henry were the cause of the bloodshed at Lexington and Bunker Hill. . . . Whoever opposes tyranny and wrong with words will often cause a conflict of deeds to follow. But where rests the responsibility? Not on those who oppose evil, but on those who maintain and defend it. Therefore, not on anti-slavery teaching, but on pro-slavery teaching, North and South, . . . rests the responsibility of this tragedy."

The real "causes of this sad affair" are, (1) "slavery itself, especially the newly developed purpose of three hundred thousand slaveholders to force support of slavery upon the nation;" (2) "the false conservatism of the North, . . laboring steadily to let down the sentiment of freedom, . . . and so giving moral aid and comfort to the slave power;" (3) "the low condition of the religion of the country. In such a conflict as that between slavery and freedom, Christianity organized in churches, embodied in Christian men and women, should have come forward, to speak the truth in love. . . . Unfortunately, little of this has been done. . . . We have been taught from a thousand pulpits that man's lower law must be obeyed, and not the law of conscience. On the other hand, when the truth has been uttered, it has not been always uttered in love to the slaveholder, but often in bitterness. . . . In saying this, I do not refer to professed Abolitionists alone. . John Brown is an Old Testament Christian, . such a man as Calvinism produced in the Scotch Covenanters, and in Cromwell's Ironside regiment, . . . with a touch of chivalric devotion and inspired enthusiasm such as nerved the arm of the Maid of Orleans. . . . One consequence of the event will be the arousing of the nation's conscience. . . . The Herod of slavery fears John Brown, in prison or in tomb, knowing him to be a just man."

Stirring times were at hand. The nation had become far more extensively aroused to the magnitude of the issues involved in the question of slavery than the political leaders were willing to believe. The nomination of Abraham Lincoln had been made in the determination that Southern aggression should at least go no farther; and thoughtful people hoped confidently, and believed generally, that that would be but the beginning of the end. On the eve of the election, Sunday, November 4, 1860, Mr. Clarke gave an address in his church, "crowded largely with voters," on the great issues involved, and urged support of Mr. Lincoln. A few days later it was known that Mr. Lincoln had been elected President by a large majority over the party of slavery, so long in the ascendant. Then came days of intense excitement on the part of the South, as it saw the sceptre departing from its hands; days of almost equal excitement at the North, through apprehension of what the South would do; and of readiness, on the part of some prominent Northern leaders, to make the greatest concessions to avert the peril. In a sermon, whose date is not given, but evidently preached at this time, when meetings "to save the Union" were called and held on all sides, Mr. Clarke said: "The object of these union meetings seems to be, not to denounce the spirit of disunion at the South, but the spirit of freedom at the North. Those who conduct and address them propose, apparently, to pacify the Southern slaveholders, by persuading or compelling Northern citizens to put a stop to all discussion of the subject of slavery.

The great danger to the stability and perpetuity of the Union is in the growth of slavery. . . . Slavery is the destructive element in our institutions; and genuine conservatism ought to oppose it always. . . . Slavery is necessarily aggressive. It is conscious that it can only live by extending itself, and therefore it always aims at new conquests. . These qualities of slavery have caused, in succession, nullification in South Carolina; the cruel and faithless robbery of the Indian lands in Georgia; the expense and misery of the Florida war; the iniquitous annexation of Texas; and the still more iniquitous war with Mexico. The founders of our Constitution were all agreed that slavery was soon to come to an end; but, instead of that, it has been steadily extending itself, and is now the controlling element in the policy of the country."

The annual meeting of the Massachusetts Anti-Slavery Society, in January, 1861, occurring at the moment when the political managers were holding these Union meetings, could not be overlooked by them, and they determined to break it up. Accordingly the galleries of Tremont Temple, in Boston, were crowded with lawless and ruffianly men, evidently instructed to act in concert at signals from their leaders. The meeting was opened quietly, President Francis Jackson in the chair. After the usual services Wendell Phillips reported a series of resolutions, largely made up of quotations, in favor of freedom and emancipation, from Daniel Webster, Henry Clay, Rev. Dr. Channing, and representatives of Georgia in the first American Congress. These being declared before the meeting, for its consideration, Rev. James Freeman Clarke, pastor of the Church of the Disciples, was the first speaker. He said, "They being dead, yet speak! I am glad to hear a speech from Dr. Channing here this morning. I am glad to hear Daniel Webster speak, as he spoke when he was in his best estate. I am glad to hear Henry Clay speak here to-day, as Henry Clay spoke when in his youth, when he loved freedom, and when his heart beat high in behalf of human liberty. They are gone; we remain. We are to finish their work. We are here to be faithful to their ideas. What is life worth, what is it good for, if it is not to serve the truth, and to uphold some principles of truth, justice, and honor?

"We come here to-day, friends, because the times are dark, and because, in these dark times, men are trying to make them darker by shutting out the eternal lights which come from God's heavens [applause], — because they would substitute for these everlasting lights of justice to all, and freedom for all, some base earth-born swamp-created meteors of mere expediency, — which is *not* expediency, even for the present hour. [Applause.] I have come here to-day, not hoping to be able to add a word to what all of you, old veterans in the cause of freedom, know already; but I come to give my simple witness in defense of those everlasting principles. I do not want to hear anything new here to-day. I want to hear the same great truths, which you have been uttering now for twenty-five years, uttered over again to-day in this hall. When I was asked, some time since [six or seven weeks before] to attend the meeting in commemoration of the work of John Brown [applause and hisses], though I reverenced John Brown, though I believed him to be a man in whom truth and justice were incarnated [a voice, "Amen," applause, and hisses] so that we beheld them in visible form before our eyes, yet I did not come, and I did not wish to come. I did not think it best to hold that meeting. [Applause.] I did not think it desirable at that time. I said, 'No; I would rather not attend,' and I did not come. But if I had known what was to happen here that day, I certainly would not have stayed away. [Loud applause and some hissing.] If I had supposed, for a moment, that an attempt was to be made, here in Boston, to put down an honest expression of opinion, upon that or upon any other subject, in a meeting of that kind, certainly I never would have hesitated, for a moment, to come here, and stand with those men on this platform. [Cheers and hisses.] Whatever else we can spare here in New England, we cannot do without free speech. [Loud applause.] That lies at the foundation of all our rights, of everything that is worth having in the land."

The noise and tumult now became so great as to make it difficult to speak or to hear. Nevertheless Mr. Clarke, in cool and steady manner, "said all he had intended to say." It was an eloquent defense both of free speech and of the faithful service which the Anti-Slavery Society had rendered thereto during many past years. "I see no danger," he said, "except from yielding up our principles."

Then came the war. He was not taken by surprise. He had seen its approach. He had remonstrated against that lack of Northern firmness which invited the South to each new act of aggression. His habitual self-possession must have had a special joy and gratitude, that his friend, John A. Andrew, at that crisis-hour, was Governor of Massachusetts. We cannot be mistaken in thinking that they often conferred together, and that Mr. Clarke's counsel and coöperation were valued by Governor Andrew.

In the "Examiner" of July, 1861, he writes on "The War," then but newly begun, and filling all hearts with anxiety. Speaking of its causes, he says: "The system of slavery must now be recognized by all as the origin and fountain of our evils." Briefly he recounts the successive demands, encroachments, and usurpations of slavery in our national affairs, so invariably submitted to by the Northern States. His hopefulness, faith, and forecast of victory, at this early and certainly not reassuring period, should be remembered. "It is our duty at the present time to be full of hope. . . . It is the duty of all patriots to resist the new attempts to compromise, to concede, and to surrender principle for the sake of peace. . . . We see in this war that we, as a people, are not what we should be; we see our want of true life, our need of more generosity, nobleness, magnanimity. . . . God is guiding events still; they are moving forward to a better future than has been seen yet." In that future Mr. Clarke discerns "emancipation and the end of slavery. Thus Christ always comes in the clouds of heaven; but he *comes*, and the world advances to its great and perfect destiny.'

On Sunday, April 21, 1861, — the Sunday following the departure of the Sixth Massachusetts Regiment for Washington, in obedience to the first call of President Lincoln for troops, — Mr. Clarke preached on "The State of the Nation." "True," he said, "the traitors who have had control of the administration for the last four years . . . have left us without money, troops, vessels, or arms; have laid their plots safely; and are wholly ready for a conflict for which we are wholly unprepared. Very likely they will succeed at first. We may be beaten at first; again and again perhaps defeated and disgraced. *Our* disasters will come at the beginning of this war; *theirs* are to come by and by." Could the actual facts have been more exactly foretold? "One of two things," said he that day, — "either slavery is to come to an end in this struggle, or else the free and the slave States must agree to separate." But in any event, he concluded, "slavery is sure to fall; for it is a sin against God, and a crime against man." This sermon was printed in full in the "National Anti-Slavery Standard" of New York.

At this time he published, in pamphlet form, a letter, addressed to Hon. Charles Sumner, entitled "Secession, Concession, or Self-Possession — Which?" the writer, "A Massachusetts Citizen." The following extract gives its key-note: "We can never purchase a permanent settlement of the controversy between freedom and slavery but by firm resistance to its encroachments. Every other solution of the difficulty must fail hereafter, as it has failed heretofore. Only, the longer the solution is deferred, the worse our position will be."

From a sermon preached by him in Boston, September 26, 1862, being the Sunday following President Lincoln's first proclamation relating to slavery, a sermon to which he gave the title "The Plagues of Egypt and America," a few extracts must be given: —

"The proclamation of Lincoln has been properly called the most important state paper issued in this country since the Declaration of Independence. It fairly and fully commits the government and people to universal freedom. It is not to be taken back again, no matter what happens. I should have been glad if it were made immediate. I should have been glad if put on principles of justice and right, not of mere war necessity. . . Nevertheless the deed is done. Prospective in form, in essence and influence it is immediate. The sword has cut the knot which policy could not untie. No more fear now of any false peace. The South now can never forgive Abraham Lincoln. . . . No more false and treasonable policies at the North. All men must choose their side now. No more deceitful compromises. . . . We, at the North, can breathe freely; we are not obliged any longer to support slavery with one hand, while we fight it with the other."

He shows the parallels of the plagues of Egypt and America with much ingenuity, and the lesson, alike in both cases, namely: "Let my people go, that they may serve me." And it is interesting to note how, at the very outset of the war, he was looking forward to see how "to build the future fair." "There will be a vast deal for us to do, after this war is over, in educating the blacks, in colonizing the slave States with a better society, in building up good institutions there. If this nation rises to a sense of its duty and opportunity, it will become the pole-star of mankind, the leading race of humanity, the christianizing people of the earth."

He gave striking proof of his interest for the colored people, as well as of his regard for justice, in the matter of the enlistment of colored troops in this war. "While we paid," he says, "the white troops thirteen dollars a month and clothing, the colored troops received but ten dollars, from which three dollars were taken for clothing, leaving but seven dollars for their pay. Governor Andrew felt great indignation at this unjust discrimination. He showed me a letter he had written to the Massachusetts Senators in Congress, requesting them to urge upon Congress and the President a redress of this inequality. 'I will not rest,' said he to the Senators, 'until this injustice is removed. I will not allow you any rest until it is removed.' I told Governor Andrew that I was going to Washington, and that I would take the letter to Mr. Sumner and Mr. Wilson, and would try to see the Attorney-General, who then was James Speed, the son of my old Louisville friend, Judge John Speed. I was to preach in the hall of the House of Representatives the following Sunday; and I took occasion to describe in my sermon the character and conduct of those colored troops. I told how the Massachusetts legislature had voted to send money to the colored regiments in South Carolina, to make up the full amount for all the time they had been in the service. These troops had steadily refused the inferior pay, and had gone without pay for some time. The State agents who carried the money explained to the troops that Massachusetts was not willing that they should serve without full pay; and they were to be told that Governor Andrew was anxious that they should receive the State money. The soldiers consulted among themselves, and one was appointed to reply. He said they thanked the State of Massachusetts, and Governor Andrew, and the gentlemen who had brought the money, but they did not consider themselves as troops of Massachusetts. They were United States soldiers, and would not take the Massachusetts money, nor even the ten dollars offered by Government, though their families were suffering for it, until they could have what was justly their due; meantime, they meant to do their duty just as well as if paid. When I had told that story, I said to the members of Congress in my audience, 'If this had been done by Greeks or Romans, it would be told in our school books, and our children would have been taught to read it as an example of heroism. But as it is done by colored soldiers, we do not think much of it. Nevertheless, in the sight of humanity and of history, I would rather be one of those colored soldiers, doing my duty as a man, and refusing the money till I could get justice with it, than a member of Congress, receiving my pay regularly, and sitting in my comfortable seat, and not able to muster courage to pass a law to pay those soldiers their just debt.' I supposed," adds Mr. Clarke, "they would be displeased · but instead of that they applauded."[1]

The work which he and the Church of the Disciples did for the freed people, through the whole period of the war and in the following years, should be at least referred to here. Early relief was sent to them, — supplies of whatever was most needed as they entered on the new life of freedom, and teachers, who would not only teach them in matters of useful knowledge, but also carry a Christian sympathy and a true human interest in their welfare into their humble homes.

Still more should it be said, though it is sufficiently obvious, that the source and spring of all Mr. Clarke's labors against slavery were in his Christian belief, in his religious sense of duty. There, in the depths of his nature, was the primal fountain of his early testimony, on slave-tilled soil, against slavery, and of his persistent, brave, and ever hopeful action against it to the end. He once expressed this broad, inclusive idea of duty thus: "I have known very good people, of culture and education, who might have done good in a large

[1] *Anti-Slavery Days*, p. 217.

circle, but who became very narrow by adopting, as their rule of life, the idea of 'doing the nearest duty.' With this rule," he said, "they cared only for the circle just about them. The interests of society, of humanity, of the universal Church, of the age, were indifferent to them. They did not care for the cause of truth, peace, freedom, human virtue, human happiness. The sufferings of the slave, the prisoner, the insane, the ignorant were not in the sphere of their nearest duties, and so were unheeded. I have seen people of the highest refinement, ornaments of their own homes, who cared for nothing beyond them, and who might have learned a lesson from the poor negro woman whose heart was interested in the missions of her church in India and Burmah, and who sheltered under her roof, at the risk of ruin to herself, the fugitive slave."[1]

At the dedication of the West Roxbury Soldiers' Monument, September 14, 1871, he gave the address. In it he described the power with which the National Government had had to contend: "The slave power: an oligarchy of about four hundred thousand slaveholders, owning some four millions of slaves, worth three thousand millions of dollars. . . . United by common interests, with the single paramount purpose of maintaining and extending slavery, it ruled the South with a rod of iron, allowing no freedom of speech, of the press, or of the pulpit. By means of this perfect union, it had obtained the control of the National Government, and, before 1860, had taken possession of the whole national organization. It annexed Texas in 1845, defeated the Wilmot Proviso in 1846, passed the Fugitive Slave Bill in 1850, repealed the Missouri Compromise in 1854, obtained the Dred Scott decision in 1857. It controlled both Houses of Congress, possessed the Executive, and directed the decisions of the Judiciary; so holding in its hand the army and navy of the Union.

[1] *Christian Register*, October 31, 1889. *Selections from his MSS.*

"But, on the other side, there had grown up, with wonderful rapidity, a mighty opposing force . It was the anti-slavery opinion of the North, which had been opposed first by mobs, then by ridicule, lastly by arguments, but had conquered them all. As Herod the king, in the midst of his power and glory, feared John the Baptist, 'knowing that he was a just man,' so the slave power, which feared nothing else, feared the anti-slavery platform. William Lloyd Garrison might have used the words of Pope, and said: —

'Yes, I am proud; I must be proud to see
Men, not afraid of God, afraid of me.'"

And in the same connection he spoke of that wonderful story of Mrs. Harriet Beecher Stowe, — "Uncle Tom's Cabin," — "inspired by genius and profound conviction," which did so much to stir and concentrate the national enthusiasm and purpose. He rendered merited tribute to the services of West Roxbury (the place of his own residence) during the war, and referred to a personal contribution of his own in words we cannot omit: "In this town was recruited and drilled one of the finest of the Massachusetts regiments. I happened to be the owner of Brook Farm in 1861; and when the Second Massachusetts was about to be organized, I offered it to my friend Morris Copeland, quartermaster of that regiment, and it was accepted. . . . I never raised much of a crop upon it before; but in 1861 it bore the greatest crop of any farm in Massachusetts, in the courage, devotion, and military renown of the officers and men of that noble regiment."

In this address he expressed, as upon all other fitting occasions, his admiration of the character, ability, and extraordinary services of Abraham Lincoln, President during the entire period of the war, — a providential man.

In March, 1873, with other friends of Mr. Garrison,

Mr. Clarke addressed a letter to that gentleman, asking him to write, for publication, the history of his life, — a matter, they say, which they have very much at heart, and which they urge " both on public and private considerations," and as a much-needed " example of the genuine happiness and true success of a life devoted to a great and unselfish purpose." [1]

In the " North American Review " of January, 1875, is an article by Mr. Clarke, which may well be consulted by those who desire to learn his position and course in relation to slavery, and the spirit in which he opposed it; and by any others seeking a condensed history of the origin and growth of slavery in this country, of its attempt to obtain supreme power, and of its ultimate overthrow. It takes Hon. Henry Wilson's " History of the Rise and Fall of the Slave Power " as its text. The most striking feature of the article is an account of the four days' contest in Congress, in February, 1836, for the " right of petition;" when John Quincy Adams met, single-handed, the representatives of slavery, and by his coolness, intrepidity, and force of intellect, completely and signally defeated them all. It was a memorable chapter of the national history; and Mr. Clarke relates it with spirit and interest.

Early in 1883, Mr. Clarke gave, in his church in Boston, a course of popular lectures on the " Anti-Slavery Conflict in the United States," which were very largely attended. These lectures were published in 1884, constituting the volume entitled " Anti-Slavery Days," to which frequent reference is made in this chapter.

Mr. Clarke was never a member of the Anti-Slavery Society; not because principled against associated action, for he was a member of other societies, and held official position in them. Nor could it have been because of any odium which attached to such membership in the minds of men determined to tolerate no inter-

[1] *Life of Mr. Garrison*, vol. iv. p. 257.

ference, as they termed it, with the subject of slavery. That would have had little weight with him. He was for many years an active member, and, from 1871 to 1878, the president, of the Massachusetts Woman Suffrage Association, when it had least favor in the public mind. The reason, doubtless, was that he could not fully identify himself with the Anti-Slavery Society. Its course was probably too distinctly aggressive to meet either his philosophy or his taste. It paid too little regard to the exceptional cases. It was earnest and incisive, while he sought to be calm and deliberate. We find sufficient explanation of his course in the fact that, during the years of his early interest in the subjcet, he misconceived the character and aim of the Anti-Slavery Society, as he himself says;[1] and in the unquestionable fact that, even when understanding that society better, so as to coöperate with them on many occasions, he still felt that, as preacher and writer, he had a work of his own to do, which he could more effectively do while responsible for that, and that alone. Few men, except the most devoted members of the Anti-Slavery Society, gave more time, thought, and labor to the overthrow of slavery than Mr. Clarke did. Early impressed with the sense of slavery's transcendent evils and wrong, steadily growing in the conviction that he had a duty in the case not to be put by, he never retrograded, or grew cold. How to overcome and terminate slavery was an uppermost thought with him, a problem seldom out of sight. He accepted new light; he corrected mistaken judgments. During the long days of the Anti-Slavery Society's effort to stir a national feeling and conscience for the three millions held in slavery by the Nation's united power, and when every attempt to get the ministers and churches of Boston, of all denominations, to give a helping hand almost invariably ended in a refusal, Mr. Clarke did not

[1] *Anti-Slavery Days*, p. 22.

refuse. It was known that, on some points, he differed with the society. That did not prevent their asking his aid again and again; nor him from giving it. He knew that he would be as free, on the platform of the Anti-Slavery Society, to express dissent where he differed as to join in advocacy of the patriotic and Christian principles which were the basis of that society's action. And so he did not stand aloof from the Abolitionists. He felt himself to be at one with their idea and purpose. They gladly welcomed him when he came among them; and he came without concealment and without compromise. He attended their meetings repeatedly, and made there his strong appeals for anti-slavery action. The members of the Anti-Slavery Society were little concerned with the matter of nominal membership, when one gave evidence of a heart right, a conscience alive, and an eye single to the great cause of freedom and justice. That it was so with Mr. Clarke, one who himself was a constant, adhering member of the Anti-Slavery Society is well assured, and gladly affirms. With an absolute steadfastness he put his heart and hand to every recognized and approved weapon against slavery, until it met its doom. And thus he spoke, when the work was done: "Slavery went down in that dreadful conflict, never to rise again. In a single generation, and in the lifetime of the chief agitator himself, this vast revolution was accomplished. Never in human history has there been such an example of the power of conscience in gaining a victory over worldly interest; and it ought to be an encouragement forever, for all who contend for lowly right against triumphant wrong, for unpopular truth against fashion, prejudice, and power."[1]

[1] *Anti-Slavery Days*, p. 10.

CHAPTER XIV.

THE UNITARIAN CHURCH.

THE reader has already seen that the constitution of Mr. Clarke's mind enabled him to put himself readily in the place of a person with whom he was carrying on a controversy. He was of a social nature, and indeed believed in the coöperation of many men. He worked cheerfully and happily with others, probably because he did not antagonize them. The diary, therefore, is full, as the remembrances of his friends are full, of the numerous occasions when he was present at gatherings of social, reformatory, and political parties. He gave much time to these different interests, but it was time which all told in preparation for the pulpit. It might be added that he sometimes had a longing for a wider field. I remember that in the year 1857, when we belonged to the New England Emigrant Aid Company, and were greatly interested in the fortunes of the German colony established by the Prince de Solms in southwestern Texas, he said to me cordially, "Let us both go out into that country, and spend the rest of our lives in doing something that we can see when it is done, so that we shall know what our mark on the world is, as Winthrop knew when his life was ended here." I have sometimes been sorry that we did not do so. Certainly he would have been an admirable leader in any such enterprise.

He had gone to Louisville as a missionary preacher. With his friends, William G. Eliot and Ephraim Peabody, he had established the "Western Messenger" as a literary organ which should give them an opportunity, once a month, to proclaim their views. He never regretted his work there; and to the end of his life he was found active in all efforts for giving breadth and depth to the religious life of "the West," whatever region might be called by that word of changing meaning. But he returned to Boston with the feeling that the Unitarian Church needed more spiritual life and more heat in the region of its central activity.[1] And, without finding fault with anybody else, he had undertaken, in the formation of the Church of the Disciples at Boston, to show his "Ideal Church."[2]

I have already said that his appearance in the little circle of Boston churches was not welcomed with enthusiasm by all the ministers of those churches. But by the churches of New England, inside the Unitarian communion and outside, he was cordially received wherever he was known; and before long this was true of Boston also. For the Unitarian leaders had found out that their work was not to proclaim a new theology, but to lift religion to a higher plane; and in all the churches that were alive, laymen and ministers were going about that business. For ten or fifteen years before the Civil War, the most important questions of social life were under general discussion in that region, and men and women had to make up their own minds

[1] I remember, many years ago, Dr. Channing expected and hoped for just such a revival. I made a short visit to him at Newport, and he spent all the summer day saying, "When is more life to come among Unitarians? Is life to come from Cambridge? I hope for life from it. I don't despair of Cambridge." I remember the dear, good man, before he bade us good-night, kneeled down, and prayed still for the same thing, — that the Father of all would send more life into our hearts, and wake us up to the truths of the living God. — Mr. Clarke's Speech at the Annual Meeting of the American Unitarian Association, May, 1866.

[2] At about the time, as may be observed, that Mr. William Ward amazed England by publishing his "Ideal Church."

as to their personal duty in the matter of slavery Whatever judgment may be passed on the courage or decision of the church in its other communions, the American free lances did not, on the whole, fail in the great appeal; and with the free lances, in practice, must the Unitarian Church always be classified. In such questions as came up between the annexation of Texas in 1845 and the firing on Sumter in 1861, men and women were indifferent to renewed threshings of the old straw of theology or criticism, and it would have been impossible to re-awaken an interest in discussions of foreknowledge, election, the fall of man, and vicarious atonement. Indeed, the leaders of Orthodoxy had shown their wisdom by declining further controversy on such themes.

Mr. Clarke's hope, on returning from Louisville, was that the Unitarian life, as presented with that eagerness, tenderness, and faith of which he and his friends were conscious, would win the sympathy of evangelical believers, and that it would prove that the gulf was not, after all, so wide between a free theology and that which still held to the Calvinistic formulas manufactured for New England churches in the days of Whitefield. In the early days of the Church of the Disciples, there were advances made by him towards those whom New England calls the "Orthodox," which, if they had been wise, they would have received more cordially than they did. I have already mentioned that Rev. Edward N. Kirk, of the Mount Vernon Church, preached in Mr. Clarke's pulpit one Sunday.[1] To Mr. Clarke's mind, the invitation to do so simply indicated the same breadth and good faith which invited the

[1] Readers in other sections of the country will hardly understand that not ten instances have occurred in sixty years when an "Evangelical" minister of a Boston church has spoken in a "Liberal" pulpit in that city, and not five when a minister of a "Liberal" church has spoken in an "Evangelical" pulpit.

heretic Theodore Parker to preach there at another time. But to the popular mind of that little company who cared for such things, the invitation to preach meant a coquetry with Orthodoxy, for Mr. Kirk was perhaps the most distinguished preacher of the self-called Evangelical school of the place and time. He would not, in his wildest dreams, have thought of asking Mr. Clarke to preach in his pulpit.

In the happy freedom of American life, there is but little sectarianism outside of the pulpit and of the denominational newspapers. So soon, therefore, as Mr. Clarke began to print his books and his sermons, they found their way right and left, and eventually they were read more widely among people who knew little about the Unitarian Church than among those who were enrolled in its communion.

The Unitarian Church itself, so soon as it was relieved from the ungracious task of controversy as to the text of Scripture, was in all quarters rising to understand its true position, as the "Church of the Holy Spirit." In practice its business is to do what it can to bring in the kingdom of God. To find out how that should be done, each child of God must look for His direction and listen to His voice, sure that the pure in heart will see Him, and that He is not far from any of them. Wherever they find help for such communion with God, or for such duty to man, it is their business to seek it. This may be in Thomas à Kempis; it may be in Kant's Critique; it may be under the stars, on Ben Nevis; it may be in putting up the widow Flaherty's stove. It might be in reading the Greek tragedies; it might be in work over the compound microscope; it might be in the battles of the Abolitionist platform; it might be in listening to the Ave Maria, in the Sistine Chapel. The Unitarian Church was finding out that it was not a "sect" or "denomination," and never could be; but that it was in accord with all children of God who were seeking him anywhere.

In Boston, its ministers had worried themselves with the question, already alluded to, whether Theodore Parker, with his iconoclasms, could be received into this wide communion of the sons of God. And they undertook to accentuate their disapproval of his doctrine of miracles by deciding not to invite him to preach the Thursday lecture. This was given by different clergymen, and was attended by the ministers who had assembled for their weekly club, and by a few others, the larger proportion being women. There were often not more than fifty present, though, if the preacher were especially attractive, there might be from three to five hundred. This was the only public sentence which could be inflicted on the preacher who afterwards called himself the minister of the "Twenty-eighth Congregational Society." For all Unitarian ministers served pure Congregational churches. And, in the true Congregational order, no church can make a creed or covenant for any church but itself, or in any way enforce one. Mr. Clarke marked his dissent from the counsels of his seniors by exchanging pulpit services, as has been said, with Mr. Parker. By the people at large his attitude was never misunderstood. It was seen that he was practically standing for that which he had always maintained theoretically, — the position of catholic freedom. Between himself and Mr. Parker there was an entire understanding, and each had confidence in the other's sincerity. Their close connection in political matters, particularly on the anti-slavery platform, often brought them together. But each of them knew that in the pulpit neither would make the same proclamation as the other.

Speaking roughly, the period of his residence in Meadville, while he was recovering his health, marks the division line between his work as the minister of the Church of the Disciples alone and his work as a leader of the Unitarian Church in America. The reader has seen how much he did, in a literary way, in those years at Meadville; and from that time forward he is to be spoken of as a man of letters. In the proper place I will put as nearly complete a list of his publications as we have been able to obtain. It will be seen how many of them belong to these years of what one calls retirement at Meadville. Their publication followed rapidly, and now he begins to be known throughout the country.

"The Doctrine of Prayer" was circulated widely among thoughtful people of all communions, and was read with such interest that many were moved to write personally to the author. This gave to him the position he was well adapted to fill, of mediating between different communions, and of showing to each what were the merits of the other. It was a good thing for us (of the Unitarian Church) that we had a man who brought us and the Orthodox people nearer to each other, and there were few among us in whom the Orthodox had the same confidence that they had in him. He understood the language in which the Evangelical churches speak as few Unitarians do, and was indeed able to speak it himself with perfect sincerity. His nature was so thoroughly poetical that he knew what was meant as a poetical expression; and he did not hold down a strain of Dr. Doddridge or an ejaculation of Dr. Finney to its literal and grammatical meaning. "The Truths and Errors of Orthodoxy" was a second book which did great good in showing to earnest persons, on both sides of the imagined gulf between the Liberal and the Evangelical churches, that it was not very much of a gulf after all. Indeed, wherever people read his books, they found out, what may be regarded as a general truth, that most intelligent Christians, so far as their everyday religion goes, are in practical agreement, though probably without knowing it. When they come to state occasions, and to the full-dress uniform of established creeds and confessions, they appear, of course, in a different array.

He rightly apprehended the need and the determination of the Unitarian Church in the region in which he was brought up. This was made clear enough by every change in its pulpit in the ten years after he came to Boston from Louisville. In place of the ethical, critical, and analytical preaching of the past generation, came in such preaching as that of Ephraim Peabody, F. D. Huntington, J. I. T. Coolidge, S. H. Winkley, Starr King, Frederic T. Gray, and R. C. Waterston. No one who heard either of these preachers ventured to say that the Unitarian pulpit was cold or hard in its utterances. Mr. Huntington and Mr. Coolidge found, as they thought, the working forces of the Unitarian Church unworthy of their missionary eagerness, and they were unwilling to be compromised by the latitudinarianism inevitable in a communion which has no creed. They left the Unitarian Church, therefore, for the Protestant Episcopal Church, which they have ever since adorned. Starr King, in 1860, went to California, where, in 1864, he died, as a soldier might die in battle. Mr. Peabody and Mr. Gray were called to higher service in the very prime of human life. With all of these ministers, as with Mr. Winkley and Mr. Waterston, Mr. Clarke always held relations of personal friendship. And if any impression has been given that at the outset the Church of the Disciples seemed an intruder among its decorous fraternity of the older Boston churches of the Liberal communion, the reader should understand that nothing was needed but a knowledge of its activity and devotion, and an acquaintance with its earnest and catholic minister, to remove every petty jealousy which watched its birth.

He became a director in the Unitarian Association in May, 1845. This association is at once the Missionary Board and the Publishing Board of the American Unitarian Church. Its activities then were very small compared with what they are now. Such as they were, they were quickened and helped forward by his good sense and energy. And then, as always, he had at heart the interests of the divinity school at Meadville, and the increase of the number of liberal pulpits in the West.

At the meeting of the Unitarian Association in 1859, a plan which he had himself favored was brought forward, by which the general secretary of that association should work without salary, and the only salaried officer should be an office clerk. It was understood, when this plan was proposed, that Mr. Clarke should be the general secretary who was to serve on these terms. The association rejected the plan, however, and chose him general secretary, fixing the salary at not less than two thousand nor more than three thousand dollars a year, including his traveling expenses. After this vote was passed, Mr. Clarke was elected. He says in the next annual report that had he been present he would have declined the office; but he decided to accept it for a year. He made it a condition, however, that he should not resign the pastoral care of his own church, and that he should be allowed to preach at home at least one Sunday in every month. Upon these conditions, which were cheerfully acceded to by the executive committee, he endeavored to fulfill during a year the duties of the office. Instead of two or three thousand dollars, he thought it right to take in all twelve hundred dollars. But the result of the year's experience with him was to confirm, on the whole, his opinion in favor of the proposal which was rejected the previous year.

The association, however, did not return to that plan, but retained his services, by agreeing that while he was still to perform the home duty he need leave his own pulpit but one Sunday in every month. The truth was, that the wisdom of his administration and the inspiration which he gave were widely felt. His conduct of the "Monthly Journal," of which he wrote the greater part himself, brought him into relation with many of the most intelligent persons in all the churches; and whoever wishes to study his work, either as a minister or as a theologian, will do well to possess himself of the volumes of that journal which he edited.

FROM THE "MONTHLY JOURNAL" FOR AUGUST, 1860.

Having just returned from a tour in which we preached in Cincinnati and Pittsburgh, and attended the commencements at Antioch and Meadville, we would like to give the readers of the "Monthly Journal" a brief account of a few of our observations.

Our annual May meetings were over. Mr. Calthrop was ordained at Marblehead; a few farewell words to Theodore Parker had been spoken; and, traveling-bag in hand, we departed for Cincinnati.

I wish I could magnetize all the readers of the "Monthly Journal" with the electric life of the great West. While the influence is yet strong within me I would communicate something of the strange power which comes to us from that surging, rushing flood of human activity. By it we are lifted above mere forms and conventional barriers; we communicate more freely, soul with soul. The weight of years and of cares falls from us as we descend the Alleghanies. .

There is no way to get rid of our ignorance and narrowness but by going to see other parts of the country with our own eyes. All the union meetings ever held do not do half as much to preserve the Union as a single railroad. Go and see. Look with your own eyes at the marvelous life, ever flowing forward, of this bit of Anglo-Saxondom. . . .

From 1833 to 1840, I used to travel some three thousand miles every year, mostly by steamboat and stage-coach. On the rivers and lakes we went by steamboat; but we traversed Ohio, Kentucky, Illinois, Pennsylvania, Virginia, and New York by stage-coach. For six or seven days together I have ridden in a stage-coach with the same party of travelers. I often crossed the Alleghanies in Pennsylvania, Maryland, and Virginia in the old and slow stage-coach; sometimes walking for hours in advance of the carriage; sometimes crossing the summits at midnight, when they were covered with ice and snow; sometimes, in the early dawn of a summer morning, looking abroad from a high mountain water-shed, over a vast wilderness of forest, here and there spotted with little green farm-openings, through which the white road wandered on to the far horizon. Or sometimes we would, at the same hour, see the morning star above us in the clear, deep sky; while, below, the whole valley would be full of white mist, lying like a vast lake, through whose surface the hilltops came up as islands. And oh, what singular combinations of travelers! merchants going East to buy goods; Methodist ministers going to their stations; gamblers from Texas; river pilots; drovers returning home after selling their cattle; atheists, Presbyterians, shoulder-hitters, Roman Catholic priests; women going to look for runaway husbands; men with bowie-knives sticking out of their jackets; men with Bibles in their pockets. But, wild and heterogeneous as our party often was, we usually became interested in each other after a day or two; and it is strange how sorry we were to part even with our whiskey-drinking and blaspheming companions.... The scholastics disputed concerning this question: Whether, when angels have occasion to go from one place to another, they are obliged to go through the intermediate spaces. However it may be with angels, it is certainly true concerning railway travelers that they are not in any intermediate places while going from Dan to Beersheba. They alight, like birds, at one point, then at another; all between goes for nothing.

> "All beside was empty waste;
> All was picture as he passed."

Thus, leaving Boston, I alighted at New York, then at Cleveland, then at Cincinnati, then at Antioch College, then at Pittsburgh, and lastly at Meadville. . . .

Leaving the Queen City at seven on Tuesday morning, we reached, at ten o'clock, the scene already made famous through the labors of Horace Mann. Here we found Dr. Bellows; Rev. Nathaniel Hall, of Dorchester; Father Taylor; Mr. Artemus Carter, of Chicago; Dr. Hosmer; Mr. Hosea, of Cincinnati; John Phillips; and other old friends of the institution.

On Commencement Day we heard the parts of twenty-eight graduates, of whom a number were young ladies. All the parts were instinct with high aims and earnest purpose. The soul of Horace Mann could be traced through all. These young men and women contemplated life as a scene of duty, where responsibilities awaited them, great laws were to be obeyed, and a grave work was to be done. Not a tone or word approaching to frivolity fell from their lips. The young girls, with modest self-possession, sweet and hopeful as a summer's morning, gave a graceful variety to the aspect of a Commencement platform.

Some people fear the consequences of having young men and young women taught together in the same college; but these fears are removed by a short observation of the practical working of the system. . . . No one at Antioch observes any bad consequences to arise from this communion of young men and young women in study. They look at each other, not in the misty light of fanciful attraction, but in the plain and commonplace relation of fellow-students, — reciting algebra, Virgil, and Horace in common, making common blunders in Greek, and equally perplexed by conic sections. . . .

I held a kind of three days' meeting in Pittsburgh, preaching on Friday, Saturday, and Sunday, to congregations which filled the little hall where service was held.

From Pittsburgh I went, *via* Cleveland, to Meadville, to be present at the Commencement of the theological school. There also I found Father Taylor and Dr. Bellows, and in their genial and glad society realized again how great a blessing there is in Christian fellowship. To the earnest young men about to leave the theological school these brethren spoke words of counsel and good cheer. We found at Meadville the same tone of strong, manly purpose as at Antioch. There was no "suspense of faith" perceptible there.

TO E. E. HALE.

William H. Channing once said of Z., "What shall be done with an artist who is not an artist?" So I say, "What shall be done with a minister who is not a minister?" My most difficult experiences are caused by being obliged to see and to hear from so many who wish for work and cannot get it, and for whom I feel the greatest sympathy. Our friend of whom you write is elegant, refined, able to criticise a novel, a poem, or a picture, well acquainted with the best opera music, but cannot succeed in preaching a Christian sermon so as to take hold of human hearts and minds.

In like manner I had a reproachful letter two days since from Y., inquiring why I did not give a man like him, with his large culture and thorough discipline of mind, some work to do? He has ample culture and discipline, and ten times the knowledge which the young men just out of the divinity school have, but if he does not get preaching it is evident that he cannot preach.

As to the West: a man who cannot succeed here is sure not to succeed there. Such a man as our friend X. is the very last man for the West. F. is worth ten of him; Augustus Staples is worth twenty. Essays on "the True, the Beautiful, and the Good" are in no demand out of the vicinity of Boston.

But certainly there is a place for every one. This is my unwavering conviction. But two things are necessary: (1) to find the right place; (2) to be willing to go to it, and to work in it.

In the earlier days, — at the instance of Henry Ware, Jr., Dr. Gannett, and other leaders, — the habit had been formed among the Unitarians of holding what they called the "Autumnal Convention." It was a queer type of the stateliness of their movement, as it then existed, that this title was chosen, where the Friends would have said "the Yearly Meeting."[1] Already, at the "Autumnal Convention" of 1863, Mr. Clarke had made an address, which is reported in the "Monthly Journal" for November of that year. He spoke of the inconsistency between our historic position and traditions as a denomination and our convictions; "our convictions have always been progressive, our traditions tame, timid, and conservative. . Now the denomination is awakened. Dr. Bellows, by his herculean labors; Dr. Eliot, our dear conservative; Hosmer, who left his peaceful home in the Connecticut Valley to bear the private's gun on his shoulder through the wearisome campaigns; Conant, whose plaintive voice, calling out at night on that dreadful battle-field, 'Are there any wounded here?' still rings in our ears; Knapp, and other hearty laborers, have thoroughly aroused it. See to it that it does not go to sleep again. Now let everything that can be done to help the human race be done. Don't stop to criticise, but *work*."

It will be more convenient to speak of his work during the war in another chapter. Here it may be said that the labors of such men, with the Sanitary Commission and in other agencies connected with the hospital and the army, had a great effect in bringing about in the Unitarian Church a higher sense of its responsibili-

[1] A good essay might be written on The Unitarian Language.

ties in the matter of missionary work. Under the lead of Dr. Bellows, at a special meeting of the Unitarian Association, in December, 1864, in Hollis Street Church in Boston, measures were taken which led to the establishment, in April, 1865, of a National Conference of Unitarian and other Christian churches. From that time this National Conference has been the representative body of the Unitarian Church of America.

In the preliminary arrangements for this conference, and in the formation of its constitution, Mr. Clarke was a central actor. When, on the 4th of April, 1865, the delegates to a national Unitarian convention met in the city of New York, he gave the first address ever delivered to the united body. His appointment to give this address indicated the place which he had gained in the affection and confidence of the denomination. The delegates, lay and clerical, were men of widely different opinions, and the existence of right and left wings in the body was perfectly well known. But in Mr. Clarke each side had confidence. In most critical issues he had shown his readiness to give freedom to the boldest inquirer, and yet the character of his own writing had given him especial favor, not only among Orthodox Unitarians, but among churches which would hardly grant the Christianity of any other Unitarian.

The sermon itself, which was published at once, met the occasion entirely. It was the key-note of the harmonious convention which followed.

Mr. Clarke was chosen a member of the National Council formed by this convention, and remained an active member of that body as long as he could do so under the constitution which formed it.

EXTRACT FROM THE CONVENTION SERMON.

Christian brethren, members of the National Unitarian Convention, why have we thus come together? Have we come together as Unitarians for the pleasure of standing alone and of being called heretics? Are we Unitarians because we like being shut out from the sympathy of the church? No. We often long for the larger communion of the universal church. Nor do we stand here as Unitarians because we cannot see how much of truth and of good there is in the churches from which we differ.

We, too, desire to have our share in that deeper life born of God, coming mostly through the mediation of Jesus of Nazareth, which changes duty into love, work into freedom, and puts the spirit into the heart whereby we call God our Father. There is no rapture of piety in the Catholic or Protestant church, no mystic ecstasy, no inspired insight in any of the great cloud of witnesses belonging to the Christian family in heaven and earth, but we humbly acknowledge its sweetness and strength, and long to appropriate it in our own life. We are not Unitarians because we do not see the good and truth there is in Orthodoxy.

But we are Unitarians, we are willing to be called heretics, because we see a work to be done which we ought to do. Our very existence, indeed, does good as a standing protest against that exclusive spirit which makes essentials out of matters of form and matters of opinion.

This convention is of Unitarians; and we accept as Unitarian Christians all who claim that name. We do not make ourselves responsible for each other's opinions. Probably we differ very widely from each other in many points of belief. The question is, Can we unite together in Christian work? We can work with Atheists in the Sanitary Commission, to help the wounded and dying. We can work with Deists in the Temperance Society, to save our brethren from ruin and despair. We can work with slaveholders and defenders of slavery in the hospitals, with Roman Catholics in the Freedman's Aid Society, with Calvinists on the school-committee. We do not compromise our faith in Theism, Christianity, Anti-slavery, Protestantism, or Unitarianism by so doing. And so if some of our brethren here are Naturalists; if they disbelieve miracles; if they carry their criticism on the New Testament farther than I do; so long as we have work to do in which we agree, we can cordially unite. So long as they wish to bring men to God by the teaching and life of Jesus, let us be glad to coöperate, and not be afraid of compromising ourselves thereby.

The lines which unite Christians are not the theological parallels of latitude, but the isothermal lines of faith. I often find myself in the same religious climate, in the same isothermal line, with men from whom I differ very widely in my religious creed.

And therefore I hope that, though we meet as a Unitarian convention this year, we shall meet next year on a much broader basis, which shall include all liberal Christian churches who may desire to coöperate with us. We and they can be what we choose at home, have our own names, creeds, and methods, but can meet once a year in a national convention, with all who believe in a broad coöperation for Christian work.

The church is the body of Christ. It is an organization through which the spirit of Christ can work. If, hitherto, it has preached him in the pulpit, rather than gone with him to seek and save the lost; if it has taught doctrines about him, rather than carried him to a world lying in wickedness; if it has rather called on men to "come to Jesus" than taken Jesus to find and help them where they are, the time has come, we think, for a change. We wish to take part in the great and opening civilization of the new day and hour. We wish to do something for such a Christianity as the world has never yet seen, a Christianity which shall fill all life with the sense of God's presence; which shall cast both Death and Hell into a lake of fire; which shall give us a new heaven and a new earth, wherein dwelleth righteousness.

If we are to do our work, we must have not less faith, and prayer, and piety than others, but more. Unitarians ought to live nearer to God than any others. Our faith should lead us to live in the spirit and walk in the spirit. Above all technical religion, mere cant of piety, we ought to live from God and to God all the day. Our views of God and man should fill us with a love which prays without ceasing, which in everything gives thanks which does all to the glory of God, which feels his presence hour by hour, moment by moment, and says secretly and sweetly, "*Abba*, Father," all day long.

We shall have men of this faith when we begin to do more work. Faith leads to work, work also leads to faith. He who does a great Christian work casts himself on God for strength. Our working men will also be praying men.

In 1877, at the request of the American Unitarian Association, Mr. Clarke gave, in Music Hall, on successive Sunday evenings, a course of six lectures, which were afterwards published in book form and called "Essentials and Non-Essentials in Religion."

CHAPTER XV.

THE WAR.

As soon as the war came, every man's plans gave way to his duties in the national cause. Men who had not known each other by sight found themselves working side by side; and even men who had distrusted each other found they were close friends. In the new life of the hour, Mr. Clarke's intimacy with Governor Andrew and the interest which he took in the Sanitary Commission brought him personally into relations with soldiers and with the arrangements made for caring for them in the field.

When the life of Governor Andrew is written, and let us hope it will be written soon, we shall have as fine an instance as our history can show of the way in which a pure idealist comes to the front in a republic like ours, and takes the lead if he be fit for it, even if he be quite indifferent to the methods of partisans and indeed ignorant of them. His life-long friend, Mr. Chandler, has left an amusing account of their experiences as poor young men, when they both first arrived in Boston. The landlady, in Howard Street, to whom they applied for lodgings, gave each of them the choice of a small attic, without a window, which had one bed, or of half a double-bedded attic which had a window. For some reason Andrew had the first choice, and he preferred darkness with solitude. Starting from circumstances as simple as this story suggests, with no forces but such as personal character and ability gave, Andrew found himself, in 1860, Governor of Massachusetts. Throughout his life in Boston he lived on the most intimate terms with Mr. Clarke. He joined the Church of the Disciples in the same year in which it was founded. When the secession from that church, which has been referred to, took place, he announced that he was a "stay-inner," and not a "come-outer." More than once, when Mr. Clarke was not present on Sunday, he conducted the religious services. He also taught a class in the Sunday-school, and for a time was its superintendent.

Mr. Andrew's name was so thoroughly identified with all the philanthropies that it was freely said when he was elected governor that he would put an end to the militia system of Massachusetts. But he was the man, as it proved, who found it his duty and his pride to enlist the largest army Massachusetts ever raised, and to maintain it in the highest efficiency. Once and again, Mr. Clarke visited Washington with Governor Andrew, having indeed duties of his own in the work of the Sanitary Commission and of the hospitals. As secretary of the Unitarian Association, he had the oversight of the publication of some army tracts, which got the name of the "White Tracts," and were said to be warmly welcomed by the soldiers.

At the very beginning of the war, Dr. Bellows founded the Sanitary Commission, with reference to its use in keeping up the interest of the country in the army, as well as for the service which it would render in hospitals and in the field. Mr. Clarke took his share of work in this organization, and was, from the first, an officer in the Massachusetts branch. But in truth, every such church as his was in itself an organization, ready made, for assisting in the duties of the war, whether recruiting for the army, or the care of soldiers, or the instruction of freedmen, or their welcome in New England, or, when things came nearer to a close, the care of refugees, and the introduction of some system of education at the South.

A number of the young men of the Church of the Disciples served in the army. Of these, some whose names are still fondly remembered died on the field of battle. Young women from the church were in hospital service, and men and women both were personally engaged in the instruction of the freedmen, for which those at home were providing the supplies. I do not know that Dr. Clarke was ever under fire in the war, but the correspondence for the four years is full of details which show how close was his personal interest in all its movement.

Up to the last minute, even those who had been watching for years the storm-cloud gather, and had uttered their warnings to the blinded nation, still hoped that the doom might be averted. Toward the end of 1860, after the election of Lincoln, in a pamphlet called "Secession, Concession, or Self-possession, — Which?" Mr. Clarke says: —

"The Sibyl has visited our country and our rulers many times during the last twenty years. She came at the time of the annexation of Texas, and offered us prosperity, union, and freedom. But the price which she asked we thought high; we could not afford to pay it. It was a courageous and firm resistance to the demands of the slave power.

"In 1850, the Sibyl came again, and offered us somewhat less at the same price. If we were then courageons enough to exclude slavery by law from the Territories, we should encounter difficulty. The slave power would resist and threaten, but there would be no disunion. But again we thought the price too high, and we did not pay it. We had another offer in 1856, which we declined. And now, in 1860, the Sibyl comes again. She offers us far less than at first. We can still have freedom and national prosperity, but not union. Some States have decided to leave us; but they may leave us peacefully, and many of the slave States may remain with us. But, if we are afraid to pay the price, the Sibyl will come again and again, offering less each time; and we shall have at last to come to her terms: for the name of the Sibyl is Opportunity."

The next spring the storm-cloud broke.

The following notes from the diary illustrate the direction which events gave to his daily life: —

April 13, 1861. Fort Sumter surrendered.

April 15. President's proclamation calling out seventy-five thousand men.

April 16. 3d, 4th, and 6th regiments meet on Boston Common.

April 19. Massachusetts men attacked and killed in Baltimore by the mob. Spent two or three hours in the governor's room at the State House.

In giving an account of this 19th of April, Mr. Clarke said: "I was in Governor Andrew's room in the State House when the news was coming, by telegraph, of the attacks on our troops in Baltimore. While I was there, Edward Everett came in. He had been nominated for vice-president by the Union Whigs, a party opposed to the Republicans who nominated Lincoln. Forgetting party hostility, he said: 'I have come, Governor Andrew, to offer you my services in any way in which you can make use of them.' Another friend, a classmate of mine, who was not a Republican, came in and handed his check for ten thousand dollars to Governor Andrew, to be used as he might think best for the common good."

FROM A SERMON PREACHED APRIL 21, THE NEXT SUNDAY AFTER THE ATTACK ON FORT SUMTER.

If the true position of a nation is its highest moral attitude, then we may say that these free States were never in a better condition than they are to-day. The end is not yet; no, and though they take Washington, take our President prisoner, seize the archives, and install themselves in the Capitol, that is not the end. So long as the magnificent spirit which actuates the whole North to-day continues, the spirit of devoted patriotism, of perfect unanimity of sentiment, of generous self-sacrifice, of calm, quiet courage, which does not boast at the beginning nor flinch at the end, so long the nation is safe

This is a sort of Pentecostal Day, in which the whole multitude are of one heart and one soul; nor says any one that aught that he possesses is his own, but we have all things in common.

For the sake of national prosperity, for the sake of outward union, for the sake of a mere mercantile peace, we have here at the North been conniving for years at a system of despotism more cruel than exists elsewhere on the face of the earth.

Now we are punished in just those three points. Our prosperity has received a terrible check, our Union is dissolved, and our peace has terminated in what threatens to be an awful war.

Let us stand by each other now in these dark hours, trusting in God's eternal justice and truth. He that is for us is more than they that be against us.

During the dark hours of the Civil War, all Mr. Clarke's faith and hope were needed; but he had foreseen that defeats during the first period of the war were to be expected; and his confidence, born of trust in the divine Providence, never failed. A friend told, twenty years later, how he had met Mr. Clarke the day after the battle of Bull Run, and how, even on that black day, when every one else was disheartened, his serenity was unshaken.

Some of his parishioners noticed that whenever anything very discouraging happened, he was sure the next Sunday to rise up in the pulpit, looking full of hope and courage, and when the time came for the first hymn, he would say: "We will sing the hymn beginning,

'Give to the winds thy fears!
Hope, and be undismayed!'"

They learned to watch for the accustomed words; and one of them said, "We lived on that hymn all through the war; everybody in the church learned it by heart."

FROM HIS DIARY.

June 2, 1861. Afternoon to Brook Farm, to "Camp Andrew" to preach.

June 9. Preach at Camp Andrew in afternoon.

June 16. To Brook Farm, preached fourth time, — text, "Be not weary."

[He owned Brook Farm, and had given the use of it for the camp of the Massachusetts Second, while it was recruiting and preparing for the front.]

July 8. Gordon's regiment left Brook Farm. Went up there before breakfast.

July 22. News of defeat at Bull Run.

July 23. State House; General Schouler.

Sept. 26. National fast. Preached on "Slavery and the Union." Church very full.

Oct. 1. Delegate to Republican Convention at Worcester. I presented two emancipation resolutions. Both set aside.

Oct. 21. Battle of Edwards' Ferry [Ball's Bluff]. Took telegram to Dr. Holmes about his son.

Oct. 29. Funeral of William Lowell Putnam.[1] I spoke.

[1] Who had died in the battle of Ball's Bluff.

FROM HIS ADDRESS AT THE FUNERAL OF WILLIAM LOWELL PUTNAM.

In the fatal battle a week ago, Putnam fell while endeavoring to save a wounded companion, — fell, soiled with no ignoble dust — "*non indecoro pulvere sordidum.*" Brought to the hospital-tent, he said to the surgeon, who came to dress his wound, "Go to some one else, to whom you can do more good; you cannot save me," — like Philip Sydney, giving the water to the soldiers who needed it more than himself. And still more striking, as showing his earnest conscientiousness, is the fact that he refused to allow Sturgis to remove him, saying: "It is your *duty* to leave me. It is your *duty* to go to your own men, and leave me here." And his friend was obliged to carry him away in spite of this protest.

How hard that these precious lives should be thus wasted, apparently for naught, through the ignorance or the carelessness of those whose duty it was to make due preparation, before sending them to the field! How can we bear it?

We could not bear it, unless we believed in God. But it is not any blind chance, nor yet any human folly, which controls these events. All is as God wills, who knows what the world needs, and what we need, better than we can know it. And the death of Christ has taught us that it is God's great law that the best shall be sacrificed to save the worst, the innocent suffering for the good of the guilty. This is the law, ordained before the earth was made; and every pure soul sacrificed in a struggle with evil is another "lamb slain from the foundation of the world."

And do we not see, in these great sacrifices, that the heroism itself is already a great gain? Is it not something to know that we do not belong to a degenerate race? Is it not a great blessing to know that we also, and our sons, are still as capable as our fathers were of great and noble sacrifices, — that Massachusetts still produces heroes, — that these boys of yours, trained perhaps in luxury, can, at the call of their country, die cheerfully for their land ?

FROM HIS DIARY.

1861. Nov. 12. Depart for Washington. Meet Govcruor and Mrs. Andrew at New Haven.

Nov. 13. To Philadelphia with Governor Andrew Colonel Howe, and Colonel Ritchie.

Nov. 15. Visit the Capitol with William H. Channing.

Nov. 16. Call upon Abraham Lincoln.

Nov. 17. Call upon President Lincoln; hear William Channing preach; walk to Fort Albany to preach to the Sixteenth Massachusetts.

Nov. 18. To see review at Upton's Hill. See distant skirmish.

Nov. 19. Brigade review.

Nov. 20. Grand review, — 53,000 men.

Nov. 24. [At home.] Preach sermon on "Washington in November." Church crowded.

These entries are intermixed with "Bible-class," "Visited seven schools," "Baptized William and Helen," "Ministers' meeting," and other affairs which would seem to be of peaceful life.

At this time Mr. Clarke was general secretary of the American Unitarian Association. In the "Monthly Journal" of December, 1861, he gives the following account of his ten days' stay in Washington during the previous month.

My last visit of any length to Washington was in 1851, — ten years ago. In those days it was a city to weep over. It was a city of politicians and place-hunters. The influence of the Government and of office-holders was so preponderant that all other powers gave way before the power of place. .

One thing, however, was essential to all aspirants for office: they must believe in slavery, or, at least, must believe in giving slavery all it asked. The bitter mockery then known as the "Compromises of 1850" had been passed. The Fugitive Slave Law of Senator Mason had been universally accepted as constitutional and right. Great men of all parties had agreed that anti-slavery agitation was ended. The conscience, reason, and heart of man were to be forever silenced on this subject.

I recollect going into the Senate chamber one day, and sitting behind the chair of Mr. Clay. It was his last session in Congress. He spoke, that morning, with great contempt of the "Free-Soil" party; and said, "We have put them down, down, down, — so low down, that they will never rise again." Yet now the principles of this party, so low in 1851, have, in 1861, taken possession of the White House and the Capitol.

In those days, to be a Free-Soiler was equivalent to exclusion from the common courtesies and privileges of Washington. All public offices, all places in the Cabinet, all important committees in the Senate and House were held by their opponents. At the house of Gamaliel Bailey, editor of the "National Era," a little knot of Free-Soilers would collect every evening. There I used to see Giddings, Seward, Chase, Hale, Julian, Horace Mann, and a few others. Meantime the great East Room of the White House was nightly crowded with ambassadors, heads of departments, military and naval officers, and brilliant women; so crowded that it was difficult to see any one at a distance from you, except two men who towered head and shoulders above all the rest, and were visible from any part of the room, — General Scott and Samuel Houston. . . .

Such was Washington in 1851. How is it now, in 1861?

Ten years have passed, and what a change! The crowds who then thronged Presidential levees are either fled, or "gone to salute the rising morn." That "rising morn" is the same Free-Soil dynasty which, ten years ago, met in Dr. Bailey's little upper chamber, — that same party which I heard Henry Clay then declare to be "put down, down, down for ever and ever!" The two foremost men in the Cabinet of Mr. Lincoln are two who used to meet in that room, Seward and Chase· another, Henry Wilson, is chairman of one of the most important committees. Everything has passed into the hands of the party which was then DOWN, — White House, Capitol, Departments, Army, Navy, Treasury, — everything but the Supreme Court, and that sits helpless for good, powerless for evil. Young politician, believe in IDEAS!

Blinded by some divine Nemesis, the slave power, which had all in its hands, flung all away. Dividing its party at Charleston, it gave the Republicans the President; by seceding from Congress, it gave them a majority in both Houses; by making war on the Union, it gave them the support of a united North; holding the sword and purse of the Union, the army and navy, the Senate and House, it threw them all away. Where are the voices once so loud and arrogant, so domineering and overbearing? Departed all, and departed forever! New men, new scenes. The new era has taken to itself new halls in the extended Capitol. But I willingly lingered in the scene of those great debates, which the pen of History shall make immortal. I stood in the place where was the desk of John Quincy Adams, and thought of the time when the brave old hero stood alone for three days, attacked by all the Southern bullies and Northern dough-faces, — he alone against all, and conquering them all. . . .

The whole aspect of the city is changed. It is like a city of Europe, — like Berlin, or Vienna, or St. Petersburg, — but with a difference. For this of ours is not a mere standing army, to be wielded blindly in the interests of despotism, but an intelligent army of freemen, come to protect liberty and law. It is the nation itself which has taken up arms, and come to Washington to defend its own life and the ideas of the fathers. It has come to defend the Declaration of Independence, and the Constitution, laws, and traditions of the land.

Therefore the most interesting thing in and about Washington is the army, considered as a collection of individuals. I enjoyed talking with the soldiers in the camps, in the hospitals, and in Washington. I talked with many of them from all parts of the land, — Michigan, Minnesota, Kentucky, Pennsylvania, Massachusetts, Vermont, New York; Irish also, and Germans; and I never talked with men who seemed animated by a more earnest purpose; never with men more serious, manly, and unpretending. Rogues and villains there doubtless are in this, as in all armies; but they are a small minority. The mails go from every camp, weighed down with letters for friends at home. From Port Royal, the other day, the steamer brought fifteen thousand letters, an average of one for every man.

In Fort Runion, which is the *tête du pont* of the Long Bridge, there is a company of Marblehead men in garrison. Nearly every one of them has had fever and ague, for the fort is on the edge of a swamp. But the men said they were very willing to stay there, since any other company would have to be seasoned as they had been, and they were already acclimated. There was true heroism in this. . . .

Saturday, November 16, ———. Went in a carriage with three friends (one of them being W. H. Channing, and another the Boston correspondent of the "New

York Tribune") over the Long Bridge, on a visit to some of the camps in Virginia. Our passes, good for ten days, and admitting us everywhere within the lines, had been procured from General McClellan. We first went to Fort Runion and Fort Albany, both garrisoned by the Massachusetts Fourteenth, and under the command of Col. William B. Greene. Colonel Greene is a graduate of West Point, and has been successively in the Florida War, as United States officer of regulars; student of theology in the Baptist Seminary, Newton; Unitarian minister at South Brookfield, Mass.; and author of various profound metaphysical, theological, and politico-economical works. From Fort Albany one overlooks the Potomac and a wide extent of country. It is a powerful fortification, defended by high earthworks, deep ditches, a tangled *abattis* of limbs of trees, and heavy pieces of artillery. The colonel summoned his regiment together, and asked them to sing some of their songs and hymns for the party; introducing to them more particularly Mrs. John A. Andrew. Among these songs the most conspicuous was the famous John Brown song, —

"John Brown's body lies a-mouldering in the grave;
His soul goes marching on.
Glory, glory, hallelujah!"

Several times afterward did we hear this song sounding among the woods of Virginia; and surely it seemed true in the deepest sense. John Brown's soul is marching on! For what is the soul of John Brown but his unconquerable hatred of slavery, and his fervent desire of seeing it abolished? And is not that desire and feeling marching on? Is not slavery recognized more and more as the cause of the war, the deadly foe of the Union, the poison in our cup, the enemy of true democracy and true Christianity, and something which must be destroyed, if the life of the nation is to be saved? . . .

To say this, or something equivalent, to Massachusetts men, on the banks of the Potomac, in Old Virginia, was accounted by me a privilege. The colonel asked us to address the men, and we did; but at this time we spoke of the pride which Massachusetts took in her soldiers, — of the credit they brought to the old State by their discipline in camp and courage in the field. We told them of the women at home, who could be happy only when doing something for their soldiers; and of the heroic deaths of the brave officers, Massachusetts boys, who, amid their own sufferings, thought only of the welfare of their men, and of their heroism. A lady of the party said a few words, suited to the scene and hour. . . .

During the evening, Governor Andrew took me, with two other gentlemen, to call on the President. The porter at the White House told us that he had gone out, but would soon be back. So we went on through gallery and corridor, blue room, council room, and parlor, — all lighted, and all empty. The doors stood open; but not a soul could be anywhere seen. The only signs of occupancy which we found were two pairs of little shoes standing outside a door, indicative of children sleeping quietly within. Happy children, who can play all day in a palace as in a cottage, and sleep all night undisturbed by the uneasy cares which deny rest to kings and presidents!

Selecting the room which best suited us, we talked together until the President, returning home and hearing our voices, came where we were. What is the impression which his appearance, manner, and conversation make on one? This: of an unassuming country gentleman, modest but self-possessed, with sagacity and full powers of observation, but without the least touch of political manœuvring. Mr. Lincoln is no politician; does not pretend to be a great and accomplished statesman; but is an honest, candid, modest, sagacious

American citizen, who means to do his duty as well as he can.

Sunday, November 17. In the afternoon of this sunny Sunday, I walked over the Long Bridge to hold a religious service with the Massachusetts Fourteenth, in Fort Albany, in compliance with an invitation brought to me on the previous evening by three of the soldiers. It so happened that I stood to address the troops with my face to the Potomac and the city of Washington; and the soft lights of evening gathered over the scene as the service went on, and the voices of the soldiers arose in song, while "the sounding aisles of the dim woods" of Virginia rang to the anthem of the free soldiers of Massachusetts. It was a thrilling scene, and one long to be remembered by me.

After preaching, parade-drill; and after this came what the colonel called the "cultus of the flag."

The soldiers were drawn up around the flag-staff: the band saluted the flag; the men presented arms. Then the flag was lowered by four men, and carefully folded into a triangular form; then carried by one of them in his arms reverently, while the others walked beside him; and the soldiers formed an escort for it to headquarters, where it was put away for the night on a shelf.

The result of this visit to Washington was, on the whole, gratifying. Far more gratifying was this visit in 1861, in time of war, than the other in 1851, in time of peace. Then all was outward prosperity; but inwardly all was corruption. Now outwardly everything denotes disaster and calamity; but inwardly there is a brave and generous purpose. Soldiers go to the war impelled by this motive; their friends at home feel its influence. .

It is very sad to go through the hospitals, and see the young men maimed for life; unable any more to take part in youthful sports; never again to ride or run or swim or skate or dance. They go out with a youthful beauty which touches all hearts; they come home disfigured and deformed. What does not the nation owe to those who incur these risks for its sake?

Nevertheless, war is like a fever, in which nature makes an effort to throw off some deep-seated evil worse than the fever. Our nation was gradually becoming corrupt. The poison of slavery was penetrating every part of the social system. It corrupted the great political parties, it polluted the church, it demoralized trade, it debased society.

Is it not a grand thing to see all this flood of evil checked, even by the storm of war?

Thus may Washington, redeemed and purified, yet become our holy city! God grant that the immense woes and wrongs of war may at least produce this happy result, a community saved from the corruptions of prosperity and peace.

FROM SOME OF HIS SERMONS OF THIS PERIOD.

It is, perhaps, the highest kind of courage, this of standing at our post, no matter whether we seem to succeed or to fail. For this, we dwell so often, with tearful eyes, on the story of the unequal fight, when young men stand firm at their post, though conscious that it is in vain. The three hundred at Thermopylæ, the six hundred at Balaklava, the Fifteenth and Twentieth Massachusetts at Ball's Bluff, — their heroism affects us more deeply than that of the men who share the triumphs of victorious days.

Such moments of heroic courage indicate to us what is the real nobleness of life. It is to do all, and then stand; to stand firm to our duty, loyal to right, faithful to justice and truth, whether men hear or forbear. This makes it worth while to live. If a man only lives for success, he is poor and cowardly when disaster comes. Then we hear him finding fault, complaining, lamenting, fearing everything; throwing doubt on everything; talking like the book of Ecclesiastes, not like the book of Revelation.

Having learned to stand by the flag, we may also learn to stand by what the flag symbolizes; to stand up for equal rights, universal freedom, for justice to all, for a true democracy.

The nation says, coming to itself, "I am a nation with ideas and duties, and I am here to do them." And that is what it has not said before for the last thirty or forty years. Patriotism is the self-consciousness of a nation; and while we were only individuals, struggling for our own selfish good, we had no patriotism, and could have none.

God does not take away the Red Sea, nor the wilderness, nor Jordan, but goes with us through them all, — a cloud by day, a pillar of fire by night.

What deeper wound in the heart than the sense of an irreparable loss? But within these two years we have seen the best blood of the land, the purest and noblest children born in our Northern homes, go out to die, with their fathers' blessing and their mothers' kiss. These children, for whose coming God prepared this fair land, that they might open their infant eyes on the beauty of its hills and valleys, its lakes and forests; for whose childhood past generations of thinkers, from Plato and Aristotle down to Pestalozzi and Horace Mann, have been providing methods of education, — these young men, purified in the calm atmosphere of virtuous homes, developed by the training and discipline of schools, of study, of books, of travel, the costly fruit of the latest century and the most advanced race, go to die in a field of unavailing destruction. I visit their mothers or sisters, their fathers or brothers, when the fatal news arrives. I go with fear, dreading to meet a great and hopeless anguish. I find heaven there. I find the peace of God in their souls. I go to carry sympathy, and words of comfort; but I receive instead inspiration. The boy, falling on the battlefield, renews all the tales of Greek and Roman heroism. We can burn our "Plutarch." We do not need to read hereafter the stories of Themistocles, of Aristides, of Leonidas. Your brothers and sons are to be spoken of in history forever, and are to be the illuminating lights of the coming age.

FROM HIS DIARY.

January 1, 1863. President Lincoln's proclamation, freeing the slaves. [Announcement had been made of this proclamation on the 22d of September, to take effect on the 1st of January.] Tremont Temple; I speak. Tea at Mrs. Ellis Gray Loring's. [Mr. Loring was one of the original Abolitionists, a member of the Church of the Disciples, and a near personal friend.] Evening, go to meet the Educational Commission at Mrs. Cabot's. [This was a commission which had in charge the sending of teachers to the freedmen at Port Royal and other points occupied by the national forces.]

TO N. AUGUSTUS STAPLES.

January 1, 1863.

I shall be in Washington on the second Sunday in January, and cannot exchange with you on that day. I am sorry it happens so, for I wished to have an exchange with you.

This is the great day which separates forever the people of this Union from slavery and slaveholding, — for the border slavery will fall of itself soon.

Glory to God in the highest, and on earth, peace, good will to men.

FROM HIS DIARY.

Sunday, January 4, 1863. Preach New Year's sermon on the proclamation. Afternoon, Lord's Supper. Leave for Washington at 11.10.

Jan. 7. Tom, Lilian and I leave [Philadelphia] for Washington at 11.35.

Jan. 8. To the Capitol; President's levee. Call on Mr. Sam. Hooper, dine with Judge Thomas. [Hon. Benjamin F. Thomas, then member of Congress for Mr. Clarke's district.]

Jan. 11. Preach in the Senate Chamber; good congregation. Lilian and I drive with Mrs. S. Hooper to the contraband camp. Dine at Mr. Hooper's with Mr. Sumner and Captain Bliss.

Jan. 12. Smithsonian; Sanitary; Capitol; Senate, House, and Library; Long Bridge.

Jan. 13. Carriage with Henry Huidekoper and Colonel and Mrs. Ashurst to Arlington Heights, and to Colonel Wells' camp at Alexandria.

He thus records one of the incidents of this visit to Washington.

I went one Sunday afternoon to the contraband camp, [near Washington] where are collected the negroes, men, women, and children, who have escaped from slavery. Small-pox being among them, we could not go into their houses; but they gathered around the carriage, and their superintendent asked them to sing for us: they sang hymns, one woman giving out the lines, and the rest singing, swaying their bodies with a slow motion backward and forward. At the request of the superintendent, I said something to them; and they replied, "Yes, sir," "That's right," "We will, sir," and so on; and when I ended they said, "Thank you, sir." Then one or two of the men told their experiences in slavery, and how they escaped, and how they had left behind their friends and children, tears streaming from their eyes, and others crying too; for all had left some behind; and the ladies in the carriage cried with them. Lastly, an old negro man prayed, leaning, like Jacob, on the top of his staff; and all the rest knelt on the ground, in the mud, and solemnly said "Amen," or else sang a sort of chanting assent, in places where they were moved to, — a low under-song, as it seemed, of sympathy. We all noticed, while they sang, what a profoundly reverent expression was on their faces; surely such as I never saw on the faces of white men. This visit to these poor people, Hebrews in the wilderness, who had come out of Egypt, but had not yet reached the promised land, was very touching. I was told that they easily found work in the District, the able-bodied men and the good female house-servants very easily. I asked one colored woman, just from Virginia, if they had heard down there, among the slaves, of the President's Proclamation. She said, "Oh, yes, massa! we all knows about it; only we dars n't let on. We pretends not to know. I said to my ole massa, 'What's this Massa Lincoln is going to do to the poor nigger? I hear he is going to cut 'em up awful bad. How is it, massa?' I just pretended foolish, sort of."

In July, 1863, Mr. Clarke went to Gettysburg, to find a young relative who had been wounded in the battle and was reported missing. He writes: —

The more I look at it, the more I deem the battle of Gettysburg the most decisive ever fought on this continent. On Tuesday afternoon, four days after the battle, I spent an hour on the field.

I walked up the road from the town toward the cemetery. All along the way lay soldiers who had been killed. . . . Poor desolated homes, South as well as North! Long will they look in vain for those dear to them as ours to us.

All the churches had been turned into hospitals. The pews were floored over, and the men lay close together with every variety of wounds, but all so patient and so quiet that it touched one's heart to see them. After two or three hours' search I found my young nephew, a Harvard graduate of 1862, among the ten thousand wounded in and around Gettysburg. He commanded a regiment of four hundred men in the first day's battle, when the First and Eleventh Army Corps held back for four long hours the whole of Lee's army. This regiment, with two others, making twelve hundred in all, held back five thousand men. They were shelled for an hour, and then were under a fire of musketry from the whole five thousand for another hour. Most of the officers were wounded, some of them two or three times. Of four hundred men belonging to this regiment, only a hundred and five came out untouched.

Our officers and soldiers understand more and more that the conflict is between liberty and slavery, between civilization and barbarism, between Christianity and Antichrist. What else supports them, and gives them such patience and fortitude? It is the most marked feature of the war, this supreme peace of men who seem to have lost everything that makes life worth having. I saw men maimed, crippled for life; but they all said, "No matter, we beat them." I saw a man who had lost both his eyes; but he was cheerful, even merry. One man who had lost a foot said, "I would rather have lost the other than not have won the victory." When I saw my nephew, who had lost his right arm, cheerful and contented; when I saw all these young soldiers, many of them badly wounded, so modest and so manly, without exultation, but with this earnest satisfaction in having done something really great, — I could not grieve any more for their loss. I saw that each lost limb, each wound, each scar, was the Cross of the Legion of Honor, to be worn always, as a proof that they had deserved well of their country; as a proof to themselves that they had not lived in vain.

TO HIS SISTER IN CANADA.

JAMAICA PLAIN, *September* 5, 1863.

H. J. H. and A. C. H. came here yesterday, — the former to go back to college, the latter to the High School. They spent their vacation in catching Morgan. They, with F. W. H. and the two B.'s, joined a Meadville company which volunteered to go to protect Pittsburgh. When there, they were sent to guard the line of the Ohio against Morgan's retreat, helped catch him, and were sent to guard him on his way to Columbus. That is the way boys spend their summer vacation in the States.

Of a young soldier who belonged to the Church of the Disciples, and was killed in May, 1864, Mr. Clarke said: —

Henry May Bond went to the war, and returned to it again, from a pure sense of duty. He had no taste for military life; in his modesty he distrusted his own fitness for the service; but he thought it his duty, having served his time in a nine-months' regiment, to enlist again. In a letter to a brother officer he says: "In the hour of personal danger I am strong and courageous only in the faith that, should it please God to take my life while in the discharge of what I deem to be my highest duty, all will be well with me. I should be worth nothing to my friends or my country without that faith in God." So the good, brave boy lived, cheerfully and patiently; so, cheerfully and patiently, he died.

TO E. C. C.

June 18, 1864.

. . Do you remember David W. Norton, who joined our church eight years ago, and afterwards went to Chicago? He became major in an Illinois regiment, fought in all the chief battles, and was killed, June 3, by a rebel sharpshooter, while in front of our lines with the general, sketching the enemy's lines. Monday I went to Mount Auburn to the funeral. Yesterday I received a cane he cut for me on Lookout Mountain, after the battle.

. . . Do you see how bravely the colored soldiers have fought at Petersburg? They have been praised by the generals on the field for their courage. Still, Government can pay them only seven dollars a month! I talked with Governor Andrew about it after church last Sunday. He said, "I wrote last week to Charles Sumner and Thaddeus Stevens that I should pursue this matter without rest or pause; that I should neither forget nor forgive any neglect or opposition in regard to it; that I would not die till I had vindicated the rights of the colored soldiers." . . .

TO E. C. C.

WASHINGTON, *June* 29, 1864.

I came to this city last Friday, preached in the Capitol on Sunday, and have been seeing a number of persons since then. I have had one or two good talks with Mr. Chase about public affairs; also with Charles Sumner. As I am *locum tenens* of Chaplain Charning, I have the *entrée* of the Senate and House as I please, so that I can go in and sit on one of the sofas behind the members, and talk to those I know as they pass me. Our Mr. Boutwell made a very good speech a few days since. Mr. Sumner has succeeded, within the past week, in getting through Congress laws to repeal the laws authorizing a coast-wise slave-trade; to repeal the fugitive slave laws; to allow colored people to testify before the United States courts; and to establish a Freedman's Bureau.

To-day I am going to the front as one of a Sanitary Relief Corps. I go to Fortress Monroe, City Point, — the lines, — and Norfolk; stay three or four days, and return to Baltimore on Monday. I hope to see and hear a good deal in these three days. I wish I had you with me. We have never traveled much together, and I should enjoy having you by me.

TO A. H. C.

NEW YORK, *April* 4, 1865.

What good news! These things seem to come as apples fall when they are ripe; we pull at them in spring and summer and they hold on, but at last drop of themselves so quietly that we hardly notice it. Abolition of slavery, fall of Charleston, fall of Richmond, — when they arrive they are like things foreordained from the foundation of the world. But there is a sad story to follow of losses, — another great flood of grief to rush over the land, giving its pathetic minor to the music of thanksgiving. But let us hope that the end has come . We heard of the fall of Richmond, at Springfield. It startled Henry B. Rogers into such unwonted enthusiasm that he clapped a hand on each of my shoulders, and half embraced me. "Negro troops too," said he, "think of that!" I did think of it, with grateful tears, in my heart if not in my eyes, to that great Wisdom who does all things well

I shall see Dr. Bellows this morning, — ride down Broadway to Wall Street, and see how the city looks, then come and work on my sermon till the last minute. Let us trust that whether it be good or bad, the Master may make it good to the hearers in its influence and results.

And the peace came that summer.

FROM A SERMON OF OCTOBER 22, 1865.

Yesterday, the Fifty-Fourth Regiment of colored troops marched through Boston, on its return from the war, and was disbanded. Ah, could we do our work as that regiment has done its work! They have helped to achieve the safety of the nation and the deliverance of their race.

FROM A SERMON OF DECEMBER 7, 1865.

On this day of Thanksgiving, while thanking God for all his other gifts, let us thank him most of all for good men — men loving justice, truth, freedom, Christianity, more than comfort or peace; men ready to live and die for an idea; enthusiasts for goodness and right.

Good men save the State; but they only save it when other men are capable of being moved and led by their example. A time comes, in the downfall and corruption of communities, when good men struggle ineffectually against the tendencies of ruin. Hannibal could not save Carthage. Marcus Antoninus could not save the Roman Empire. Demosthenes could not save Greece, and Jesus Christ himself could not save Jerusalem from decay and destruction. Nations can go too far to be saved. The great hope of this land is in the fact that the mass of the people mean right, and, unless misled by demagogues, will do right. But, for this hope to be realized, all Christians and all patriots must work together.

CHAPTER XVI.

EDUCATION.

THE reader of Mr. Clarke's autobiography has already seen how central and vital was his interest in public education in his early life. He had been a teacher soon after he left college. At Louisville, he gave his personal attention to elevating the public schools, and became superintendent of schools there early in 1839. So soon as his home was established at Jamaica Plain, he took a personal interest in the public schools of that neighborhood, and was chosen for successive years upon the school committee, until Jamaica Plain was absorbed by the city of Boston.

In the year 1863 he was appointed by Governor Andrew a member of the State Board of Education, to succeed Governor Boutwell. The Board of Education in Massachusetts has the entire control of the Normal Schools and of the Art School. He retained this position until December, 1869, when he resigned. He was one of the active members of that board. He drew upits annual report for the year 1868, and in reference to the time allotted for study, he proposed that eight hours' application, including the time spent in school, be fixed as the outside limit of brain work of Normal School pupils.

In the year 1867 he was appointed a professor in the Divinity School of Harvard College. It was understood that he was not to live at Cambridge, but was to be present two days in the week,[1] and a good deal of free-

---

[1] *In* the year 1867-68 he gave two days; after that only one day.

dom was given him in the selection of his subjects. In the quinquennial catalogue he stands as "Professor of Natural Theology and Christian Doctrine," — a wide range which in another line of life would be called a pirate's commission. In the annual catalogue, at the same date, his title stands, "Professor of Ethnic Religions and the Creeds of Christendom." Mr. Clarke used this commission almost as broadly as it was given. The outcome of this work which has most interest for the reading public is found in the two books, "Steps of Belief" and "Ten Great Religions," of which he laid the foundations in lectures prepared at this time for his classes. Besides these, which, at the time, were called lectures on "Comparative Theology," he delivered a course on "Christian Doctrine." Afterwards he prepared several lectures on "The Roman Catholic Church," and on other subjects. The lectures on subjects specially Christian form a considerable part of his courses. In the autumn of 1869, his subject was "The Apostle Paul."

His duties at the divinity school required him to spend at least one morning every week with the students. He enjoyed the work, and especially his relationship with the young men. Indeed, his intercourse with students who were preparing to be preachers was always interesting to him; and as family ties often drew him to Meadville, where is situated the only divinity school of the Unitarian Church of America,[1] he maintained a friendly intimacy with the students he found there, as well as with those at Cambridge.

In 1866 he was chosen by the legislature of Massachusetts an overseer of Harvard College, and when that board of overseers was reconstituted in 1873, so

---

[1] The Unitarian Church of America also endowed the Cambridge divinity school, which is now supported by the endowment; but it is distinctly understood that the school shall be undenominational, and its professors may be taken from any Christian communion.

that the alumni should choose the overseers, he was one of the first elected. The alumni continued to elect him as often as they could, until his death.[1] Under the constitution of the board, a person who has served for two terms cannot be reëlected for a third, without a year's interval.

The board of overseers of Harvard College is one of those boards of which the instincts of Massachusetts men are very fond, which has very few powers, but a great deal of power.[2]

It would be hard to overstate the importance of the public supervision exercised by the board of overseers. Experience proves that our main hope for the permanence and ever-widening influence of the university must rest upon this double-headed organization. The English practice of setting up a single board of private trustees to carry on a school or a charity of some founder or founders has certainly proved a bad one; and when we count by generations, the institutions thus established have proved short-lived. The same causes which have brought about the decline of English endowed schools would threaten the life of the university were it not for the existence of the board of overseers.

Mr. Clarke was a loyal child of the university, who felt the value of the training to himself. He could always be relied upon for active work in the business of the overseers, and was always glad to take his share of the details of the work. He early formed very broad plans for the divinity school, plans which he saw

---

[1] That is, they chose him at the elections of 1866, 1873, 1880, and 1886.

[2] Doctor Dwight says of Harvard and Bowdoin Colleges, that each of them is governed by two boards, whose business it is to quarrel with each other; but that Yale College is more fortunate. The arrangement at Yale was for one board, which did as Doctor Dwight bade it.

made real in part, while for a part the future is still responsible. He was himself, by well-formed conviction, a positive Unitarian, but no man was more loyal to the Church Universal than he, as indeed a loyal Unitarian should be.[1]

It may be possible that a man who believes in the Westminster Confession, with all his mind and heart and soul and strength, shall do justice to the theological views of Emerson and Parker, and can be trusted in a theological school to present such views fairly. But it is not probable.

On the other hand, it will not often happen that a professor chosen for his duty because he has repudiated High Calvinism in all its works and ways will give precise respect to the just gradations and the nice dependencies of the Westminster Confession.

Mr. Clarke, therefore, all his life long, was hoping and planning for a real "University of Theology" in Cambridge, where every important communion should be represented by some one who could state its views, its dogmas and its plans, and even its rituals, in such a way that the members of that communion should think themselves fairly represented. He did not propose to have twenty or thirty professors who had no strong convictions on these dividing subjects. Rather, he wished to have as many as possible who had strong convictions. The man who wrote "Ten Great Religions" was not the man who would wish to have the professors of a divinity school ignore the existence of all religions except Christianity. And the man who

---

[1] The only origin of the word *Unitarian* for which there is historical authority must be looked for among the *Uniti* or *Unitarii* who, after the Synod of Thorde, gave their assent to the plan of *Unity* there agreed upon, as a method of mutual toleration among Catholics, Calvinists, Lutherans, and Socinians. *H*istorically, there can be found no authority for referring the origin of the word to a distinctive belief in the unity of God, which is, indeed, believed in by Trinitarians quite as earnestly as by Unitarians.

wrote "Truths and Errors of Orthodoxy" would be sure that what is known as Orthodoxy was fairly interpreted, by its very best advocates, before the pitiless jury of intelligent young men.

In 1864, Mr. Clarke was made chairman of a committee to consider this subject. He was indefatigable in obtaining information, writing to and consulting with professors and officials of other universities. In the report drawn up by him, and presented in February, 1865, to the board of overseers, he says : —

What your committee are prepared, at this time, to recommend to the corporation and government of the university is, simply to extend to the department of theology the system of university lectures already inaugurated in other departments.

Let the corporation invite members of different denominations to guarantee an adequate remuneration to lecturers taken from among their own best scholars. The most eminent men might thus be brought to Cambridge, from among the Presbyterian, Baptist, Methodist, Episcopalian, or other denominations, to give, each, a course of lectures on some branch of theology. . . .

If there be such a thing as a university, it ought to have a department of theology; and this department ought to contain professors of every chief school of opinion. What would some of us not give for an opportunity to attend such a school even now ? What would not all earnest and truth-loving young men, longing for solid knowledge in religion, not sacrifice for such an opportunity ?

This war is breaking up sectarianism. Now is the time to institute such a measure, — to try whether in this Christian land we cannot have one school of Christian theology where the student can hear differing and opposing views calmly and honestly stated.

TO E. E. HALE.

March 14, 1867.

I inclose you a copy of some letters received by me when attempting to do something to enlarge the theological department of the university. You may, perhaps, use to advantage the opinions of some of these gentlemen in your correspondence about the Methodist and Free-Will Baptist schools. How fast things move! It is only two years since Dr. Walker and some of those to whom I wrote thought all attempts at bringing together the sects at Cambridge chimerical. Now, there seems already a prospect of having there the schools of three other denominations beside the Unitarian, — the Episcopal, Free-Will Baptist, and Methodist.

He favored every detail of the arrangements which have led to some approach toward such a university in the present constitution of the Cambridge schools of divinity. The divinity school in which he himself was educated now maintains six professors and three other teachers, and the students are permitted to attend the lectures given in all the branches of the university by more than two hundred professors and instructors. Of the special staff of the divinity school itself, it is understood that three professors are of the Unitarian communion, two of the Baptist, and one of that branch of the Congregational Church of New Enggland which has never accepted, as the other has, the Unitarian name.

During the winter of 1867–68 he lectured on Tuesdays and Thursdays to the students at the Cambridge Divinity School. In one of his reports (after mentioning the Tuesday lesson) he says : —

On Thursdays I had a lesson with the Senior and

Middle classes in Christian doctrine, beginning with Anthropology, and proceeding to Theology proper, Christology, Soteriology, and Ecclesiology. Each of these courses consisted of about thirty lessons.

During the present year (1868-69) I visit the school only one day in the week, viz., Tuesday. Finding it impossible to give two days to this work, I informed the corporation, through the president, that I was ready to resign altogether, or to give one day instead of two. The president told me that they preferred to have me come one day rather than not at all.

Accordingly, I now hear the whole school every Tuesday, in Natural and Revealed Religion.

The course will consist of about forty lessons. The first part will relate to the controversy between Atheism and Theism; the second, to that between Deism and Christianity; the third, to that between Catholic and Protestant Christianity; the fourth, to that between Orthodox and Liberal Protestant Christianity. My method is to give out, at the end of each lesson, three or four questions, which are the subject of the next lesson. To these questions I request each member of the class to prepare concise written answers. The answers, being read, are discussed. This occupies about an hour. I then read my own answer to the questions, which occupies from twenty minutes to half an hour.

I find the young men interested in their studies. They seem to put their minds seriously to the investigation and discussion of these questions.

Rev. C. W. Wendte, at that time a pupil, has given us these recollections: —

During my stay at the Cambridge divinity school in 1868-69, Mr. Clarke was lecturer or professor. His coming was an event. His fresh, unconventional methods, his simplicity, piety, and friendliness were delightful to the students, and inspired new life in the school.

His courses in Speculative Theology were awakening and kindling, and led to earnest discussion between the students and the professor, and among the students themselves.

A second series of lectures was on "The Great Religions of the World," and here Dr. Clarke departed from the traditional methods of the school. As in the previous course, his style was conversational rather than formal, and the lecture proper rarely occupied more than a third of the time which was devoted to the subject. At the beginning he assigned to two or more of the class, for their study and report, one of the ten great religions treated. He then selected a question or topic for the evening meeting; *e. g.*, "What does this specific religion teach about God," or "moral obligations," or "immortality?"

TO A PROFESSOR IN A THEOLOGICAL SCHOOL.

What we want is a ministry who look upon their business as really important, and are thoroughly in earnest about it; who would rather be preachers and pastors than anything else in the world. . . .

You must give the young men a chance to express freely their notions, even though they seem to you to be crude and foolish. You must encourage them to inquire and think in their own way, rather than in your way, for if they do not, they will not think at all. I judge of others by myself. If I have ever gained clear and satisfactory convictions, it has been by following out my own thoughts. The mind of a young man who is at all in earnest must go through a process of fermentation, and throw off a deal of scum in that way. The business of a wise teacher is to guide and regulate the process, not to try to prevent it.

He had always desired that among the departments of university instruction more attention should be given to the study of modern languages, and in January, 1865 (the same winter in which his report in regard to enlarging the divinity school was offered), he presented a report on this subject. He says: —

Your committee's conviction of the importance and the needs of this department compels it to state emphatically its opinion that injustice is done to the cause of education, and to every class which graduates, by the low position assigned to modern languages in the university. While Latin, Greek, and mathematics are made obligatory studies during the freshman and sophomore years, and Latin and Greek during the junior year, modern languages are made elective. During the first year no place is given to them even as elective studies. During the sophomore year French is permitted, but only as an extra. During the junior year one modern language may be taken instead of mathematics, and another instead of chemistry, and during the senior year Italian is also allowed as an elective study. Your committee cannot but consider that the course in this respect has changed for the worse in recent times; for formerly modern languages were required studies, even in the freshman year. . . .

Your committee has no prejudice against the Greek language; its object in this comparison is only to show how little is done for modern languages. It is difficult to see the benefit that it will be to a class of a hundred young men to know how to write Greek prose, but surely no one can doubt the benefit that it would be to them to be able to write and speak French, German, Italian, or Spanish. Probably no graduate ever will have occasion to write another line of Greek composition; but if the young man be a lawyer, ability to speak German may help him to clients; if he be a merchant, to be able to write French or Spanish letters will be of assistance. Perhaps half of every class, sometime in their lives, will have occasion to travel abroad, in which case to speak the language of the country, however imperfectly, will add infinitely to the pleasure and profit of the journey. And whether the graduate becomes lawyer, physician, clergyman, or man of science, he will find constant benefit in being able to read with ease books and periodicals in each of the modern languages. . . .

Grant everything that can be said in favor of the study of Greek — the beauty of the Greek language, the richness of its literature, its use as a mental discipline: the question remains, Which is the most useful? . . . And may not the intellect be disciplined by useful study, as well as by useless? We consider the time given to Greek composition as wholly wasted except as far as the mental discipline is concerned. It does not help, but actually hinders the acquisition of the Greek language and acquaintance with the Greek literature. Every one knows that to learn to read a language and to learn to write it are two wholly distinct mental operations. If a young man spends his strength and time in learning to write Greek, he has just so much less time and strength for learning to read it. One of your committee lately went to New York in company with a young lady, and noticed that she had taken with her a copy of the Greek Iliad to read by the way. How many graduates of our university would be likely to have done this? Probably very few graduates of Harvard can read a Greek book with facility after having devoted a large part of seven of the best years of life to this study. Yet this young lady made no claim to distinguished scholarship. She had studied Greek simply in order to read Greek books. Cousequently she had given no more time to philology than was necessary for this purpose. If the time now devoted to grammatical minutiæ, to the subtilties of Greek words and the pedantry of Greek prosody were spent in reading the literature, and if after the first year Greek were made an elective study to be taken only by those who had a taste for it, we should find many more of our graduates amusing themselves on their journeys with Plato or Homer.

And we cannot but take this occasion to enter a protest against the constant tendency to make grammars larger, and consequently worse. The size of grammars has become a sore evil in education. There is not an intelligent teacher in Massachusetts but will tell you that if the Latin and Greek grammars contained a quarter of their present contents, they would be four times as good.

Your committee knows perfectly well that in reply to all this it will be told about "mental discipline." Mental discipline, however, ought not to be made the excuse for every useless and irrelevant study which takes the place of what would be useful when learned, as well as a discipline in learning.

Mr. Clarke was also interested in the admission of women to Harvard College, and in 1872 prepared a report on this subject. Although he was chairman of this committee, he was in a minority; and his report, therefore, was a minority report. He had obtained information from President White of Cornell University, from Oberlin College, from Ann Arbor, from Washington University at St. Louis, and other colleges, as well as many normal schools. He considered the result of his investigations favorable to the admission of women to Harvard; but the other members of the committee differed from him, and the plan was rejected.

In 1873 the admission of women to the medical school of the university engaged his attention. On this subject he writes to Rev. E. E. Hale: —

JAMAICA PLAIN, *March* 7, 1873.

The more I think of it, the more important it seems to me that the arrangement shall be made by which the female medical school shall become a department of the medical school of Harvard University. For this end I am ready to work; but, unfortunately, I am going to Troy to-morrow for theatre preaching, and have promised to stay there and read on Monday evening, and so shall not be back until Tuesday night. After that I will coöperate with you in raising the $40,000.

. I think it important that before beginning the subscription we should have some definite assurance from the trustees of the medical college on the one hand, and the corporation of Harvard University on the other, that by raising the $40,000 the union can be accomplished. Perhaps you already have all the guarantees that are necessary and attainable at this stage of the proceeding.

If you decide to do anything, and want my aid, let me find a letter here on my return, telling me what you wish me to do.

He had at heart every change in the customs of the university which should give more worth to its degrees, by making them expressions of the simple truth, and not forms of respect or compliment. With this view he once draughted the following resolutions, the spirit of which has passed into some of the changes made in the university since that time, although in this precise form they never were accepted by the board of overseers.

Resolved, That this board recommend to the corporation,

1. That all the degrees given in the university shall be attainable by examination.

2. That no honorary degree shall be conferred as a compliment to mere official position.

3. That to obtain by examination the degree of Doctor of Laws, or Doctor of Divinity, residence shall not be required, and that residence may be dispensed with in the case of Master of Arts.

4. That in these three departments the university may accept, in place of examination, and as an equivalent therefor, any valuable work in art, law, or divinity, which work shall be specified in the diploma, mentioned when the degree is conferred, and recorded in the quinquennial catalogue.

All his life, Mr. Clarke maintained an interest in astronomical science, and he was personally fond of observing the stars. He enlarged his apparatus for this purpose from time to time, and in the year 1877 built a little platform above his study for an observatory, and mounted there a telescope with a four-inch object-glass, which he used, to his great delight, in the study of the heavens. No member of the board of overseers of the college took more personal interest than he did in the Harvard Observatory, and he was for many years chairman of the visiting committee.

The reader who is trying to see how he divided his time in the last twenty years of his life must give one day in fourteen of each winter to meetings of the board of overseers, or to visits of examination at Cambridge.

During the same years he was one of the trustees of the Boston Public Library. This service interested him extremely, and he was one of the most active of the board, — always in sympathy with every improvement which brought the treasures of the library more easily into the hands of the people, where they belong. Nothing interested him more than the observations which show what people want to read, which are, of course, an admirable test of the range of public education.

His desire to extend the popular knowledge of astronomy, and the habit of observing the stars, led him to publish a series of maps of the northern heavens, with a lantern, devised by himself, by means of which the observer may trace the forms of the constellations, and determine the name of a star without having to return to the house to examine an atlas of the heavens. On one side of the lantern slides may be inserted, the light within the lantern shining through perforations in the pasteboard. The differing sizes of the holes indicate the different magnitude of the stars, and their relative positions give the forms of the different constellations. All astronomical maps try to represent something; but they do not try, as these do, to represent it to a student who is out of doors, and who from the nature of his study wishes to be in darkness.

A story is told of one of his family who was waked in the middle of the night by hearing steps on the roof near her chamber. In the morning Mr. Clarke acknowledged that he was the midnight wanderer, and asked why she did not come out to join him. He had been watching through the night for an occultation of Jupiter. This was in January, 1886.

He was well-nigh a perfect teacher. His Bible-classes, and his classes of history and literature, which in the work of his church he regularly carried on, were stimulating and suggestive. He was so fond of young people that they could hardly fail to learn from him. "Everything I know of the Norse mythology," said a young student, who will one day be teaching others in the same line, "I learned from him as we sat together, summer evenings, on the piazza."

His book called "Self-Culture," which embodies not only his theories, but a great deal of the practical expericuce of his life, has found, probably for that reason, a very general welcome. Up to this present time it has passed through fifteen editions. Perhaps this book may be considered one of his best contributions to the cause of education.

He read French and German with perfect ease, but he could not readily carry on a conversation in either language. He has told of his trying, in Italy, to get some explanation about the tonsure from one of the clergy in a church which he was visiting. For this purpose he put his questions in his best Latin. The priest thought that Mr. Clarke wanted some one to whom he could confess, and eagerly exclaiming, "Si! si!" rushed off to find a priest for the confessional.

The reader will observe in the letters and diaries frequent allusions to drawing. He was never very skillful in drawing, but he enjoyed using his pencil, and often drew the outlines of a mountain or lake view, or of a building which he wished to preserve in his memory.

In a short speech at the Commencement Dinner of 1886, he gives a review of the progress which Harvard College had made since he knew it first: —

It is said that old men are apt to think that the former days were better than these. I have known Harvard College since 1825, — that is, for sixty years, — and I find it has been improving all the time. I have been on the board of overseers since 1863, except a single year, in which I was excluded by the act of incorporation, and these have been years of remarkable progress in the university.

1. The choice of the board of overseers by the alumni. When I entered the board, the members were chosen by the legislature. There was a great deal of effort used to be elected; but as soon as a man was chosen, he seemed to lose all interest in the matter. Only one or two meetings were held in the year, and many never came even to those. The reports of the visiting committee were often hastily written at the meeting at which they were to be presented. Since the board has been chosen by the alumni the greatest improvement has taken place. We have had as members some of the

best men in the State and the best friends of the college. The meetings have been frequent, and the discussions earnest and interesting.

2. Another important improvement has been made in introducing the elective system. The difference between good teaching and poor is that the good teacher leads, and the poor one drives. The most essential qualification of the good teacher is enthusiasm, of the scholar, interest. When the students at Harvard were forced to pursue a plan of study which was unattractive, they had to be driven; now they have only to be led.

3. Modern languages. When I came on the board of overseers modern languages were systematically discredited. There were four times as many teachers for the two ancient languages as there were for the four modern languages, and a much lower rank was given for proficiency in modern languages than for the same proficiency in Latin and Greek. The doors to the knowledge contained in Greek and Latin books were wide open, but those which admitted to the science, art, and literature of France, Italy, Germany, and Spain were hardly opened at all. Now these languages have full justice done them. In the same way, scientific pursuits have been generously encouraged.

4. The system of voluntary recitations and written examinations is, in my opinion, a great improvement. Formerly, the only business of a teacher was to hear recitations, and make marks for merit. Now, he has the opportunity of teaching. This is one of the greatest educational discoveries of modern times, — that the business of a teacher is to teach.

CHAPTER XVII.

WORK IN THE PULPIT.

IN Mr. Clarke's earlier letters and diaries, when he was still under the rather benumbing influence of the college life of those days, he alludes more than once to his determination to acquire the power of preaching without notes. In Louisville, particularly when he first arrived there, he saw that the habit of the place required ready ability for extempore speaking, and at the first regretted his own deficiency. But so far as such deficiency existed, he soon conquered it. He could not have been in a better school than was afforded him by his seven years in Kentucky. And those who remember his active life, from the time he was thirty years old, remember him as a person who "thought on his feet" with great precision, who spoke easily and effectively, keeping always in sight the end which he had in view at the beginning. The reader will note Mr. Higginson's reference to this power in another chapter of this volume.

He tried the two methods of preaching, namely, extemporizing from brief notes, and writing his sermon in full. Gradually he came to the conviction that by the latter method he was able to say more in the same time, and to say it in a better way. There was also the additional advantage in this method, that what he wrote was ready for publication; but this was a secondary consideration.

He was accustomed to write the greater part of his sermon on the morning of the day on which it was to be delivered, rising early for that purpose; but the sermon had often been carefully thought out during the preceding week.

The sermons of the last fourteen years of his life were printed regularly, as they were delivered. A great number of those preached earlier were also printed. There are five collected volumes of sermons: "The Hour which Cometh," "Go up Higher," "Every-Day Religion," "Common-Sense in Religion," and "Self-Culture."

It is to be observed in them that he addressed himself simply and directly to the subject in hand, without introduction in the shape of apology, or explanation of his reasons for dealing with it, and his sermons contained none of the "fine passages" which are the terror of the judicious, when the judicious are among the listeners.

His church was filled with hearers, who may be described under two classes, wholly distinct from each other. First, there was the "old line" of the Church of the Disciples, a body of worshipers, recruited from almost every class of society, who were interested in his studies for the truth, and followed them in the order they took in his mind. To them there was an organic and vital connection between one sermon and the next, whether the sermons were announced as belonging to one series or not. They were sorry to lose any one step in such a series, and were singularly regular in their attendance on Sundays. The fundamental principle of a "Free Church" made it easy for people who had few other social ties in Boston to feel at home in the Church of the Disciples, and the congregation had probably a larger share than is usual of new-comers to the city, who began their attendance because attracted by its ready hospitality, and continued it because drawn by the sturdy, straightforward earnestness of the preacher, and his entire indifference to popular opinion or the arts of sensation.

The other class of attendants were strangers visiting in Boston, and other persons, who had read one or many of Mr. Clarke's theological books. The readers of these books, who perhaps had never met with the writings of any other Unitarian, naturally wanted to see and hear him, and they found their way on Sunday morning to the Church of the Disciples.

It would be difficult to say how many of his sermons were printed. They were often on practical subjects which adapted them to the time, so that reporters and editors were glad to obtain the manuscript, and on his part there was not one shred of literary vanity which hindered him from giving a manuscript for publication. The thing was to be of use. If any one wanted to extend its usefulness, that was enough. He received, therefore, with satisfaction, a proposal from Mr. Parker, the editor of the "Saturday Evening Gazette," to print his sermons regularly. This paper is published on Saturday at midnight, or later, and was for a long time the only Sunday paper in Boston. On the 25th of October, 1873, the "Gazette" announced the beginning of the series which was continued during the autumn, winter, and spring for fifteen years. There were about five hundred subscribers, I have been told, who took the paper simply for these sermons. They were read aloud, in Sunday services, as Mr. Clarke had occasion to know, in many lands.

From the outset there was a demand for the sermons, not only from the public, but from clergymen of other denominations. Almost every day's mail brought orders for back sermons, new subscriptions for the year, and sums of money with orders to send the "Gazette" to some address named as long as the money would pay for them.

Among the sermons published during the last years of his life there has been a large demand for the one on "The Mind of Christ," January 22, 1888; for the series on "The Unitarian Faith;" "Christ and Christianity;" the "Sermon on the Mount;" the future life, especially "The Old and New View of the Hereafter," and "Homes in Heaven and on Earth;" and the closing series on "The Lord's Prayer."

The intended publication of the sermons in the "Gazette" was announced in these words: "In his denomination Mr. Clarke is recognized as, perhaps more than any other, the leading mind, and is held in high estimation by all classes of Christians. What he says possesses value and interest to a large portion of the community. The stand he has recently taken in favor of independence, manliness, and purity in the politics of the nation has also much enhanced his reputation, and will have the effect to increase the importance attached to his pulpit utterances. The sermons will be continued from week to week in our columns. . . . The subject of to-day's sermon, which is the first of the series, will be 'Possessed with a Devil.'"

More than five hundred sermons were published in this series, the last being the last sermon on the Lord's Prayer, which was read to the Church of the Disciples, May 27, 1888, by Mr. Darwin E. Ware.

When Mr. Clarke was in Boston he regularly called at the printing-office and read his own proof, seldom altering a word.[1] All the printers whose acquaintance he thus made personally were fond of him, "indeed they loved him. They took pleasure in obeying his lightest wish, and never forgot or neglected it. He liked to talk, and sometimes to tell stories. His story of Booth and the pigeons is remembered in the printing-office. His talk there on death was always inter-

---

[1] After he had written anything, a sermon, a lecture, an essay, an article for a magazine or newspaper, he never wished to go over it again to improve the form. He disliked to give his time to a question of mere literary excellence. The moment he had finished what he had to say he wanted to turn his thoughts to some new work.

esting, courageous, and consoling." He would not have his sermons printed in type as small as nonpareil. He said he respected old eyes as well as young ones. He wanted to have one fixed place, the same in every issue. If any poetry were to be placed in the corner above the sermon, he sometimes selected it himself.

He insisted that no advertisements of whiskey or champagne should be placed under his sermons, or in the columns next to them, and sometimes told the editors of other "antipathies," which he hoped might be respected in the "make-up."

His expectation and wish in early life were to lift the world around him by his work as a preacher. And, as has been said, the work in which to the end of his life he was most interested was that of the Church of the Disciples. But, while his success as a preacher was marked, he was known as an author by thousands who never saw his face or heard his voice. And the reader knows how many of the great needs of his time and country acknowledged the help which his prudent counsel, his unflinching courage, and his daily effort gave them.

In his book called "Self-Culture" he has related the following incident: —

"When I lived in the West, there came a phrenologist to the town, and examining the heads of all the clergymen in the place found us all deficient in the organ of réverence. More than that, we all admitted that the fact was so; that we were not, any of us, specially gifted with natural piety or love of worship. Then he said, 'You have all mistaken your calling. You ought not to be ministers.' But I, for one, protested against that sentence, for I knew that though I had no natural tendency to worship or pray, I had come by experience to know that I could not live without prayer. Though I did not pray from sentiment and feeling, I was able to pray from conviction and faith."

Some of his friends and hearers have recorded the impression made upon them by his preaching at different periods of his ministry.

Margaret Fuller, who in 1838 was teaching a school in Providence, Rhode Island, wrote in her diary on November 25 of that year: "My friend of other years, J. F. C., has been here and preached; he will be here two more Sundays. I rejoice in it, both for the pleasure of his conversation and his preaching.

"He *is* a preacher. In the first place he is really a Christian, revering what is above, loving and pitying what is below, and in manly sympathy, esteem and tolerance meeting what is on a level with him. He does not appeal to the love of beauty, to the fancy, or the restless intellect. His style is somewhat unpolished; his sentences somewhat deficient in natural flow; no exquisite sentiment exquisitely expressed fills the ear and melts the heart. He convinces rather than persuades. In 'simple force direct' he challenges respect and confidence from his hearer, who at once believes that this man will never palsy his own tongue, or seal up the ear of another by the utterance of unfelt truth. J.'s mind is, I think, wholly practical in its tendency. It is quite a strong mind, an aspiring mind, an active, and becoming a clear mind, but its cry is for 'action, action, action.' I never heard better prayers than his. He really prays in church."

John A. Andrew, after hearing him preach for the first time, in 1841, wrote to a friend: —

"I have forgotten to give you my impressions of Rev. J. F. Clarke. In the first place I liked the flavor of the *man*. He carried his service as though he felt it a good thing to worship God and wanted the people to feel the same. I liked his sermon thoroughly. It was upon well-seasoned speech. 'Let your speech be always with grace, seasoned with salt, that ye may know how ye ought to answer every man.' And the sermon was itself a good illustration of the theme. Its spirit was Christian to the core, and did not disturb my Orthodox conscience in the least. I think I felt the catholicity of the man: he did not say a word that could be fairly understood to touch any man's honest convictions ungently. The whole service I enjoyed heartily; and not the least agreeable experience was the being invited to seats at least half-a-dozen times while I was waiting for my friend at the entrance."

In 1869, a young man who had just graduated from the Cambridge divinity school, and who has ever since been a faithful and efficient minister, wrote: —

"And, dear Mr. Clarke, will you let me tell you how much the services of the Church of the Disciples have helped and cheered me during the past two years. I could not attend as frequently as I wished, yet I never came without being made truer to myself, and so to God.

"I have so many pleasant memories in connection with your Sunday-school that it would have been very pleasant to be with them once more. It always gave me new inspiration and strength to see how devotedly some of those blessed teachers labored for the little children.

"And I wish to say also that although I have felt it my duty to disagree with you on some points of theology, yet I have always listened to your preaching with genuine interest and benefit. You have been very helpful to me, and I feel regret that my anticipated removal is to take me away from a church whose members I love and whose minister has brought me nearer to humanity, and so, nearer to God.'

This characteristic incident is related by Rev. J. W. Chadwick: —

"I have many pleasant memories of Dr. Clarke, and one which, I am sure, is all my own. Just before the 'Battle of Syracuse,' as Mr. Abbot calls it, I met Dr.

Clarke at Albany, in the early morning. There was an hour or more to spare before the train started westward. 'Let us take a walk,' he said; and we strolled away together, and in a short time came upon a little conventicle in which a religious service was going on. We went in, and found a company of twenty or thirty people, looking somewhat dreary and depressed, a very humble set of worshipers, of what special sect or creed I do not know, nor why met at such an early hour. The talk was very poor, with much iteration of the conventional phrases of the conference meeting. When there came a pause Dr. Clarke stood up and asked if he might say a few words. Permission was granted, and he moved forward till he faced the little company. Then he spoke for about ten minutes with a sweetness, a tenderness, a serious beauty that I never shall forget. He said in conclusion, 'We have never met before, and it is not likely we shall ever meet again, but I am glad to have taken part in your meeting and to have spoken to you a few words.' We went out. I had almost heard the people listen as he spoke. He made their faces shine."

The following friendly tribute is from Rev. S. W. Bush: —

"I knew him for more than forty years, but was brought into closer relationship with him when editing the 'Christian Register.' Then I loved and revered him more and more. For years he was one of our regular contributors; but we never could induce him to write unless he had something to say. Even when his own opinions were controverted he would only reply when it was necessary to put the subject in a clearer light. He was one of the easiest of public speakers to report, because his thought was arranged in logical order, and presented with point and directness. He had what Matthew Arnold calls 'lucidity.' He threw light on the subject in hand, and with sentences easily understood.

"He was one of the fairest men in the discussion of a subject I ever knew. This was still more evident in his private judgment of an opponent. We had many illustrations of this in the editorial office."

FROM REV. THOMAS L. ELIOT.

I recollect once going into a conference meeting at Saratoga, after traveling alone all the way from Portland, Oregon. The first words I heard were from Mr. Clarke. He was speaking of how people orphan themselves, and forget that God is their Father. He said, "I met a lady the other day who began to pour her troubles bitterly into my ears. She had no one to help her; no one understood her. I asked her, 'Have you not forgotten your best friend? Have you told your troubles to God?'" I have never forgotten the tone in which Mr. Clarke spoke; the reverence and assurance seemed to take all loneliness out of the world, and make the hour a real meeting of the spirit of Trust and Grace; tears ran down my cheeks, and some one began the hymn, —

> "Love for all, and can it be,
> Can I hope it is for me?"

FROM A CHARGE AT AN ORDINATION.

We recognize the fact that we belong not only to the finite, but the infinite, — that around the world of time is that of eternity; we wish to root our lives in the deep soil of infinite ideas.

"Come," they say to you, "come and be the friend of our souls. Seek for truth, and help us to seek for it. We have nothing to draw with, and the well is deep; help us to obtain that living water. The world is too much for us; we are too much away from God. Oh, if thou canst lead us into that state of nearness to God in which he shall be to us as a father, and obedience to him the law of our life, the friendship formed to-day will be of all others the most blessed!"

Truth is the food of the soul, thought is the garment of life; but "the life is more than meat, and the body than raiment;" and a man whose aim is high, and his heart in it, shall find his hearers fed as are the birds of the air, not by man, but by God.

Expect to see men born again under your preaching; expect this, and you will witness it. But be patient,— be very patient. You do not know how much is to be done, and how much God is doing. Be then both hopeful and patient, expecting everything that God is able to give, satisfied with anything that he chooses to give.

I charge you to be a *builder*. You might acquire more notoriety by pulling down, but you will do the most good by building up. . . . While you are a reformer, cultivate the moderation which avoids ultraism, not by neutrality, not by lukewarmness, not by taking neither side, but by taking a hearty interest in both sides of truth. . . . It is easy to see and denounce the extravagances and iniquities of others, but to go before them, showing them a more excellent way, — this is harder.

Finally, my brother, I charge you to study and to preach Christ. You will find God in nature and history; you will find God in the intuitions of eternal truth which move your own soul. . But except you also preach God in Christ, there is a large portion of human experience before which you will stand helpless. To the sinner God comes with pardon and comfort only in that manifestation of love which has beamed upon the world from the cross of Calvary. Learn to know and to preach Christ as the friend of the sinner, as a manifestation of God's love to the despairing prodigal. Announce a present Saviour, a present salvation, to those on whose conscience the burden of sin lies heavy, and you will find that your words will go from your lips freighted with a power of persuasion which will soften the hardest heart and bend the most stubborn will.

On the evening of February 28, 1884, he spoke to the students of the Cambridge divinity school on "The Evolution of the Minister." Near the close of this address he said: —

Work grows more interesting all the time. The work of the Christian minister becomes so interesting that he hates the idea of dying. We always have a great deal more to say, a great deal more to do, and take more interest in saying and doing.

The greatest possible blessing to the minister is to believe that whenever a duty comes to him there is a power somewhere to help him to do it; that there is a great fountain of spiritual life ready to flow into his soul whenever he really needs it. I think we have a right to believe this. If a duty comes to us which we feel unable to perform, then is the time to say, "I cannot do it without help; but because the Lord has sent me this work he will give me wisdom and strength and love for it." We should never be discouraged; we should be able to say with the apostle, "When I am weak, then I am strong.'

FROM THE "MONTHLY JOURNAL," ON THE "EDUCATION OF A CHURCH."

The business and work of a church is to grow; to grow up in all things into its head, who is Christ. It is a delightful work, than which there can be nothing more satisfying. "The most beautiful of lives," says Lord Bacon, "each day to find one's self somewhat better." Where there is growth, mental and moral, all the evils of life disappear; the grand sense of progress abolishes them all. This destroys the evil of age, for what if the body grow old, since the heart and thought continue young; this, the evil of poverty, since the soul is growing rich, and is able to make others so; this, the evil of sickness, since what is the harm of sickness while health reigns within; this, of solitude, since the mind is compassed about with a cloud of companions; this, of bereavement, since to the open eye of faith our loved ones have only gone before where we are following. A church with an advancing life, deepening its convictions every year, enlarging its knowledge, growing more generous, more loving, more full of good works, filled with a deeper humility while it ascends into a loftier piety, like the lofty cedars of Dryden, which

> "as far upward shoot
> As to the nether heavens they drive the root,"—

such a church would deserve the name adopted of late by a religious society, and might truly call itself a church of "Progressive Friends." Progress with friendship — what more could one desire?

FROM A LETTER TO A YOUNG MINISTER, WHO HAD ASKED HIS ADVICE ABOUT MINISTERIAL WORK IN THE WEST.

Pastoral work is that which tells. If a church is to be built up strong, united, active, it is by action on individuals, not upon congregations. Preaching is their baptism; pastoral work is their confirmation. The ceremony of confirmation in the Episcopal Church is only the outward sign of a great reality; the reality is the change by which a hearer of the word is changed into a doer.

Do not complain of being persecuted. Persecution in our days is a joke. I never feel ashamed of being a Unitarian, except when I hear Unitarians complain of being persecuted.

Let negation be for the sake of subsequent affirmation. Do not let denying end in denial; but always pass on to something positive.

Treat reforms frankly and kindly in the pulpit as you would in the parlor. Do not be savage to show your independence. Regard those who differ from you as your friends, not as opponents to be refuted and put down.

The end of Christian preaching is to make men abound in hope through the power of the Holy Ghost. It is not to make them abound in opinions through the power of argument, nor to abound in anxiety through the power of the law, nor to abound in self-satisfaction through the power of rhetorical flatteries; but it is to make them abound in hope through the power of the Holy Ghost. It is to bring them to God, and make them feel his divine nearness; to lift them out of darkness into light; to enable them to feel their sins forgiven, and their hearts full of peace and joy.

FROM HIS SERMONS.

This is a very simple test of genuine faith in Christ. If you have faith enough in Jesus as the Christ of God to enable you to undertake his work of saving your fellow-men from sin and misery here and hereafter, you may be sure that you have the true faith. But if you have not the courage to do this work, then, though you preach faith in Christ as the Omnipotent God, and utter that doctrine with the tongue of men and angels, yet you prove by your own cowardice in the presence of evil that you have no real faith in him as an actual Saviour of actual men and women.

Do you know of any case of vice or sorrow which it seems almost impossible to relieve or cure? Go and see if God will not work a miracle through your mind and heart, giving your actions and words a power not their own, so that you can make the blind see, the lame walk, and raise up the dead. You must go in faith, however, trusting entirely that if the thing ought to be done God will give you strength to do it. You must go also in the spirit of prayer; not, necessarily, with the prayer of words, but with that essential prayer which consists in keeping one's self in a condition of faith and hope, leaning on God.

Of all the holy things which God has made, the most holy is man himself. He is the temple of God; for the spirit of God dwells in him, and wherever a human being stands, there stands something greater than the Temple at Jerusalem. God has made man in his own image, with power of insight, capacity of affection, energy of action. The mysterious depths and heights of his nature we do not yet half understand. His expericuce in this world has meanings and objects of which, as yet, we have hardly an idea. His destiny in the other world, the depths of being which he shall sound, the heights of knowledge which he shall climb, eternity alone can reveal.

The churches keep alive this sense of the greatness of humanity.... If I did not go to church for anything else, I should go for this. The sermon might be stupid; then I should not listen to it. The prayers might not suit me; then I should pass them by. The music might grate on my ear; I should try not to hear it. One would stand before me greater than the Temple; greater than its liturgy, its prayers, its priests, its ritual, — my brother man, bowed before my Father, God.

That which makes this earth seem solid is not the rocks and mountains that are in it, but the love that is in it. Love, joining hands with faith and work, makes our life rich and full. These three, neither of them alone; work which is done in love, love which is born of faith. And it is a blessed thing that the longer we live thus the more beautiful the world becomes, the more rich and precious our life seems. It is the young who are oftenest tired of life. As we live on, we seem to grow younger, not older; we find ourselves coming nearer to God and man; we grow more like little children in our hearts. Beautiful is age when it does not become hard and cold, but grows evermore full of faith and love. The old man looks backward through a life in which he has learned to know the wonders of nature; to know the heart and thoughts of many varieties of human beings; in which he has done faithfully his part in the world in his own place. He looks back over the long perspective, and he sees how kindly God has led him on; how he has been taught by disappointment and success; how he has gone deep into his own heart, gathered up wisdom, become truly free by self-control and self-direction; how he has ceased to think of God as Power and Law only, and come to think of him as Friend and Father. And he wonders that he ever could have been weary of life; he feels the infinite riches of the universe, and thanks God, in the depths of a happy heart, for the gift of existence.

CHAPTER XVIII.

VARIED ACTIVITIES.

1865-1880.

THE war had broken up every man's plan of life. Whatever other obligations he might have, his duties to his country, if he were a man of honor, took precedence of all others. And with Mr. Clarke, as with the rest of his countrymen, whatever work might occupy him during that period, it was carried on with the underlying aim of making it serve his country's welfare. But when the war was over, the interests to which he had given his time in previous years were continued on a larger scale than ever, until he began to feel the pressure of years a little before his death. His diaries speak of work in the cause of education; of frequent visits to the Normal Schools at Framingham, Bridgewater, and Salem; of meetings of the Board of Education, meetings of the Freedman's Aid Society, meetings of the board of overseers of Harvard University; of lectures to the Cambridge divinity students; of history classes in his own church; of Sunday evening lectures; of Wednesday evening lectures on the Apostle Paul; these entries and many others show that his life was a busy one.

If one can say it good-naturedly, it is fair to say that with the emancipation of the slaves, some of the old war-horses of the anti-slavery movement found themselves at a loss as to their own personal future. They were glad the slaves were free, but they did not know what they were to do next. So the fond mother of an only child is glad when her daughter is married to the man she loves; but all the same, when the bride is gone, she finds her own home very empty and her days long. Cynical Philistines, therefore, would tell us that the old anti-slavery leaders looked round in their hunger for a new philanthropy, and picked up woman suffrage. But no man can say this of Mr. Clarke. He is on record as committed to this cause from a very early period, and his interest in it belongs to the whole system of his life.

Colonel Higginson has kindly given us a careful sketch of his relations to this reform.

J. F. C. AND WOMAN SUFFRAGE.

Every one who was brought into intercourse with James Freeman Clarke in the woman suffrage movement must recall his presence with pleasure, partly from the important service he rendered to it, but more because his action on this point was, like all else he did, the simple outgrowth of his peculiarly straightforward and equable nature. For instance, he always rested its main argument not on the assumed superiority of woman, — an argument which proves too much, yet into which so clear-headed a man as Theodore Parker conspicuously fell, — but on the simple ground of her equality of gifts and needs with man, and hence her right to be represented in government equally with him. If, as Theodore Parker maintained in his "Discourse of Woman," the voice of women on all subjects will be incomparably superior to that of men, the question will naturally arise whether it is better to risk demoralizing a creature so elevated, by admitting her to a sphere where man has, perhaps, been lowered. But if we take the ground, as Dr. Clarke was accustomed to do, that she is simply to be viewed as a human being, with the shortcomings, risks, and limitations of a human being, and that she will undoubtedly make mistakes and exhibit inconsistencies as a voter, then the case is a great deal stronger.

I remember that this strong, common-sense quality of his mind was once strikingly shown in a speech made, I think, at a Washington convention in 1871. Some question had been raised as to how women would be likely to vote if enfranchised, and he undertook in his accustomed straightforward way to answer it. He explained that no such anticipations were at all necessary to the argument, which rested on natural right or recognized need. He pointed out, also, the difficulty of prophesying as to any newly enfranchised class. "But," he said, in substance, "there are a few things which can safely be predicted." Then it would have been natural to expect him to go on by lauding the elevated qualities of women and showing how admirably they would vote, as if by intuition, when they got the opportunity. Not at all. He said, amid general attention, "The first visible result of women's voting will probably be a great increase of majorities in all elections. The reason is plain. Women, being new to politics, will very largely imbibe their first opinions from their fathers, brothers, husbands, or pastors. A few, from independent thought or even from natural contrariety, will vote against these advisers, but the bulk of women will vote with them. Hence, at the first elections, wherever there has before been a Republican majority of fifty, there will be likely to be a Republican majority of a hundred. Wherever, on the other hand, there was a Democratic majority of a hundred, there will now, very likely, be one of two hundred. If there is any especial local or temporary excitement, among the men, the new voters will be apt to throw themselves into it, with the ardor of their sex, and will swell the majority very greatly, one way or the other. But this will be temporary, and women will soon learn to vote according to their own individual judgment, as men do."

I have stated all this in substance, as well as I can, but the point was then wholly new to me, and new points were rather uncommon in that discussion, for those of us who had been long in it; so that it impressed me very much, and I am sure of having retained the essential features of the statement. And any one who studies the history of the vote of Boston women on the school question, for instance, last year and this, will already find a striking illustration of Dr. Clarke's foresight. The vote last year had the character of a crusade, and was essentially the carrying out by women of a movement initiated, wisely or otherwise, by men; whereas already, as it seems to an outside observer, those same women are voting more discriminatingly and are applying their own judgments to the views of their pastors and their husbands.

I remember in connection with that same convention an admirable instance of Dr. Clarke's sensible and good-natured way of dealing with vexed questions. The convention took place during what has always been known as the "Woodhull period" of the agitation; and the feeling of the local advocates of woman suffrage in Washington was strongly enlisted in favor of Mrs. Woodhull and her methods, to which the organization which we represented was quite opposed. On coming to the hall where the convention was to be held, we found that the representatives of the Woodhull party had practically taken possession of the approach to the hall, and had a table where their documents were being sold and distributed, while the seats within the hall were already flooded with their publications. All remonstrance was in vain; it only increased the excitement; and some of the members had begun to talk of appealing to the police for protection, when Dr. Clarke arrived, and, on hearing the grievance stated, said serenely, " I think we had better take no action about it. If you will let me explain the matter to the audience, I think that I can easily make it understood." Accordingly, soon after the meeting was opened, he got up and said, in his usual clear and simple way, looking round upon the audience, with the utmost good-nature beaming through his spectacles, words like these : " As the officers of this society came into the hall, we noticed lying about on the seats and in the passage-way a great many publications with which we have nothing to do. None of us have read them, and they may contain something exceedingly good, of which it would be very unjust for us to claim the credit. Or they may contain something that we should disapprove, and it would then, of course, be unjust to hold us responsible. At any rate, they are none of ours, and the audience must judge of them by what they say, and of us by what we say." This moderate and kindly statement, with a little dash of humor behind it, put the whole thing in a satisfactory position and predisposed everybody towards a candid hearing ; so that the convention went on to a triumphant success, which might have been wholly lost if it had begun with a wrangle. I have thought of it more than once, since then, when I have been at political conventions with Dr. Clarke, and have seen him disarm opponents by some pithy and good-natured statement, which secured victory, or at least peace, without the crossing of bayonets. I was not present at the Republican convention where he helped to turn the scales in an important debate by the remark, " A bolt is always in order," but I suppose it to have been an exercise of the same fortunate faculty. It is, as all public speakers know, one of the rarest of gifts.

Dr. Clarke always appeared to great advantage in any public discussion. In the quiet of his own study, carried on by strong convictions, he could sometimes work himself up into quite a polemic vigor, and was not always, I think, quite just to theological antagonists; but whenever he was brought face to face with a man, even if a strong opponent, his natural kindliness always came uppermost, and he met controversy with imperturbable good-nature. This is, I think, opposite to the common experience, for many men who can write mildly enough are carried beyond themselves by meeting their adversary face to face on a platform. At any rate, Dr. Clarke was of peculiar value on the woman suffrage platform; not merely from his entire independence and courage, — qualities which came so naturally to him that it hardly seems worth while to speak of them, — but from his breadth of view, strong common-sense, good-nature, and good judgment.

CAMBRIDGE, *December* 11, 1889.

The letters which follow give a glimpse of the years between 1865 and 1881.

TO S. S. C.

February 24, 1865.

I shall send you to-morrow a copy of my lecture on Mr. Emerson's religious speculations. I have had it printed in "The Traveller." . . .

March 6.

My time is so taken up that I do not write more than a page before I stop to do something else. Shall I give you my diary for last week, exclusive of calls, etc.? Sunday, — Wrote and preached a sermon; attended a funeral; heard a Bible-class of twenty young men in Church History; went to a meeting for Women's Hospital, and made a speech. Monday, — Went to meeting at office of Charles G. Loring, about Children's Aid Society; to meeting about another society; drove to Brookline to see my friend, Mrs. Wells. Tuesday, — Saw engineer about making road to Brook Farm; wrote ordination sermon; went to Westboro to deliver it.

Wednesday, — Came from Westboro; wrote the annual report of the school committee of West Roxbury; presided two hours at school committee; presided at social meeting of church in evening. Thursday, — Prepared lesson for class in history till 11.35; to Boston, and then to Newton, to see sick lady; back to Boston, and to history class from 3 to 5. Friday, — Spent some time with Governor Andrew; saw General Macy about Eliot's going into the army, which he wishes to do; evening to hear Agassiz' lecture. Saturday, — Meeting of board of overseers at State House, in forenoon, etc.

Everything seems to come at once. Meeting of board of education; meetings of board of overseers, of school committee, of executive committee of A. U. A., of Freedmen's Aid Association, of Children's Aid Association, of Protective War Claim Association; putting through a road to Brook Farm, which takes no end of talking; visiting public schools; writing report on divinity school; report of school committee; report on modern languages. . . .

TO HIS DAUGHTER, WITH HIS COPY OF "COLERIDGE, SHELLEY, AND KEATS."

June 4, 1865.

This book I bought in 1830, when I was twenty years old. I had just left college, and entered the divinity school. I was poor, and it was a good deal to me to pay $7.50 for a book. But the American edition of this work had not then been published, nor had there been then printed, even in England, a complete edition of either of these poets. So I imported a copy of this Paris edition, and had a great deal of pleasure out of it. During the winter of 1830-31 I lived with my mother in Ashburton Place, and after keeping school all day at Cambridgeport, I passed the evening with my family in my brother Sam's room, he being confined to bed with rheumatism. After I went to my room at night, at eleven or twelve o'clock, I would read awhile in this book, and I hope that you may have as much pleasure out of it as I had then.

TO A. F. C.

December 22, 1867.

Governor Andrew's death seems to make all things different to me. I have had him so long for adviser and friend that I miss him every day. . . .

I have begun my work at Cambridge. I find the young men very pleasant, and I get along with them very well. But it takes a great deal of time. I am to preach the election sermon next week, — a great institution. . . .

He was always glad when an invitation came to him such as he here mentions, because it gave him a fitting opportunity to address a large audience on the subject of national sins and national obligations. On this occasion he spoke of the application of the principles of Christianity to legislation; of the reform needed in the management of prisoners; of the government of children in the public schools; and also, at some length, he advocated giving suffrage to women.

TO A. H. C.

PIGEON COVE, *July* 15, 1869.

I have written a note to Mr. Call to ask him to advertise (for next Sunday) a sermon on "Woman Suffrage, in reply to Dr. Bushnell." I hope you will see no objection to this. Some one ought to say it, why not I? I have Dr. Bushnell here, and am reading him. If it rains more I shall write my sermon.

Cora and I roamed about together a great deal yesterday. I took her out in a boat, we went in to swim, we went into the woods, and I read to her from Mrs. Stowe; then we went and lay on the rocks.

In 1869, Mr. Clarke went to Illinois to see a total eclipse of the sun, and afterwards took a trip over the prairies with his brothers, three of whom lived in the West.

TO L. F. C., IN EUROPE.

MILWAUKEE, *August* 12, 1869.

As I did not go to Europe to see Switzerland with you, I determined to go to Illinois to see the total eclipse of the sun

Burlington is in Iowa, on the Mississippi, not far from the central line, and a corps of astronomers were already collected to observe the phenomenon. A large field was assigned to them, and a police force to guard it; and therein your uncle Sam and I took our places with my telescope, which I carried out with me.

It had rained for two days, but the great day came without a cloud. Never was such a field-day for the astronomers; they were prepared to attack the sun along the whole line of total obscuration from Alaska to North Carolina. Parties were posted with telescopes, spectroscopes, and photographic instruments on both sides of Behring's Straits, at Sitka Sound, on the Pacific; in Montana, Nebraska, Iowa, Illinois, Kentucky, Indiana, Virginia, and North Carolina.

At last, at the predicted moment, the moon impinged on the edge of the sun's disk. It moved on, eating out a larger and larger piece, till at last the sun became a crescent; the sky grew gray, the air chill, the foliage and grass became leaden, all faces gathered paleness. The crescent became an edge of light, a line of light, but still it blazed and dazzled. Suddenly it broke into beads of light, then these disappeared till only one remained. This one point blazed with a brilliancy dazzling the eye, and then disappeared! At that moment came a phenomenon which no language can describe. Suddenly, in place of this dazzling, blazing sun, there was seen, in mid-heaven, a black sun, surrounded by a luminous waving border of the purest white light. This corona or halo did not blaze nor dazzle, like direct sunlight. Pure and snowy in its celestial beauty it waved around the black sun and flashed out on every side far into the darkened heavens. On the right of the sun, at the same moment, appeared Mercury. Venus glittered above, and other stars. They suggested to me the lines in an old English play: —

> "Let it be mentioned
> They served but as small tapers, to attend
> The solemn flame of this great funeral."

The sky had seemed cloudless up to the moment of complete obscuration. But then, along the horizon, in the north and south came out suddenly a mass of angry, stormy, yellow clouds, as though some great fire were blazing on the prairies, or a terrific thunder-storm were at hand. Just then, too, on the lower edge of the black moon came out a spot of ruby or carmine color, a little protuberance which grew larger and larger very rapidly, while similar rosy clouds grew out into the white corona on other parts of the lunar circumference. These were masses of burning hydrogen gas, blazing up from the surface of the sun into the solar atmosphere, and one of those which we saw was computed to ascend a hundred thousand miles while we were looking at it. Conceive what a frightful hurricane of flame this must be to be seen so large, and moving so fast, at the distance of ninety-six millions of miles! And yet these enormous tornadoes of flame are so insignificant compared with the sunbeams that a single ray of sunshine hides them all. They have never been seen except in a total eclipse.

Hundreds of photographs were taken at the different points, and these we shall be able to see. But the eclipse itself was such a wonderful phenomenon that I would willingly have gone the next day twelve hundred miles farther to see it over again.

TO A. H. C.

August 19, 1869.

I am at present in Kinnikinik township, Wisconsin, about ten miles east of Hudson on the St. Croix River, and twenty north of Prescott on the Mississippi. Five brothers and our nephew Freeman are in one room, lying about the floor at a farmhouse; grouse fields and trout brooks all about us. Around are picturesque bluffs, like the cliffs above the Rhine, with miles and miles of fertile valleys between, great fields rolling in waves of golden wheat. Abraham and I arrived yesterday afternoon, and before dark we six brought in twenty grouse, some of which we had for breakfast. I have not fired a gun before since 1850, in Meadville.[1] The air is as pure and fresh and delicious as that of Mount Desert. I drink in health at every pore.

HUDSON, WIS., *Sunday, August* 22, 1869.

We left "the farm" last evening, and came here to pass Sunday; Sam came Friday. . . . To-day I shall go to church and enjoy the comfort of listening to a service. This town is on Lake St. Croix, an expansion of the St. Croix River. It is in the midst of great wheat-growing farms, and is a thriving place. Being also in the midst of trout streams, deer-licks, and grouse, the inhabitants seem to make sport their business, and treat their business as sport. Every man you meet is ready to turn the key in his office door, put up a placard "To be back to-morrow," and go with one gladly to hunt or

[1] During his earlier visits to Meadville he would occasionally take his gun when he went to walk in the woods, which were full of game; but in December, 1850, he writes to his mother from Meadville: "*I* have been obliged to promise the children not to go a-gunning any more, they felt so badly when I brought home birds or a rabbit. I brought a rabbit the other day, and Ellie came to me with a very solemn face and whispered, '*Papa,* you have broken the Golden Rule, you have, really.' *I* thought he was more than half right."

fish. The landlord of this hotel spent yesterday afternoon fishing in the lake with Sam. .

I should be very willing to turn my face homeward to-morrow, but I wish to tempt William to prolong his stay. . I waded two hours on Friday in the Kinnikinik River, and caught two trout, a trout an hour. William waded four or five hours, and caught about twenty.

HUDSON, WIS., *August* 23, 1869.

. . . We are going down the river to-day on our way to Milwaukee. Yesterday I went in the morning to the Presbyterian church, and heard a good sermon on " Recreations," defending their legitimate use. In the evening I went to a different church, and heard a discourse from the text, "Keep thy heart with all diligence, for out of it are the issues of life." The preacher argued that Solomon must have known the circulation of the blood, and hence the Bible was inspired! He thought also that Job must have known that the solar system is moving toward the Pleiades when he said, "Canst thou bind the sweet influences of the Pleiades?" I hope I do not use such foolish arguments as these. . . .

MILWAUKEE, *August* 26, 1869.

We waited at Prescott till about eleven P. M. for the St. Paul steamer on its way down the river. By that time the weather had become beautifully clear, and a moon nearly full threw the most enchanting light on the river and the high hills on its banks. William and I sat on the guards enjoying the lovely night, and talked till almost three o'clock about old times, — his journey thirty years ago from Mackinaw up to the head of Lake Superior in a canoe, and then down the Mississippi, when there was scarcely a white settler above Prairie du Chien. Then I slept an hour, and rose at four and watched the morning slowly dawning over the river and hills. During the forenoon we passed scenery so fine that I think it worth a journey here to see it. We reached La Crosse at one P. M., and were obliged to stay there till nine P. M., waiting for a train. The day was intensely warm. I went out and found a place where, under the shade of some trees, we could enjoy a cool draught of air. It is true the trees had been cut down and sawn into boards, and the location was between two piles of boards of sweet piny perfume and terebinthine aroma. A thunder-storm toward night cooled the air somewhat.

I shall go to Chicago, preach there on Sunday and then set out for home.

TO HIS SISTER, IN ROME.

December 28, 1869.

Boston pursues its ancient way and is what it was, only more so; lectures here and lectures there, learned societies, literary reunions, no end of new publications; meetings, — morning, noon, at dewy eve, and silent night. The city rushes and roars with business, like the Ohio in a freshet, or the yellow Tiber : —

> . . . " retortis
> Littore Etrusco violenter undis."

. . . All night the city rushes with ardent crowds in pursuit of knowledge at lectures, or in pursuit of pleasure at theatres and balls.

As for me my business this winter is as follows : I am giving four series of discourses, viz., four sermons on the questions between atheists and theists, four on the questions between Christian theists and others, four on the questions between church authority and that of reason, four on the questions between broad and narrow Christianity. These on Sunday mornings. I am preparing for publication in the spring, volume i. of "Comparative Theology of Ethnic and Catholic Religions," to be published by Fields & Osgood. I hope to finish it in time. Then I write something for each number of

Hale's new magazine, which has swallowed, silently, with capacious throat, both the great "Christian Examiner" and the little "Monthly Journal." . . I have my weekly lecture to the divinity students at Cambridge, my Wednesday night lecture to my church, pastoral visits, and occasional theatre preaching, and lyceum lectures.

"So happily the years of Thalaba go by."

TO E. E. HALE.

November 8, 1870.

I expected to see you last night at the [Examiner] Club. I write to say that I am engaged to lecture on Thursday night at Grantville. I am sorry if this disappoints you, and will go to you some other time.

Did you find my little poem? And what do you think of appending the moral, —

> The Christ-like child seekest thou? Go not apart —
> But be a child thyself, and he is in thy heart.

Please let them send me the proofs of "Wanted, a Statesman."

TO W. G. ELIOT.

August 19, 1871.

Thank you, dear William, for your very kind and bright letter. I cannot stop now to answer it; but I will only say that if you have been tempted to envy me for anything I have been enabled to do, I also have often experienced that amiable sentiment when I have considered your magnificent work. I suppose we all underrate what we have, and overrate what we have not. But the man of action, who can translate thought into life, who can root it in institutions, who can direct and control men, is at least equal to the man of books.

> "Weak-winged is song,
> Nor aims at that clear-ethered height
> Whither the brave deed climbs for light."

The man who has done your work and developed such power need not wish for any other man's gift.

TO A. H. C.

WASHINGTON, *December* 9, 1871.

I had a good time in Philadelphia, — went to see Dr. Furness and the Lesleys; to Germantown to see Rebecca Bond. Saw the philosophical-instrument maker about my lantern. Mr. Lesley was much pleased with the lantern, and said the only wonder was that it had not been invented before. . . . I came to Washington on Thursday, and lectured for Mr. Hinckley Thursday evening. Mr. Boutwell, Mr. Twitchell, and other gentlemen were there and asked me to come and see them. I have spent an hour with Charles Sumner in his house, where he showed me all his pictures and works of art.

Last evening we had a very good opening meeting of the [Woman] Suffrage Association. The speakers were Mrs. Stone, Mrs. Howe, and myself. The hall was full of an attentive audience, including Senators and other members of Congress. To-day the meeting goes on, morning, afternoon, and evening. I shall lunch with Mr. Twitchell, and then, perhaps, go with him to see the President. For Cora's sake I shall see the Agricultural Museum, and for my own sake the Congressioual Library. To-morrow I preach in the Unitarian church in the morning, and in the theatre in the evening.

TO HIS SISTER, IN ROME.

February 15, 1872.

To-day is with us a sacred anniversary. Shall I ever forget that morning when our dear child's life was slowly ebbing away, and all that love and thought and prayer could do was — nothing. It seems yesterday only, and the unappeasable sorrow, the wound that will never close, is in our hearts all the same as then.

So much he might have been, done, become. So much to his mother, sisters, brother. Such a tie he was to this world and the next. . . . The "scar of that deep-stabbed woe" may be hidden, but it aches still after twenty-three years.

Dear Sarah, why does the time go by, and we have no more to say to each other? The stream of time rushes along so rapidly as it nears the cataract that two boats, though near each other, are effectually separated by the forceful river.

TO E. E. HALE.

October 9, 1872.

I have found an article in the "Revue des Deux Mondes" for August 1st, giving an account of the opening of the University of Zurich to women in all departments, especially in the medical faculty. It speaks in high terms of the success of the enterprise. I have translated it, and thought of preparing an article on the general subject, in which it is to be introduced. Would you like it for your "Record of Progress"?

TO HIS SISTER.

JAMAICA PLAIN, *March* 5, 1873.

To-day Anna and I went to the State House, where I made a little speech before the committee to which was referred Mr. Whittier's petition, urging the legislature to rescind their vote of censure on Charles Sumner. Mr. Whittier had asked me to go and speak. . . . We have been having a series of interesting meetings in our church on Wednesday evenings, on the charities of Boston. The subjects, thus far, have been:

"What is doing here for animals?"
"What is doing for young men?"
"What is doing for street-boys?"
"What is doing for infants?"
"What is doing for the poor?"

To each of these meetings I have invited experts, — persons connected with the various charities, — and they have compared notes, and given much interesting information. We have had Catholics and Protestants, Orthodox men and Unitarians, — and the lion at these meetings has lain down with the lamb, and the lamb has not been inside of him, either. .

TO HIS SISTER.

April 9, 1873.

Our dear old friend "Don"[1] has gone to the place, wherever it may be, that good dogs go to. Surely he has a right to some happy home, if ever a dog had. He never was cross, never out of temper; he overflowed with love and devotion to all of us. To be near us was happiness enough for him. The best people have their moods, — Don never had any. He died of gradual decay; he has been fading away "to the land of the leal" for some months. Life had become a burden to him, — his bright eye was growing dim, his joyful nature torpid. At last, on Fast Day, April 3, he crept away to the shelter of a large tree, and laid himself down at its root, led by that curious instinct which tells dogs when their death is at hand. There he lay, without moving or eating, till the afternoon of Friday, April 4, and then sank gently into death. A few minutes before he died he lapped a little water from Lilian's hand. We buried him under the tree next day; and our hearts have been sad ever since. He was one of the family. It will seem lonely not to see him about the yard when we come home. I shall put a stone over him, with his name and the words, "*Amavit multum.*"

[1] "Don" was a Newfoundland dog, who had passed all his life in the family.

TO A. H. C.

LOUISVILLE, KY., *May* 5, 1873.

It seems very natural to be writing from Louisville — though the Louisville of to-day is widely different from that to which I came forty years ago. It is now a splendid, beautiful city. Mr. Heywood's house, where I am, is better than any house that then existed in Louisville; more tasteful, convenient, and desirable as a residence. It stands in the midst of a green garden, with shrubbery around it. We reached Louisville at eight A. M. on Saturday, and I called the same day on Judge and Mrs. Pirtle, Mary and Eliza Speed, Mrs. Speed and Martha, her daughter, and Philip and Emma. They were all glad to see me. Yesterday I gave a lesson to the Sunday-school, of which Mr. Munn is superintendent, preached morning and evening to large congregations, and took tea at Judge Pirtle's. The judge is very deaf, but has the same sweet smile he used to have. Mrs. Pirtle is sick, confined to her chamber, but saw me there; and one of her grandchildren was baptized yesterday afternoon. . . .

TO A. H. C.

LOUISVILLE, *May* 6, 1873.

Yesterday I spent another hour with Eliza and Mary Speed, took tea with Philip and Emma, and went to a sociable at the church, where I gave some reminiscences of former days in Louisville. I have shaken hands with a hundred people, for Mr. Heywood wishes me to see all his friends. . . . Eliza Speed told me how staunch a patriot her mother had been during the war, and how her little nephew, Philip's youngest son, had refused to shout for Seymour when his schoolfellows, rebels, held him out of the upper window of the schoolhouse, and threatened to drop him if he would not. I drove out with Mr. Heywood, Mr. Belknap, and Judge

Ballard, to dine with Joshua Speed, Mr. Lincoln's friend. Joshua told me many anecdotes of Abraham Lincoln, and gave me a letter of his. On my return, I saw a Colonel Whitman, who was in Kansas with John Brown, and told me anecdotes about those days. .

In Louisville I have bathed in memories of the past, and, as Dryden says, "The weight of years and cares fell from me" in these recollections of youth, hope, and the beginnings of experience. How poor life would be without such recollections!

TO MRS. G. S. HILLARD.

NEW YORK, *June* 18, 1873.

MY DEAR MRS. HILLARD, — I received your note yesterday, and am very glad you asked me to go and see X. I will certainly do so. I always feel when any request comes to me to see any one in trouble, as though the Lord sent it to show that he takes an interest in me. Some persons think their sins forgiven when they have a feeling to that effect. I think God forgives us our sins whenever he allows us to do anything for each other. So, when such a request as yours comes to me, I seem to hear the Lord saying, "Son, be of good cheer, thy sins are forgiven thee!" . . .

TO HIS SISTER.

JAMAICA PLAIN, *July* 11, 1873.

My trip to the West was very pleasant. I went to Chicago, Milwaukee, Louisville, Cincinnati, and Meadville. I went with good Mr. Heywood to Louisville, and passed three or four days, preached twice, and found many old friends, as warm-hearted as ever. I had a delightful time. Among other visits I enjoyed one to Joshua Speed, who went to Illinois when about twenty-two or twenty-three years old, and kept a store in Springfield. One day Abraham Lincoln came into his store, and said, "Mr. Speed, I have opened an office in this town, and I have a bedstead, but I want a mattress, pillow, blankets, and sheets. I cannot pay you now, but perhaps I can after the next court; what will be the cost?" Mr. Speed replied, "Seventeen dollars," and Mr. Lincoln looked alarmed. Mr. Speed said, "You need not pay me till you are ready, Mr. Lincoln; there is no hurry about that; but, if you prefer, you may share my room overhead; it is a large room." "How do you get to it?" asked Mr. Lincoln. Mr. Speed pointed to stairs in the corner. Mr. Lincoln went up, deposited his saddle-bags in the corner of the chamber, came down, and said, "I've moved in, Mr. Speed." They occupied the same room five years, and Mr. Speed remained always Mr. Lincoln's most intimate friend. He said that Lincoln was free from all vices. He never drank nor gambled, but spent his time in hard study over his cases. Mr. Speed told me many other interesting stories about Lincoln.

TO H. W. BELLOWS.

December 22, 1873.

I was delighted to receive your cordial and friendly note, and to learn that you were well enough to read my book and to write to me about it. I received a letter the same day from Mr. Weeden, who said that all you needed was six months' rest, and that then you would be as well as ever. This was good news, for we cannot spare you yet, nor for a long time to come. I do not think they need you as much in the other world as we do. Therefore I beseech you to take a good six months' rest somewhere, where no one can get at you; where you cannot preach, lecture, write, or be consulted with on any business, theological, philanthropic, literary, social, or political. Let us keep on working together here, and when our work is well done, perhaps we can go together and visit our friends on the other side of the beautiful river which men call the stream of

Death, but which the angels doubtless call that of Life infinite and eternal.

I thank you heartily for the warm sympathy you have always felt with every effort of mine to say or do anything useful. It has been very grateful to me, and has encouraged me to new endeavor. . . . There is one point in which you and I are alike, — in our efforts, we have always written, spoken, and acted to do good, not thinking of literary position or fame.

TO HIS SISTER.

JAMAICA PLAIN, *February* 12, 1874.

It gave us all unmitigated pleasure to hear of your Nile-boat trip. Next to going myself, is my joy in knowing that you are there, and perhaps I am more glad at having you in Egypt than if I myself were meditating in the tombs of Beni Hassan, or examining the hieroglyphs of Karnak. There are cases when the law maxim, "*Qui facit per alium facit per se,*" applies to sight-seeing; and one of these is when we have such an observing and recording friend as you are to do our traveling for us, and save us the trouble of going to " Arabia the stony, Sabæa the gummy."

It is a pleasure to think of you lazily creeping along on the surface of the River of the Pharaohs, surrounded by reminiscences of Moses and his bulrushes, and basking with the crocodiles in unchanging warmth, while we shiver over our registers, and pass through the classical routine of colds, coughs, rheumatisms, bronchial affections, and pulmonary disabilities. You amuse yourselves with pyramids and sphinxes; while we have nothing more venerable than our Old South Church.

See, then, with all your eyes; listen, with all your ears; and be able to give us, when you come back, the last news from the Fourteenth Century B. C. Meantime we must give you all the news we can of our busy ant-hill life in Boston. . . With the exception of colds, which this year are more numerous and obstinate than usual, we are well here. Lilian enjoys her class with Mr. Hunt. Our church is full every Sunday, so I do not think that any apoplexy is getting into my sermons as yet. They are now being printed every week in full in the "Saturday Gazette;" and I have directed them to be sent regularly to you in Rome; but I do not suppose that you will receive any of them at the upper cataracts, or find advertisements of them placarded on the ruins of Denderah.

Recently I made a visit to the Schuylers in New York, and spent a week there, enjoying myself much. They had a little dinner-party for me every evening. Two very interesting English people were also guests in the house, Mr. and Mrs. Laurence Oliphant.

Mr. O., after having figured as London man of society, author, traveler, diplomate, now belongs, with his wife and his mother (Lady Oliphant), to a religious community on Lake Erie, under the leading of T. L. Harris. I also saw, in New York, Clarence King, the California mountain-climber and geologist, who showed me his photographs of the Sierra Nevada. . . . In Boston, I go to two clubs, the Examiner Club, where we discuss grave moral and social questions, and the Thursday Club, where we have scientific lectures and papers. . . .

We see by the papers this morning that the Massachusetts Senate has repealed the vote of censure on Charles Sumner, passed by a previous one. The House will probably do the same. The real motive of the censure on Sumner was his opposition to Grant, and the people have compelled the political leaders to rescind their anti-Sumner resolutions.

There are people in Boston who think, with Rob Roy, that

> "Of old things, all are over-old;
> Of new things, none are new enough."

So they are for pulling down the Old South Church, and cutting down the Paddock elms on Tremont Street.

To you, who are looking at buildings erected 3000 B. C., this may seem a small matter, but we are fighting in sermons and newspapers for our antiquities, trying, but I fear trying in vain, to check that desolating tide which will soon make of Boston a third-rate Chicago.

If we have to lose the Old South Church, perhaps you can console me by bringing me some Egyptian antiquity. I authorize you to buy for me an authentic mummy of Joseph or Cleopatra, or a papyrus autograph of the decree ordering Pharaoh's baker to be hung, or of that allowing Moses to go with the Israelites out of Egypt. Even the signet ring of Menes, if you come by it, or a scarabæus which belonged to Sesostris, would content me. But do not trouble yourself to find these little souvenirs of the past. After all, a piece of Roxbury pudding-stone is older than any of them.

Well, dear Sarah, have a pleasant time; and when you get back to Rome, I shall think you are close by. You must feel then as if you had emerged from a grim past into modern times. The papacy will appear a thing of yesterday, and the Arch of Titus of the day before yesterday. We shall welcome you back, with joy, to our "little life of strut and rave," and all our "pasteboard passions and desires."

He has told us in his Autobiography about the college class of '29, to which he considered it his good fortune to belong. Mr. May was (and is) secretary of the class.

TO SAMUEL MAY.

JAMAICA PLAIN, February 6, 1874.

DEAR SAM, — It is very good of you to speak of me as you do; but I seem to myself to have been a very poor sort of a worker, and I can almost take to myself Wordsworth's lines,

> " But he is weak, both man and boy, —
> Hath been an idler in the land,
> Contented, if he can enjoy
> The things which others understand."

The things I most wished to do, I have never done; the things I have done best, I have only half done. I have lived "*au jour le jour*," and merely tried to do the nearest duty. The first sermon I ever preached had for its text (it was preached in the school) what I meant for the motto of my life, " Whatever thy hand finds to do, do it with thy might." I have kept this ideal before me, though I have never fulfilled it, — whatever my hand found to do, the thing which lay at hand; not what the heart desired, not what the ambition aspired to, not what the will chose, but what the hand found. I have always believed in Providence, and so have never desponded; I have always trusted in the essential good-will of my fellow-men, and have not been deceived. This life I have held to be sweet, and the next life at least as good as this. Cheerfulness and contentment have kept me well, so far as I have kept well, both in body and mind. I have come nearer to God every year, finding in Him love which is always law, and law which is always love. My creed has grown shorter every year, until I now put it into four words, " From God, for man."

Some day, when I am taken from you, in outward presence, but not in heart, — for wherever in God's universe I may be, I shall think of our dear class still, — you will perhaps read to them this note, kept in your book till then, and so they will hear me once more speaking to them, and telling them to believe that we shall come together somewhere in the vast beyond.

Truly yours,

JAMES FREEMAN CLARKE.

In 1874 a bronchial trouble obliged Mr. Clarke to go to the South. He left home March 18th (accompanied by Mrs. Clarke), and was absent nine weeks. During the journey he everywhere investigated the condition of the colored people, went to their schools, attended service at their churches, and talked with them while they were at work in their little patches of prospective corn or cotton. At Beaufort, S. C., they visited Mr. Clarke's parishioner, Miss Botume, who for ten years had been teaching a colored school near there. On Sunday they attended the afternoon service in the schoolhouse, five miles distant, and at its close Mr. Clarke spoke to the earnest little group of worshipers. Before separating, the people crowded into one of the recitation rooms and had a "shout," which consisted of a sort of chant, accompanied by a measured, shuffling movement, round and round in a circle. It was not easy to distinguish the words, but one of the women repeated over and over, "Oh, Lord, I 'se *so* lonesome, Oh, Lord, I 'se *so* lonesome." After the shout, every one in the schoolhouse, men, women, and children, shook hands with Mr. and Mrs. Clarke. One of the women said, "I hope you 'll arrive safely at home, if ever you live to get there." Many of them had kind words to say, and all seemed like friends. On Monday, the whole day was passed at the school, which was on Old Fort plantation, a picturesque place, which takes its name from a Huguenot fort, whose remains are still visible. On this plantation Dr. Nehemiah Adams wrote his "South Side View of Slavery." His favorite seat was shown, in a grove of live-oaks, from whose branches depend the long, swaying drapery of the Southern moss. Mr. Clarke measured one of these trees, and found the distance between its outermost tips to be 120 feet. During the war these weird trees witnessed a memorable scene. On the first day of January, 1863, the colored people came from every direction, — from Beaufort, Port Royal,

St. Helena, Lady's Island; from "the Main;" from every accessible place, — they and their white friends, and the United States troops in the vicinity assembled in this grove, and there one of the officers read to the group President Lincoln's Emancipation Proclamation, which took effect that day. As the last words left the speaker's lips, there burst forth the hymn, "My country, 't is of thee." From this moment it was *their* country also. The war was only half over, but in those sea islands the battle of Hilton Head had restored the control of the United States government.

Mr. Clarke felt a personal interest in the people on Old Fort plantation, having heard the story of their lives from Miss Botume,[1] and now he walked about the place and saw them peacefully cultivating their little patches of ground. One woman, who was at work near the schoolhouse, invited Mr. Clarke to plant some cotton-seed, and said she would send him the first ripe boll, which promise she fulfilled.

Their next visit was to Miss Laura Towne on St. Helena island. When the sea islands had come back into the possession of the United States government, Miss Towne had gone down there to remain for life with the freed-people, to teach and counsel and in every way help them in their efforts to rise in the world.

On the island was a church which before the war had been used by the planters, not however to the exclusion

---

[1] One good old man, Smart Washington, had by his labor accumulated enough to build a little cabin, and he and his wife took in a paralytic woman, who had no claim upon them except her helplessness. One day, when "Uncle Smart" was at work elsewhere, his little cabin took fire, and as the efforts of the occupants were all needed to save the paralytic, it was burned to the ground. When the old man returned and saw the ashes of his much-prized little home he bowed his head and said: "If it be Him will it ought to be my pleasure, and it *shall* be." It is perhaps unnecessary to add that when Mr. Clarke told the story from his pulpit, and added that a hundred dollars would build another cabin, the church responded by sending the old man that sum and something over for other necessaries.

of the colored people, for a place in the church had been set apart for them. Now the congregation was wholly of colored people and their teachers from the North. The pulpit was usually occupied by a colored minister; but he, on being introduced to Mr. Clarke, politely invited him to take his place on the following Sunday. That, as it happened, was Easter, and also Mr. Clarke's birthday, and away from his own pulpit and people he was glad of the opportunity offered him of preaching in the church on St. Helena.

He remained over Monday, in order to be present at a monthly meeting of an organization formed among the children to promote temperance.

During a drive on St. Helena island a dwelling-house was pointed out, from the upper balconies of which the families of the planters had watched the battle of Hilton Head, on the issue of which depended their continned possession of their homes or their flight to "the Main."

Mr. Clarke spent some weeks in North Carolina, and returned by Richmond, Washington, and Philadelphia, reaching home May 22d. He was in his pulpit on Whitsunday, which was the 24th.

TO HIS SISTER.

October 26, 1874.

We were beginning to wonder a little where you were and what doing. . . . Your letter explained what we might have understood: that when one goes in pursuit of Dante through the mysterious recesses of the Apennines, where he seemed to love to hide himself, one is apt to get away from post-offices and such modern contrivances. Why did he journey off to such an extent? Why did he write his "Divine Comedy" in such a multitude of castles, and climb the stairs of the stranger to such an amazing extent? But I suppose that in those days any one in Italy opposed to the pope was hunted about very severely and hardly knew where to lay his head. Since I last wrote you I have been to the Unitarian Conference at Saratoga, to Chicago and Milwaukee with Cora, to Portland, to the Republican Convention at Worcester, to Keene, N. H., to preach, to the top of Monadnock, to Lowell to preach, and to Concord, N. H., to a wedding.

TO HIS SISTER.

June 6, 1876.

I received your good, long letter on my return from Kentucky, where I went with Cora and Eliot, and stayed at the house of Philip and Emma Speed. I was glad to have my children see the kind friends of my earlier days, who continue as kind as ever, and, with their children, welcomed mine with all their old Kentucky hospitality. After having assisted at a Western conference of Unitarians I went with E. and C. to the Mammoth Cave, which they both enjoyed. Then C. and I returned to Philadelphia and spent a week with Tom, going every day to the exhibition, which is certainly an extraordinary and wonderful sight. It is "the Parliament of man, the federation of the world."

The nations from all the five continents and all the islands have met in a grand cordial emulation in doing the works of peace, — "Parthians, Medes, and Elamites," speaking in one tongue of useful labor.

I go again to Cincinnati this week as a delegate to the convention of Republicans to select a candidate for the presidency. We shall try to get a good man this time.

TO J. T. FIELDS.

JAMAICA PLAIN, *August* 19, 1876.

Mrs. Clarke and I are to go to the Adirondacks on Tuesday. Then farewell, for a time, bustle and business, fuss and free-trade, preaching and politics, saving the Old South, and such like vanities. Welcome, then, long solitary rows on the lakes framed in lonely mountains, sweet sleep on hemlock boughs, unbroken days, with time enough and to spare, days not chopped up into mince-meat by the multitudinous avocations, thicker than leaves in Vallombrosa. We shall return, no doubt, homesick for all these tormenting daily cares; homesick also for our friends, among whom we gratefully reckon yourself and the fair lady whom you call "The Dame.'

TO HIS SISTER.

December 3, 1876.

I sent you my Thanksgiving sermon, in which as you may see, I said a good word for our Southern brethren. I have received several letters about it, mostly approving; among others, one from that old anti-slavery war horse, Parker Pillsbury, who thanks me warmly for it.

This has been my "Annus Politicus," and I am glad it has come to its end. It is curious that I, who dislike politics, and have so much else to do that I like, should be dragged into it, *nolens volens*.

TO E. E. HALE.

September 29, 1877.

DEAR EDWARD, — Why do you ask me to do for love of you what I cannot do because the "stern daughter of the voice of God" has given me something else to do?

I should have enjoyed going to Springfield; I should three times over have enjoyed doing anything for you, but I was obliged to deny myself the meeting because of the absolute necessity at this season of avoiding distractions, and keeping my poor brain to its work. For the time is short in which I am to finish my tasks, and there are, at this season, somewhat less than twelve hours in the day.

Therefore sadly and unwillingly, but as one who has profited by James Walker's teaching, I am obliged to say No, but am still yours, JAMES.

TO HIS SISTER.

April 6, 1878.

I went on Thursday evening to our club, where Prof. A. Agassiz gave a highly interesting account of his deep-sea dredging in the Gulf of Mexico. . . We also had an interesting account of the fur-seal islands off Alaska. . . . But the most extraordinary feature of our club this evening was the exhibition, by Professor Dalton, of a phonograph. . . . It seemed a pure piece of magic, and when I thought of this realization of Munchausen's story of the notes frozen in a bugle, I saw that imagination could conceive of nothing which science would not realize.

TO HIS SISTER.

April 11, 1878.

I send you herewith a curiosity, some of the first cotton raised by free labor on Jefferson Davis's plantation in Mississippi. When our troops got possession of the country one of Davis's slaves, named Dick Montgomery, a very smart fellow, bought his master's plantation, to which he afterwards added two more. This cotton was some of the first raised by him, and was brought to me by a friend, Mr. Lombard, who also told me that this Montgomery became rich, and when Jefferson Davis once came to a place on the river near the plantation, Montgomery went in his carriage and brought his old master and friends to the new house he had built on the site of the old one, which our troops had burned. He gave them a sumptuous entertainment, and insisted on waiting at table as of old. This is an example of the delicacy and real gentlemanly feeling often found among the colored people.

Mr. Clarke's seventieth year found him in the full enjoyment of active work. But perhaps its approach had reminded him that he must not delay putting into outward shape those books that he most wished to finish. The publication of these, as he approached the year 1880, came at shorter intervals. In 1877, he printed a volume of sermons," Go up Higher." In 1878 were published " Memorial and Biographical Sketches," " Essentials and Non-Essentials," and the little book, " How to Find the Stars." In 1879 came " Common-Sense in Religion."

His seventieth birthday was kept by a happy meeting of his friends at the Church of the Disciples. It was a pleasure to him that his life-long friend, William Henry Channing, was able to be present. When he and others, among whom were Rev. Henry W. Foote, Mrs. Julia Ward Howe, and Dr. O. W. Holmes, had brought tributes of friendship in poem, song, and story, Mr. Clarke himself was asked to let them hear his voice.

After dwelling for a few moments on the earlier incidents and influences of his life, he said: —

On leaving college I hesitated about a profession, at first intending to study law. I cannot be too thankful that I was finally led to decide for the ministry. Never for an hour have I regretted it. To spend one's life in communion with the loftiest themes of thought, to have work bringing us into intercourse with the wise and good of all times, to be offered year after year opportunities of helping and blessing our fellow-men, to be able sometimes to be a mediator to others of God's truth and grace — what can be a better lot than this ?

I do not mean to say, by any means, that I have always accomplished, or even attempted, the good I might have done. Looking back to-day, I see enough of time lost, opportunities neglected.

> "Let the thick curtain fall;
> I better know than all
> How little I have gained,
> How vast the unattained."

I am thankful that I was brought up among Unitarians. . . . I have never known the day when God did not seem to me a Father and Friend, Christ a human brother and heavenly teacher, and life made for perpetual progress. . . . If sometimes life has seemed a burden and the way dark, I have never blamed Providence or destiny. For this I thank my training.

I am thankful, too, that when the time came for me to begin my work as a minister, I did not remain in New England, but went out to Kentucky, and there stayed seven years. . . . It was a good thing to speak to people who were unaccustomed to the thoughts familiar to me. I could thus test and try all I knew and see what it amounted to. I was deprived of my usual supports, and had to depend on myself. I was surrounded by those who thought my creed only infidelity under another name, and others to whom all religion seemed only a sham or folly. This was hard, but useful as a discipline. I could take nothing for granted; I must be able to give a reason for everything I believed. And I also found there noble friends, generous and loving hearts, whose friendship has been a joy to me always.

And I am glad that, when I left Kentucky and returned to New England, instead of being settled in an old church, I united with friends in forming a new one. . . . This church was founded in April, 1841, with forty-eight members. Its creed was faith in Jesus as a teacher and master, its aim the study and practice of Christianity. We have worked together in this spirit and purpose during nearly forty years, and I think our church has done some good, — not so much as we might and ought to have done, but yet something. I have had great joy in this church, and have been helped by it in many ways.

The seashore had a great attraction for Mr. Clarke,

and in 1879 he had built a house on one of the headlands of Cape Ann, twenty-seven miles from Boston. From that time his summers were all passed at this seashore home, with the exception of the one spent in Europe.

MAGNOLIA, MASSACHUSETTS, *July*, 1880.

Magnolia super Mare, Magnolia by the Sea; so called because the swamp magnolia grows and flourishes near by in the depths of the wild woods of Cape Ann. Like the rest of this romantic coast, it combines magnificent rocks and cliffs with umbrageous woods and far-resounding shores. Here one can take his rest aloof from care. As I sit on a piazza facing the blue ocean, see the white surf on Kettle Island, hear the long roll on the beach close by, I feel as if all the anxiety and worry of life were far away. Here it is always afternoon.

TO S. C. C.

August 15, 1880.

To hear from you, or Sarah, or Abraham, always makes me happy for the rest of the day. I am aware of a certain feeling of content, which, when I analyze it, resolves itself into the influence of your letter. What a blessing it is that we should have been spared so long to each other, and that we should never have had any of those estrangements which are not infrequent in families.

We are enjoying our quiet and lovely home here very much. All around is ocean, old gray rocks, deep green foliage of the most luxuriant masses of thick-set bushes and vines, which are crowded so close as to make an almost impenetrable barrier, except where a foot-path goes through. I am now sitting (6 A. M.) on the piazza; and as I write I look up and see the long stretch of pale blue ocean before me, with a vast sky of tender clouds. To the left is the curving beach, on which the pulse of ocean beats regularly in slow throbs of heavy surf waves. We are expecting a visit from the sea-serpent, for he is at present cruising round this cape.

In the winter of 1880-81, he gave at the Lowell Institute a course of lectures, which were published soon after under the title of "Events and Epochs in Religious History." His topics included the life and times of St. Augustine, Savonarola, Luther, Wesley, George Fox, the Christian Monks, the Buddhist Monks, the Huguenots, Jeanne d'Arc, and an account of the Catacombs. Stereopticon illustrations of these last were given, and also of the rock-cut temples of Central Asia, and of abbeys, monasteries, etc. Anything which interested him in his studies he wanted to communicate to others. Of the life of Jeanne d'Arc he had made careful study at an earlier period, and in addition to such authorities as were to be found in our public libraries, he had obtained, from France, Wallon's account of her trial, — every question addressed to her, every answer made by the poor maiden, brave when facing the terrors of war, but finding it harder to meet the cruel looks of her accusers and judges.

CHAPTER XIX.

CLOSING YEARS.

1881-1888.

IN the year 1881 came the fortieth anniversary of the Church of the Disciples. On the 27th of April, the birthday of the church was celebrated by an assembly of the congregation which was large, united, and enthusiastic. There appeared no sign of any decline of strength on the part of the minister as he entered upon his seventy-first year. On Sundays he often preached twice, and except in his summer vacation, conducted two classes. He completed and published "Thomas Didymus"[1] and "Events and Epochs in Religious History." In February, he visited Washington, and preached there, and in March, in October, and again in November, he visited New York. In June he went to Grand Manan, and later in the summer to Newport; but he spent most of the summer at Magnolia. He prepared in the first half of the year twelve written lectures on St. Paul, which he delivered at his church. He also conducted two classes — one in the evening for men, and one in the daytime for women — on Christian history, taking one century at each lesson.

And the picture of those years of his life of which we have spoken in earlier chapters is incomplete unless one recalls the talk, serious or slight, which went on in the office of "The Atlantic Monthly," or in the contributors' reading-room. Mr. Lowell had edited that magazine for years, and after him Mr. Fields. In his remi-

[1] Afterwards called *Life and Times of Jesus*.

niscences, Mr. Fields has shown something of his own humor, and of that range of recollection which made him the most charming of story-tellers and conversers. From the "Old Corner Book-Store," at the foot of School Street, the publishers had removed to what was called the "new corner," where Hamilton Place opens from Tremont Street. In a pleasant parlor overlooking the Common, the favored contributors might find the latest books or magazines, might make an appointment, or write their letters. Best of all, they met each other there; and of the little group who dropped in as they went up-town and down-town, it may well be imagined that none were more welcome than Mr. Clarke. I remember an occasion when, meeting Dr. Holmes there, I offered to tell him of an "astonishing coincidence." He defied me to tell one so remarkable as something which had just happened in his experience. We arranged an impromptu eclogue on the moment, in which Mr. Clarke was appointed to be the Palæmon who should decide in our great discussion.[1]

The Examiner Club is a favorite club for conversation in Boston. It was formed in the year 1870, and Mr. Clarke was one of its first members. At the time of his death he was the president. The New Englander will readily see the interest of a club in which, not to speak of men still living, Governor Andrew, Mr. Emerson, Mr. G. P. Bradford, Dr. E. H. Clarke, James Freeman Clarke, Mr. Goddard of the "Advertiser," Mr. Henry James, Professor Rogers of the School of Technology, and Mr. Whipple were active members. Yet again, the Thursday Club interested him, and often were glad of the services which he so willingly rendered. This is a club of one hundred of the most active

---

[1] Both Dr. Holmes and I were at this time story-tellers for the magazine. The truth of history requires me to state that Mr. Clarke awarded the premium to neither of us, but gave it to Mr. Aldrich, who had interjected a third story.

men of the time who live in Boston or the neighborhood. It is their business to keep each other informed of the last news in science, art, and literature, as they learn of it in their different occupations. In the intimacies of this club, Mr. Clarke's contributions were generally of subjects bearing on education or history. In preparing this volume, we have availed ourselves of notes which he made for some of his historical reminiscences at its meetings.

The year 1882 begins with the course of lectures on the "Religions of the World," delivered in the Lowell Institute. The regular Sunday services go on, and the attendance at meetings of the college overseers, the library trustees, and other boards. On the 30th of April he took part in the services at Mr. Emerson's funeral. In March he made a visit to Washington, where he preached on two Sundays. On the 13th of May, he sailed on the "Atlas" for Europe, with Mrs. Clarke and one of his daughters. He had accepted an invitation to preach before the British and Foreign Unitarian Association on their fifty-fifth anniversary. His visit in London was made very agreeable by the society of people whom he was glad to meet. The party then visited Paris, spent a month in Switzerland, returned by the Rhine to England, and he was in Boston again on the 12th of September. He went to the Unitarian conference at Saratoga the next week, and made a visit in New York.

In the next year, 1883, the entry "Bad cold" appears frequently in the diary, and gives the first signal of failing strength. There is one stormy Sunday, when he did not go to church in the afternoon, — the first entry of that kind which I have noted. But the regular service at church continues unbroken. The morning sermons for the months of winter and spring were a course on Unitarian belief. In the same year he collected and revised for press the materials for a course of talks on anti-slavery days, which had interested large companies. The second volume of "Ten Great Religions" was published. He wrote a "Manual of Unitarian Belief," which has since had a wide circulation. He made visits to New York, to Newport, and to Meadville, spending the summer months mostly at Magnolia. On the 6th of October is a note that he attended a "meeting of Independents," at Young's Hotel.

The 21st of July was the fiftieth anniversary of his preaching that first sermon on the duty next our hand. He notes the anniversary, and on that day begins the Autobiography which the reader has enjoyed.

He was now obliged to hold himself a little in check, and to feel that he could no longer do what he did when he was a young man. But the services at church are performed with unbroken regularity through 1884. In the spring he made a visit to his invalid brother at Marietta, in Georgia, and on the way preached in Washington and, on successive Sundays, in Atlanta and New York.

Mr. Clarke was dissatisfied with the nomination of the Republican convention in July, and placed himself at once on record as one who would not support it. He believed that the old issues between North and South, which had governed the politics of the country since the beginning of the century, were substantially settled. He was especially interested in civil-service reform and in every action which looked toward the rescue of official appointments from machine politics. At first there seemed reason to fear that he might have to stand apart from his old anti-slavery friends in his determination not to vote with the Republican party; but, as it proved, he did not stand alone. He united with some of his anti-slavery friends and with other gentlemen who had heretofore acted with the Republicans. They did not organize as a party, but preferred to consider themselves Independents; and by this name they came to be known in the political world. Eventually, they determined to unite with the Democrats in the election of Mr. Cleveland.

To satisfy himself as to Mr. Cleveland's position and intentions, he visited him at Albany. When he returned from Albany to the Unitarian national conference at Saratoga, he was asked by a few of the ministers there to give them his impressions. They met in a private room, and from more than one of those present on that occasion we learn that Mr. Clarke said, in substance, that he was convinced Mr. Cleveland was an honest, hard-working, capable man, who believed in civil-service reform, and had sufficient strength of purpose to be true to it in spite of outside pressure. For this reason he felt it his duty to support him.

He found at the end of the canvass that he was not in the minority of the people of the country, as he had expected to be, but that the Independents and their allies had succeeded.

The parish work, which he would never willingly forego, continues, and the diary was never more full of subjects for sermons than in this year. But it seems to me to show some signs of fatigue. There is the "bad cold" again occasionally, and the entries are shorter and fewer than in earlier years. It is pathetic to see four such entries as these together: —

Friday. Bad cold. Stay at home all day.
Saturday. At home all day.
Sunday. Thermometer minus 4°. Sermon on "Vis inertiæ [as if he knew anything about it!]: its good and evil in nature and in life."
Monday. My cold continues. At home all day.

On the 24th of January, 1885, he conducted, at Arlingtou Street Church, the funeral services of his lifelong friend and companion in study, William Henry Channing.

On the 21st of the month he went to New York, and was present that evening at a meeting of the Harvard Club. The visit was only for a few days.

His determination to work steadily in composition appears from the memorandum that his amanuensis is to attend two hours each day for four days in the week. His seventy-fifth birthday was celebrated by the Church of the Disciples in a re-union at the church, of three or four hundred persons, and he marks it as "very pleasant."

On the centenary of the introduction at King's Chapel of the Revised Book of Common Prayer, the 12th of April, 1885, he was present at that church, and gave an address on the life of his grandfather, Dr. Freeman, who arranged that book of service, and was for near half a century the minister of that church.

On the 11th of May, 1885, there met at Hartford, Connecticut, a "Congress of Churches." It originated in the catholic wish of some Broad Church Episcopalians and liberal Orthodox Congregationalists to bring about a better understanding between different Protestant communions in America, or at least among their members. They had the courage and consistency to invite Mr. Clarke. And no occasion could have given him more satisfaction, or been more in harmony with the spirit of the work of his life. On the 13th he read to this congress a paper on "The Historical Christ as the Centre of Christian Theology."

He spent the summer at his happy home at Magnolia, enjoying, almost every day, his favorite recreations of walking, driving, and sailing. On the 5th of July, the entry in his diary is, "Up at 4.30. 5 to 7, writing sermon. 10.30, preach dedication sermon of Union Chapel [at Magnolia]. Chapel crowded. Letters in evening."

On the 16th of August, the tireless entries in the diary are: —

Things to be done this winter : —

1. Books. (a) Ticknor's [the publisher] book on 'Self-Development.

(b) A. U. A. Sursum Corda.

(c) Ellis' [the publisher] Vexed Questions.

(d) Previous Questions.

Things to be done in the church this winter : —

1. Afternoon Bible-class on Monday.

2. S. S. lectures on Picturesque Palestine.

3. Literary lectures, on Wednesday evenings, on such subjects as Spenser, Milton's " Areopagitica," Bacon's " Advancement," Sir T. Browne, Byron, Shelley, Coleridge, Goldsmith, Gray, etc.

4. Sermons on special subjects, same as " Previous Questions."

The Sunday services at the Church of the Disciples are renewed on the 13th of September, when he preached a sermon, " What is a church for ? " Sometimes the diary notes — what it might often have noted — " a large congregation." It should be remembered that this means eight or nine hundred persons. In the afternoons he meets a " class of young men." And he now begins the preparation for his Palestine lectures, as indicated in the plan made in August. There is no break in the parish duties, — indeed, they seem, if possible, more sedulously cared for than ever. One notes the advanced age of the persons whose funerals he attends. The friends who united in young life to form a living church are passing to higher life.

In 1886, the steady line of his out-door work is twice interrupted by " jaundice," of which an earlier attack had been noted in 1885. But an attack of illness seems to mean little more to him than staying at home. The end of the year notes, " Books published in 1886 : 'Every-Day Religion' (a volume of sermons), 'Vexed Questions,' and 'The Problem of the Fourth Gospel.'"

There is an entry of letters written, "from 900 to 1,000," — a pathetic and lamentable contrast to the happier entries of earlier years, when he wrote letters because he wanted to. He is now experiencing the weight of correspondence, which St. Marc Girardin so well calls "the burden of our modern civilization," — a burden so heavy that men wonder whether Rowland Hill were, indeed, a benefactor of his kind.

The "First Unitarian Society" in Philadelphia were to dedicate their new church building on the evening of Tuesday, February 9, 1886, and a conference of the ministers and others assembled on that occasion was to be held during the two succeeding days. Mr. Clarke was invited by Rev. Joseph May, pastor of the Philadelphia society, to preach the dedication sermon. He arrived in Philadelphia on the Saturday previous, and on Sunday preached twice for Mr. Mangasarian, an Armenian who had lately established an independent church in Philadelphia. On Monday he called on Dr. Furness and a number of other friends. When Tuesday came he had a hoarse cold, but by remaining quietly in-doors all day he was able in the evening to give the sermon which he had prepared for the occasion.[1] He was to have taken part in the conference, but this satisfaction was made impossible by the state of his throat, and on the morning of the tenth he left for New York, and after resting there for a night, reached home on the eleventh.

On the following Sunday he preached in his own pulpit.

The summer, as was usual with him now, was spent at Magnolia; and the more regular course of life was broken only by a visit to Newport. When the autumn's work began he organized a temperance union in his church, and he also mentions, with interest, addressing

[1] His diary of the Wednesday previous was, "Up at 4.30 [A. M.], writing sermon for Philadelphia."

a full house one night at the Howard Athenæum, a theatre in the heart of Boston; "not one half of them regular church attendants."

It is a manly record of determination to do his duty to the last. It is not until the 20th of Jannary, 1887, that he gives up preaching. For the rest of that winter and through the spring the pulpit of the Church of the Disciples, from which he had seldom been absent, was supplied by the ministry of different friends. He was not confined to the house, nor did he shrink from occupatiou. During forty days of this confinement there is mention of a hundred and ten letters written by him. And a sermon was regularly sent to the "Gazette," for that larger congregation which read his words every week, in other parts of the world. He continued his contributions to different newspapers. It is an invalid's life which is recorded, with hardly a reference to weakness or illness. On the 15th of June he went to Magnolia. He resumed his work on the Autobiography, and advanced it nearly to the point where the reader has found it discontinued. In this summer he records excursions, longer or shorter, in the "Sheila," the yacht of his friend Mr. Foote, who, as it proved, was not to survive him long, and whose friendship and companionship were the source of great pleasure to him. For the first time, I think, he prepared in advance for the pulpit service of the winter by writing sermons in summer, and before he returned to Boston he had written six. The subjects are, "Rejoice Evermore," "The Labor Troubles," "Dorothea Dix," "Jesus as the Spiritual Leader of the Race," "Paganism in Christianity."

On the 2d of October, to the joy of his people, he resumed his place in the pulpit, and preached the sermon, "Rejoice Evermore" From this time, with but two exceptions, he preached every Sunday until the 4th of March, generally with the memorandum in the diary that some member of the church, or some other friend, assisted in the service.[1] As late as November of this year, he wrote, as he had done for so many years, the report of the committee on the Observatory to the overseers of Harvard College.

Nor is there any self-indulgence as the winter comes on. "To Boston; carriage two hours; seven calls," "Dinner of Class of 1829;" "Letter with Christmas song to R. C. H.;" "Sent G. H. Ellis two sermons, 'Temperance Efforts and Temperance Methods' and 'The Pew System';" "Bible-class at my room at church;" such are memoranda of four successive January days. "How to get the best out of the coming year" is the resolute title of the sermon of January 8; and, on the same day, fitly enough he baptizes a little girl by the name of "Hope."

On the 22d, after he had preached as usual, as he returned home to Jamaica Plain, the horses in the carriage took fright "and dashed against a lamp-post, bruising Anna, and cutting my cheek. Dr. Emma L. Call attended to me" Such is the simple entry in his diary. Dr. Call, who fortunately happened to be passing, accompanied him to Jamaica Plain and took a stitch in his eyelid. His diary adds, "On account of accident I have been obliged to stay at home all this week and abstain from reading and writing;" and Thursday he says, "Amanuensis writes my sermon." The accident did not prevent his preaching the next Sunday, "Know Thyself" being his subject. There follow, in regular order of successive Sundays, with only one interruption, four sermons on the Lord's prayer; the texts being, "Thy Kingdom Come," "Daily Bread," "Forgive us our Debts," "As we forgive our Debtors." The last of these was delivered on the 18th of March, the Sunday after the well-remembered "blizzard," which blocked all railroads and broke all telegraph wires, so

---

[1] His parishioners, Rev. S. B. Cruft and Mr. Darwin E. Ware, read the service for him during several months.

that "our only access to New York from Boston is by cable to London." This is his entry of the 14th.

A few letters, written during the years of which we have spoken, follow.

TO W. G. ELIOT.

October 31, 1881.

DEAR WILLIAM, — 'T is All-Hallow E'en, and I have seen a ghost. I opened my portfolio, and there lay two letters of yours unanswered, and the ghost I saw was that of your face looking at me, and saying, "How long, James! how long?" But then I knew you would never say it; it was only a ghost and no reality.

How good of you to write such sweet, bright, tender, sparkling letters. You have forgotten all about them, but they were just like your talk... I wish that you and Mrs. Eliot would come and make us a visit next summer at our little house by the sea, on the shore of Cape Ann. William Channing came last summer, and it would make us all very happy to see you. I sit on the piazza and look at the ocean; that is the chief work I do in the summer.

Did you know I have two grandchildren? Eliot's children, one a little girl, over two and half years, and one a little boy called James Freeman, eight months. They are as charming as they can be.

With love always, JAMES.

TO W. G. ELIOT.

November 9 and 27, 1881.

Half an hour before your pleasant letter came I had finished a little dedication to you of my next book, "Events and Epochs in Religious History." I hope you will not be displeased at my showing in this way the many years of affection which have united us. Thanksgiving is over, and we have been made glad and gay by a visit from Eliot, his wife and two children. It was delightful to have the little things about.

Dear William, I always read your letters with delight. They bring back the old days when we were full of vitality and hope. Perhaps in the next world we shall be like little children again, and have a fresh supply of juvenility. Do not forget your promise to come with your wife and stay with us next summer at the seashore. You need not do anything but sit on the piazza and look at the sea.

I have a terrible piece of work before me in writing a new course of Lowell lectures. It will make the second part of "Ten Great Religions," and must be finished by the end of January.

TO A. H. C.

NEW YORK, *November* 20, 1881.

I wish to show in my Lowell lectures the real religion of humanity, and how God is with all nations, teaching them something of himself.[1] . . .

TO W. G. ELIOT.

April 3, 1882.

DEAR WILLIAM, — I am seventy-two years to-morrow, and congratulate myself that you and William Channing are still on this side with me. Let us stick together as long as we can. I send you some of his symbolisms. How he throws himself into all sympathies! I am expecting to see him before long, for I shall sail from Boston, May 13, to be away two or three months. .

---

[1] Among some manuscripts of that period was a loose sheet headed: Before writing the *Lowell Lectures.*

"*H*owbeit, when he, the spirit of truth shall come, he will lead you into all truth.

"This work of twelve lectures on the religions of the world may do great good or little, as it is done. May I be helped to put out of my heart any wish but this, that the truth of God and the good of man may be served by them. May I be led by the Spirit to say the best and most needed things — whatever may confirm love to God and to man. May I rely on that promise of my master and friend."

LONDON, *May* 29, 1882.

Our voyage was rather long, cold, foggy and disagreeable, and we were glad last Thursday morning to be at Liverpool, where we took a train at once for London. Lilian joined us Friday evening, coming from Paris, where she has had a pleasant time with Mrs. William B. Greene and Ellen Hale.

Yesterday (Whitsunday) we four went to Hampstead where I preached for Dr. Sadler, a fine old gentleman, in a very pleasant, picturesque English chapel.

Hampstead is lovely, half city and half country. We went, after church, to dine with Professor J. Estlin Carpenter. His father, Dr. William B. Carpenter, was present, and was very agreeable, talking about Darwin, Carlyle, and many others whom he had known.

June 17, 1882.

We have been in London three weeks; and it seems more like three months, so many new impressions have succeeded each other, so many people have we seen, so many places visited. Did you ever notice this curious mental phenomenon, that a succession of novelties makes the time go by very rapidly, but also causes it to appear very long in looking back? Each day goes by like a flash; but, when gone, it has the air of a week. On the other hand, when one has little to do, the days drag heavily along and the hours have leaden feet; but when gone, leaving nothing to mark them in the memory, they shrink to a span.

This week was the close of the Oxford term, and we spent the greater part of two days there. I think there can be no other place in the world like Oxford. Quiet and peaceful for the most part, with an air of monastic seclusion; every college a cloister, a separate community, with its own hall, chapel, library, quadrangles, dormitories, gardens, kitchens, dining-room, — the effect is of a town of convents. These gray old buildings take us back five hundred years. Eaten by the teeth of time, that mighty rodent, they speak of the numerous generations come and gone. Pass under this low Gothic portal in the wall: a bell chimes as you enter, a gift of John of Gaunt perhaps, or of bluff King Harry. Cross it and pass into another old gateway, and open an old oaken door. You are now in the chapel, where storied panes, richly colored, admit the poet's dim religious light. Opposite is the dining-hall, with portraits on the walls of the eminent scholars, statesmen, soldiers, ecclesiastics, who have been students in these halls. Then comes the library. The books have that unreadable air which belongs to a very old collection. The fashion of this world passeth away in books, as well as in all other things. How proud were the authors of these mighty tomes of their work! Now, who reads them? An ancient and a mouldy smell comes from them: let us go into the gardens.

Every hall has its garden or park, often running down to the river, gay with flowers, bordered by stately elms.

We were desirous of being present at the Commemoration Services, which correspond to our College Commencement. Tickets to the theatre were in demand, but through the great kindness of Dr. Acland, Regius Professor of Medicine, we had seats for our whole party. The distinguished guests of the university who came that day to take their honorary degrees were Sir William Hamilton Muir (the Sanskrit scholar), Goldwin Smith, Robert Browning, Dr. Allen Thompson, and Mr. Watts, the artist.

At Oxford I had the pleasure of seeing Dr. Jowett Dr. Acland, Professor Westwood, Mr. Seligman, authority on libraries, and Max Müller, besides other interesting people.

In London I have met with very many interesting people, to some of whom I had letters. Dr. Bradley,

Dean of Westminster, showed me through the curious rooms and passages of the Deanery and explained the monuments of the Abbey. I have also met with Stopford Brooke, Mr. Haweis, Matthew Arnold, John Bright, Miss Octavia Hill, Thomas H. Gill, Miss Swanwick, Miss Frances Power Cobbe, and others.

Mr. Clarke and his family spent some days with Mr. and Mrs. Edwin Lawrence, whose hospitable home is so gratefully remembered by many traveling Americans. Here they saw John Bright, and others whom they were glad to meet. They made several visits to Professor and Mrs. J. Estlin Carpenter. They also spent some hours with Rev. and Mrs. Philip Wicksteed. Indeed, those who contributed to the happiness of their stay in London were too numerous to be named here, and the days were too few to see as much as they wished of these friends.

Mr. Clarke had long been a lover of the hymns of Thomas H. Gill, and they had exchanged letters and books. Now they met face to face. Mr. Gill came rapidly into the room, and, seizing Mr. Clarke's hand, said in Greek, "As unknown and yet well known." Then followed a long and happy talk.

William H. Channing was living in London, and he and Mr. Clarke met almost every day.

LONDON, *June* 18, 1882.

Yesterday I went in the morning to hear Canon Farrar, who preaches in St. Margaret's, Westminster. The church was crowded in every part, every foot of standing-room being occupied. The sermon was a noble tribute to Garibaldi, and was as free and strong as if it had come from the lips of Theodore Parker. The services which preceded the sermon lasted about an hour, and were full of repetitions. . . . But, when Canon Farrar ascended the pulpit and began to preach, the change from formalism to freedom was instantaneous. He seemed to clear the air of these mediæval mists by the first words he spoke.

On the Sunday evening previous we had heard a very different preacher, Mr. Spurgeon. Intellectually his sermon had nothing in it. Yet there was a crowded house, said to contain six thousand persons. The force which brings them together, and holds them there, is the manifest belief of Spurgeon that these people need and can have an immediate salvation, and his direct, strong, simple purpose of doing all in his power to bring them into the love of God.

What a contrast was this evening to another evening a week later, with James Martineau! We passed some quiet hours with this pure, clear, and profound thinker, who is still working on at the age of seventy-five in calm serenity. He is as deeply interested as ever in the religious thought of the time, and in the education of young men for the ministry.

PARIS, *July* 2.

In London I found what I had wished much to see, an early autograph copy of Gray's "Elegy." Several autographs of this poem exist. One is in the British Museum. By the kindness of Sir William Fraser, its owner, I examined at my leisure what seems to have been the earliest sketch of the poem. He has also many other curiosities in his collection, — the original manuscript of Scott's "Marmion;" the copy of the first edition of the "Vicar of Wakefield," given by Goldsmith to Dr. Johnson; Dr. Johnson's own copy of his own story "Rasselas;" and a whole library of curious works of this sort.

In the house of another English gentleman I saw a package of autograph letters by Oliver Cromwell. They came from the house of Richard Cromwell; and as I spelled them out, one by one, they interested me much.

One, written to his son Richard, when a youth, gave him advice as to his reading, and, among other books, recommended him to read Walter Raleigh's "History of the World." I saw also in the same collection a letter written by Mary, Queen of Scots, on the night before her execution. It was, I believe, to the mother of her first husband. It was a long letter, carefully written, and showed how self-possessed she must have been in view of her approaching death.

Mr. Clarke went twice to the House of Commons. On one occasion the Egyptian and the Irish troubles were both under discussion, and he heard questions put by the different members to Gladstone, and his replies. A fiery member rose, and made a speech in favor of boycotting, and this proved to be Parnell.

The party reluctantly turned their faces toward the Continent, saying, in the words of Francis Higginson, "Farewell, dear England! Farewell the church of God in England, and all the Christian friends there!"

They spent ten or twelve days in Paris, and Mr. Clarke, as was his habit, went into many of the churches.

"How imposing are these Catholic churches! What beauty and majesty in their vast proportions and lovely details! As we enter these solemn aisles a sense of religion enters the soul. We drop our cares, our desires, and for a few moments feel the presence of eternity. The Catholic Church represents the element of worship latent in every soul, and represents and serves it so well that it retains its hold on millions. It omits too much the other elements of Christianity. It does not help the progress of man; but, when the deeper and larger religion comes, it must retain all there is of good in this church, and add all that is now wanting. May that day dawn soon!"

From Paris they went to Switzerland, where Mr.

Clarke enjoyed showing his daughters the beautiful scenery which had so impressed him on his first visit in 1849.

INTERLAKEN, *July* 9, 1882.

. . . In Bâle one sees the portraits by Holbein, and is struck, as in the early Italian masters, with the fullness of expression in each face. These masters understood little of the technicalities of art, but they knew what they wished to do. They did not draw a face in order to show their skill, but to fix on their canvas the character of the man. And there he is, with his courage, his determined purpose, his patient, immovable stress of will, hardened by long struggles, tested by sharp encounters, hardened in the fires of misfortune and pain. Or there is the pure, saintly face of some aspiring and devoted woman, a divinely tempered soul, whose conversation was in heaven. You look at these faces and you know them as if you had lived with them; and you say, "This is what the artist is for; not to display his skill on trivial subjects, not to paint shallow men and frivolous women in aristocratic salons, but to seize and keep the higher moments of life, its richest experience, its memorable hours."

The picture in this museum which interested me most, and to see which was worth a visit to Bâle, was a portrait of Luther in miniature, by his friend, Lucas Cranach. It represents him as a young man, not with the burly form and heavy features to which we are accustomed, but with clearly-cut, well-defined contours of face, an earnest and somewhat melancholy expression, and eyes as of one who looked at a grave task laid on his conscience and heart.

The Lake of Lucerne I saw for the third time, and neither memory nor imagination can paint it more wonderful than it is. It combines all charms, the sublime majesty of its black cliffs and granite pyramids, the tender loveliness of its shaded shores, the dazzling splendor of the snow-fields above.

From Switzerland they went to Holland, where they spent ten or twelve days. This country had a special interest for them because Mrs. Clarke's father came from there. But, beside the pleasure of meeting their relatives, they liked its scenery; and with Fromentin's "Maîtres d'Autrefois" for a guide-book, enjoyed its treasures of art.

As faithful descendants of the Pilgrims they visited Leyden, and at Scheveningen tried to find the exact spot from which the Pilgrims had set sail; but to their disappointment they found that the sea had devoured it.

Mr. Clarke spent a few days in London on his return from the Continent, and took this opportunity to go to Nazing, a village from which came some of his ancestors, and also the Apostle Eliot, related to the family through the marriage of his sister to William Curtis, an ancestor of Mr. Clarke. Though only a few hours from London, everything, roads and fields and houses, appeared as they might have done when Eliot and his friends took their last look at the place before setting out for America. Mr. Clarke went at once to the top of the tower in the old church.

"In ascending I had to push my way through the remains of the nests made by many generations of rooks.

As I looked down from the tower I saw Epping forest in the distance, and nearer, the common, where tradition tells us that Boadicea defeated the Roman army. In the little church are still shown the oaken seats on which John Eliot and William Curtis sat as boys. . . .

"Perhaps some of you may have visited Nazing. Those who have not will like to hear of the village, where originated the Curtises and Heaths, of Roxbury, and so many more with whose names we are familiar, and especially which gave birth to John Eliot, that sweet and holy soul, who gave letters and grammar to a before unwritten language; who translated the Bible into this strange tongue; who had it printed; who taught the Indians to read it; who went among the rude savages without fear, and who made them his friends. The pure light of his loving faith shines among the more lurid lights of New England Puritanism, —

> 'Velut inter ignes
> Luna minores.'

"I also went to Waltham Abbey, six miles from Nazing. This is a church so ancient that a part of it dates back to a period before the Conquest. Somewhere in the churchyard repose the remains of Harold, the last Saxon king.

"Waltham Abbey is fourteen miles from London, and is on the river Lea, a stream made famous as the place where Izaak Walton loved to fish."

On the 12th of September, Mr. Clarke was back in Boston, and on the following Sunday he preached in his own pulpit.

TO HIS SISTER.

November 8, 1882.

We are all well and have gone to work again as usual. The moment I was at home I was called upon to attend to various duties immediately. I felt as the horses in the engine house may be supposed to feel when the fire-bell strikes, and their harness drops upon them. I found myself as suddenly in the traces.

TO HIS SISTER.

JAMAICA PLAIN, *March* 12, 1883.

I was much pleased to see your catalogue of books. As soon as I get the vacant half hour (which Mr. F—— said he should have after his death, and designated as a time when an importunate person might call, and he would attend to him), I shall try to look up some books to fill your evident *lacunæ*. Last night I preached to a full Music Hall for an hour, and was not tired. . . . Anna and I are reading the correspondence of Emerson and Carlyle. It is interesting. But we are rather startled at the stately, elaborate style on both sides. Every letter seems a *tour de force*. There is nothing of the *currente calamo* about either. Even the impetuous T. C., who in his books rushes on at hap-hazard, and often in his haste seems to go head over heels, appears daunted by R. W. E., and tries to write back in the same vein.

TO REV. JOHN CORDNER.

BOSTON, *March* 15, 1883.

I am, with many others, much interested in the attempt to procure a central, commodious, and suitable building for the use of the Unitarian body. This should have been done long ago, and we have suffered much from not having had it . A home for the denomination is what is needed in order to be the centre of our chief activities.

I am not a sectarian, I believe, in my regard for the Unitarian body. I feel great sympathy with the other denominations, and see how grand is the work they are doing. But we also have our one talent, and ought not to bury it in the earth, or to hide our Lord's money. It is not ours, it is his. Wherever Unitarianism has gone it has aided education, philanthropy, and all humane reforms. Let us do everything we can for that which has done so much for us.

FROM W. H. CHANNING.

June 14, 1883.

You shall certainly have all your letters now in my possession. But the great Boston fire cost you and me more than you dreamed of; for a portmanteau, filled with the assorted correspondence of friends, and of my own note-books, etc., went up in tinder that tremeudous night, though the flames stopped at the very next wall, in Exchange Building, State Street, after licking up our "sweet morsels" with the final sweep of its ruddy tongue.[1] Of late years you have found time to write very little to me, though some of your brief notes indicate the quality of our friendship.

And in using this sacred name, the wish grows strong that in your story you will interweave enough of bright memories of this old classmate and compeer of yours to let the growing boys and youth of our dear New England see how very sweet, beautiful, and heavenly a life-long unbroken friendship is. Tell them somewhat of our old Cambridge days; of the Cincinnati and Louisville era, when we were co-editors of the "Western Messenger;" of the anti-slavery and Brook Farm times, so rich with mighty issues. But follow your own impulse, and that will be best.

TO WILLIAM G. ELIOT.

December 14, 1883.

I feel as you do about the work we might have done, and have not. I sometimes think I made a great mistake in being settled over a church, instead of devoting my life to preaching in the byways and out of the way places to the unchurched people, outside of any healthy organization. By giving them the sincere milk of the gospel, all summed up in the words, "Come unto me and I will give you rest," apart from all theologies or anti-theologies, Jesus the dear Christ, the well-beloved son, the brother and friend and helper of us all, I think that a new revival ought to come. But I take the same comfort that you do. The Lord has his own servants, and will send by whom he will send. He has let us do something, and we ought to be grateful.

---

[1] The greater portion of Mr. Clarke's letters to his friend, William G. Eliot, were also destroyed, by the burning of Mr. Eliot's house in St. Louis.

In the spring of 1884, a great sorrow came to Mr. Clarke in the death of the dear grandson of whom he has spoken in his letters. He missed the sunshine which the child had brought into his life, but deeper than the sense of loss was his conviction that "what God gives he gives forever."

FROM W. H. CHANNING.

Ascension Day, May 22, 1884.

MY DEAR JAMES, — Let this blessed day of hope for heavenly reunion with our ascended friends be marked in my calendar as a festival, by wishing you joy for the success with which you have been favored in your book on "The Ideas of Paul." Only my continued weakness, from two months and more confinement to my bed and room, making all effort to write a painful burden, has delayed an earlier expression of my thanks. But you will be glad to know that this beautiful volume has been one of my "morning companions" ever since it reached me, and has inspired as well as comforted me, in your own sense of the word comfort. . . .

TO HIS SISTER.

MAGNOLIA, *July* 5, 1884.

We are all anxious about our little Anna, Eliot's youngest child, who is extremely ill with the whooping-cough. She has the best care, and Dr. Charles Putnam is staying with us all the time he can, day and night. . . .

I have attacked my Autobiography, and find I need your help, and that of Sam, about Newton in our childhood. Will you write out all you recollect, especially about grandfather and grandmother Hull, and the curious characters then in Newton. I want that preserved, and you two can do it.

July 16, 1884.

The doctor told us yesterday he thought our baby had turned the corner, and was on the mend. Her cough is less frequent and not so severe as it has been; so we feel very much relieved. . We have no news, for the baby and its condition have absorbed us.[1]

TO REV. J. H. ALLEN.

JAMAICA PLAIN, *February* 17, 1885.

I received your very kind letter, and it gave me great pleasure. Your description of the interest you took in the group of which Theodore Parker, William Henry Channing, James H. Perkins, George Ripley, etc., were members, and with which I also had the pleasure of being associated, was peculiarly pleasing, and touched me nearly. How strange are the influences which act on us! There was our poor little "Western Messenger," which found you out at Northboro, and found our dear brother Conant in Chicago, and in which we put the best life we had. How well James H. Perkins wrote! When it was printed in Louisville, I had to be publisher, editor, contributor, proof-reader, and boy to pack up the copies and carry them to the post office. But I enjoyed it.

And you read "Theodore" too, and went to Amory Hall! I have scarcely ever heard of any one's reading "Theodore," but if you liked it, perhaps others also liked it. Every man who writes a book or preaches a sermon casts his bread on the waters, — happy if, as now, he finds it again after many days.

It was very kind of you, my dear Allen, to write to me as you have done, and your friendly appreciation of

---

[1] When not too ill, the infant was carried about, lying on a pillow, in the arms of different members of the family, and her grandfather would walk up and down the hall, holding her, and reciting in Latin the *Odes* of *Horace*. The tones of his voice had the effect of soothing her.

some of my past efforts warms my heart. We do not care for praise as we grow old, but we always are made happy by sympathy.

"Common as light is love,
And its familiar voice wearies not ever."

On Mr. Clarke's seventy-fifth birthday his parishioners invited him to spend a social evening with them and the occasion, as usual, was like a family festival, though it included also a few friends not belonging to the church family. It was held on the 6th of April, and the next day he wrote to his sister : —

We had a large and pleasant reception last night, and your very affectionate telegram added much to our satisfaction. There were four hundred persons present. Innumerable roses, lilies, violets, etc., perfumed the air, and all went merry as a marriage bell. The ages ranged from that of Mr. Henry B. Rogers, eighty-three, and Mr. William Amory, and Mr. John C. Park, over eighty, down to two little daughters of Laura Howe Richards. . . .

TO REV. J. W. DAY.

MAGNOLIA, MASS., *September* 7, 1885.

Thank you for your kind note, and for what you say of the good you received from my services. No greater satisfaction can come to us than from such an expression as that. No matter how old we are, it always gladdens us to think that we have been helped to help others, on this, the highest plane of being. That you may receive many such assurances is my best wish for you.

TO W. G. ELIOT.

February 13, 1886.

DEAR WILLIAM, — I read with delight and emotion your charming little story about the fugitive "Archer."

It is one of the "mémoires pour servir" for the history of an epoch already so far passed by as almost to belong to a Paleontologic age. . . .

With constant love.

TO S. C. C.

MAGNOLIA, *August* 25, 1886.

I have had a very slow recovery from my indisposition. I have been confined to this house for more than four weeks, — half of my vacation. But, as I like to look on the bright side of things, I looked for it in this event, and then I remembered that many of the gayest people went into "a religious retreat" once a year, the world quite shut out for a month. So I said I will consider this as my religious retreat, and be content. . . .

TO HIS SISTER.

JAMAICA PLAIN, *January* 24, 1887.

I have just seen in the paper the death of William G. Eliot. How our dear friends leave us! We seem to be at the foot of the procession. What a true and admirable life William led! How fixed to his principles! It might have been said to him as to Simon, "Thou art a rock." And yet what a sweet and playful nature withal! His serious work would have made him stern, did not this cloud have a silver lining Our relations were more of the affections than of the intellect. I leaned on his life, on his true heart, on his unflinching will, on his untiring devotion to everything right and good. .

TO HIS SISTER.

JAMAICA PLAIN, *May* 9, 1887.

You perceive by this that I am a step on my way towards convalescence. But I do not write much as yet. In fact, I think this is my second letter in my own autograph. I now see one or more friends each afternoon, drive out every morning, and walk a little when the weather allows. The weather is warm, and has tempted out the great flowers of my soulange magnolia. There are hundreds of flowers upon it. The orioles have come from the South, and fill the air with their music. We hope to go to Magnolia early in June. . . .

TO HIS SISTER.

June 8, 1887.

A week ago (Whitsunday) I went to church, and baptized some children, saying a few words, and I was none the worse for it. Yesterday I went to Boston to attend to a little business. To-day Cora and some of the family go to Magnolia to open the house, and Anna and I expect to go down next Wednesday. I dare say the change of air will help me. We shall have a full house, — fourteen in all, including the three children. . . .

TO HIS SISTER.

MAGNOLIA, *August* 21, 1887.

Your letter from Milwaukee gave me a new idea of the immense and rapid progress of those Western cities. The only case like these is that of Melbourne, founded in 1835, and now containing nearly 300,000 inhabitants, splendid streets, noble buildings, and a richly endowed university. The reason I know about this is that this summer, as usual, Anna and I travel round the world in books. We drop down in South Africa, we climb the Alps of New Zealand, are half killed by drought in Australia, and then cool ourselves by a little Arctic adventure. How kind it is in all these good people to travel for us!

We have lately mourned the death of Dorothea Dix, a wonderful woman, whose tranquil confidence, force of character, tact, and devotion to her work accomplished such wonders. She wished W. G. Eliot or me to write her memoir, but I am unable. If I ever write my own biography, it is all I expect to do.

I am getting better, but not as fast as I could wish. I drive and sail almost every day.

Our home here is full, and happy with the glad voices of children, — happy also that they are all well this summer.

TO HIS SISTER.

MAGNOLIA, *September* 1, 1887.

Autumn has arrived, and we have had cold winds and chill rains during a large part of August.

Do you wish to know the method of my days? We all breakfast together, including Eliot, Alice, Sue, and little Anna. Then I usually drive Eliot to the station; he goes to Boston every day. After I have been to the station I drive over to the post office, and often go out to sail with Mr. Foote, who has been most kind in urging me to go. I have sailed with him already twenty-two times this summer. When my family see the boat returning they come for me in the carriage. In the afternoon I sometimes call on our pleasant neighbor, Mr. Jefferson Coolidge, or visit Mrs. Towne, Mrs. Hemenway, or Mrs. James T. Fields at Manchester.

I have prepared some sermons for winter, and hope to begin to preach about the first of October.

Mrs. Putnam has taken great interest in hunting through the old print-shops in London to find portraits for me of the persons whose autographs I possess. She has sent me a large number, such as I could not find here. The autographs become much more interesting when accompanied with portraits of the writers.

Of a morning with him on the "Sheila," during this summer, Professor H. H. Barber gives us this picture.

The last time I met Mr. Clarke will be always memorable to me. He was at his summer home in Magnolia, and several of us were visiting another dear friend there, Henry W. Foote, and on this beautiful summer morning Mr. Foote signaled to his neighbor, whose house was at the other end of the beach, and Dr. Clarke drove round for a sail.

At first he seemed very feeble and said little, but sat by himself in the shadow of the sail, looking out over the sea. Before long he came to where we were sitting, and began to talk. He related many reminiscences of his life in Meadville and Louisville, and of the remarkable persons and scenes of his experience in the latter place. As he talked his voice grew stronger and his eye brighter, and for the forenoon he was our friend in his most genial and instructive mood. When he left the yacht he said, "I have had a very pleasant morning, but it seems to me that I have done most of the talking." It was our happiness that he had done most of the talking.

As I sailed along the shore last summer, and saw both of the homes where these dear friends had lived, I remembered Mr. Clarke's verses which a friend has repeated to me, and which hold in part, at least, the lesson of both these good lives.[1]

TO HIS SISTER.

September 16, 1887.

And now our season is at an end, and we are going to Boston next week to see some very kind London friends whom we expect to meet there.[2] It is getting cold here. I have been steadily gaining health and strength, but continued bad weather has given me the hoarseness and cough which I am too apt to suffer from in the winter and spring. . . . I am charmed with the tone of youth, hope, and active interest in good

[1] The reference is to the poem called *White-capt Waves*, which will be found in another chapter.
[2] Mr. and Mrs. Edwin Lawrence and Rev. R. Spears.

things and people which pervades your letter. You remind me more and more of our dear mother in this. . . . How glad we shall be to see her again! and our father and William and Abraham and dear Herman and Emerson, John A. Andrew, and fifty more. How sad it would be to suppose that death were a wall instead of a door! But to believe in a great future world, we must first, I think, believe in God; for if we have been made by an infinite wisdom, we have been made for something more than just to begin a career and then to be cut off. That would be too inconsequential. Here are you, as much interested in life and art as ever. I, at seventy-seven, full of plans of work that would take a dozen years to complete. We are, my dear sister, just at the beginning, not at the end.

TO HIS SISTER.

JAMAICA PLAIN, *November* 7, 1887.

I was glad to have your pleasant letter of October 30th, in which you speak of Cabot's Life of Emerson. It is a capital book; but it seems as if one could never hear enough about Emerson. How little of continuity in his thoughts! and this it seems he knew and regretted. But I think he might have consoled himself by what Lord Bacon says, that "knowledge, while it is in aphorisms and observations, is in growth; but when comprehended in exact methods, it may be further polished and illustrated, but it increaseth no more in bulk and substance." Yes! I am working away, though not violently. Last week I took a vacation, and wrote no sermon.

We are all well as usual. The three grandchildren are very sweet. Anna has been opening our place to the light by felling a number of large trees. One elm, which I planted myself, was seventy-four feet high. Before felling it I took its altitude by a method grandfather Freeman showed me when I was a boy, by placing a mirror horizontally on the ground, at such a distance from the tree that I could see its top in the mirror standing as far from it as the height of my eye from the ground. I then had two similar right-angled triangles, in each of which the length of the base was equal to the height, and so had only to measure the distance from the mirror to the foot of the tree to have its height. After that I enjoyed the idea of trigonometry. How wise he was!

TO F. H. HEDGE.

JAMAICA PLAIN, *January* 12, 1888.

I read through, immediately on its arrival, the pamphlet you were so kind as to send me. I was much interested in it, as I am in everything you have ever printed. Your thoughts are a great stimulus to my intellect; they set my thoughts in motion. Most of what you say seems to me eminently true and wise. Some things I hesitate about. I do not like trying to leave the received view of personality for the etymological one.

We cannot go back to the primal meaning of words, when a different one has been accepted. For instance, I could hardly justify myself in calling a man from whom I differ intellectually a *"miscreant"* by saying that I only meant a "misbeliever."

Personality has come in all philosophical speech to mean the living unit which combines thought, feeling, and will, in a perfect monad.

I like your criticism on Matthew Arnold and his definition of Deity.

TO HIS SISTER.

JAMAICA PLAIN, *March* 9, 1888.

Sitting before your picture of "The Jungfrau" one afternoon lately, the sun stole over it, and brought out a multitude of lovely details, introducing new values and lighting up the great silver peaks till they seemed to swim in a rosy radiance. The light quivered over the vast mountains; and when a cloud went over the sun, the mists collected round the summits and hid them for a moment, and then drifted away, and the snowy fields emerged again, and once more were bathed in the tender light. It was really like being on the spot. I enjoyed it so much that I wished you to know of it. . It has been a severe winter. Except on Sundays, I have not been to Boston for a month.

CHAPTER XX.

THE MAN.

At Mr. Clarke's ordination, on the 21st of July, 1833, Rev. F. W. P. Greenwood preached the sermon from the text, "Now the God of hope fill you with all joy and peace in believing, that ye may abound in hope, through the power of the Holy Ghost."

A manuscript copy of this sermon has been preserved among Mr. Clarke's papers, and as it lies before us we see this sentence: "If we know God and believe in him, we shall be filled with all joy and peace in believing, for he is the God of hope." These words read like prophecy. We have seen that in the earlier years of Mr. Clarke's ministry he had his periods of discouragement, but these grew less and less frequent, and in after years he literally "abounded" in hope. In the darkest hour of the war he did not despair; under the most depressing circumstances of life he always saw light shining on the future. We think that the influence which he had on those who heard him preach came in a measure from this inspiring element of hope. While we listened to him all good seemed possible to us.

This hope was no blind optimism, but had its roots in faith, — faith in God, faith in man. His faith in God as the Father of every soul which he has created was entire, and was the deep foundation on which all else rested, a foundation which could not be moved. To him God was an ever-present friend, to whom he could turn at any moment for guidance and help; and this trust in the Infinite Love was the staff on which he leaned in all times of weakness or perplexity. Sometimes, after returning home on Sunday, he has said, "When I went into the pulpit this morning I felt weak and unequal to the service, but I asked that the souls before me might be fed with better food than I could give them, and my weakness disappeared, and I was helped to say the right words." This was his habit also in other and more difficult circumstances, and this assurance of the nearness of God was the secret of his great happiness in his work. The sense of responsibility for results, under which so many faithful souls are weighed down, was made less heavy to him by the conviction that what was demanded of him was faithfulness, but that to an over-ruling Providence belonged all the issues of life and work.

And he had faith in his fellow-men.[1] He delighted in reading the lives of saints and heroes and martyrs of every age and every land, Pagan and Christian, Catholic and Protestant. They all testified to the divine life, manifested in the human; and all were a prophecy of the future of the race. When he was last in London, the monument in Westminster Abbey which appealed most to his feelings was the simple stone to the memory of David Livingstone, one of the martyrs, of whose influence among the simple Africans he could not speak without emotion.

Through the weaknesses and faults of human nature he saw the hidden good which would one day conquer the evil; if not here, then elsewhere. Did any one treat him rudely he would say, "That is only want of tact; he did not mean it." Did he happen to hear of

---

[1] A younger minister wrote to him in 1864, "I want to thank you for words you said to me when first I came to you six years ago. You bade me take the expectant attitude; to expect men and women to be generous and noble. *I* think that *I* have done so, and the result has been as you said: *I* find them generous and noble."

an unkind remark, "He has not the gift of language; that does not really express his meaning." Did a public orator take unwarrantable liberty with facts, "The danger of a platform speaker is the temptation to aim at immediate effect."

But he would speak to a man face to face about his faults, though he would not listen to any discussion of them if the man were absent. This frankness early won him the regard of other lovers of truth. A few days before the death of his good friend Judge Speed, Mr. Clarke saw him in his chamber. After he had taken leave, the judge followed him with his eyes as he left the room, and then turning to those standing by his bed-side, he uttered the one word "Truth-teller." When this was repeated to Mr. Clarke, by one of the family, he was much moved.

Under his own roof every one, of whatever age, was left free to do what seemed to him right, and it was taken for granted that whatever was done had been done with good intentions. There was no criticism, no faultfinding. When mistakes happened it was not difficult to confess them, for no subsequent allusion would ever recall the circumstance.

And this was also true in regard to his relations with the world outside of his home. It was enough if a man saw that he was wrong and turned to the right; no word in after years would ever remind him of a painful past. Often we have heard Mr. Clarke say, "You cannot help a man unless you first love him;" and to him this first step presented no difficulty. This too, came from his unwavering faith, his illimitable hope.

He said of himself that by nature he had a quick temper, but that while still a child he had resolved to conquer it. To those who remember how he bore himself under provocation in after life, it will be difficult to believe, without his own authority for it, that his patience and serenity were not gifts of nature. B. P. Winslow, his college chum, afterwards his parishioner, and always his friend, maintained that during his life at the university he manifested a remarkably good temper.

It was his good fortune to have a forgiving disposition. This saved him from harboring at any time a sense of personal injury. If a false accusation caused a momentary feeling of indignation, the feeling subsided almost as quickly as it rose. He had better things to think of, and he did not waste his time in considering what others said about him.

On one occasion a public attack was made upon him by a man whose misrepresentations had the effect of wounding him; and he departed from his better method of silence, and sat down to write a reply. But the habit of dwelling on all that is best and noblest in every one was too strong for him; and, as his adversary had been active in a number of important reforms, Mr. Clarke's pen was soon led into a glowing eulogy of the man and his services. By the time he had written a few pages in this strain, he was not in a mood for controversy, and was glad to forget the whole matter.

But though he readily forgot a seeming injustice, he did not forget the kindness which met him everywhere, and which he often declared to be out of all proportion to his deserts. "We none of us deserve to be loved," he said, "but being loved makes us more deserving than anything else can."

Some of his friends smiled at his once saying he thought the young people of to-day had better manners than was formerly the case. He had lately returned from his summer's vacation, and "all the young people were so kind, so attentive, so respectful, so courteous."

Words of apology, and of frank confession of error or fault, so difficult to many, were easy to him. He was always ready, almost eager to say, "It was *my* fault" — "*I* was to blame" — "Forgive me" — "I am sorry, dear friend, to have done anything that grieves or wounds you."

When friends asked him his secret for keeping young and vigorous he would sometimes reply with a smile, "I never worry." When the "Herald of Health" wished to obtain articles on the "health and working habits of prominent thinkers, as described by themselves," Mr. Clarke wrote, May 9, 1885: —

I find myself at the age of seventy-five still able to do a good deal of work, and I attribute it, under Providence, to the following causes: —

1. I am not of an anxious temperament; I do not worry. I am not, to any great extent, annoyed by disappointments or failure; and it has never disturbed me when I have been censured, so long as I believed I was doing right.

2. I have a great faculty for sleeping. Although able to keep awake, when necessary, without injury, I can always fall asleep at any moment when sleep seems desirable. These fragments of rest are, no doubt, of great service to me.

3. I have always, from childhood, been fond of outdoor exercise. I began to ride on horseback when about eight years old; and when a lad I joined with delight in all out-of-door sports, — skating, swimming, rowing, and playing ball; and also in indoor athletic exercises, such as fencing, boxing, and gymnastics. But all these belonged to an early period of my life.

4. I have few fixed habits and am fond of change. When I have done anything in one way for a few times, I enjoy doing it differently. But if this tendency has its advantages, it, on the other hand, prevents me from receiving the benefit which comes from established methods of work.

5. Although, when young, I smoked, I have not used tobacco since I was about twenty. In half a century I

have only smoked two cigars, and those only because I happened to be where the air was malarious.

6. Finally, I love work, and especially brain work. My professional duties as a clergyman have been to me a source of great happiness. I have also written several books, and many articles for the press; and I believe that this kind of work has been beneficial to my health.

There is an impression that it was his custom to postpone all consideration of his sermon until an early hour on Sunday morning. This is a mistake. In his diary of January 1, 1866, he says, "I believe I never before began and finished a whole sermon *before breakfast* on Sunday morning, though I have often done it before church." But he had his sermon in his mind during the week, and it was gradually taking shape before Sunday came. Indeed, he more often than not began to write his sermon at least as early as Saturday. His diaries show this, and in late years the sermon, partly written, usually lay on his study table Saturday night, ready to be continued about four o'clock on Sunday morning.

In his little story of "Deacon Herbert's Bible Class," the minister begins his sermon on Tuesday morning, and we may infer that Mr. Clarke would recommend this as a good plan. But what he says is true, that he, himself, had no fixed habits, and was very spontaneous in his methods of work.

In a less important department of life he said of himself, "I am very methodical, but very disorderly. I have a place for everything, but put nothing in its place. I arrange systematically for every different thing, and then mix all things together. I have a cabinet for sermons, and put into it newspaper cuttings and carpenter's tools. Portfolios and boxes, marked and labeled, never contain the things they are said to, but something else. So with pigeon holes for letters, answered and unanswered."

We may perhaps be allowed to say here that though no harm resulted from this want of order while his possessions were few and his memory at its best, yet, when the manuscripts, printed articles, pamphlets, paper cuttings, and other furnishings of a minister's study had been accumulating for years, it was sometimes difficult to lay his hands on an article wanted at a moment's notice. But whether the search were successful or not, his good nature was never to be reckoned among the things lost or mislaid. If he found what he wanted he was pleased. If not, he cheerfully managed to do without it.

However spontaneous he may have been in his methods of work, there was a unity in his character from boyhood to the end. His progress was continually along the same lines of development. There were no abrupt departures in new directions. Changes there were, certainly; but these came gradually. One of the most noticeable, when we compare the earlier years with the later, was in his growing neglect of controversy. In the "Western Messenger" days, and for years after, he seemed to enjoy an opportunity to stand face to face with an opponent over any matter which, with the enthusiasm of youth, he regarded as of importance. He appeared to hold his lance ready at a moment's notice for the service of any worthy cause in need of a champion. But as he found that the years were not long enough for the more important work which he had at heart, the unnecessary skirmishing lost its attraction. Sometimes the old zeal would revive, and he would write a reply to something which had attracted his attention in a book or elsewhere, but when finished the manuscript would often be thrown aside. "I have had the satisfaction of writing it," he would say, "I do not care about its being printed." And finally even this outlet was unnecessary. The fire of youth had given place to the maturer wisdom which comes with an ever-widening field of thought and action.

But the central convictions with which he began his ministry were the same which he held to its close, only strengthened by the experiences of his life. And from first to last his aims were essentially the same, though the years brought a better knowledge of methods.

On his seventieth birthday, a friend who had known him for sixty years alluded to his first appearance at the Latin School. His youthful look was then enhanced by his curls, which a fond grandmother had not allowed to be cut off. The boys at first thought that the new scholar would be a promising subject for their "chaff." But James had an elder brother who was not a non-resistant, and he had counseled the little fellow, in case there were any aggressive measures, to "strike out from the shoulder." This advice was followed, and as a result he was soon accorded his rightful place in that miniature world, the Boston Public Latin School. We would not mention this boyish incident, but that it shows, though on a very low plane, the fearlessness of nature which, in after years, led him to climb to the top of Salisbury, and Antwerp, and Strasburg spires, and on a much higher plane of life to advocate unpopular reforms, and to stand firm in any course which seemed to him right. He always had the courage of his convictions, and this too had its root in faith, a firm belief that in the end good must overcome every form of evil.

We have spoken of his ready sympathy with children, and the ease with which he put himself into relations with them. They felt that he loved them, and they responded, as children will, when they see that their teacher is also their friend.

When he had been a year in the divinity school the death of his father made it necessary that he and other members of the family should earn something for the support of the household. He accordingly left Cambridge, and during one winter kept a school at Cambridgeport, living, however, in Boston, with the family. Among his pupils was a boy who was very slow in learning arithmetic, and much time and patience were required before the child could be made to see the properties of figures. It was a happy moment for both teacher and scholar when success came at last; and it was pleasant to hear Mr. Clarke tell of this experience, into which he had evidently put much heart and thought. "Ah," he said, "people talk of the pleasure of teaching a bright child; that is nothing to the pleasure of teaching a dull one. When you have tried and tried, apparently without success, and then see, at last, the poor little face brighten up with the illumination of a new idea, that is a real delight."

On one occasion when he had taken part in a school celebration where a number of addresses were on the programme, he came home and told exultingly how he had saved the children from being obliged to listen to some of the addresses which had been planned. He had noticed that they were growing tired, and, when his turn came for talking to them, his speech consisted only of a proposal that the exercises should be considered ended, and the children released.

"Oh, how they shouted and hurrahed when I finished my little speech," he said, laughing heartily as he told the story.

Of the readiness with which he put himself *en rapport* with a class of boys usually irrepressible, this illustration is furnished us by Rev. J. L. Seward. "Mr. Clarke was once addressing a great audience in Huntington Hall, Lowell. The crowd comprised the most intelligent and the least intelligent inhabitants of the city. The boys in the gallery had greatly disturbed previous meetings by walking out with much noise in the midst of the services. On the night of Mr. Clarke's discourse the customary pedestrianism began. Looking at the gallery, he said in his inimitable way, 'Young men, I presume some of you hardly know why you came here at all to-night, and perhaps you feel badly cheated by the performance; but I hope for the sake of these good friends who try to listen that you will bear your disappointment with as much patience as you can, and let us have peace.' The effect of his words was magical, and scarcely another fellow left the hall."

He had a happy faculty of guiding meetings for discussion. A minister whom he was advising to hold meetings for social conversation on religious subjects replied, "That is all very well for you, James, for if any one were to say the most absurd thing that can be imagined you would answer, 'Yes, from some points of view there seems to be something in that,' and you would really find something quite interesting in it. But not everybody can do that."

"I should not be afraid to say anything in his Bible-class, however stupid," was the remark of one of the younger members of the class.

He had especial skill in presiding over meetings where differing elements were to be harmonized. We recall an occasion when, at the Meionaon, he was presiding over a meeting free to all comers, Orthodox or atheist, Methodist or Unitarian, minister or layman, man or woman, learned or ignorant, the only condition being that no one should occupy the floor more than five minutes. It happened that the first person who wanted to speak was a man whom many present did not wish to hear, and there were noisy demonstrations to that effect. Mr. Clarke reminded the audience that the meeting was free to all, and, turning to the speaker, said courteously, " I will hold up my watch at the end of five minutes, and I am sure the gentleman will then yield the floor." The audience became quiet, and the man after speaking five minutes sat down.

During the years in which he was a trustee of the Boston Public Library, he had the good of the institution much at heart, and was regular in his attendance at all business meetings. But the work was not wholly without compensation, for he enjoyed the atmosphere of a great library, and spent many happy hours there. A little story of one of his visits in the early years of his connection with it is thus told by an officer of long standing in the library. "His habit was to walk in and look about quietly, with a pleasant smile and a courteous word to all that he met. He would occasionally take a book from the shelf, glance over it, read a little, and always carefully return it to its place. I said to him one day, 'Why do you trouble yourself to do that? The attendant will do it.' 'No,' he replied, 'I will not make him any extra work.' One day his saunterings and browsings were anxiously watched by a young attendant, new to the place, and seriously impressed by the notices that 'Visitors must not handle the books without permission,' and very much troubled by the doings of this pleasant-looking gentleman, who did not seem to realize that he was breaking rules. After a short time she reluctantly approached him, and said, 'Excuse me, sir, the public are not allowed to handle our books.' The poor child could hardly recover her breath after this great effort, when Dr. Clarke, turning in his leisurely manner, said, 'But I am not the *public*, I am a *trustee*,' and as she hastily endeavored to excuse herself for having questioned his rights, he said, 'There is nothing to excuse, but everything to commend; you are faithful to a trust.' I was near enough to see and hear, but they were not aware of my proximity. Dr. Clarke never forgot the girl; his name for her was 'our faithful girl,' and he often inquired for her in his visits."

Of his interest in young men entering the ministry, Rev. A. D. Mayo writes: "I went into Freeman Place

Chapel one evening, and Mr. Clarke, seeing me, invited me to come into the pulpit and preach. Out of this kindly welcome grew up a delightful acquaintance for the remaining six years of my first ministry in New England. To me, a young man entering the profession without the usual preparation, his fatherly kindness and interest were, naturally, the most prominent feature of his gracious personality. I recognized his gifts as a preacher and writer, but this sight of him was subordinate to the affection of a young man so generously accepted by a revered superior. I remember, especially, one day when a long out-of-door talk with him confirmed my purpose to seek a Western ministry."

He believed that every one owed to his country the duty of voting. In a letter written while still in Louisville, he speaks of the intensely warm August weather, from which cause, in connection with work for the public schools, be is "fairly worn out," and adds, "I must vote on Monday, like a good citizen, and then I think I shall leave. Half of my society have gone to the East."

During the earlier years of his residence at Jamaica Plain, the place for voting was about a mile distant, and he and his hired man were accustomed to drive there together. Mr. Clarke went first into the building, and voted the Republican ticket. Then he remained with the horse while his man went in and voted the Democratic ticket. On one occasion when the election day was stormy, Mr. Clarke suggested to his Democratic friend that they should pair off and stay at home. The man's countenance did not express assent, and Mr. Clarke made haste to say, "You are right, we will both go to the polls, and vote."

In one of these later years a lady asked him at a musical party whether he were fond of music. He told her just how far his interest went, which a connoisseur would say was not far, and added, "I am really glad I have not an interest in music, in addition to so many others; I am afraid it would be the last straw."

But he was so well rounded, and put so much heart into every duty, that he had all the joy of eventful living. In literary and social circles he was always welcome. It is a pity that we can give no adequate idea of him as a member of the social circle; of the charm of his conversation; the simplicity with which he would drop into talk on the most serious themes; while he also enjoyed, as much as any one, amusements and recreations which came to him without his going out of his way to seek them.

A lady, who is an ornament of society and a leader in educational and philanthropic circles, once took him to a great ball in Washington. She has since said that she looks back to a talk there with Mr. Clarke about the future life as one of the most helpful conversations that she ever had. To those about them they seemed to be looking at the gay throng before them, but he had fallen naturally into discourse upon a subject which was never far from his thoughts.

Of his home-life Rev. William L. Chaffin has given these pleasant reminiscences: —

As I said to you, some men look well through the telescope, but not under the microscope. James Freeman Clarke would bear examination under either, and my sight of him in his own home gave me the highest opinion of him I had.

I especially remember him as we gathered in the morning at the table. When all were there, he would have a moment's talk with God, his voice hardly raised above a whisper, yet distinctly audible, so quiet, so reverent, so confiding in his manner, that we all felt God was right there. I can remember he would say · "We thank thee, our Father, for the rest and quiet of the night, for the morning light, for the new thought, the new hope and love thou givest us," — and so on, in such a grateful and loving way that one could not help being touched and blessed.

I was much impressed by his manner towards children. You know Mr. Clarke was a good listener. One saw he was paying heed to what one was saying, and was not intent upon what he would say next. But he was a good listener to children. If they expressed foolish opinions, he did not directly correct or reprove. He would quietly ask questions, set them thinking, and gradually lead them out of their unwise notions, giving them the impression, no doubt, that they had thought themselves out of them. This maintained their self-respect, gave them confidence to express themselves, and nourished their love for him.

He was in Meadville while "Uncle Tom's Cabin" was being printed in the "National Era." One day his daughter Lilian, full of excitement, came rushing for one of her companions, and told her that another chapter of "Uncle Tom's Cabin" had come, and her father would read it to them. They went to his study, and sat together on the rug before the open fire, he in his study chair on one side, and he then read the chapter narrating the escape of Eliza. He was an excellent reader, and to these two girls it was thrilling, and made an impression never to be forgotten.

Is not this an interesting picture, these two little girls, about nine and eleven years old, sitting in the flickering firelight on the rug, eagerly intent on the story he was so glad to read to them?

My wife remembers that at Meadville, at the family gatherings, he was the leader in the entertainment of the children in that part of the day that was devoted to them, as a part of it always was. He was quite a ventriloquist, and gave them great amusement in carrying on conversations between a gentleman in one room and his hired man in another; also in imitation of the voices of animals, and in other ways.

My wife also remembers another thing very gratefully. She came as a little girl from Newburyport to go to Mr. Clarke's on a visit. He kindly met her at the station in Boston, and took her out to Roxbury in an omnibus. After a while all but they two had got out. He noticed that the little girl was blue and homesick, and drawing her towards him, he entertained her all the way out with fairy and other stories, changing what, but for his tender sympathy, would have been a dark and lonesome hour into one of the happiest hours and one of the brightest recollections of her life.

He was an ideal traveling companion, interested in everything to be seen; and, when there was nothing to be seen, producing from his inexhaustible memory story or poem to beguile the hours. He had at his command all the best poems in the English language. On a rainy day, shut up with friends in a stage-coach, he would help those about him to forget the prosaic present, and live for the time in a world of infinite beauty or grandeur. And sailing on the Bay of Naples, or sitting by a camp-fire in the Adirondacks, he would give to the scene the added charm of words in which a poet had sung the beauty of Nature. He did not, however, travel without books. His hand-bag was filled with them; and in the breast-pocket of his coat was apt to be a copy of Horace, a favorite with him from boyhood throughout his life.

Of a journey taken in his company, when going to a Western conference, Rev. S. W. Bush says: —

A party of six or eight friends traveled in an inclosed stateroom, in a parlor car, and sat around a table in the privacy of friendly intercourse. To travel with a friend in this way is to put him to a real test. If he has any weak spots they will be sure to show themselves. Mr. Clarke, under this test, was a charming companion.

While he never lost his grave and slow manner of speaking, he was a very interesting story-teller. He was a keen observer of men, and what he saw as well as what he read was stored in his retentive memory. He had the dramatic talent of impersonation and flashing wit and playfulness, so that in his talk of men he reproduced admirable portraitures of character. In addition, he had a love of the beautiful in nature, which kindled his imagination.

We reached Niagara between nine and ten in the evening. The moon was out in full splendor, and the lights and shadows produced beautiful and picturesque effects. As the cars, in crossing the bridge, slackened their speed, he sat on the steps of the sleeping-car and gazed in silence at the falls, with their deep roar, while the spray danced in the moonbeams. Not a word fell from his lips. The next morning, before breakfast, he read us a poem which he had written.

With all this he recognized the adage of the wise man that there is a time to speak and a time to be silent; so he never wearied us by incessant talk, but had his refreshing pauses. The more intimately one knew him, the more impressed he was with the thorough reality of the man. He was as true and genuine in the palace car as a familiar traveling companion as he was when preaching in the pulpit at Milwaukee, before the Western conference.

But though his memory was retentive of the books he had read, the poems he had enjoyed, the scenes through which he had passed, it did not serve him so faithfully in regard to faces, and he sometimes had the mortification of failing to recognize friends for whom he had a sincere regard. He once spent some days at Paris in the same hotel with members of a family whose house had not long before been a delightful home to him when on a visit to Washington, and of whose kindness he had often spoken. After he had met them two or three times without recognition, the lady very magnanimously sent him her card, and thus gave him an opportunity to explain his strange conduct. He was exceedingly mortified at having mistaken a valued friend for a stranger.

Also, when absorbed in any scene, he would perhaps not remember the people who had been about him. One day, in company with a few friends, he spent a number of hours in visiting the Girls' Industrial School at Lancaster. In the evening he went to the weekly meeting of his church at the vestry, and after greeting one and another of those present, said to a parishioner whom he had long known well, "I wish you had been with us to-day at Lancaster." "I *was* with you to-day at Lancaster," the lady calmly replied.

To those in daily intercourse with him, his abounding life gave a sense of the value of existence. One saw how much the day might be made to hold. He was always working, studying, producing, — enjoying nature, art, books, people. He climbed mountains, sailed, rowed, and sat up all night on the roof of the house to observe the stars. He talked with theologians, he played with children. He liked to go on journeys, but was apt to return a day or two before the time set, entering the house with a radiant air of satisfaction at finding himself once more in his own home.

To the end of his life he continued to have the expectant outlook of youth.

By those who knew him chiefly as a thinker and writer, or who heard him preach on special occasions, the trait which has been most often mentioned was his breadth of view, his fairness, his habit of looking at a question on all sides. Among his fellow-workers on boards or committees, he was liked because of his practical wisdom and his good-natured adaptiveness. In political work, his fearlessness, his happy gift of self-possession, and his ready reply during discussion, made him a useful coadjutor.

But there were other traits, which will remain longer in the memories of the nearer circle with whom he came into more intimate relations. He was what our orthodox friends would call a "lover of souls," and this gave to his services in the pulpit, or in missionary work, a tenderness and sweetness such as that spoken of by the minister who had shared his visit to the morning prayer-meeting in another city. He knew that he himself could not live without the sense of God's nearness at every moment, and he earnestly endeavored to bring the same help and comfort to every other heart. And from his implicit trust came that abounding hope of which we have spoken, which surrounded him as with an atmosphere of sunshine. His hearers would leave the church to take up again the duties and cares of life with a more cheerful courage. A friend, who spent last summer in Maine, found in a country place a working-man who seemed in advance of the people about him, and asked him the secret of this difference. He replied, "It is owing to a sermon that I heard James Freeman Clarke preach here years ago; that was an era in my life."

His cheerful faith and warm sympathy gave him the power to bring comfort to the sorrowing, and to impart hope to the dying. When he was still young in the ministry, one of his heaviest burdens was to be called upon to bear tidings of bereavement to a happy family circle unconscious of loss. After a time, out of his feeling of helplessness came the habit of leaning wholly upon God in all times when a more than human wisdom was needed, and by many, we think, he will be remembered, more than in all other ways, as "the comforter."

When he compiled his service book, he put into the funeral service some of the usual psalms referring to death; but before long he ceased to use these. He knew from his own experience that we never believe so little in death as when we stand by the open grave, and in those hours he appeared to reach a yet deeper faith and a higher hope. While he spoke, the heavens seemed opened, and things unseen and eternal were made real to sorrowing hearts. Death was swallowed up in life.

CHAPTER XXI.

THE END.

By the advice of his physician Dr. Stedman, Mr. Clarke went, in the latter part of March, 1888, to Lakewood, in New Jersey, to escape the harsh spring winds of New England. He enjoyed the drives he was able to take at Lakewood, and occasionally a very short walk. But the greater part of his days were passed on a lounge. He liked to have Mrs. Clarke read to him, but he was able also to read himself, and even wished to share with her and his daughter anything in his book which he especially enjoyed. The diary for April 1st says: "A. read aloud the last two chapters of John's Gospel, and the extracts from Martineau in the 'Christian Register.' At eleven 1 walked a short distance, rested fifteen minutes on a door-step, and walked back. After tea, A. read aloud Dr. Furness's sermon in 'Christian Register.'"

That his daughter in Jamaica Plain might receive something from his own hand on his birthday he wrote: —

Lakewood, April 3, 1888.

. . . This is my birthday note to you, brimful of love to yourself and our beloved ones. I am glad I have been allowed to live so long. My life has been very fortunate and happy; and if now I can do no more work, I am content to rest amid the love of friends, which is the best part of our human life.

When April 4th came he at first felt a little like an

exile; but this feeling vanished as tokens of affection arrived from members of his church in Boston, and from relatives and friends in other places. His room was bright with flowers, and he was made happy by receiving these and other messages of remembrance. The last poem which he wrote, and with which this record of his life ends, was dated on this birthday.

On the 17th of April he sent to the "Christian Register" an article on the Revised Version of the New Testament.

The diary is broken with the "spraying of the throat" and "bad fever attack." On the second of May, with the nominal end of the hard New England winter, he returned home.

He was still able to drive out. On the 9th of May he married two young friends. On the 13th of May he preached "for the first time," as he says in his diary, and, as it proved, for the last time. The text was, "Lead us not into temptation." After the service he sat in front of the pulpit, and took the hand of many friends. As he drove home he said, "How good that was; how delightful to see them again!" On the 22d of May he makes the memorandum, "Finish sermon." As late as the 11th of May he had written a note to the "Transcript," suggesting that a statue of Sir Henry Vane should be placed in front of the new Public Library. The diary stops, with declining strength, on the 27th of May. The day before, Dr. Cheever had told his family that there was no hope of recovery.

Dr. Clarke had looked forward to one more summer at Magnolia, like the seven happy summers which he had already spent at his own house there, and to sailing with Mr. Foote on the "Sheila." But, when he knew that there was to be no renewing of physical strength, all his hopes turned toward the future, and he longed to pass into that other life where he never doubted that he should feel as much at home as here. When his friend, Judge Allen, called one evening, Mr. Clarke asked to see him. He wished to take his hand once more and to tell him of the good he had received from his friendship. He was able to take leave of one or two other dear friends, but his strength was rapidly failing, and he could say very little. During the last days of May the annual meetings of the Unitarian denomination were being held, and on the evening of the social festival those present were told from the platform that he would never meet with them again. A hush fell on the assembly, and when a message of love and remembrance was framed, the thousand men and women present rose and stood while it was read. He was able to hear the message, to look at the flowers sent with it, and to be cheered by this token of sympathy from friends who had been so dear to him.

Though too weak to talk, he could sometimes listen to a few words. A sentence was read to him from a letter which expressed gratitude for help which had come from his writings. He said softly, "I have been greatly blessed."

One day, after lying quiet a long time, he said, "Please repeat to me the hymn, 'Abide with me.'" He had evidently been thinking of it, but there were a few words he could not recall.

He expressed his undoubting trust in a reunion hereafter with those who had gone before and those who were yet to follow him. From day to day his bodily strength failed, but his mind was perfectly clear to the last, and faith, hope, and love endured.

Before midnight on Friday, the 8th of June, 1888, he ceased to breathe.

The reader of this biography has before him not one in a hundred of the memorials of unselfish, loyal work for man and devotion to God, which it has been my pleasure to examine in the years since he died, while I have been trying to select what might be best fitted for this biography. It is an instance of a life where a man gave every day steadily to this or that duty for mankind, entering upon it with positive pleasure because it was duty, and with a determination to do it as well as he could, quite indifferent to the credit or the blame which might be awarded to it by the world. His physical constitution, in early life, was not strong. But the determination to be of use in God's world seems to have mastered bodily ailments, and, for much of his life, he was in well-nigh perfect working order. "He is my despair as he is my admiration," was the testimony, while he lived, of one of his classmates and near friends, who has himself rendered the highest service to mankind. Such work as came to him to do he did with an energy and directness which almost commanded success. And then, if he were praised, or if he were blamed, so far as men saw, it was all one. I have seen him receive severe and sharp criticism of his course or his writing, with the same good-natured smile with which he would have received a compliment. "Very likely it is as you say, but I did as well as I knew how." It was simply impossible to quarrel with him; he found fault with himself, and he saw no reason why others should not find fault with him.

In compiling from the large range of manuscript memorials, I have found it difficult — it has proved impossible — rightly to preserve, in so small a space, the proper perspective of his life. It does not follow that because his enterprises in any regard do not take much space on paper, they did not take a large place in his thought, in his heart, in his estimate of duty. He would spend as much time on the comfort of a newlanded exile as he would spend upon a speech to a thousand men, or as he would give to the occultation of a planet. His friends may find that I have passed by work and success which they value as important. I can only ask that they will see how wide was the field from which I was to select. It is not a life which presents only a few salient points for study. It is the life of an unselfish child of God, of tireless determination, giving himself in every hour for the service of mankind.

ON DEATH.

"Therefore we come at last to think nothing about dying, but more and more about living. We do not desire to die in order to go to God, for God is with us here, on this side as much as on the other. The nearer death comes, the less we believe in it. Though an unhappy style of religion has sought to make death terrible, it has not succeeded in doing so. God fills the heart with a better faith. He teaches us that he, the infinite presence, the boundless tenderness, whose joy is to pour himself out in nature as a ceaseless creator, to make his myriad creatures full of gladness here, is the same God who will be with us there. What matters it when we cross the line which divides this world from the next? It is only an imaginary line, like that which divides two States of our Union. We pass from Massachusetts into New Hampshire, and we do not know it, for there is the same scenery around, the same sky above, the same sort of people, speaking the same language. So it will be when we pass into the other life. There will be the same God above, the same soul within, the same beauty around in nature, like work to do, similar objects of knowledge, loving hearts, benign friendships, and an eternal progress. Therefore we keep up all our activities to the end, and though the outward man perishes, the inward man is renewed day by day."

"If in a long life I have gained anything which is worth keeping, it is the knowledge and friendship and love of pure, generous, noble souls. Am I to lose that great inheritance? Am I to go into the other world poor, lonely, homesick? I do not so understand the lessons of experience or the facts of observation. When all other memory fades from the mind of the dying, when his thoughts are bewildered, the impressions of time effaced, he still shows by a faint pressure of the hand that love remains. The last look of the dim eye seeks the faces of those he loves. The last faint whisper of the failing voice is a murmur of blessing on those dear ones. Love is stronger than death: will it not survive the grave?

"Yes, when I open my eyes on a new world I expect to come once more into the company of those who have been my inspiration, my comfort, my joy, in this life. I shall learn what these years have been teaching them, and they will again be my friendly companions and helpers. I shall see again the parents and the dear children whose love has sweetened my life. I shall be a little child once more myself. And I hope to come very near to my Master, Jesus, and to have my errors corrected, and be taught the alphabet of a higher language of truth. Not all at once; for the laws of gradation and limitation will probably apply there as here. But if faith and hope and love abide, then there will be always more of knowledge, more of work, and more of love in the divine beyond."

"Soft as an infant's sleep shall be the coming of death to you and to me. Sweet shall be the rest which falls on the soul weary with work and the body exhausted by years. Tenderly shall the death-cloud envelop us, and hide all familiar things from our failing sight. And when we awake again, with no abrupt transition, with no astonishment, we shall find ourselves gently led into new being, in the midst of old and new friends. We shall be in the presence of a more divine beauty than that of this earth, and with faculties opening into greater power to meet the new knowledge and the new work of that next world, that vast beyond."

PROTECTING SHADOWS.

I sit beneath the elm's protecting shadow,
    Whose graceful form
    Shelters from sunshine warm;
While far around me, in the heated meadow,
    The busy insects swarm.
Better than any roof these softly swaying leaves,
Opening and closing to the passing air,
Which from afar the fragrant breath receives
    Of forest odors rare.
    And, as the branches sway,
Revealing depths on depths of heavenly blue,
The tempered rays of sunshine, glancing through
In flickering spots of light, around me play;
While little birds dart through the mazy web,
    With happy chirp and song,
    Fearing no wrong,
To their half-hidden nests above my head.
Thus, without motion, without speech or sound,
I rest, — a part of all this life around.

Beneath the shadow of the Great Protection
    The soul sits, hushed and calm.
Bathed in the peace of that divine affection,
No fever-heats of life, or dull dejection
    Can work the spirit harm.
    Diviner heavens above
    Look down on it in love.
And, as the varying winds move where they will,
In whispers soft, through trackless fields of air,
So comes the Spirit's breath, serene and still,
Its tender messages of love to bear
From men of every race and speech and zone,
    Making the whole world one;
Till every sword shall to a sickle bend,
And the long, weary strifes of earth shall end.

THE END.

   Be happy then, my heart,
   That thou in all hast part, —
In all these outward gifts of time and sense,
In all the spirit's nobler influence,
   In sun and snow and storm;
In the vast life which flows through sea and sky,
Through every changing form
Whose beauty soon must die;
In the things seen, which ever pass away;
In things unseen, which shall forever stay;
   In the Eternal Love
   That lifts the soul above
All earthly passion, grief, remorse, and care
   Which lower life must bear.
   Be happy now and ever,
Since from the Love divine no power the soul shall sever:
  For not our feeble nor our stormy past,
  Nor shadows from the future backward cast;
Not all the gulfs of evil far below,
Nor mountain-peaks of good which soar on high
   Into the unstained sky,
Nor any power the universe can know;
Not the vast laws to whose control is given
The blades of grass just springing from the sod,
And stars within the unsounded depths of heaven,
Can touch the spirit hid with Christ in God.
For nought that he has made, below, above,
   Can part us from his love.

April 4, 1888.

WRITINGS OF JAMES FREEMAN CLARKE.

BOOKS.

Theodore; or, The Skeptic's Conversion. Translated from the German of De Wette. Boston, 1841.

Service Book. For the Church of the Disciples. Boston, 1844.

History of the Campaign of 1812, and Defence of Gen. William Hull for the Surrender of Detroit. Boston, 1848.

Eleven Weeks in Europe. Boston, 1852.

Memoirs of Margaret Fuller, written in connection with W. H. Channing and R. W. Emerson. Boston, 1852.

Christian Doctrine of Forgiveness of Sin. Boston, 1852.

Christian Doctrine of Prayer. Boston, 1854.

Karl Hase: Life of Jesus. Boston, 1860.

The Hour which Cometh. A volume of sermons. Boston, 1864.

Orthodoxy: its Truths and Errors. Boston, 1866.

Steps of Belief. Boston, 1870.

Ten Great Religions. [Part I.] Boston, 1871.

Exotics. A collection of translations in verse. Boston, 1876.

Go up Higher; or Religion in Common Life. Boston, 1877.

Essentials and Non-Essentials in Religion. Boston, 1878.

How to find the Stars. Boston, 1878.

Memorial and Biographical Sketches. Boston, 1878.

Common-Sense in Religion. Boston, 1879.

Events and Epochs in Religious History. Boston, 1881.

The Legend of Thomas Didymus, the Jewish Skeptic. Boston, 1881.

Self-Culture. Boston, 1882.

Ten Great Religions. Part II. Boston, 1883.

The Ideas of the Apostle Paul. Boston, 1884.

Anti-Slavery Days. New York, 1884.

Manual of Unitarian Belief. Boston, 1884.

The Problem of the Fourth Gospel. Boston, 1886.

Vexed Questions in Theology. Boston, 1886.
Every-Day Religion. Boston, 1886.
Sermons on the Lord's Prayer. London, 1888.
Deacon Herbert's Bible-Class. Boston, 1890.

MAGAZINE ARTICLES.

THE CHRISTIAN EXAMINER. — Robert Hall, 1833. The Pilgrim Fathers, 1843. Fourierism, 1844. History of the Doctrine of the Atonement, 1845. Joan of Arc, 1848. Brownson's Argument for the Roman Church, 1850. Furness's History of Jesus, 1850. The Christian Review on Original Sin, 1852. Natural Depravity and Total Depravity, 1852. Polemics and Irenics, 1854. H. J. Huidekoper: A Memorial Sketch, 1854. Adams's South Side View of Slavery, 1855. James on the Nature of Evil, 1855. The Progressive Friends, 1856. President Lord's Defence of Slavery, 1856. Comparative Theology of Heathen Religions, 1857. Bishop Hopkins on Slavery, 1857. The Revival of 1858, 1858. The Free Colored People of the United States, 1859. The War, 1861. Buckle's History of Civilization, 1861. Henry James on Creation, 1863. Military Drill in Schools, 1864. The Two Carlyles; or, Carlyle, past and present, 1864. Open Questions in Theology, 1866. Bushnell on Vicarious Sacrifice, 1866. The Fourth Gospel and its Author, 1868. Jean Jacques Rousseau, 1868. Are there Two Religions in the New Testament? 1869.

THE ATLANTIC MONTHLY. — Adventure with Junius Brutus Booth, September, 1861. A New Chapter of Christian Evidences, March, 1869. Brahmanism, May, 1869. Buddhism, June, 1869. Zoroaster, August, 1869. Confucius and the Chinese, September. 1869. Mohammed, November, 1869. Have Animals Souls? October, 1874. Parton's Life of Voltaire, August, 1881.

THE NORTH AMERICAN REVIEW. — Western History, 1836. Hall's Statistics of the West, 1837. Wilson's Rise and Fall of the Slave Power in America, 1875. Harriet Martineau, 1877. Law and Design in Nature, 1879. Rational Sunday Observance, 1880. Did Shakspeare write Bacon's Works? 1881. Affinities of Buddhism and Christianity, 1883. Why I am not a Free Religionist, 1887.

OLD AND NEW. — The Perfection of Jesus, 1870. George

D. Prentice, and Kentucky Thirty-five Years ago, 1870. Wanted — a Statesman, 1870. Renan's Paul, 1870.

ADDRESSES, SERMONS, AND ARTICLES IN PAMPHLET FORM.

Letter to Unitarian Society in Louisville. Reform and Conservatism. Slavery in the United States. The Pilgrim Fathers. Character of George Keats. Protest against Slavery, signed by Unitarian Ministers. Principles and Methods of the Church of the Disciples. Phi Beta Kappa Poem. Story of a Converted Skeptic. Charge at Ordination of T. W. Higginson. Dilemma of Orthodoxy. An Important Question. The Church: as it was, as it is, as it ought to be. Discourse at Dedication of Freeman Place Chapel. James Freeman. Rendition of Burns. Polemics and Irenics. Jesus Christ the True Corner-Stone. False Witnesses answered. The Unitarian Reform. Theodore Parker and his Theology. Causes and Consequences of the Affair at Harper's Ferry. A Look at the Life of Theodore Parker. Secession, Concession, or Self-Possession — Which? Christ and his Anti-Christs. Two Ways in Religion reviewed. Aspects of the War. The Word in the Beginning with God. Address at the Tercentenary of Shakspeare. Is Evil Eternal? Abraham Lincoln. Address to Agricultural Society. The Duties of Massachusetts (election sermon). On giving Names to Towns and Streets. Dedication of West Roxbury Soldiers' Monument. A True Theology the Basis of Human Progress. Peter at Antioch. Fourth of July Oration. One God, the Father. The New Theology. Materialism and Atheism. Work of Unitarianism in the Past, Present, and Future. Coffee Houses and Coffee Palaces. Channing: Address at Dedication of Memorial Window at Newport. R. W. Emerson. Unitarian Belief and Fellowship. Five Points of Calvinism and Five Points of the New Theology. Sin against the Holy Ghost. Introduction to the Gospel of John. Old and New Ideas concerning the Divinity of Jesus. Is Probation or Education the End of Life? The Sabbath, Sunday, or Lord's Day — Which? Old and New Views concerning the Bible. The True Coming of Christ. Agnosticism *vs.* Positivism. The Hercules and Wagoner of To-day. The Scientific Basis of Prayer. The Meaning and Value of the Lord's Supper at this time. Some Reasons for believing in a Future Life. The Mutual

Obligations of Science and Religion. From Faith to Faith. A Happy New Year. The Ministry of the Letter and the Ministry of the Spirit. Melchizedek and his Moral. The Wrath of the Lamb. Rejoice Evermore. Dorothea L. Dix. Anarchy and Law. Temperance Efforts and Temperance Methods. The Pew System and the Free-Seat System. The Mind of Christ. What God gives He gives Forever. The Broad Church. Christ and other Masters. The Old and New View of the Hereafter. Lost Opportunities. Be not Weary in Well-doing. Homes in Heaven and on Earth. The Joys of Christmas. How to get the Most out of the Coming Year. I make All Things New. Man doth not live by Bread alone. What do Unitarians believe about God? about Jesus Christ? about Sin and Salvation? about the Holy Ghost? about Heaven and Hell? about Conversion and Regeneration? about Divine Providence and Human Freedom? in regard to the Supernatural Element in Christianity? in regard to Vicarious Sacrifice? The True Doctrine of Liberal Christianity. The Brotherhood of Man. The Atonement. The Bible. Why am I a Unitarian? Orthodox Views of the Atonement. Inspiration of the New Testament. Revivals. Has Unitarianism done its Work? Church-going: Past, Present, and Future.

NOTE. — No attempt has been made to give a list of Mr. Clarke's articles in the "Western Messenger," the "Monthly Journal," the "Christian World," the "Christian Inquirer," and the "Christian Register."

INDEX.

Abbott, Jacob, 72, 108.
Abington, 234.
Abolitionists, 220, 222, 223.
Acland, Dr., 309.
Adams, John Quincy, 122, 233, 248, 277.
Adams, Nehemiah, 229, 347.
Adams, Samuel, 237.
Agassiz, Professor, 163, 165, 329.
Agassiz, A., 352.
Alaska, 351.
Alcott, Bronson, 138, 188.
Alcott, Miss, 138.
Aldrich, Thomas Bailey, 358.
Allston, Washington, 143.
Alps, The, 177, 178, 181.
"American Citizen, The," 230.
"American Churches Bulwarks of American Slavery," 230.
"American First Class Book," 33.
"American Slavery, as it is," 215.
Amory Hall, 159.
Amory, William, 381.
Andrew, John Albion, 6, 141; proposes a contribution for defense of John Brown, 205; extracts from birthday address, 209, 210, 211; writes against war with Mexico, 227; saying in praise of John Brown, 236; governor of Massachusetts, 268, 269; indignant at injustice to colored troops, 244, 289; connection with Church of the Disciples, 269; call on the President, 280; death of, 330, 386.
Andrew, Mrs. John A., 275, 279.
Antinomian, An, 74.
ntioch College, 261.
"Anti-Slavery Days," 214, 218, 221, 232, 245, 248-250.
Anti-slavery leaders and woman suffrage, 324.
Anti-slavery opinion, growth of, 226.
Anti-Slavery Society, 248-250.
ntwerp, 182, 183.
April 19, 1861, 271.
"Arithmetic, First Lessons in," 31, 32.
Arnold, Matthew, 371.
Ashurst, Colonel and Mrs., 285.
"Atlantic Monthly, The," 357.
August 1st, 234.
Augustus, John, 148.

Autobiography, 1-80; 81, 83, 84, 95, 96, 135, 164, 292, 345, 360, 365, 379.
Autumnal Convention, 263.

Bacon, Mr., 133.
Bailey, Gamaliel, 232, 276, 277.
Baltimore, 271.
Banks, Governor, 228.
Barber, Prof. H. H., 384.
Barnard, 161.
Barrett, Hepzibah, 2.
Barrett, Samuel, 156.
Bartol, Cyrus A., 122, 156.
Basel or Bâle, 181, 374.
Beaufort, S. C., 347.
Beecher, Dr. Lyman, 94.
Beethoven's symphonies, 140.
Bellows, Henry W., 86; editor of "Christian Inquirer," 150, 227; letter to, 169; letter from, to J. F. C., 183; met at Antioch, 261; at Meadville, 262; herculean labors of, 263; founder of Sanitary Commission, 269.
Bentley, Dr., 87.
Berne, 181.
"Bible against Slavery," 222.
Bible-class, 159, 162.
Bigotry, 40.
Biographies of ministers, 136.
Birney, James G., 217, 220, 224, 230.
Bond, George W., 207.
Bond, Henry May, 288.
Bond, Rebecca, 337.
Boston, 137, 138, 140, 335; association of ministers, 163; churches in, 144, 151; coldness about slavery, 154.
"Boston Courier," 235.
Boston Latin School, 26, 28, 83, 396; Public Library, 304, 399, 409.
Botume, Miss, 347, 348.
Boutwell, George S., 289, 292.
Bowditch, Dr., 193.
Bowdoin College, 294.
Bowdoin prize dissertation, 85, 86.
Bradford, G. P., 358.
Bradley, Dr., 370, 371.
Breckenridge, General, 100, 224.
Breckenridge, John, 76.
Briggs, Charles, 96.
Briggs, George W., 156, 157.

Bright, John, 371.
Brisbane, Mr., 138.
British and Foreign Unitarian Association, 359.
Brook Farm, 139, 247, 273, 328, 329.
Brooke, Stopford, 371.
Brooks, Preston, 171.
Brosowski, 106.
Brown, John, 205, 206, 237; famous song on, 279.
Brown, Sir Thomas, 39.
Brown, William W., 172.
Browning, Mr. and Mrs., 195.
Browning, Robert, 370.
Buckingham, Joseph T., 235.
Buckminster, Martha, 3.
Buckminsters of Framingham, 3.
Burns, Anthony, 228, 233.
Burr, Aaron, 120.
Burritt, Elihu, 172.
Bush, S. W., 315, 403.
Bushnell, Dr. Horace, 330.

Cabot, Dr. Samuel, and Mrs., 6, 194.
Call, Dr. Emma L., 366.
Call, Mr., 330.
Calthorp, Mr., 259.
Cambridge Divinity School, 88, 89, 213, 214, 252, 297, 330.
Canal-boat travel, 59.
Cape Ann, 355.
Carlyle, Thomas, 115, 120, 121, 125, 127, 377.
Carpenter, Prof. J. Estlin, 369, 371.
Carpenter, Dr. William B., 369, 371.
arter, Artemas, 261.
Chadwick, J. W., 314.
Chaffin, William L., 401.
Chandler, Mr., 268.
Change in church life, 146.
Channing, Prof. Edward, 45.
Channing, George G., 150, 159, 227.
Channing, Dr. William Ellery, 87; letters of, 114, 118; intercourse with, 122, 123; description of, 124, 142; counsel and sympathy of, 142, 156, 157, 159-161; guiding influence of, 213; extracts from "Slavery," 218, 219; his letters quoted, 221-223; desires more spiritual life, 252.
Channing, William Henry, description of, in youth, 35, 36; classmate and friend of Mr. Clarke, 46, 86, 141; letters to, 101, 102, 107; connection with "Western Messenger," 125-127, 223; ordination of, 129, 130; eloquence of, 140, 141; writes in "Life of Margaret Fuller," 141, 142, 188; prayer at Church of the Disciples, 187; art criticism, 262; preaches in Washington, 275; visit to camps in Virginia, 278; letters from, 377, 379; a life-long friend, 353, 371, 380; funeral of, 361.
Chapman, George, 50, 67, 96.
Chase, Salmon P., 232, 276, 277, 289.
Cheever, Dr., 409.
Chicago, 64, 135.

Children's Aid Society, 148.
"Christian Examiner," 206, 229, 230, 241, 336.
"Christian Inquirer," 150, 169, 170, 184, 227, 228.
"Christian Register," 150, 246, 315, 409.
"Christian World," 163, 227.
Christians, practical agreement of, 256.
Church, elements of a, 168; an ideal, 252, 253; principles embodied in, 158, 160, 161.
Church of the Disciples, 146; name, 146, 147; without a choir, 147; fundamental principle, 147, 148; Wednesday evening meetings, 148; a free church, 149; first service, 149; increase of, 150; not representative of locality, 151; withdrawal from, 152; friendly relations, 152; organization, 160; social meetings, 164, 165; dedication of chapel, 167; sale of building, 187; meeting in 1851, 193; reëstablished, 201; cordial social life of, 202, 203; Dr. Holmes's description of, 203, 204; a missionary church, 205; new building, 211; protest against war with Mexico, 227; work for freed people, 245; activity and devotion of, 257; Governor Andrew, an earnest member of, 269; members of, in the army, 270; a favorite hymn, 273; two classes of hearers, 309, 310; its Sunday-school, 314; meetings on charities of Boston, 338, 339; a birthday meeting at, 353, 354; Sunday services at, 363, 365.
Cincinnati, 115, 231.
Clarke, Abraham, 64, 333, 355, 386.
Clarke, Mr. A. F., 162.
Clarke, Barnabas, 2.
Clarke, Cora, 337, 350, 383.
Clarke, Dr. E. H., 358.
Clarke, Eliot, 329, 333, 367, 384.
Clarke, Hepzibah, 2.
Clarke, Herman, 165, 169, 179, 194, 337, 338.
Clarke, Mrs. J. F., 132, 188, 194, 347, 350, 375.
Clarke, James Freeman, Autobiography, 1-80; 81, 83, 84, 95, 96; home in boyhood, 14, 22, 82, 83; education, 16-18, 83; reading, 19-21; Boston Latin School, 26, 30; college life, 34, 36, 41, 42, 44, 84, 85; painful experience, 45-47; reasons for going West, 50; first sermon, 51; memories of travel, 51, 55-59; overturns, 52-54; Niagara, 60; Trenton Falls, 63; Chicago, 64; Louisville, 66, 68; extempore sermons, 69, 70; homesickness, 71; important question, 72; religious books read, 72; sermons written, 73; evening meetings, 73; interest in a certain phase of belief, 74, 75; school-boy lines, 84; Bowdoin prize essay, 85; judicial temperament, 86, 92; early friendships, 86, 90; at Cam-

INDEX. 423

bridge Divinity School, 88-90; reading Goethe, 90, 91; a poet, 91; Puritan dramas planned, 91, 92; text of sermon, 92; prayer, 93; paper on Robert Hall, 93; at Louisville, 95-99; "Western Messenger," 97, 108, 109, 115, 124-126; sermon on dueling, 98, 225; ordination, 99; admiration of the West, 103, 104, 109; books planned, 102, 105; interest in Poles, 105, 106, 108; studies, 106, 108; sermon preached on steamboat, 110, 111; objects seen, 113; at Mobile, 113, 114; Kentucky History, 115; letter to Carlyle, 115; in Cincinnati, 115, 129, 130; Sunday-school, 118; discourse on temperance, 118; a long journey, 120; at a child's funeral, 122; meeting with J. Q. Adams, 122; love of work, 125; admiration of Emerson, 124; delight in preaching, 128, 133; agent of public schools, 131, 132; various occupations, 131; marriage, 132; leaving Louisville, 132, 135; Meadville, 132, 135, 136; route to Meadville, 136; life in Boston, 137; interest in all movements, 139; friendship with W. H. Channing, 141; position on slavery question, 141; respect for Wendell Phillips, 141; description of Margaret Fuller's "Conversations," 142; at Dr. Channing's, 142; repartee, 144; not a proselyter, 145; modest opinion of his own importance, 146; compiler of hymn-book, 147; idea of a free church, 149, 155, 156; memoranda, 149, 150; regular duties as minister, 150; contributor to weekly papers, 150; exchange with Theodore Parker, 152, 255; friendly relations with seceders, 152; baptisms by immersion, 153; director of Unitarian Association, 153; chaplain of Mass. Senate, 153; fearless discussion of slavery question, 154; vindication of Gen. Hull, 155; project of a new church, 155-157; first service, 157; discourses, 158, 159; organizing, 158, 160, 161; interference to protect a horse, 159; journals, 161-163; interest in prisoners, 163; in Free-Soil movement, 163; contributes to the "Christian World," 163; questions before Boston association of ministers, 163; his children, 165; lecture on Joan of Arc, 165; biographical discourses, 166; poem before Phi Beta Kappa Society, 166; seashore enjoyment, 166; a row on Concord River, 166; sermon at dedication of Freeman Place Chapel, 167; plan of lectures on reforms, 167, 168; diary, 167, 168; death of his son, 169; a summer in Europe, 171; delegate to the Peace Congress, 171-173, 176; three things he wished to see, 171; rules for seeing works of art, 172; incident of Salisbury spire, 173, 174, 176; passion for high elevations, 174, 177, 181, 375; life on board ship, 174; lines written in the mizzen-top, 174; excursions in England and Wales, 175; Westminster Abbey, 175; Salisbury Plain, like an Illinois prairie, 176; Stonehenge, 176; Alps, first view of, 177; Strasbourg minster, 177; ascent of the Rhigi, 177; thunder-storm, 177; walk round the Jungfrau, 178; emotion in little church in Untersee, 179; ascent of the Gemmi, 179; view of Mont Blanc, 180; down the Rhine to Cologne, 181; at Berne, 181; in old church at Basel, 181, 182; love for crypts, 182; day at Heidelberg, 182; in Antwerp, 182, 183; characteristic landing at Long Wharf, Boston, 183; "The House that Jack built," 184; a long illness, 186, 187; gap in ministerial life in Boston, 187; last service in the Church of the Disciples, 187; severe disappointment, 187; at Meadville, 188, 190, 191, 194, 197; journeys, 188, 189, 194; Memoir of Margaret Fuller, 188, 189; preaching, 189, 192; publications, 189, 191, 206; life with his children, 191; his pleasant study, 191; intercourse with theological students, 191, 192; abhorrence of slavery, 192; at Niagara Falls, 193; visit to Boston, 193; second trip to Europe, 195; a winter in Italy, 195; lines on the "Riviera di Ponente," 195-197; tie with the Church of the Disciples unbroken, 197; message from Nice, 198-200; renewal of Boston pastorate, 201; Sunday-school, 201, 202; social meeting, importance of, 202; interest of, how preserved, 202, 203; views of church membership, 205; a missionary, 205; correspondence, 206; question of permanent home, 206, 207; purchase of Brook Farm, 207; house at Jamaica Plain, 207, 208; trees, 207, 208; fiftieth birthday, 209-211; a citizen of Kentucky, 214; anti-slavery lessons from slaveholders, 214; visits to slaveholding friends, 217; opposition to slavery, 218; attitude as editor of "Western Messenger," 218, 219, 223, 224; judgment of slavery, 220, 224, 225; opinion of Abolitionists unfavorable, 222; not advocate of immediate emancipation, 222, 223; writings against slavery, 226-229; review of Dr. Lord, 230; of Bishop Hopkins, 231; interest in colored people, 231, 232, 243, 244; discourse on rendition of Anthony Burns, 233; speech, Aug. 1st, 234, 235; is censured, 235; sermons against slavery, 236; high estimate of John Brown, 236; address on eve of Lincoln's election, 238; speech in Tremont Temple in 1861, 239-241; sermon on the state of the nation, 242; pamphlet entitled "Secession," etc., 242, 270; sermon on the

424 INDEX.

"Plagues of Egypt and America," 243; in Hall of Representatives, Washington, 244, 245; address at dedication of soldiers' monument, 246; admiration of President Lincoln, 247; letter to Garrison, 248; not fully identified with Anti-Slavery Society, 249; social nature, 251; ideal church, 252; how received by Boston ministers, 252; speech at annual meeting of Unitarian Association, 252; hope on returning from Louisville, 253; books and sermons widely read, 254; division line in work, 255; publications, 256; qualifications as mediator, 256; member of Unitarian Association, 257, 258; writer in "Monthly Journal," 259; Western tours, 259, 260; opinion of co-education, 261; address at autumnal convention, 263; convention sermon, 264-267; lectures in Music Hall, 267; intimacy with Gov. Andrew, 268, 269; member of sanitary commission during the war, 269, 270; extracts from diary, 271, 273, 275, 284, 285; April 19, 1861, 271; sermon after attack on Fort Sumter, 271, 272; hopefulness after Bull Run, 272; address at funeral of William Lowell Putnam, 274; visit to Washington, 275-281, 289; in Virginian camps, 279-281; extracts from sermons, 281-283, 291, 320-322; at contraband camp, 285; at Gettysburg, 286, 287; of sanitary relief corps, 290; interest in public education, 292 professor in Divinity School, Cambridge, 292, 293, 297, 298; an overseer of Harvard College, 293; a loyal child of the university, 294; plans for improvement of Divinity School, 295; reports to board of overseers, 296, 297; lectures, 299; report on study of modern languages, 300, 301; on the study of Greek, 301; admission of women to Harvard, 302; resolutions on conferring degrees, 303, 304; interest in astronomy, 304, 305; trustee of Boston Public Library, 304; a "perfect" teacher, 305; book called "Self-Culture," 305; acquaintance with French and German, 306; use of pencil, 306; speech at Commencement dinner, 306, 307; extempore speaking, 308; sermons, 308-311; habits at printing-office, 311, 312; incident related in "Self-Culture," 312; preaching described by Margaret Fuller, 313; by John A. Andrew, 313; by young graduate, 314; incident at Albany, 315; tribute from S. W. Bush, 315; from Thomas L. Eliot, 316; charge at an ordination, 316, 317; address at Divinity School, 318; extract from the "Monthly Journal," 218; varied activities, 323, 328, 329, 350, 366; interest in woman suffrage, 324-326, 328, 330, 337; dealing with vexed questions, 326, 327; election sermon, 330; misses Gov. Andrew every day, 330; trip to the West, 331; notice of an eclipse, 331, 332; gunning, 333; fishing, 334; extracts from diary, 333, 334; series of discourses, 335; a sacred anniversary, 337; before committee at the State House, 338; sadness at death of Don, 339; Louisville visits, 340; memories of the past, 341; college class, 345; text of first sermon, 346; creed in four words, 346; journey to the South, 347; visit to Old Fort plantation, 347; sermon on St. Helena island, 349; publications, 353, 360, 363; seventieth birthday, 353, 354; love for the seashore, 354, 355; lectures at Lowell Institute, 356, 359, 368; lectures and classes, 357; visits to "Atlantic Monthly" office, 358; member of Examiner Club, 358; contributor to Thursday club, 359; visit to Europe, 359; parish work, 359-361; interest in civil service reform, 360, 361; at funeral of Wm. H. Channing, 361; seventy-fifth birthday, 362, 381; address on life of Dr. Freeman, 362; paper before Congress of churches, 362; home at Magnolia, 362, 364; plans for work, 363; correspondence 364, 365; at conference in Philadelphia, 364; sermons, 365, 366; an accident, 366; his grandchildren, 367, 379, 380, 384; diaries in England, 369, 370; people met in Oxford and London, 369-371; preachers heard, 371, 372; curiosities seen, 372, 373; House of Commons, 373; churches of Paris, 373; Switzerland, 374; Holland, 375; visit to Nazing, 375; praise of John Eliot, 376; letters destroyed, 378; a great sorrow, 379; on death of Wm. G. Eliot, 382; life at Magnolia, 384, 385; method of taking altitudes, 387; his faith in God, 389; faith in man, 390; a "truth-teller," 391; characteristics, 391, 392, 411; description of himself, 393, 394; no fixed habits, 393, 394; unity in his character, 395, 396; first appearance at Latin School, 396; fearlessness, 396; sympathy with children, 396, 397, 403; incident at Lowell, 397, 398; skill in presiding, 398; a visit to Boston Public Library, 399; interest in young men entering the ministry, 400; welcomed in social circles, 401; talk at a ball, 401; his home-life, 402; a good listener, 402; a picture in study at Meadville, 402; an ideal traveling companion, 403; an interesting storyteller, 404; at Niagara, 404; his memory, 404, 405; other traits, 405, 406; a comforter, 406; six weeks in New Jersey, 408, 409; article on revised version of New Testament, 409; preaches for the last time, 409; scene at annual social festival, 410; trust in a reunion hereafter, 410; "he ceased

INDEX.   425

to breathe," 410; on death, 412, 413; "Protecting Shadows," 414, 415.
Clarke, Lilian, 194, 285, 344, 369, 402.
Clarke, Rebecca Parker [Hull], 6-8, 10.
Clarke, Samuel, 2, 3.
Clarke, Dr. Samuel, 5, 6, 8, 9, 81, 82.
Clarke, Samuel C., or "Sam," 10, 82, 84, 329, 331, 333.
Clarke, Thomas, mate of the Mayflower, 2.
Clarke, William, 64, 334.
Clay, Cassius M., 223, 224.
Clay, Henry, 80, 239, 277.
Clerical manners in the West, 103.
Clergymen's lives difficult to describe, 136.
Cleveland, Grover, 361.
Cobbe, Frances Power, 371.
Cobden, 172, 176.
Colburn, Warren, 31, 32.
Coleridge, 39, 45, 87.
College, years in, a preparation for life, 43.
"Collegian, The," 35.
Colonization Society, 219, 221.
Colored people, condition of, 231, 232.
Colored troops, 244, 289.
Compromises of 1850, 276.
Conant, A. H., 162, 263, 380.
Concord, 166.
Congregational church, 11; minister, 13; churches, 255.
ongregationalism, theory of, 145.
Congress of churches, 362.
Constant, Benjamin, 139.
Conventions, 138.
Coolidge, J. I. T., 257.
Coolidge, Jefferson, 384.
Coolidge, Joseph, 5.
Coolidge, Joseph, Jr., 5.
opeland, Morris, 247.
Copy of Coleridge, Shelley, and Keats, 329.
Coquerel, Athanase, 172, 176.
Cotton, influence of, on slavery, 154.
Cotton, John, 88.
Cranch, C. P., 126.
Cranch, Edward, 130.
Cromwell, Oliver, 372, 373.
Cromwell, Richard, 372.
Cruft, S. B., 366.
Crypts, 182.
Curious literary deception, 33.
Curtis, Anna, 4.
Curtis, Benjamin Robbins, 34, 35, 46.
Curtis, Charles Pelham, 5.
Curtis, James Freeman, 5.
Curtis, Martha, 3, 4.
Curtis, Obadiah, 3, 4.
Curtis, Sarah, or "Sally," 4, 14, 21.
Curtis, Thomas, 4.
Curtis, Thomas Buckminster, 5.
Curtis, William, emigrant from Nazing, 3-5, 375.

Dalton, Professor, 282.
Daniel, Book of, 139.

Dante, 349.
Daviess, Joseph Hamilton, 80, 99.
Davis, George T., 36, 39.
Davis, Jefferson, 352.
Day, J. W., 381.
Deguerry, the Abbé, 172.
Dennie, William, 3.
Detroit, surrender of, by Hull, 83.
Devens, Charles, 10.
De Wette, Dr., 181.
Dewey, Orville, 169.
"Dial, The," 143.
Dictionaries, superstition of, 17, 29.
Divinity School, Cambridge, 88; of Unitarian Church, 293.
Dix, Dorothea, 383.
Dixwell, Epes S., 83.
"Doctrine of Prayer," 256.
Don, 339.
Drake, Dr., 130.
Dred Scott case, 228.
Dueling, 98, 101, 225.
Duncan, Garnet, 32.
Dwight, Dr., 294.

Eclipse described, 331, 332.
Edgeworth, Maria, stories of, 18, 19.
Education, Board of, 292.
"Elegy in a Country Churchyard," 372.
Eliot, John, 3, 25, 375, 376.
Eliot, Samuel A., 140.
Eliot, Thomas L., 316.
Eliot, William G., 86, 95, 129, 130, 251, 263; letters to, 104, 336, 367, 368, 378, 381.
Emerson, Ralph Waldo, 22, 84, 86, 89; conversation with, 85; letters to, 115, 120, 121, 124, 128; letters from, 123, 126; praise of, 124; poems, 124, 125; remark of, 133; a lecturer, 140; writer in "Life of Margaret Fuller," 142, 188; frequenter of foreign bookstore, 143; religious speculations of, 328; member of Examiner Club, 358; funeral of, 359; correspondence with Carlyle, 377.
Epping Forest, 375.
Erasmus, bust of, 182.
Espy, Professor, 135.
"Essentials and Non-Essentials in Religion," 267.
European tour, the effects of, 186.
Everett, Edward, 271.
Examiner Club, 336, 344, 358.

Faith, 104.
Farley, Frederick A., 129, 130, 161.
Farrar, Canon F. W., 371.
Farrar, John, 37.
Female medical school, 303.
Fields, James T., 350, 357, 358.
Fields, Mrs. James T., 384.
Finney, Dr., 256.
First sermon, 1, 51, 93.
First twenty years, 1.
Flag, "the cultus" of, at a Virginia camp, 281.

426   INDEX.

Florence, 139.
Follen, Dr. Charles, 43, 214.
Foote, Henry W., 353, 365, 384, 385, 409.
Foreign bookstore, frequenters of, 143.
Fourth, The, 121, 122.
Fowle, William B., 33.
Fraser, Sir William, 372.
Free-Soil party, 163, 206, 276.
Freeman, Rev. James, 3, 4; excellence as a teacher, 16-18, 83, 387; house of, 22, 25; of King's Chapel, 81, 82, 213, 362.
Freeman, Martha [Curtis], 4, 13.
Freeman Place Chapel, 166, 167, 188, 194.
Freiburg minster, 177.
Fresh Pond, 45.
Fruitlands, 138.
Fugitive slave law, 227, 228, 276.
Fuller, Margaret, 71, 125, 313; letters to, 99, 100, 105, 107-110; life of, written, 91, 141, 188, 189; classes for conversation, 142, 143.
Furness, Dr., 337, 364, 408.
Furness, Mr. and Mrs., 109.

Gannett, Dr. E. S., 157, 158, 161, 163, 263.
Garden pleasures, 14, 15.
Gardner, Governor, 228.
Garibaldi, 371.
Garrison, William Lloyd, 220, 221, 247, 248.
Gemmi Pass, the, 179.
German books, 87.
Gettysburg, 286, 287.
Ghost story, a, 7.
Giddings, Joshua, 232, 276.
Gill, Thomas H., 371.
Girardin, Emile de, 172.
Gladstone, 373.
Goddard, Francis E., 32, 96.
Goddard, Mr., 358.
Goodwin, Simeon S., 66, 67.
Gospels, the four, 88.
Gould, Benjamin A., 31, 83.
Gray, Frederick T., 122, 149, 257.
Greene, Colonel William B., 279.
Greene, Mrs. William B., 287.
Greene, William, 130.
Greene, Mrs., 130.
Greenwood, F. W. P., 389.
Grimes, Mr., 6.
Guyandotte route, the, 57, 96.
Gymnastics, 43, 44, 85, 174.

Hale, Edward Everett, 138, 302, 336, 358.
Hale, Ellen, 369.
Hale, John P., 232, 276.
Hall, Nathaniel, 261.
Hampstead, 369.
Harvard club, 362; college, 34, 41, 84; emulation the motive appealed to, 37, 40-42; boards of, 294, 306.
Haweis, Mr., 371.
Hawthorne, Mrs. [Peabody], 143.

Hawthorne, Nathaniel, 143, 166.
Hayden, Lewis, 193.
Hedge, Frederick Henry, 86, 91, 120, 142, 143, 169, 387.
Heidelberg, 182.
Hemenway, Mrs., 384.
Hemp, field of, 77.
"Herald of Health," 393.
Herbert, George, 198.
Henry, Patrick, 237.
Heywood, Mr., 340, 341.
Higginson, Francis, 373.
Higginson, T. Wentworth, 308, 324.
Hill, Miss Octavia, 371.
Hillard, George Stillman, 84.
Hillard, Mrs. G. S., 341.
Hills, influence of, 22.
Hilton Head, 348, 349.
Hinckley, Mr., 337.
Holidays, 234.
Holland, 375.
Holley, Horace, 67, 94, 95.
Hollis Street Church, 263.
Holmes, Oliver Wendell, 35, 84, 203, 273, 353, 358.
Home for aged colored women, 148.
Home, temporary, for children, 148.
Homer, Anna [Curtis], 4.
Homer, Dr. Jonathan, 12, 13.
Hooper, Samuel, 285.
Hopedale, 139.
Hopkins, Bishop John H., 229-231.
Horses in Kentucky, 52.
Hosea, Mr., 261.
Hosmer, Dr., 261, 262.
Houston, Samuel, 276.
Howe, Colonel, 275.
Howe, Mrs. Julia Ward, 337, 353.
Hubbard, Gurdon, 64.
Huidekoper, Anna, 132.
Huidekoper, Henry, 285.
Huidekoper, Mr., 95, 190, 375.
Hull, Abraham, 24.
Hull, General William, 83; hospitality of, 22, 23; vindication of, 155.
Hunt, Mr., 394.
Huntington, Frederick D., 257.
Hutton, Dr., 175.

"Ideal church," 252.
Indiana-Place Chapel, 211.
Indians, "western Orientalists," 110.
Infidel, so called, 77, 117.
Inspiration, literal, of Old Testament, 74, 75, 77.
Irwin, Mr. and Mrs., 109.
Italy, 195.

Jackson, Francis, 239.
Jackson, Dr. James, 194.
James, Henry, 358.
Jameson, Mrs., 127.
Jefferson, Thomas, 215.
Joan of Arc, 165, 166, 356.
Jowett, Dr., 370.
Julian, 232, 276.
Jungfrau, 177, 178.

INDEX.

Kansas, 203.
Keats, George, 107, 121.
Keats, John, 107, 329.
Kemble, Fanny, 109.
Kentuckians, 79, 98, 99, 103, 121,
Kentucky, 52, 78, 79, 94, 95, 98, 103, 132 ; forests, 100, 121 ; slavery in, 214, 218, 219, 224.
" Kentucky History," 115.
Kettle Island, 355.
" Key to ' Uncle Tom's Cabin,' " 215.
King, Clarence, 344.
King, Starr, 257.
King's Chapel, 81, 82, 362.
Kinzie, Mr., 64.
Kirk, Edward N., 153, 253, 254.
Knapp, 263.
Kossuth, 194.

Laboratory, 25.
" Lady of the Lake," 15, 16.
Lake Leman, 181.
Lakes, the, 64, 65 ; Zug and Lucerne, 177.
Lancaster, 405.
Lane, Mr., 138.
Latin Grammar, 16, 29, 30.
Latin School, 26, 28, 396.
Latter-day Saints, 139.
Lawrence, Mr. and Mrs. Edwin, 385.
Lay preaching, 162.
Lesley, Mr., 169, 337.
Letters : to
    Margaret Fuller, 99, 100, 105, 107-110, 115.
    W. H. Channing, 101, 102, 107, 116, 117.
    W. G. Eliot, 104, 336, 367, 368, 378, 381.
    G. T. D., 108, 120.
    H. T. D., 111, 112.
    Editor " Western Messenger," 111.
    Mr. and Mrs. G. T. D., 119.
    R. W. Emerson, 120, 124, 128.
    A. H., 121, 123, 125, 126, 128, 129, 131.
    A. H. C., 133, 156, 175, 193, 290, 330, 333, 337, 340, 368.
    His sister, 155, 211, 288, 335, 337-339, 341, 343, 344, 349-352, 376, 379, 382-387.
    S. S. C., 165, 185, 328, 355.
    H. W. Bellows, 169, 184.
    Mrs. A. F. C., 193.
    Church of the Disciples, 198-200.
    T. W. Higginson, 208.
    E. E. Hale, 262, 297, 303, 336, 338, 351.
    N. Augustus Staples, 284.
    E. C. C., 289.
    Professor in a theological school, 299.
    A young minister, 319.
    His daughter, 329, 408.
    L. F. C., 331.
    Mrs. G. S. Hillard, 341.
    H. W. Bellows, 342.
    Samuel May, 345.

J. T. Fields, 350.
Rev. John Cordner, 377.
Rev. J. W. Day, 381.
Rev. J. H. Allen, 380.
S. C. C., 382.
F. H. Hedge, 387.
Lexington, Ky., 94, 109.
Leyden, 375.
Lieber, Dr. Francis, 61-63.
Lincoln, Abraham, 78, 218, 238, 243, 247, 275, 277, 284, 341, 342.
Lind, Jenny, 193.
Livingstone, David, 390.
Locke, John, philosophy of, 39, 89.
Lombard, Mr., 352.
London, 89, 369.
Longworth, Mr., 130.
Lord, Nathan, 229, 230.
Loring, Caleb, 4.
Loring, Charles G., 328.
Loring, Edward G., 228.
Loring, Mrs. Ellis Gray, 284.
Louisville, 66, 68, 94, 98, 100 ; a lady of, 75, 76 ; life at, 96 ; Unitarian Society at, 96, 97, 133 ; visits, 340.
" Louisville Journal," 218.
Lovejoy, Elijah P,, 222.
Lowell, James Russell, 357.
Lowell, John, Jr., 130.
Lowell Lectures, 368.
Lucerne, Lake of, 178, 374.
Lundy's Lane, 24.

Mackintosh, Sir James, 178.
Macy, General, 329.
Maffitt, 109.
Magnolia, 355, 362.
Mammoth Cave, 189, 190, 300.
Mangasarian, Mr., 364.
Manliness, true and false, 45.
Mann, Horace, 10, 48, 232, 233, 261, 276, 283.
Mann, Mrs. Horace [Peabody], 10, 143.
Marblehead men, 278.
Marsh, Professor, 39.
Marshall, Mrs., 216.
Martineau, Harriet, 109.
Martineau, James, 372.
Mary, Queen of Scots, 373.
Massachusetts Anti-Slavery Society, 235.
Massachusetts Fourteenth Regiment, 279-281.
Massachusetts Woman Suffrage Association, 249.
May, Joseph, 364.
May, Samuel J., 156, 213 ; letter to, 345.
Mayo, A. D., 399.
McClellan, General, 279.
McDuffie, Governor, 216.
Meadville, 132, 135, 136, 256, 261, 262, 293, 402.
Meetings for discourse, 73, 74.
Melbourne, 383.
" Memorial History of Boston," 206.
Mexico, war with, 227.
Mickiewitz, Casimir, 105, 107.
Miller, William, 139.
Milwaukee, 383.

428   INDEX.

Mineralogy, 106.
Mississippi River, 110.
Mobile, 112-114.
Money, allowance of, 24, 25.
Mont Blanc, 180.
Montgomery, Dick, 352.
"Monthly Journal," 263, 275, 336.
Morgan, 288.
Mormons, 139.
Muir, Sir William Hamilton, 370.
Müller, Max, 370.
Mumford, Thomas J., 189.
Museum, 24.

"National Anti-slavery Standard," 234.
National Conference of Unitarian Churches, 264.
"National Era," 276, 402.
National road from Wheeling, Va., 11, 12, 379.
Nazing, 375.
Negro flogging, 111.
New England, 50, 86, 87, 94, 97.
New England Emigrant Aid Co., 251.
New Jersey, 408.
"New York Observer," 163.
"New York Tribune," 279.
Newcastle railroad, 100.
Newton, town of, 11, 12, 379.
Newton, Stewart, 127.
Niagara, 60, 61, 188, 189, 193, 404.
Niebuhr, Baron, 62.
Nonantum, 25.
North, Anti-slavery opinion of the, 247.
"North American Review," 248.
Norton, Andrews, 88.
Norton, David W., 289.
"Notes on the State of Virginia," 215.
Novels, 21.
Novelties, 147.

Ogden, William B., 64.
Old Corner Bookstore, 358.
Old Manse, 166.
Old South Church, 345.
"Oldtown Folks," 23.
Oliphant, Lady, 344.
Oliphant, Mr. and Mrs. Laurence, 344.
Orthodoxy, leaders of, 253, 254.
Osgood, Samuel, 162, 169, 184, 227.
Otis, James, 237.
Overseers of church, 147.
Overseers, Boards of, 294, 306.
Owen, Robert, 138.
Oxford, 369, 370.
Oxford movement, The, 139.

Paddock elms, 345.
Palfrey, John G., 90, 141, 214, 233.
Park, John C., 381.
Parker, Mr., 310.
Parker, Theodore, 151, 152, 193, 227, 254, 255, 259, 324, 371, 380.
Parkman, Francis, 96, 157, 161.
Parnell, 373
Patterson. Mr., 65.
Peabody, Ephraim, 95, 161, 251, 257.

Peabody, Nathaniel, daughters of, 10; house of, 143.
Peace Congress, 171-173, 176.
Peers, President, 102.
Peirce, Benjamin, 34.
Pennsylvania route, 96.
Perkins, James H., 36, 130, 169, 380.
Petersburg, 289.
Philadelphia, 337, 350, 364.
Phillips, John, 261.
Phillips, Jonathan, 223.
Phillips, Wendell, 84, 141.
Phonograph, 352.
Phrenology, 47-49.
Pierpont, John, 32, 96.
Pillsbury, Parker, 351.
Pittsburg, 261, 262.
Planters, hospitality of, 57, 58.
Play, 18, 27.
Poles in Louisville, 105-107.
Popkin, Dr., 36, 37.
Port Royal, 278.
Positive Doctrines of Christianity, 168.
Potomac, 279, 280.
Prentice, George D., 98, 99, 101, 135, 218.
Prentiss, 103.
Presbyterian ministers, 95.
Protestant Episcopal school, 139.
Public schools, 28.
Putnam, Dr. Charles, 379.
Putnam, William Lowell, 273.

Quincy, Josiah, 237.

Railroad lines, 96, 140.
Rand, Edward S., 10.
Reading room, West Street, 143, 144.
Revelation, Book of the, 139.
Revised Book of Common Prayer, 362.
"Revue des Deux Mondes," 143.
Richards, Laura Howe, 381.
"Richmond Examiner," 216.
Richmond, fall of, 290.
Ripley, George, 122, 133, 143, 156, 380.
Ritchie, Colonel, 275.
"Riviera di Ponente," 195, 196.
Rob Roy, 344.
Robbins, Chandler, 102, 193.
Rogers, Henry B., 157, 290, 381.
Rogers, Professor, 358.
Rowan, John, 98, 99.
Rubens, pictures by, 183.

Sadler, Dr., 369.
Salisbury Cathedral spire, 173.
Salisbury Plain, 176.
Sanitary Commission, 263, 269.
Sargent, John Osborne, 30, 31, 156.
"Saturday Evening Gazette," 310, 311, 344.
Savoy Alps, 180.
Schleiermacher, 63.
School prizes, 22.
Schuylers, the, 344.
Scott, General, 276.
Scott's poems, 15, 19; and novels, 19.
Sectarianism, 254.
Seligman, Mr., 370.

INDEX. 429

Seward, J. L., 397.
Seward, William Henry, 232, 276, 277.
Shackford, Mr., 151.
Shakespeare, 20.
"Shark," 136.
Simmons, George F., 169, 223.
Slade, 232.
Slave power, The, 246, 277.
Slavery in Kentucky, 78, 79, 98; affected by cotton-growing, 154; Southern ideas about, 216; protest against, 226.
Smith, Bishop, 102.
Smith, Goldwin, 370.
Smith, Dr. Nathan, 81.
Social experiments, 139.
Socialism, 184, 185.
Society, redemption of, 138.
Sohier, Edward D., 44, 45.
Soldiers, at Washington, 278.
Solms, Prince de, 251.
"South-side View of Slavery," 229, 347.
Sparks, Jared, 10.
Spears, R., 385.
Speed, James, 218, 244.
Speed, John, 76–79, 217, 244, 391.
Speed, Joshua, 77, 78, 218, 341.
Speed, Mrs. and Martha, Mary and Eliza, Philip and Emma, 340.
Spurgeon, 372.
Spurzheim, Dr., 47, 48.
St. Gothard road, 178.
St. Helena, Island of, 348, 349.
St. John, Mr., 130.
St. Paul, 102.
Stage-coach journeys and adventures, 51–61, 96; drivers, 52, 53.
Staples, N. Augustus, 262.
Stedman, Dr., 408.
Stetson, Caleb, 226.
Stetson, Mrs., 130.
Stevens, Thaddeus, 289.
Stevenson, J. Thomas, 228.
Stone, Mrs., 337.
Stonehenge, 176.
Stowe, Harriet Beecher, 23, 215, 247, 330.
Strasburg minster, 177.
Stump-speaking, 79, 80.
Sumner, Charles, 84, 141, 171, 233, 242, 244, 289, 337, 344.
Sumner, S. B., 130.
Swan, Mrs. Hepzibah [Clarke], 2, 22, 55.
Swedenborgian chapel, 156, 157.
Sycamore, 68, 69.

Taverns in the West, 57.
Taylor, "Father," 156, 261, 262.
"Ten Great Religions," 295.
Texas, annexation of, 153, 154.
Text-books, 20, 21.
Theology, 39, 40, 87.
Thomas, Benjamin F., 285.
Thompson, 161.
Thompson, Dr. Allen, 370.
Thoreau, Henry D., 188.
Thursday Lecture, The, 255.
Towne, Miss Laura, 348.

Towne, Mrs., 384.
Translations, use of, 42.
Travelling in 1833, 51, 52.
Trees, in Western forests, 55; hostility to, 69; live oaks, 347.
Trenton Falls, 63.
Trotter, Mr., 101.
Truths and errors of Orthodoxy, 256, 296.
Twitchell, Mr., 337.

"Uncle Tom's Cabin," 189, 402.
Unitarian Association, 153, 257, 264, 267, 275; church, 233, 253, 254, 263; doctrine, 50, 72; leaders, 152, 252; ministers, 226, 227; pulpit, change in, 257; society, in Louisville, 96, 97.
Unitarian, origin of word, 295.
Unitarianism, 377.
Unitarians, 265.
Uri, bay of, 178.

Vailly, M., 24.
Vandyck, 183.
Vane, Sir Henry, 409.
Vaughan, Mr., 130.
Verses, 123, 126, 127
Victor Hugo, 172, 176.
Vine Street, Boston, 84.
Virgil, 31.
Virginia, 279–281.
Visits, 14, 25.

Walker, Amasa, 172.
Walker, Dr. James, 37, 96, 139, 140, 297, 351.
Waltham Abbey, 376.
Ward, William, 253.
Ware, Darwin E., 311, 366.
Ware, Henry, 88, 214.
Ware, Henry, Jr., 89, 162, 214, 263.
Warren Street Chapel, 162.
Washington, 276–278.
Washington, George, 215.
Washington, Smart, story of, 348.
Waterston, R. C., 149, 156, 157, 257.
Watts, Mr., 370.
Webster, Daniel, 216, 228.
Weeden, Mr., 342.
Weld, Theodore, 215.
Wells, Mrs., 328.
Wendte, C. W., 298.
Wesley, John, 215.
West, The, 103, 104.
"Western Messenger, The," 97, 109, 115, 124–126, 162, 218, 222, 223, 251, 378, 380.
Westminster Abbey, 371.
Westminster Confession, 295.
Westwood, Professor, 370.
Whipple, Edwin P., 358.
"White-capt Waves," 385.
White Mountain Notch, 7.
"White Tracts," 269.
Whitman, Bernard, 67, 96.
Whitman, Colonel, 341.
Whitsunday, 233.
Whittier, John G., 221, 338.

Wicksteed, Mr. and Mrs. Philip, 371.
Wilder, Dr., 135.
Wilson, Henry, 244, 248, 277.
Winkley, S. H., 257.
Winslow, B. P., 187.
Winthrop, John, 88.
Winthrop, Robert Charles, 84.
Woman suffrage, 324-326, 330; association, 337.

Woman, admission of, to college, 302.
Woodhull, Mrs., party of, 326.
World, end of, prophesied, 139.

Yale College, 294.
Yandell, Dr., 135.

Zug, lake of, 177.
Zurich, university of, 338.

THE WORKS OF
JAMES FREEMAN CLARKE, D.D.

Ten Great Religions. Part I. An Essay in Comparative Theology. With an Index. Crown 8vo, $2.00; half calf, $3.25.

CONTENTS: Ethnic and Catholic Religions; Confucius and the Chinese; Brahmanism; Buddhism, or the Protestantism of the East; Zoroaster and the Zend Avesta; The Gods of Egypt; The Gods of Greece; The Religion of Rome; The Teutonic and Scandinavian Religion; The Jewish Religion; Mohammed and Islam; The Ten Religions and Christianity.

Nothing has come to our knowledge which furnishes evidence of such voluminous reading, such thorough study and research, and such masterly grasp of the real elements of these religions as does the volume before us. James Freeman Clarke has accomplished a work here of solid worth. — *Missionary Review* (Princeton).

Dr. Clarke has here given us an outline of the history of each of the religions that have exerted the most influence in space and time. . . . A book of consummate merit and surpassing interest. — *Christian Register* (Boston).

He treats the ten condemned faiths in a spirit of the fullest reverence, anxious to bring to light whatever of good is contained in them. — *The Nation* (New York).

Ten Great Religions. Part II. Comparison of all Religions. Crown 8vo, $2.00; half calf, $3.25. The two Parts, half calf, $6.50.

CONTENTS: Introduction — Description and Classification; Special Types — Variations; Origin and Development of all Religions; The Idea of God in all Religions — Animism Polytheism, Pantheism; Idea of God in all Religions, Ditheism, Tritheism, and Monotheism; The Soul and its Transmigrations, in all Religions; The Origin of the World, in all Religions; Evolution, Emanation and Creation; Prayer and Worship in all Religions; Inspiration and Art in all Religions; Ethics in all Religions; Idea of a Future State in all Religions; The Future Religion of Mankind.

WORKS OF JAMES FREEMAN CLARKE — (continued).

The last few years have done much to throw light upon the religions of the world, and especially those of the East. Of these researches the author has availed himself, and he has given the world a book unique in design and execution; in its attempt to trace the doctrines we have named through all religions the work has no predecessor. — *The Churchman* (New York)

Common Sense in Religion. 12mo, $2.00.

CONTENTS: Common-Sense and Mystery; Common-Sense View of Human Nature; On the Doctrine Concerning God; The Bible and Inspiration; The True Meaning of Evangelical Christianity; The Truth about Sin: Common-Sense and Scripture views of Heaven and Hell; Satan, according to Common-Sense and the Bible; Concerning the Future Life; The Nature of Our Condition Hereafter; Common-Sense View of the Christian Church; Five kinds of Piety; Jesus a Mediator; The Expectations and Disappointments of Jesus; Common-Sense View of Salvation by Faith; On not being Afraid; Hope; The Patience of Hope; Love; The Brotherhood of Men.

Dr. Clarke has much to say which commends itself to our judgment and our feelings. There is a certain vigor in his thought, and an absolute clearness in his style, together with an evident and rugged honesty and strength of conviction underlying all, which make him an impressive teacher, even when we cannot bring ourselves to accept his instructions. — *The Congregationalist* (Boston).

Events and Epochs in Religious History.

With Maps and Illustrations. 12mo, $2.00; half calf, $3.50.

CONTENTS: The Catacombs; Buddhist Monks; Christian Monks; Augustine, Anselm, Bernard; Jeanne d'Arc; Savonarola, Luther, Loyola; The Mystics; German Pietists; Fénelon, Swedenborg, Emerson; George Fox; Huguenots, Waldenses, Albigenses; John Wesley; Moravians and Methodists.

It contains an historical account of some of the most striking phases of religious life and character, chiefly, but not exclusively Christian, together with extended critical studies of the great leaders in the religious movements of which the author treats. . . . He has gathered a great amount of interesting material from the various sources of history and of biography, and has presented them in a striking light, making an eminently readable and instructive book. — *New York Observer.*

The Ideas of the Apostle Paul. Translated
into their Modern Equivalents. 12mo, $1.50.

A thoughtful study of the life, character, opinions, and influence of the Apostle Paul. So many theological doctrines are based upon Paul's Epistles, or buttressed by them, that a careful examination of them by so competent and candid a scholar as Dr. Clarke is peculiarly welcome.

A work on this subject from this source does not need my commendation. But I permit myself the pleasure of expressing the satisfaction I have derived from its catholicity of sentiment and its deep spirituality. — Professor C. H. TOY, *of Harvard Divinity School.*

Every-Day Religion. 12mo, $1.50.

Twenty-nine Essays, discussing, with the simplicity, wisdom, and practical good sense characteristic of Dr. Clarke, the religion of daily life in the family, the neighborhood, in business, in society, in politics. It is a thoroughly wise and helpful book.

They are full of thoughts that are as pertinent in the parlor as in the pew, and which speak as fittingly in the marketplace as at the altar; and this is accomplished, not by bringing the sanctuary down to the level of the world, but by bringing the world up to the level of the sanctuary. If the thoughts are for every day as well as for Sunday, it is because the preacher would have all days alike made holy. "How to make the most of life" is the subject of the first discourse, and the keynote of all. — *New York Tribune.*

Self-Culture. Physical, Intellectual, Moral,
and Spiritual. 12mo, $1.50; half calf, $3.00.

Twenty-two lectures, discussing with admirable breadth and insight the methods of educating the powers of observation, reflection, imagination, conscience, affection, reverence, temper; education by books, amusements, and love of beauty, and seeking for truth.

"Self-Culture is written from the standpoint of universal ideas and the broadest truth. It bears the impress of ripe scholarship, and yet is so simple in style and clear in statement that no attentive reader can fail to comprehend the meaning or learn the lesson intended. Its philosophy of life is sound and its spirit such as all men approve. The work will be found in the best sense a useful handbook for parents, teachers, and the thousands of young persons for whom it was prepared. And in speaking thus, we could hardly give stronger utterance to our admiration of the author's practical wisdom, deftness, and force of diction, and remarkably clear and intelligible apprehension of the problems considered. The volume will prove a godsend to multitudes to whom it will open a hitherto unknown path to education and true culture. — *Boston Transcript.*

Memorial and Biographical Sketches. Including Governor Andrew, Charles Sumner, Dr. Channing, Theodore Parker, Dr. Howe, Dr. Gannett, Dr. Susan Dimmock, and others. 12mo, $2.00.

The nineteen essays, articles, sermons, and addresses which make up this volume are marked by the sterling qualities, the common-sense, manliness, earnestness, and tenderness which have given Dr. Clarke his enviable reputation in his native city and State. — *The Nation* (New York).

Exotics. Poems translated from the French, German, and Italian, by J. F. C. and L. C. 18mo, $1.00.

No equally varied collection of the minor gems of German and French lyrical poetry has hitherto appeared in English; and very few translations of equal spirit and fidelity have appeared in English at all. — *Appletons' Journal.*

The "Exotics" make a charming collection, and touch all moods of fancy, thought, and love. — *Boston Advertiser.*

A thoroughly exquisite book without and within. — *New York Christian Advocate.*

_{*} *For sale by all Booksellers. Sent, post-paid, on receipt of price by the Publishers,*

HOUGHTON, MIFFLIN AND COMPANY,

4 PARK ST., BOSTON; 11 EAST 17TH ST., NEW YORK.